Waqf in Central Asia

Waqf in Central Asia

FOUR HUNDRED YEARS IN THE HISTORY
OF A MUSLIM SHRINE, 1480–1889

R. D. McChesney

PRINCETON UNIVERSITY PRESS

PRINCETON, NEW JERSEY

Copyright © 1991 by Princeton University Press
Published by Princeton University Press, 41 William Street,
Princeton, New Jersey 08540
In the United Kingdom: Princeton University Press, Oxford

Library of Congress Cataloging-in-Publication Data

McChesney, R. D., 1944–
Waqf in Central Asia : four hundred years in the history of a Muslim
shrine, 1480–1889 / R. D. McChesney.
p.   cm.
Revision of thesis (Ph.D.)—Princeton University, 1973.
Includes bibliographical references and index.
1. Islamic shrines—Afghanistan—Balkh Region—History. 2. Charitable
uses, trusts, and foundations—Afghanistan—Balkh Region—History.
3. Mazār-e Sharīf (Afghanistan)—History. I. Title.
BP187.55.A3B345   1991   297'.35—dc20   90-47769   CIP

ISBN 0-691-05584-X (alk. paper)

This book has been composed in Linotron Caledonia

Princeton University Press books are printed on acid-free paper
and meet the guidelines for permanence and durability of the
Committee on Production Guidelines for Book Longevity of the
Council on Library Resources

Printed in the United States of America by Princeton University Press,
Princeton, New Jersey

10   9   8   7   6   5   4   3   2   1

TO MY PARENTS

Herbert L. and Charlotte W. McChesney,

with love and gratitude

Contents

Preface

THIS IS the story of an Islamic legal institution, the charitable endowment or *waqf*, and its place in society. It is more especially the story of a single example of the institution, the endowment of a major Muslim shrine in what is today northern Afghanistan. This work traces the evolution of the waqf endowment from its foundation in the late fifteenth century until the late nineteenth century, when the Afghan government assumed administrative control of it. The region in which the endowment operated was known until the nineteenth century as Balkh—after its chief city, an ancient urban center. By the end of the century, the shrine, founded in the small village of Khwajah Khayran a few miles east of Balkh, had supplanted that ancient city as the economic, demographic, and administrative center of the region. The city that grew up around the shrine came to be known as "Noble Shrine" (*mazar-i sharif*). Today Mazar-i Sharif is the fourth largest metropolis in Afghanistan and is the administrative center of the area north of the Hindu Kush mountains.

For most of the period of this study—the 1480s to the 1880s—Balkh's economy, culture, and politics were linked not to the region to the south but to the north. It was one of the three great urban centers, along with Bukhara and Samarqand, of the area called Trans-Oxiana (Mawarannahr in Arabo-Persian). Rather than being the northernmost urban region of Afghanistan, as it is today, Balkh was the southernmost city of a political unit whose northern centers were Bukhara, Samarqand, and, for some of the period, Tashkent. For lack of a more precise term to denote this region, I have used "Central Asia" through much of this study, alternating it with "Mawarannahr" or "Mawarannahr and Balkh." To locate it more precisely, it is the region bounded by sixty-three and seventy degrees east longitude and thirty-five and forty-five degrees north latitude.

The transformation of the shrine from village holy site to urban conglomeration was largely dependent on the economic fortunes of the shrine, and these in turn were predicated mainly on the management of the waqf endowment. Such is the central thesis of this book. A complex of charitable, political, reverential, and social motives produced the original endowment in the 1480s. Once established and equipped with an administrative apparatus, the waqf endowment became a formidable economic force in the region, particularly during those times when its sacred character and the tax privileges it acquired provided its managers relative security in comparison with others conducting their economic lives without such advantages.

The subject of the Islamic institution of charitable endowments has long been the domain of scholars whose perspective on waqf is theoretical and legal. Recently, however, a number of studies have appeared stressing the social and economic significance of waqf. Waqf was never a purely legal institution, one whose features could be wholly understood by reference to legal sources. It was a social institution as well, operating in a particular society and subject, like all other components of that society, to local economic, social, and cultural influences. Just as art and architecture adapted to local tastes and economic conditions while retaining and perpetuating certain universal forms, so too did waqf. And what evolved in individual situations, as a consequence of political, social, and economic factors, was often far removed from the way in which legal scholars depicted the institution and formulated its theoretical behavior.

In order to show the evolution of waqf in society, it seemed desirable to limit the study as far as possible to a single endowment. This allows one to grasp more fully the environment in which waqf evolved and still evolves. Here I have chosen the endowment of the shrine of ʿAli b. Abi Talib in the center of present-day Mazar-i Sharif, from its origins in the late fifteenth century to its incorporation under Afghan administration in the late nineteenth century. Throughout, a consistent effort has been made not to view this corpus of waqf as an institution isolated either from the legal regulations governing it or from its environment. As it is impossible in such a study to separate the endowment from the institution it was meant to support or from the administration formed to manage it, both play central roles in this work.

The choice of the ʿAlid shrine at Balkh owes a good deal to serendipity. In 1968 I was in Afghanistan doing research on nineteenth-century Afghan history. I came across a small book by Hafiz Nur Muhammad titled *Tarikh-i Mazar-i Sharif*. The work was published in Kabul in 1325/1946 in what was probably a very small edition. It contains facsimiles with accompanying transcriptions of two documents, a decree (*manshur*) issued in 1668–1669 by the Tuqay-Timurid *sultan* of Balkh, Subhan Quli, and an edict (*farman*) of the Muhammadzaʾi amir of Afghanistan, ʿAbd al-Rahman Khan, dated 1889. Both documents concerned the administration of the ʿAlid shrine at Balkh and the waqf endowment of the shrine. In addition, Hafiz Nur Muhammad provides a synopsis of a waqf endowment established in the 1870s by a governor of Mazar-i Sharif, Naʾib Muhammad ʿAlam Khan, as well as a summary narrative on the founding of the ʿAlid shrine and information on nineteenth-century renovations and additions to the shrine.

Some months before the book came into my hands, I had visited the shrine as a tourist with no particular scholarly interest in it. The shrine dominates the city of Mazar-i Sharif and the surrounding plain and creates a very powerful visual impression. In part because of the impression left by the shrine, the book and the documents in it immediately piqued my curiosity. The book offered evidence that the shrine and its endowments had had an unbroken history of more than four centuries—five, if one brings it to the present day. Such longevity raises many questions: What are the economic circumstances that permit the survival of such an institution for so long a period? How is administrative continuity maintained for such a long period of time? What sorts of conflicts does such an institution experience and how are they resolved? What kinds of changes do the institution and its economy undergo as a consequence of changing external conditions—political, social, and economic—in the immediate surroundings? And what effect does such a long-lived institution have on its environment—on land tenure patterns, on agriculture and commerce, on urbanization, and on the formation and dissolution of social groups?

For the past two decades, I have spent a good deal of time trying to arrive at satisfactory answers to these questions. This process involved finding information that would illuminate the 223-year interval separating the documents in Hafiz Nur Muhammad's book and reconstruct the history of the institution from its founding and first waqf endowment until the time when the 1668–1669 manshur provides a comparative abundance of information. In the process, I discovered that it was necessary to create a narrative of the history of the region, for no satisfactory one now exists, and to try to sketch in the political, economic, and social conditions that had the greatest influence on the way in which the institution and its endowments evolved.

In 1973, the first product of this research appeared in the form of a doctoral dissertation submitted to the department of Near Eastern Studies at Princeton University. This book is an elaboration and considerable expansion of that first effort.

Many people and organizations have encouraged and assisted me in the course of writing this book. I owe my professors at Princeton University, in particular Michel M. Mazzaoui and Martin B. Dickson, a debt of gratitude that can never be adequately repaid. Ashraf Ghani and Aharon Layish also encouraged me and made many helpful suggestions for which I am grateful. For financial support, without which the circumstances that brought the *Tarikh-i Mazar-i Sharif* into my hands would not have occurred, I must thank the U.S. Department of Education (then part of the Department of Health, Education and Welfare) for awarding me the Fulbright Grant that took me to Afghanistan. Since then the American Council for Learned Societies/Social Science Research Council, the International Research and Exchanges Board, and the U.S. Department of

Education, while providing financial assistance for other research, have indirectly supported work on this book. To them I extend my thanks. Finally, thanks also are due the Hagop Kevorkian Center for Near Eastern Studies at New York University, which underwrote the cost of the book jacket.

Note on Transliteration

CENTRAL ASIA in the period of this book was the meeting place of at least four major linguistic and cultural currents—the Arabo-Persian, the Turko-Mongol, the Anglo-Indian, and the Russian. The first two traditions used the Arabic script to produce written forms of names and terms, the third rendered those same names intelligible to the reading public in the Latin alphabet, while the fourth reproduced Central Asian names and terms in the Cyrillic alphabet.

While Arabo-Persian names and terminology are generally consistently rendered in Arabic script, the same cannot be said of Turko-Mongol names and terms reproduced in Arabic (or for that matter English or Russian names and terms). Inconsistency (to the point of unintelligibility in some cases) is also the norm for Arabo-Persian and Turko-Mongol names and terms reproduced in the Latin and Cyrillic scripts.

Choosing among the bewildering variety of renderings of terms that have been transformed by one or another of these scripts is no small problem. Words of Persian or Turko-Mongol origin that pass from the Arabic script into the Cyrillic via the Latin or into the Latin via the Cyrillic can undergo very strange transformations. In this book, since most of the words being rendered in the Latin alphabet originally come from Arabo-Persian sources, some basic rules have been adopted for transliterating names and terms that cannot be sensibly translated. The object of transliteration is mainly to provide an alphabetic equivalent for each letter being transliterated and only secondarily to reproduce or approximate the sound. (Some Arabic letters, for example, have very different sounds when used in Persian. At the same time, a number of different letters of the Arabo-Persian alphabet may sound exactly the same when uttered in Persian or Turkish.) Of course, equivalence is based to a large extent on phonetic similarity. Here each individual letter of the Arabo-Persian alphabet will have its own Latin alphabet equivalent regardless of whether or not that letter reproduces the sound precisely. For example, I transliterate the word for Islamic judge as *qadi* rather than as *kazi* even though the latter better represents its sound as pronounced in Central Asia. Diacritics are used to distinguish letters for which there is no straightforward Latin alphabet equivalent.

In transliterating I have generally followed the system used by the *Encyclopaedia of Islam*, with a few modifications. First, the following equivalents have been changed:

$\check{C}$ = j   rather than dj
$\check{C}$ = ch   rather than č
ق = q   rather than ḳ

Second, in transliterating the Cyrillic alphabet, I have modified the *Encyclopaedia of Islam* system as follows:

й	=	i in place of y
ж	=	zh in place of ž
ч	=	ch in place of č
щ	=	shch in place of shč
ы	=	y in place of i
ю	=	iu in place of yu
я	=	ia in place of ya

Some liberties have been taken with Turkish terms. For example, the word properly transliterated as *bik*, *biki* (or *big*, *bigi*) is rendered *beg*, *begi*.

Finally, when searching for the perfect system of transliteration, the writer must also reckon with his readers. For those who know the languages and scripts from which words are being transliterated, it is often unnecessary to provide full transliteration (i.e., with diacritics for lengthened vowels and for consonants without Latin equivalents). The expert reader can mentally convert the letters based on his or her knowledge of context and language. For those who have no knowledge of the language, full transliteration is even less helpful, for it simply distracts and confuses the reader. Those best served by full transliteration are either readers who fall somewhere in between, having some knowledge of the language but not certain enough to make the automatic mental conversion of the letters, or expert readers who are interested in the precise way in which a specific text transliterates a particular name or term.

To try to meet the various expectations brought to the reading of this book, I provide full diacritics for all names and terms in the glossary, bibliography, and index. In addition, because of the particular difficulty presented by names of Mongol and Turkish origin when rendered in Arabic script, I have given some of the variant spellings of these words in the glossary and index entries.

To simplify matters further, I have opted for familiar renderings of well-known geographic names, even though they may differ somewhat from the forms that would emerge if I were to apply the above rules strictly (i.e., Herat for Harāt and Tashkent for Tashkand).

For those still interested in pronunciation, the following is an approximate guide to the way in which Arabo-Persian consonants and vowels without an obvious English equivalent were apparently pronounced in Balkh in the period of this study:

<u>th</u>	=	s
<u>dh</u>	=	z
ḍ	=	z
q	=	k
a	=	a in *pat*
i	=	i in *ship*
u	=	u in *put*
ā	=	a in *shah*
ī	=	ee in *feet*
ū	=	oo in *hoop*
ʾ		Unpronounced
ʿ		Unpronounced

Abbreviations

COMPLETE citations of the works listed below may be found in the Bibliography.

BA 2–4	Mahmud b. Amir Wali. *Bahr al-asrar fi manaqib al-akhyars* parts (rukn) 2–4 of vol. 6
EI (1, 2, S)	1: *Encyclopaedia of Islam.* 1st ed.
	2: *Encyclopaedia of Islam.* New ed.
	S: *Shorter Encyclopaedia of Islam.*
EIr	Yarshater, E., ed. *Encyclopaedia Iranica*
FA	*Al-Fatawa al-ʿAlamgiriyah*
Gaz. 1, 4	Adamec, Ludwig. *Historical and Political Gazetteer of Afghanistan*, vols. 1 and 4
IVAN	Institut Vostokovedeniia Akademii Nauk
SSR	Sovetsk(oi) Sotsialistichesk(oi) Respublik(i)
TMS	Nur Muhammad, Hafiz. *Tarikh-i Mazar-i Sharif*
TR	Sharaf al-Din. *Tarikh-i Mir Sayyid Sharif Raqim (Tarikh-i Raqimi)*

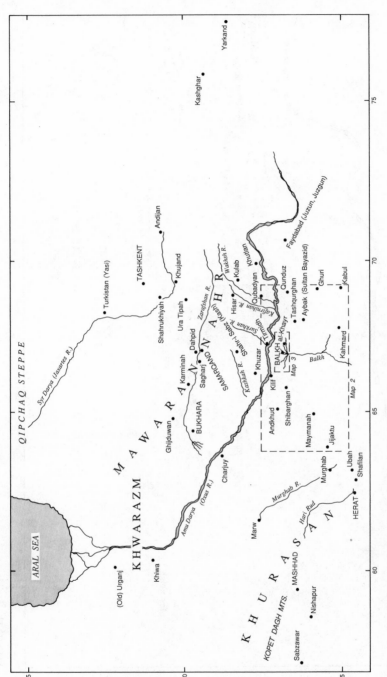

Map 1. Central Asia in the sixteenth through nineteenth centuries.

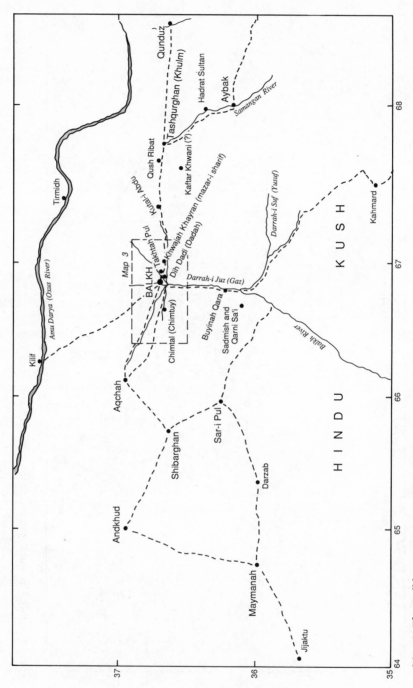

Map 2. The Balkh appanage: waqf sites of the seventeenth century.

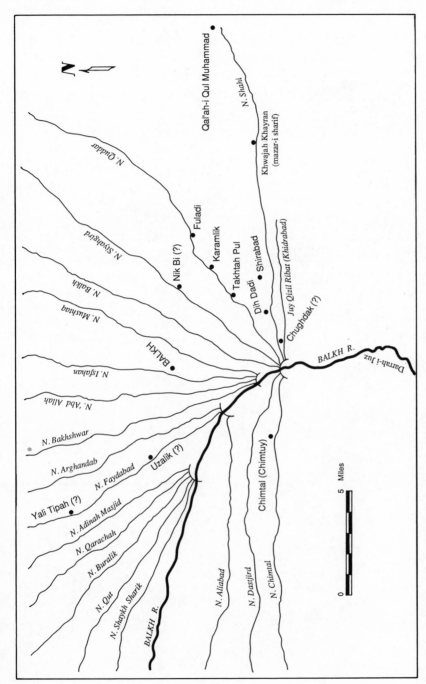

Map 3. Waqf sites in the Hazhdah Nahr system in the seventeenth through nineteenth centuries.

Waqf in Central Asia

Introduction

"IT IS IMPOSSIBLE to understand and to appreciate a juridical institution at all without having considered it beforehand in its natural milieu and without having pursued its historical evolution." So wrote Fuad Köprülü nearly half a century ago in the first article in the inaugural issue of the journal *Vakıflar Dergisi*.[1] Anyone who has spent time studying the history of Islamdom has formed some idea of the institution of the Islamic endowment, or *waqf* (*vaqf* in the western Persian-speaking regions, *vakıf* to a Turk, and *hubus* to a North African).[2] No one would question its central importance in the social and economic history of the Islamicate regions, particularly in the twelfth to nineteenth centuries, and most scholars consider it the single most important institution for the provision of community social services in Islamdom. Whether supporting education; financing public buildings and facilities; providing welfare for the poor, the indigent, and travelers; feeding birds and stray cats and dogs; or supplying communal tools and utensils, waqf has been thoroughly woven into the fabric of daily life and its ubiquitousness established by the breadth and depth of the historical record.

But despite the literature about waqf, Köprülü's challenge to consider it in its own context both temporally and geographically has remained largely unanswered. In 1942 he noted that despite the tremendous volume of studies then available on waqf it was still little understood as a historical phenomenon.[3] As late as 1965, Claude Cahen wrote ". . . no work as yet has dealt with the history, let alone the economic history, of the waqf. . . ."[4] Köprülü argued for the study of waqf from the perspective of social history and suggested an approach that would embrace the entire Islamicate world.[5] But since those words appeared in print, research and writing on waqf[6] have been affected by the general gravitation

[1] Köprülü 1938, 4.

[2] The Arabic plural form is *awqaf*. However, throughout this book I have elected to use the Anglicized form, *waqfs*, when speaking of more than one endowment.

[3] Köprülü 1942, 6.

[4] Cahen 1965, 91.

[5] Köprülü 1938, 4–9.

[6] Among the scholars whose works should be consulted on waqf in Anatolia, Iran, and the Arab region are Muhammad Muhammad Amin, Gabriel Baer, Omar Lutfi Barkan, Soraya Faroqhi, Leonor Fernandes, Ronald Jennings, Metin Kunt, Uri Kupferschmidt, Ann Lambton, Aharon Layish, and Andre Raymond.

of historical scholarship toward economic and social issues to such a point that the methodological problems that such a study would involve would render it unworkable, at least for the time being. The amount of literature available is now so massive and, more importantly, reveals such a wide range of as yet unresolved problems as to make a comparative study of the type envisioned by Köprülü impractical. In such a study, the author would have to make sense not only of the political and social histories of Islamdom from Indonesia to Mauritania but also of economic developments, including such complex and understudied topics as land tenure, market and nonmarket exchanges, agriculture (especially agronomy), and manufacturing. The essential and highly individualistic issue of terminology alone makes such a study almost inconceivable at this point. As only one example, terms for units of land may vary widely in one region over a period of a century and between regions contemporaneously. Until a complete understanding of the meaning of such terms is obtained, it is very difficult to make accurate comparative assessments of such issues as the changing proportion of different categories of landholding, the flow of land into and out of cultivation over time, and comparative crop yields, and, therefore, to assess changing economic conditions.

Certainly the direction of scholarship, guided by the same belief in the necessity of understanding the historical and "natural" milieu of waqf, has been away from the type of all-encompassing work proposed by Köprülü. Instead the focus has been on limited geographic areas[7] or on single aspects of waqf.[8] The value of the monographic treatment is in allowing the historian to consider the whole range of the transactions and interactions of waqf within a limited scope, either in time or in space, while maintaining some control over the material.

The subject of this book is the corpus of waqf administered on behalf of the shrine complex of 'Ali b. Abi Talib near Balkh. The conclusions drawn for the 'Alid shrine's waqf may prove useful to others in examining comparable cases. At the same time, it is my firm belief that the particular historical circumstances of Balkh and its surrounding region shaped the waqf institution in unique ways that could not be reproduced elsewhere. While it is hoped that the reader will find parallels elsewhere, the shrine and its waqf at Balkh should not necessarily be taken as a model for the evolution of waqf.

In the course of carrying out the research for this study, it became clear that the literature about the waqf at Balkh, as well as waqf in Central Asia generally, tended to fall into two broad categories: works of a theoretical and legal nature (generally those of Muslim legal scholarship)

---

[7] For example, see Faroqhi 1974, 1981, 1984.
[8] For example, Baer 1979, 1982; Shinar 1982.

and descriptive and analytical works. There is no fine line that can be drawn between the two categories; they deal with the same subject and often overlap. And both have a marked tendency to regard waqf, whether generally or in a specific case, as a permanent and therefore static institution, an institution that once created remains largely unchanged. Many authors, whether legal thinkers attempting to formalize the principles of waqf or scholars concerned with waqf as a phenomenon in history, have found it difficult to correlate the idea of the inevitability of change with the legal concept of waqf's immutability.

THEORETICAL AND LEGAL WORKS

Legal works include the fatwa collections, manuals of legal formularies (*shurut*), and monographs devoted to waqf. The legal school of interpretation for Central Asia in the period under discussion is that of Abu Hanifah al-Nu'man (d. 767), known as the Hanafi or Nu'mani school. The legal tradition on waqf comes down from Abu Hanifah through his two main interpreters, Abu Yusuf (d. 808) and al-Shaybani (d. 805) (the latter usually cited in the Hanafi texts by his given name, Muhammad). Through the citations found in such latter-day (late-seventeenth-century) Hanafi compilations as *al-Fatawa al-'Alamgiriyah* (*FA*); through the fiqh works which were commented upon, glossed, and super-glossed in sixteenth- and seventeenth-century Central Asia; through the works cited in manuals of legal formularies; or through biographical entries on legal scholars, in which the works they read and wrote are listed, it is possible to identify the authoritative legal works and thus the authoritative legal tradition on waqf in Balkh. Using *FA*[9] as a representative summation of the works current in Central Asian and Hindustani Hanafi law at the end of the seventeenth century, we find nearly fifty different sources cited in the *kitab al-waqf*, the chapter on waqf. In addition, the opinions of another dozen or so individual authorities or groups of authorities, such as the "shaykhs of Bukhara" and "shaykhs of Balkh" (referring to the legal scholars of those two cities in the eleventh and twelfth centuries), are

[9] Here I have concentrated on works that were considered authoritative in Balkh during the period covered by this study. Although *FA* was compiled in India, it serves our purposes for several reasons. In the first place, the bulk of its sources are Central Asian. Second, it has been published and (partially) translated, whereas Central Asian fiqh works contemporary with it are far less accessible—works like al-Khwarazmi's *al-Fatawa al-Shibaniyah* (*Fatawa Shibani Khan*), compiled for the founder of the Abu'l-Khayrid/Shibanid line in Mawarannahr, Muhammad Shibani Khan (d. 1510), or the seventeenth-century *Fatawa Subhaniyah*, compiled for Subhan Quli Khan (d. 1702). Third, these latter sources cite the same authorities as *FA*. Perhaps an analysis and comparison of the texts will show different emphases over time and between regions, but for now the Indian work serves well enough.

adduced from quotations in the works cited. The works used by *FA* fall more or less into six categories with one or two prominent subcategories:

1. Fatwa works, the authors of which select appropriate opinions from the authorities of their time and where applicable cite opposing points of view, in which case a recommendation for the mufti using the work is given.
2. A line of scholarship going back to al-Quduri's (d. 1037) *Mukhtasar*.[10]
3. A line of scholarship going back to Husam al-Din 'Umar Ibn Mazah (d. 1141),[11] author of *al-Waqi'at al-Husamiyah*.
4. A third line to *al-Hidayah* of Burhan al-Din 'Ali b. Abi Bakr al-Marghinani (d. 1197)[12] within which line there is a major subcategory of commentaries stemming from Mahmud b. Ahmad b. 'Ubayd Allah al-Mahbubi, who flourished in the thirteenth century.
5. A fourth line from Hafiz al-Din Abu'l-Barakat 'Abd Allah b. Ahmad al-Nasafi's (d. 1310) *Kanz al-daqa'iq* and *al-Kafi*.[13]
6. A group of miscellaneous *furu'* works, whose antecedents are a combination of all these lines.

Besides fiqh works, I also include in the category of legal materials the documents—waqf inscriptions, waqf deeds (*waqfnamahs* or *waqfiyat*), government decrees (*farmans, manshurs, yarlighs, 'inayatnamahs*)—directly related to waqf as well as such ancillary documents as sale/purchase agreements, lease agreements, and tenancy and development (*hikr* and *sukna*) covenants.

What nearly all these works have in common (with the exception of government documents confirming waqf conditions or attempting to correct abuses) is an a priori perspective, that is, they postulate what waqf should be, not necessarily what it became, and as such convey to the investigator an idealized, however indispensable, picture of waqf.

In its narrowly legal sense, *waqf* is the voluntary relinquishing of the right of disposal of a thing by its owner and the dedication of the usufruct of that thing to some charitable end, as a charitable gift (*sadaqah*).[14] The word *waqf* refers to the act of transferring the thing to a permanent state of impoundment, but it has come to be widely used as well for the thing impounded (more properly *mawquf*, pl. *mawqufat*, or *sadaqah mawqufah*, as the legal texts generally refer to it).[15] The act of waqf is considered

---

[10] Brockelmann 1943–49, 1:183.

[11] Ibid., 179. Barthold 1968, 326–27 and 353–55 discusses the political activities of Ibn Mazah and his successors.

[12] Brockelmann 1943–49, 1:466.

[13] Ibid., 2:251.

[14] The standard Hanafi phrasing may be found in al-Marghinani 1980, 3:10. The work was translated in the mid-nineteenth century by Charles Hamilton (see al-Marghinani 1957).

[15] Heffening 1961; Fernandes 1980, 12, where the use of the term for both the endowment and the object of the endowment in Mamluk Egypt is discussed.

by Hanafi lawyers to be accomplished and the right of alienation relinquished (implicitly to God) either when a *qadi* (judge) probates the waqf deed or when the waqf donor, in the words of al-Nasafi in *al-Kafi*, "delivers what he has made waqf to the waqf administrator [*mutawalli*] then [as a legal procedure] alleges that the waqf is not binding and the qadi issues a decision that it is."[16]

The practice of voluntarily alienating one's property for a purpose benefiting the community as a whole was ascribed to Islamdom's earliest history. Despite this, the surviving hadith texts show no unanimity on the admissibility of the practice. The ninth-century Hanafi tradition on the earliest waqf relates that Mukhayriq, who was killed thirty-two months after the Hijrah, willed all his wealth to the Prophet. The latter impounded it and made it a charitable gift. Al-Khassaf considered that act to constitute the first waqf.[17] Others see the first waqf as 'Umar b. al-Khattab's (d. 644) dedication of land at Khaybar to a charitable purpose on the advice of the Prophet.[18]

Among the eighth-century Hanafis, there was much difference of opinion, first on the admissibility of waqf and then on its irrevocability. Abu Hanifah held at first that, since the usufruct was a nonexistent thing and as it was not permissible to make a charitable gift of a nonexistent thing, then waqf was not permissible.[19] Having later adopted the view that waqf was permissible, he then saw it as analogous to an interest-free loan and therefore revocable by the bestower, a point on which his disciples, Abu Yusuf and Muhammad al-Shaybani, overruled him, at least as they were interpreted by later lawyers.[20]

Systematization of the regulations concerning waqf came in the ninth century in the works of Abu Bakr Ahmad b. 'Amr al-Khassaf (d. 875) and Hilal ibn Yahya ibn Muslim al-Basri (d. 859).[21] These specialized works attempted to define every legal issue that might arise for a waqf and supply an authoritative answer. Much later, in the sixteenth century, Ibrahim b. Musa b. Abi Bakr b. al-shaykh 'Ali al-Tarabulusi (d. 1516) offered the texts of al-Khassaf and Hilal in an abridged form.[22] By his own account, al-Tarabulusi merely restated the significant points (*al-maqasid*) made by al-Khassaf and added to these the additional things (*al-zawa'id*)

---

[16] *FA* 2:350–51.

[17] Al-Khassaf, fol. 1b; al-Tarabulusi 1952, 3. For *hadith*-reports, see the "Kitab al-wasaya" in any edition of al-Bukhari's *al-Sahih*.

[18] Heffening 1961, 625.

[19] Al-Marghinani 1908, 3:10: *Al-manfa'ah ma'dumah fa'l-tasadduq bi'l-ma'dum la yasihh wa la yajuz al-waqf.*

[20] Ibid.

[21] Al-Khassaf; al-Basri 1936–37.

[22] Al-Tarabulusi 1952.

to be found in al-Basri.[23] It should be noted, however, that for the compilers of *FA*, al-Tarabulusi was treated as an authority alongside al-Khassaf and Hilal. Unlike his predecessors, al-Tarabulusi did not follow the usual *responsa* format (*su'al/jawab*, question/answer, or *qala/qultu*, he said/I said) but attempted to extract the principal precepts contained in the texts of al-Khassaf and Hilal and present them in a more coherent manner. These and other works (the vast majority of which were Central Asian or Khurasanian in origin) cited by the compilers of *FA* were known and available to administrators of the law in Balkh during the time covered in the present work.

A necessary question for the historian, however, is whether these works represented or portrayed actual situations and whether the legal concerns expressed were, in fact, actual issues at the time in which the work was compiled or written. For example, in *Fatawa Qadi Khan*, the author refers to a case involving a hostel (*ribat*) and uncultivated (*mawat*) land on the banks of the Oxus River. The question is posed thus:

> A group rehabilitated mawat land on the Oxus. The sultan collected the *'ushr* [tax] from them. Nearby was a ribat. The mutawalli [administrator] of the ribat came to the sultan and the sultan released the 'ushr to him. Does the mutawalli have the right to spend the money on the muezzin who gives the call to prayer at that ribat, that is, to help him out with food and clothing? And does the muezzin have the right to take that 'ushr which the sultan has provided? The jurist Abu Ja'far[24] is reported to have said, "If the muezzin is in need then it is good for him. It is not incumbent on [the mutawalli] to spend that 'ushr on the ribat building [for repairs]. He may spend it on the needy but that is all. . . ."[25]

For the historian the question is: When the detail seems as concrete as this, fixing the example in a specific setting, can one assume that the example represents an actual case?

There is some evidence suggesting that one may indeed make such an assumption. The late Ol'ga D. Chekhovich of the Uzbek Academy of Sciences in Tashkent, who has published a considerable amount of documentary material pertinent to Central Asian economic issues,[26] wrote an article not long before her death in which she examined a number of Central Asian manuals of legal formularies dating to the late Middle

---

[23] Ibid., 2. Notwithstanding his disclaimer, al-Tarabulusi includes the opinions of a number of other jurists, among whom are al-Natifi (d. 1054), Shaykh Isma'il al-Zahid, Qadi Khan (d. 1196), Abu'l-Qasim al-Kufi (d. 963?), and Abu Layth al-Samarqandi (d. 993/4).

[24] Abu Ja'far al-Hinduwani, one of the "shaykhs of Balkh." He was a teacher of al-Sarakhsi and authored a collection of fatawa (Brockelmann 1943–49, 2:951).

[25] Cited in *FA* 2:472.

[26] See Chekhovich 1954, 1965, 1974, 1979.

Ages.[27] These manuals were written for court officials such as qadis and muftis as handbooks of specimen forms. In passing, they give examples of the changes in legal institutions that time and changing circumstances had wrought. Such information is often introduced by phrases like, "At the present time in Mawarannahr a certain circumstance exists that . . ." or, alluding to political realities after summarizing the legal view on some aspect of taxation, "but the rulers of our day collect such and such a tax. . . . " One qadi writing such a manual at the beginning of the sixteenth century clearly describes the then-novel system of commendation (that is, surrendering lands or other taxable property to someone who would guarantee the tax payments) and gives sample documents by which such a transaction might be legally executed.

Even if one remains skeptical that such cases were in fact a portrayal of what was really going on, one has to assume at least that the writers were dealing with issues of concern to them and their contemporaries.

Many of the issues surrounding waqf in a historical setting are not addressed in the legal materials. One of the most important developments in the history of waqf, the evolution of two distinct forms—the "public" waqf (*waqf khayri*) and the "family" waqf (*waqf ahli* or *waqf dhurri*)—is only covered inferentially. From a strictly legal standpoint the two forms of waqf are identical. Whether the object of a waqf endowment was an institution or a relative was of little concern legally. But for the historian of Muslim society, the two forms were usually of a different scale and often had dramatically different social and economic consequences. Public waqfs typically had as their first purpose support of a public institution—such as a fountain, a mosque, a hostel, a cemetery, a hospital, or a school—while private waqfs were established to aid the founder's kin and descendants. To be legally valid, such private waqfs had to establish an ultimate public purpose in the event of the extinction of the founder's line. In many cases, such as the Ahrarid waqfs of Samarqand and Tashkent, the foundation served both purposes simultaneously (what has become known as the "mixed" or *mushtarak* waqf), benefiting family members and supporting a public institution. Such waqf deeds might specify that family members would receive a certain percentage of the income either as foundation officials or as direct beneficiaries, while the remainder would be used to maintain a public institution.[28]

In general private waqfs tended to be small, somewhat more vulnera-

---

[27] Chekhovich 1980a.

[28] For instance, Khwajah 'Ubayd Allah Ahrar's waqf deed of January 25, 1470, on behalf of his madrasah at the Suzangaran Gate in Samarqand (Chekhovich 1974, 76–77 [text], 82–83 [translation]). After expenses, including taxes, the income was to be divided into sixty equal parts, ten of which were for the founder's son. The other fifty shares went for various positions at the madrasah.

ble to economic and political pressures, and, in the case of Central Asia for the period in which we are interested, of substantially less economic importance than the public waqfs. On the other hand, public waqfs (and in this study we will be considering only public waqfs), tended to be extensive, either because the object they funded required substantial appropriations from the outset or because (as in the case of al-Bakharzi's mausoleum in Bukhara) over a long period of time numerous small waqfs had accrued to the institution and created, from an administrative standpoint, one large waqf.

There were moral considerations in the case of public waqfs that also distinguished them from the family foundations and which, incidentally, made them more resistant to political and economic pressures. From an economic standpoint, too, property held as a public waqf had certain distinguishing characteristics. Two recent studies of waqf-held commercial property in our day, one in Sefrou, Morocco, and the other in Yazd, Iran, suggest that waqf-owned property was and still is less driven by market forces than private property. In Sefrou, waqf administrators kept rents on commercial properties at a very low level, effectively eliminating rent as a cost of doing business, while in Yazd it was found that rents on waqf properties tended to lag behind the market, rising and falling well behind rents on private real estate.[29] This situation was due to a number of factors, including the public views that a public waqf should not make profit the first priority and that its function was to serve the community with both its endowed institutions and its endowments. Politically, public waqfs created constituencies—the employees of the foundation, the recipients of its benefits and services, and those who might have to provide such services in the absence of the waqf. A public constituency ensured that politicians would try to avoid acts that might offend the public and at the same time would be vigilant in monitoring the administration of the waqf.

A good deal of the information that comes down to us about waqfs in Central Asia was produced by the judicial and political reviews of waqfs and their administrations. From the documentary trail left by these reviews, we find that, for a variety of reasons, the administrators of public waqfs were influential figures locally and regionally.

Little of this information can be gleaned from the legal texts. Nor does one learn from them alone which legal prescriptions or prohibitions were most influential on the administrative practices of those responsible for the waqfs, which were irrelevant to particular areas, and which were replaced or overruled by unwritten customary practices. Islamic legal scholars, including the specialists in waqf, have been concerned to a large

[29] Bonine 1979 for Yazd, Iran. Geertz et al. 1979 for Sefrou, Morocco.

extent with establishing the conformity of social institutions to the moral and ethical standards of Islam. We may assume that early lawyers, al-Khassaf and Hilal al-Basri for example, were attempting to deal with waqf as it appeared in the ninth century. That al-Tarabulusi found it sufficient, six and one-half centuries later, simply to recast his predecessors' works might indicate either that the work of the earlier lawyers was seen to be substantially complete and adequate to contemporary conditions or that as a legal institution waqf remained more or less what it had been in the ninth century. But perhaps this frames the question too narrowly. It would take a careful comparison, for example, of all the texts cited in *FA* to show beyond a doubt that there had been no significant changes in the legal status of waqf over the long period covered by these works. It is perhaps more likely that such an analysis would show that indeed there was a gradual change in waqf law in general and even perhaps radical changes in some aspects of it. (The emergence in the Ottoman regions— also predominantly Hanafi—of such phenomena as the cash waqf, the double rent, the *mursad*-lien, and the hikr and *kedek* instruments for alienating waqf probably had analogues in Hanafi Central Asia.)[30]

One finds certain broad issues and principles in the legal texts that are of special significance to this study. Some of these are addressed directly, such as the power of the mutawalli to dispose of waqf property. Others are only alluded to in the course of discussing another matter.

The first issue we will deal with is the concept of the "general good" (*maslahah*)[31] of the waqf. The primary concern of the mutawalli and, indeed, the only reason for his existence is the "general good" of the waqf. What constitutes the "general good" is to a large extent defined by the formal instrument or waqf deed of the donor. The stipulations set out there are, once validated, absolutely binding on the mutawalli. Should the donor stipulate that the endowment is never to be sold, lent, rented, or exchanged, then the mutawalli is bound by these terms. On the other hand, should the donor stipulate that the property be disposed of in a specified fashion or that the waqf income be used to acquire additional property, then the mutawalli is similarly obligated to act accordingly.[32] Should he violate the stipulations, and thereby subvert the good of the waqf, the mutawalli would be liable for dismissal by the appropriate judicial overseer, generally the qadi-judge.

In cases where express conditions are not laid down, the mutawalli,

---

[30] Mandaville 1979; Deguilhem-Schoem 1988; Baer 1979, 1982. Recently, evidence of cash waqfs in Central Asia in the late nineteenth and early twentieth centuries has been discovered. See Dzhalilov 1989.

[31] Generally on maslahah see Khadduri 1989.

[32] See for example, al-Khassaf, fol. 88b.

being by definition a judicious and capable individual (*qadir wa amin*),[33] has the power to manage the endowment to its best advantage according to the regulations found in the authoritative law manuals of his time and always subject to judicial review. For the donor, the overriding concern (after the validation of the waqf) must be the object for which the waqf was established. Since he cannot foresee conditions that might prevail after his death and since his presumptive interest is the security and perpetuity of the beneficiary of his waqf, whether a mosque, a college, a mausoleum, or social services, there would be little point in arbitrarily limiting the ability of the waqf administrator to achieve these ends. In certain cases, provision could be made for the depreciation of waqf property in the waqf deed itself. Al-Tarabulusi cites the case of a slave given as waqf along with the land on which he worked. The mutawalli could sell this slave when he had become old and use the price toward a younger slave, in order that the "general good" of the waqf might continue to be served.[34] Most future conditions, such as soil erosion or the depletion of water supplies, changing trade patterns, or natural disasters, could not be so readily provided for. It was therefore to the advantage of the donor to allow the mutawalli as wide a scope as possible for maneuvering while at the same time trying to insure that he kept his attention riveted on the welfare of the waqf.

This guiding principle is clearly outlined by al-Tarabulusi: "He [the mutawalli] is permitted no discretionary action, except when the well-being [maslahah] of the waqf is involved."[35] The maslahah could overrule all other considerations. The author of the early-sixteenth-century *al-Fatawa al-Shibaniyah*, in discussing the length of waqf leases, qualifies his opinion at least twice with the phrases, "unless the maslahah of the waqf is served by not giving permission [to extend a lease]" and elsewhere "unless the maslahah of the waqf lies in granting permission [to extend a lease]."[36] Since the welfare of the waqf was almost always involved when the mutawalli was acting in his official capacity, it is clear that the lawyers intended that he have fairly wide discretionary power, in the absence of specific donor stipulations. Such power was a practical necessity for the waqf to function at all over a long period of time. In addition, at various times and places, the judicial authorities took a broad view of the good of the waqf to override specific stipulations set down by the owner.[37]

The power of the mutawalli to dispose of waqf property, a subsidiary issue to the welfare of the waqf, has drawn the attention of outside ob-

[33] *FA* 2:399.
[34] Al-Tarabulusi 1952, 49.
[35] Ibid., 55.
[36] Al-Khwarazmi, *al-Fatawa al-Shibaniyah*, fols. 90a–90b.
[37] For example, *FA* 2:401.

servers, who have tended, in the absence of specific information to the contrary, to assume that waqf property was inalienable. It is not uncommon to find such remarks as "it is well-known that the sale, exchange, or any other alteration in the status of waqf property was forbidden by the Shari'ah,"[38] occasionally even when the writer has evidence to the contrary. Such assertions are certainly not unreasonable given the emphasis placed by the legal texts on the stability and permanence of the endowments and the formulaic prohibition of sale contained in many if not most waqf deeds. But the same texts also offer vehicles for valid alterations in the status of waqf properties. In the Hanafi manuals current at Balkh in the period of this study, there were provisions for the sale, exchange, and/or lease of waqf property either when explicitly stipulated in the waqf deed or when it was to the clear advantage of the waqf.[39]

The discretionary power to sell, lease, or exchange waqf property subject to any donor's stipulations was not, of course, unlimited but was controlled by another authority, the state, whose power is referred to somewhat obliquely but nonetheless unambiguously in the texts. The government's role is implied by the frequent references, in the fatwa works in particular, to the qadi-judge and his decisions. It also appears where there are discussions of the stipulations which make a waqf act null and void. In the chapters on the administration (*wilayah*) of waqf in both *FA* and al-Tarabulusi, for example, several circumstances are cited under which the qadi-judge is empowered to remove or appoint a mutawalli-administrator even in the face of contrary stipulations in the waqf deed. Al-Tarabulusi states, "If [the donor] stipulates that the administration of the waqf be his own, or he confers it on someone else, whether his children or others, and stipulates that neither the sultan nor the qadi may

[38] For example, Abduraimov 1970, 65–66.

[39] See *FA* 2:399–401 on the conditions for sale or exchange with or without the founder's stipulations; 401 on the right of the qadi to order the sale of waqf property when the maslahah of the waqf requires it. However, al-Mahbubi n.d., 370, a mid-fourteenth-century Bukharan work, offers a dissenting opinion: "Some of the 'moderns' allow the sale of some of a waqf if it is detrimental to the development of the rest but the most correct point of view is that [sale] is not permissible on the principle that waqf, after validation, does not admit [ever again] of ownership just as the free man does not admit of the status of slave." Here we see just what we have seen in cases of *istibdal*-exchange [i.e., abuses of the waqf]." On 369, addressing the question of istibdal, the author writes, "He [Abu Yusuf] permits exchange of waqf in the absence of an express stipulation by the donor if the income of the land has decreased. But we do not issue fatwas in accordance with this [opinion]. For we have seen innumerable corrupt practices in cases of istibdal exchanges. The tyranny of the qadi has made it a device [*hilah*] for invalidating the majority of the waqfs of Muslims."

On leases, see *FA* 3:407. On private improvements permitted on waqf property, see Chekhovich 1964, 71–74 and Mukminova 1968, 129–30 for the terms *sukniyat* and *uskunah*, which designated such improvements in sixteenth- to nineteenth-century Central Asia. In other Hanafi regions, see Baer 1979, 1982; Deguilhem-Schoem 1988.

dismiss him from the position, his stipulation is null and void if he or whomever he designates is not trustworthy."[40] The comparable passage in *FA*, citing Qadi Khan, reads, "If the donor stipulates the administration for himself and [further] stipulates that neither the sultan nor qadi shall have the right to dismiss him, then if he were not trustworthy in his administration, the stipulation is null and void and the qadi has the right to dismiss him and to appoint another in his place."[41]

This seemingly minor point underscores an issue of major importance in the history of waqf. The state is an acknowledged party to the legal operation of waqf. The mutawalli of the waqf might not be a person designated by the government at the outset, but it is clear that in the discharge of his duties he not only has to conform to standards established in the law manuals but also has to behave according to the "Shari'ah-minded" norms of the political authorities. The head of the government, whether a local amir or the khan himself, was bound by moral and legal standards as well but remained the final arbiter in controversial cases. It was to him or to his official, the qadi, that questions of the welfare of the waqf eventually came. Some rulers closely identified themselves with the interests of the waqfs under their regimes and established bureaucratic agencies to supervise their operation. The title *mutawalli 'amm* (public or general mutawalli) was adopted in certain places by political leaders to signify both their arbitrary role and their moral commitment to a particular waqf or group of waqfs even though they did not participate in day-to-day management.[42]

Besides an interest in the sound administration of waqfs, governments also retained a fiscal interest in the tax liability of property made waqf. Like the issue of the disposal of waqf property, the retention of tax liability in waqf property has drawn comment from historians. An apparent bias toward the view that waqf properties were by their nature tax-exempt persists to the present despite what would seem to be overwhelming evidence to the contrary. If one is to generalize, the view most supported by legal and historical evidence is that lands liable for taxes retained that liability on being made waqf. Similarly, property that was not liable did not acquire any tax liability on being made waqf. This would seem to be the rule, to which of course there are numerous exceptions. The law manuals generally assume that property subject to tax (*kharaj* or *jibayah*) remains so when transferred to a waqf. One of the questions raised in the manuals is whether or not the mutawalli may bor-

---

[40] Al-Tarabulusi 1952, 50.

[41] *FA* 2:409.

[42] Shah 'Abbas (r. 1587–29), for example, so designated himself in the waqfs he founded at Mashhad and Isfahan. See McChesney 1981, 169, 172. The Afghan amir 'Abd al-Rahman Khan assigned himself a similar title (see chapter 13).

row against the waqf property if he has insufficient funds to pay the taxes when they fall due.[43] One of the few cases (if not the only one) in which tax exemption seems to have been assumed was when a cemetery or mosque was at issue. The *FA*, citing *Fatawa Qadi Khan*, says that it is correct that kharaj land becomes exempt from kharaj if the owner makes it a cemetery, and that the same holds true in the case of a commercial building (*khan*) or house whose income is dedicated to a cemetery.[44]

That governments resisted efforts to reduce or remove tax obligations is shown in Central Asia by the case of the Ahrarid waqfs, extensive properties left by the celebrated fifteenth-century Naqshbandi figure, Khwajah 'Ubayd Allah Ahrar (d. 1490). In the nineteenth century, his descendants, still administering the waqfs, complained of the heavy tax burden they bore.[45] Ahrar himself once reportedly described the extent of some of his properties not by acreage, price, or yield, but by the amount of tax he paid.[46] At the time he made the remark, the lands in question were not yet waqf but it seems safe to suppose that the waqf on which his descendants were paying taxes had also been among the taxed properties to which the khwajah had wryly referred.

For a mutawalli there was obviously an interest in obtaining tax exemption for waqf lands or, in the case of new waqf lands added to an already existing stock, to see that they were as unencumbered as possible. So besides exemptions from sympathetic politicians, there evolved a complicated legal method for converting tax-liable into tax-exempt property before making it waqf.[47] The procedure was being used at least as early as 1556.[48] Citing evidence in two fourteenth-century fatwa collections (*al-Fatawa al-Tatarkhaniyah* and *Khizanat al-muftin*), a judicial document ruled that the permanent exchange of one-third of a piece of 'ushr land (land taxed at 10 percent of its yield) or two-thirds of a piece of kharaj land (land taxed in this case at 20 percent of yield) for a tax

---

[43] *FA* 2:424; al-Tarabulusi 1952, 57. The Baillie abridged translation of *FA* has a footnote on p. 622 that says "According to the *Land Tax of India*, waqf land is generally liable to the kharaj." Lambton 1969, 234 notes that in Iran, "before the grant of the Constitution, vaqf land was subject to taxation unless granted immunity by a special decree or farman." In an Afghan source of the early twentieth century, we find some evidence that waqf land may have had its own specific tax levy, at least in Afghanistan at that time. In the archives of the Afghan sardar 'Inayat Allah Khan (son of the amir Habib Allah Khan, who reigned from 1901 to 1919), there is a petition for relief from an assessment on waqf that reads in part, "For several years they have annually assessed us forty *sir* of wheat and forty-eight *sir* [one *sir* = about seven kilograms] of white straw as *maliyat* [tax] on waqf. Since we do not have a single iota of waqf land we ask to be relieved of this levy" (Shokhumorov 1980, 103).

[44] *FA* 2:472.

[45] "Vakufy v Tashkente," in *Turkestanskie Vedomosti*, 1884, 10:32.

[46] Ivanov 1954, 11, quoting Wa'iz-i Kashifi, *Rashahat 'ayn al-hayat*.

[47] See Chekhovich 1955.

[48] Ibid., 227.

exemption on the remainder was valid.[49] The amount of land that had to be surrendered permanently in order to receive tax exemption on the remainder thus depended on the original tax liability. The greater the tax claim of the government, the less the residual value to the owner.

One of the two cases cited by Chekhovich in which such a procedure was used to create tax-exempt land illustrates precisely how tax exemption could be gained for a piece of land about to be made waqf without reducing the size of the land. In a waqf deed dated 1618, Qadi Mirza Beg, a judge in Bukhara, donated two parcels of 'ushr land as waqf on behalf of a mosque. Before the waqf was established, however, the judge first sold the two parcels to a third party. Then, acting as attorney for the khan, Imam Quli Khan (r. 1612–1641) (whose complicity in the transaction is taken for granted), the judge sold to the same third party a parcel of state land (mamlakah-i padshahi). The sum paid for the total (both the 'ushr land and the state land) was eight thousand tangahs. Immediately, the buyer surrendered the state lands to the judge, as attorney for the khan, in exchange for tax exemption on the remainder (the two pieces of 'ushr land he had bought from the judge). For eight thousand tangahs, the judge then repurchased his property, which was now no longer subject to 'ushr but was deemed completely tax-exempt (milk-i hurr-i khalis—literally "pure, free private property") and then converted it into waqf. In such a transaction, the government was compensated for the loss of tax-producing land while the waqf administration acquired unencumbered property.[50] The eight thousand tangahs paid to the government represented one-third of the value of the 'ushr land before conversion.

The tax status of waqf property was always a matter of interest to both the mutawalli and the government. Occasions when government tax policy and practices conflicted with the perceived fiscal privileges of a waqf administration are often captured in the documentary record. A recurring theme in the relations between the administration of the 'Alid shrine and the government in Balkh during the period of this study is conflict over taxes. Had there been no such disputes, we would know far less today of the history of the 'Alid shrine and its waqf.

The questions of tax liability and tax policy went far beyond the classical Islamicate taxes, the kharaj and the 'ushr. The men who governed Balkh during the long period covered by this study collected many other levies as well. Virtually everything that had or produced value was at one time or another subject to taxation. The appeals of successive waqf administrators at the 'Alid shrine against various "nuisance" taxes give a good picture of just how extensive taxation could be at particular times.

[49] Ibid.
[50] Ibid., 233.

Tax policy was, of course, closely tied to the form and philosophy of government prevalent at any given time in Balkh. If one can generalize about four centuries of government at Balkh, perhaps the one supportable conclusion one can draw is that public opinion showed a discernible preference for greater local control and a marked disinclination for distant imperial rule, and that this view in turn was reflected in tax policy. The records that survive of relations between the waqf administration and the government paint a picture of local disputes locally resolved. Even when the political center was Bukhara or Samarqand, decisions about waqf were made at Balkh without recourse to another authority. Such a localization of the resolution of disputes is reflected in the fact that there is no reference to a central state bureau regulating and monitoring waqfs all over the territory. In contemporary Iran, India, and the Ottoman lands, in contrast, there was always at least the semblance of centralized government regulation of waqfs through a bureaucratic agency.[51] It is not until the late nineteenth century, however, that the first such government agency is mentioned for Balkh, and even then it is an open question whether it exercised any real supervision over waqfs.[52] At Balkh, as apparently elsewhere in Mawarannahr, the control, accounting, and periodic contacts that a government agency would have required are simply not evident. When contacts with state officials are recorded, they occur at times of crises—crises in succession to the waqf administration or in succession to the government of Balkh itself, or occasions when the waqf administrators thought their fiscal prerogatives were being threatened or undermined by officials in the Balkh government.

For the mutawalli of the 'Alid waqf, such a political environment undoubtedly made his task more demanding. He had to maintain and continually renew his personal ties to the governor, sultan, or khan at Balkh. It was to his decided advantage to cultivate the friendship of appropriate government officials and influential intellectual and spiritual figures. The absence of bureaucratic supervision and a clear hierarchy of control complicated his work but expanded opportunities for exercising his own authority. Under the ordinances of Hanafi law, the mutawalli had, as we have seen, broad powers to manage his endowment to its best advantage. Subject only to specific stipulations in the waqf deeds themselves and to qadi review of the legality of his transactions if challenged, the mutawalli was free to buy and sell waqf property, lease property for use or development, hire employees to staff his administration, assess and collect rev-

---

[51] For Iran, see Minorsky 1943, 42, 78–79, 146 on the *daftar-i mawqufat*. For the Ottoman lands, see Gibb and Bowen 1957 (chapter 12) and Barnes 1987 (chapter 7). Although information on waqf supervision under the Moghuls is surprisingly scanty, it was the office of *sadr* (see Bilgrami 1984, 88–89) that was responsible for central supervision of waqfs.

[52] See chapter 12.

enues on his domains, take part in local and regional trade, establish and operate market facilities, and generally conduct himself in the manner one would expect of a large-scale landowner and businessman.

But the mutawalli's acquisition of economic and therefore political power meant a corresponding diminishment of power in the hands of others, a fact of political life which increased the complexities of his job. Without the shelter of a government agency forestalling such conflict in the first place, or providing a means to resolve it when it arose, the mutawalli was forced to assume a conspicuously public role, constantly preparing himself for recurring disputes with government officials by cultivating his contacts with the highest authorities.

We can see then that the legal basis for the evolution of waqf through time and the position of those who managed it is only partly explained in the legal writings on waqf. The Shari'ah standards provide both prescription and prohibition, but it is the particular political and economic conditions that provide (or limit) the opportunity for the real functioning of those regulations. If we wish then to know how waqf actually operated within a given environment, its "natural milieu," we need to know both the legal norms and the special local customs and conditions that affected waqf administration.

MODERN DESCRIPTIVE AND ANALYTIC STUDIES OF WAQF

The second general group of works depicting the institution of waqf in Central Asia comprises studies done by nineteenth- and twentieth-century scholars viewing waqf from a social and economic perspective. By and large it is fair to say that these scholars, being primarily concerned with waqf as a historical phenomenon and with its economic and social ramifications, have taken the legal framework for granted. The major contributions to this body of works on Central Asian waqf come in the main from Russian and Soviet scholars.[53]

Typically, their scholarship has focused on editing and publishing waqf materials, in particular waqf deeds. Accompanying analyses of these materials have emphasized the broader issues of land tenure, agrarian relations, and the economy generally. Less emphasis has been placed on the social consequences of waqf—such as the maintenance of a social welfare system or the creation of managerial elites. An important exception, however, is the recent work of Ol'ga Aleksandrovna Sukhareva, who has es-

[53] The leading Russian scholars of Central Asian waqf of the late nineteenth and early twentieth centuries were V. L. Viatkin and V. V. Barthold. Soviet scholars besides Chekhovich who have made major contributions to the study of waqf in Central Asia include M. A. Abduraimov, E. A. Davidovich, A. D. Davydov, R. G. Mukminova, and O. A. Sukhareva.

tablished the importance of waqf in the communal organization of the city of Bukhara from the late sixteenth to the early twentieth century.[54]

The publication of waqf deeds and other documentary materials related to waqf along with commentaries on the contents of the documents tends to depict the institution as a fixed phenomenon clearly observed at a particular moment but obscure in terms of its antecedents or its evolution. A single document, especially a waqf deed, is not very revealing about the evolution of the specific waqf that it describes. Let us take, for example, the waqf deed of Mihr Sultan Khanum, the daughter-in-law of the Shibanid khan and military leader Muhammad Shibani Khan (d. 1510). Published by Roziia Galievna Mukminova, a researcher at the Institute of History in Tashkent, the document in its edited form is 122 pages long. It lists some ten whole or part villages (*qariyah* and *mawdi'*), another 158 individual parcels of land, and a variety of commercial and retail establishments in and around Samarqand.[55] Although its principal beneficiary, a madrasah in Samarqand, survived for several centuries, there exists virtually no information on the fate of the waqf. The document was written sometime in the 1520s and the editor found only one reference to a single village still cited as part of the waqf in 1558.[56] The absence of information does not mean that the waqf was not operating as Mihr Sultan Khanum had envisioned. Indeed, the appointment of faculty at the madrasah in the late seventeenth century is evidence that the foundation was functioning. But we have no clue as to the condition of the waqf, its extent by the late seventeenth century, or its development during the intervening period.

This example illustrates a major problem for the student of waqf: how to trace the evolution of a particular waqf over time in order to understand how it actually worked. The documents pertaining to it, especially the waqf deeds, are in reality little more than a statement of purpose and hope. They do, however, tell us something of human memory and the economic expectations based on that memory. For example, when a founder stipulated salaries or stipends in a specific unit of currency, we may assume his expectations were that the currency would remain stable and retain its relative value—an expectation engendered by his own experience. On the other hand, when another founder at another time stipulated salaries and stipends as a share of the net income after expenses were paid, or as a percentage of the gross income of the foundation, we

[54] Sukhareva 1976. Although the author's focus is on the residential quarters of Bukhara rather than waqf per se, her frequent citation of waqf materials for her information on mosques, madrasahs, and water facilities shows waqf's central place in the economy of the city.

[55] Mukminova 1966, 26–29.

[56] Ibid., 7–8.

may assume he had a greater sense of uncertainty about the future value of current money.

But the waqf deeds tell us little about the way in which the founder's intentions were carried out. It is an uncertain assumption at best that they were carried out exactly as set forth in the waqf deed. Many waqf deeds produced no functioning foundation and in many more cases only a part of the stated waqf grant ever reached its object.[57] To trace a waqf foundation's performance over a period of time requires other records, such as court-filed attestations (*iqrars*), which tend to reveal more about the endowment at its establishment than does a waqf deed.[58] But these too have limitations. First, they are not often available, and second, they add nothing to our understanding of developments two, ten, or one hundred years later. Ideally, every waqf foundation would leave a trail of legal documents beginning with the waqf deed. Periodic changes in the administration, subsequent court resolutions of litigation, government decrees defining the prerogatives of a waqf administration, and additions to the endowments of the original foundation all meant filing evidence establishing proof of claims and, consequently, generating records. For a full understanding of how any given foundation fared in its "natural milieu," we need the entire record. Single documents, however illuminating on particular economic issues, are records of specific moments in time. But a complete documentary record of a single foundation remains elusive.

In the case of the 'Alid waqf, we have only a handful of documents, the two most important of which were compiled from an unknown number of separate documents. But it is hoped that, by extracting and analyzing both the evidential and inferential information contained in them, a useful contribution will be made toward understanding the social and economic implications of the Islamic institution of waqf over a long period of history.

[57] *BA* 4: fol. 214b on parts of a waqf foundation established by the seventeenth-century Balkh ruler Nadhr Muhammad that were never implemented. Also *TMS*, 90 for a waqf inscription commissioned by a governor of Balkh in the second half of the nineteenth century. A later waqfnamah from that same governor says that the terms of the inscription were never operative and were superseded by the waqfnamah.

[58] For example, the *iqrarnamahs* appended to Subhan Quli Khan's waqfnamah on behalf of his madrasah in Balkh (see Davydov 1960, 126).

CHAPTER TWO

The Origins of the 'Alid Shrine at Balkh

THE SETTING: LAND AND WATER

Geography and the forces of a world economy were arguably the most significant factors in determining the historical importance of Balkh. In the ancient and medieval world, the urban conglomeration of Balkh was produced by the intersection of the commercial and cultural currents flowing between the Indian subcontinent, China, and the Mesopotamian and Mediterranean basins. For some two thousand years, until a revolution in the technology of transportation made possible a worldwide reorganization of international communications, Balkh was one of the most important cities of the world.

Its economic and political importance ebbed and flowed over the long stretch of its history. Changes in the world's economy were reflected in the composition of both the urban society and the city's physical infrastructure. Marketplaces, warehouses, housing for foreign businessmen, and processing plants must have appeared, expanded, contracted, and disappeared as dictated by world economic forces. Such diverse international commodities as silk, precious metals and minerals, horses, and, for a brief but striking moment, tobacco all required distinctive and specific facilities called into and then out of existence by changing world demand. But the periodic and transient changes in Balkh caused by swings in world tastes and fashions were not of long-term consequence for the city's durability. Roman and Byzantine love of silk may have brought profits and luxuries to Balkh, but its permanence, its ability to weather the eventual collapse of its role in the silk trade or the trade in silver and rubies and to continue to service the requirements of an international exchange of goods and ideas, depended ultimately on its agrarian resources.

Agricultural activity around Balkh expanded and contracted in accordance with economic and demographic forces. This is a fairly straightforward assumption. What needs emphasis is the natural potential of the Balkh region for agricultural exploitation and its attractiveness for investment. As in most of the inhabited regions of the Arid Zone between the Mediterranean and the Himalayan massif, weather patterns placed fairly severe limitations on agricultural development. In the Balkh region average rainfall has probably never exceeded ten inches annually.[1] More-over, more than 90 percent of the yearly precipitation occurs in the months of February, March, and April.[2] The small amount of precipitation and its unequal distribution during the year would have made Balkh's site unsuitable, if not entirely inadequate, as an urban center had it not been for two other phenomena, one a matter of geography and the other a result of human engineering.

Balkh is located on the northern flank of the Hindu Kush range. The mountains run more or less along an east-west line and a few miles to the south of Balkh rise rather precipitously from a relatively uniform elevation of about one thousand feet to heights of eight thousand feet and above. Because of the difference in elevations, the Hindu Kush has been a vast reservoir for Balkh and its plain. The precipitation that reaches Balkh as rain falls as snow in the winter months on the Hindu Kush. As spring and summer temperatures gradually melt the snow, it is released into streams and then into the Balkh River (known variously as Balkh Ab, Darya-yi Balkh, Nahr-i Dahas, and Nahr-i Band-i Amir),[3] which flows north out of the mountains and onto the plain. There it has been man's achievement to organize an efficient distribution of the snowmelt for agriculture.

Where the Balkh River debouches from the mountains, at a point about ten miles south of the city, an irrigation system known as the Hazhdah Nahr (Eighteen-Canal) system begins. For the remainder of the river's course, as it flows to the northwest, it is interrupted by a series of barrages, which divert water into large feeder canals (*nahr*, pl. *anhar*), which in turn fan out to transport the life-giving substance into the city itself and its surrounding region. It is impossible to say now whether the political or administrative context led to the creation of such a system or whether the gradual creation of the system provided a framework for Balkh's economic and administrative unity. Perhaps it is reasonable to proceed under the assumption that the need for irrigation encouraged regional unity and cooperation, which in turn were crucial to the development and durability of the irrigation system. One probably should not, however, go so far as to predicate the one on the other. The irrigation system has certainly been either expanding or contracting from the moment the first attempt was made to divert water from the Balkh River. Economic and even climatic conditions and events have probably been far more decisive in its development than have the more easily documented political circumstances.

[1] *Gaz.* 4:7.

[2] Ibid. Figures are from 1966–67.

[3] *Gaz.* 4:250; Barthold 1984, 11, 15 (see note for Dahas).

The existence of a system to exploit the waters of the Balkh River for irrigation can be traced at least as far back as the tenth century.[4] The earliest known reference to the system of eighteen canals, however, is in the geography of Hafiz-i Abru (d. 1430),[5] which actually names twenty-two canals.[6] The first detailed treatment known of the Hazhdah Nahr system dates to the late-seventeenth- or early-eighteenth-century work of Muhammad Mu'min b. 'Iwad Baqi entitled *Jaridah*.[7] The sections of it pertaining to the Hazhdah Nahr system have been found elsewhere as well.[8] In the late nineteenth century, the British General Staff in India compiled detailed information on the Hazhdah Nahr system, which has been published recently in volume 4 of the *Historical and Political Gazetteer of Afghanistan*.[9] Finally, there are data on the system from as late as 1969.[10]

That the system developed and changed over time is readily apparent from a comparison of these sources. The number of canals in operation at any given time varies, the names of the canals change, the channels themselves shift, the number of villages served by the system rises and falls, and the population deriving its livelihood from the system likewise expands and contracts.

The Hazhdah Nahr system begins at a point about ten miles south of the city center of Balkh where the Balkh River passes through the gorge called Darrah-i Juz. At four points downstream, over a distance of about ten miles, barrages were built to divert water into the main feeder canals. The first barrage lay just south (upstream) of the Imam Bakri Bridge, which spanned the Balkh River and linked the east-west road running along the flanks of the mountain. At this barrage, six canals were supplied: Shahi, Quddar, Siyahgird (Siyahjird), Balkh, Dastjird, and Chimtal. The first four of these flowed to the east of Balkh, the other two to the west.[11]

Just below the bridge, another barrage distributed water to four more canals: the Mushtaq, Isfahan, 'Abd Allah, and Bakhshwar. Of these four, the Mushtaq Canal flowed to the east and the others to the west of Balkh City. Two more barrages further downstream diverted water, first for three feeder canals (Arghandab, Faydabad, and 'Aliabad) and then for

[4] *Hudud al-'Alam* 1937, 73.

[5] Salakhetdinova 1970, 227; Storey 1927–84, 2(1):132–33.

[6] Salakhetdinova 1970, 227.

[7] Mukhtarov 1980, 9–10.

[8] Salakhetdinova 1970 found identical information in two manuscripts of *TR*. More recently Mukhtarov 1980, 11–12 identified these fragments as the work of Muhammad Mu'min, author of *Jaridah*.

[9] *Gaz.* 4:249–64.

[10] Mukhtarov 1980, 106–9.

[11] Ibid., 101; Salakhetdinova 1970, 223.

five (Adinah Masjid, Qarachah, Buralik, Qut, and Shaykh Sharik (Shah Sarak or Sharsharak). All eight of these canals flowed to the west of the city proper.

According to the *Jaridah*, there was another small canal—the Qizil Ribat—which flowed to the east in the general vicinity of the Shahi Canal. This was identified as a smaller waterway, a *juy* rather than a nahr. It is perhaps identical with the Khidrabad Canal mentioned in one of the waqf documents examined in this book.[12]

Not part of the system but also drawing water from the Balkh River, according to Muhammad Mu'min, were two other trunk canals. One was in the Darrah-i Juz itself, well south of Balkh and upstream of the first barrage of the Hazhdah Nahr system. The other was at Aqchah, about forty miles west of Balkh, where the last of the water of the Balkh River was used up.

Each of the main canals supplied a number of villages along its course. The number of villages varied over time. When Muhammad Mu'min compiled his information late in the seventeenth century, 231 separate villages were irrigated by these canals. The number watered by each varied from three villages along the Qizil Ribat or Khidrabad, to five villages along both the Mushtaq and Buralik Canals, to twenty-six watered by the 'Abd Allah Canal. In addition to the 231 villages watered by the Hazhdah Nahr system, another thirteen villages were watered by the canal in the Darrah-i Juz and twenty-seven at Aqchah. In the seventeenth century then, 271 villages around Balkh City were dependent on the Hazhdah Nahr system.

In 1886, Major P. J. Maitland, while employed as a British representative to the Afghan Border Commission, collected information on the Hazhdah Nahr system. Although he still found the names of eighteen canals, one of them no longer had any villages along it. The other seventeen watered 185 villages with a total population of 14,925 households.[13]

A. Mukhtarov, who did research in Balkh in 1974, compares the seventeenth-century figures with 1969 statistics provided by officials at Balkh. By 1969, only six of the trunk canals were still in operation: Siyahgird, Arghandab, 'Abd Allah, Dawlatabad (formerly the district if not the actual channel of the Bakhshwar Canal), Balkh, and Mushtaq.[14] These six irrigated 58 villages, as well as Balkh City, with a total population of 15,644 people working 171,577 jaribs of land, or about 86,000 acres.[15]

---

[12] *TMS*, 52, 69.

[13] *Gaz.* 4:250–58.

[14] *Gaz.* 4:254 calls Bakhshwar a branch of the Dawlatabad Canal.

[15] According to Mukhtarov 1980, 124, who gives no source for the information, the present Afghan jarib is equal to 2 hectares. The nineteenth-century jarib, according to *Gaz.* 4:263, was about one-half acre. The jarib and the tanab during the period of this study were

The average of about eighty households per village estimated by Mait-land in 1886 is not inconsistent with the 1969 figures showing an average of 217 people per village on the remaining canals.

The canals served a number of functions. First and foremost, they provided the necessary means for food production. Although dry-farmed (*lal-miyah*) lands could be found in the vicinity of Balkh,[16] most cropland, and even some of the pastureland around the city, was under irrigation. The canals were also a source of power. Local grist mills (*asyab*) were powered directly by water flow, and thorns, twigs, and stubble gathered along the canals' banks were used as fuel for cooking and brickmaking and as feed for livestock. These by-products of the canal were of sufficient economic importance in the seventeenth century to be taxed.[17]

Irrigation in the region around Balkh was essential to the economic well-being of the city if not its very existence. The Hazhdah Nahr system provided the city's water supply for as many as four centuries, for at least three of which the system is fairly well documented. Such longevity probably had some effect on the organization of society. And social organization in turn may have affected the supply of water. Any relationship between society and the operation of the Hazhdah Nahr system is difficult to discern, however. A member of the Afghan Boundary Commission of 1884–1886, Captain R. E. Peacocke, thought he saw a direct connection between political power and residential position on the canals: "The course[s] of these juis [canals] through the plain are lined at intervals with villages,—those highest up near the canal heads being generally oc-

used more or less interchangeably and denoted a similar area, 3,600 square *gaz*, a square 60 gaz on a side. This was a standard measurement of area and the differences in tanab and jarib areas come from differences in the size of the gaz. In general the gaz (alternately the *dhar'*, pl. *dhira'*) over the long period we are concerned with may have ranged from about 28 to 30 inches up to 50 inches. There were various gaz measures: the "broken" gaz (*gaz-i mukassar*), the construction gaz (*gaz-i 'imarat*; see Bertel's 1938, document no. 242), the tailor's or draper's gaz (*gaz-i bazzazi, gaz-i karbasi*), and the land gaz (*gaz-i zamin*; see Mukminova 1966, 125, where the land gaz—here a measurement of surface area—is referenced in terms of the gaz-i mukassar). An early-eighteenth-century source equated 5 of the tailor's gaz (gaz-i bazzazi) to 8.75 of the canonical gaz (*gaz-i shar'i*) (Salim, fol. 220a). This is a clue to the two different gaz standards—the "canonical gaz" comprised of 24 *angusht* (finger-breadths) and the "tailor's (bazzazi) gaz" of 42 angusht. What the relationship of the mukassar, karbasi, 'imarat, and zamin gazes were to each other, how many angusht there were in each, and how these values may have changed over time remain to be determined. In the late nineteenth century, the gaz-i shar'i was put at 28 inches. In the early sixteenth century, the tailor's gaz or dhar' (*dhar'-i karbasi*) was also equal to 28 inches (71.12 centimeters) (Mukminova 1976, 18 citing V. L. Viatkin). If the ratio of 24:42 is equally valid in both periods, then the upper range of the longer gaz (the tailor's gaz referred to by Salim, fol. 220a) was about 49 inches. For comparative purposes, in contemporary Moghul India the gaz-i Sikandari of 30.36 inches gave way in 1586–87 to the gaz-i Ilahi of about 32 inches (Habib, 1982, xiii–xiv).

[16] *TMS*, 66.

[17] See chapter 8.

cupied by Pathans; those next lower down by Uzbaks or Arabs; while the further outlying villages in the plain are occupied by Arsari Turkomans, the latest settlers."[18]

The clear implication that the politically more powerful settled nearest to the canal heads does not seem to be borne out conclusively by an examination of the ethnic composition of the villages and their relative positions as listed in the *Gazetteer*, material Peacocke himself helped compile, although there may be a germ of insight here into the relationship between power and water rights in Balkh.

It seems more appropriate to conclude that the system required a high degree of administrative skill, which could only be exercised by the political authorities. The distribution of the Balkh River into the main canals and then from the main feeder canals into smaller channels ultimately carrying the water to the end user was a complex and controversial operation. Efficient water distribution meant a permanent cadre of technocrats. To avoid the problem of corruption that such authority posed, supervision by a higher power whose interests spanned the entire region was a fundamental and obvious need. The canal system justified bureaucratic development as a social and economic necessity. Without trying to establish a cause and effect relationship between the irrigation system and its management, it is clear that the canal system on the one hand and its managers on the other were indispensable to each other. Although this makes for a reasonable construct, the historian's problem is in finding the evidence for such a relationship. While archaeology can reveal the physical record, the record of human activity is usually more difficult to trace.

For the Balkh region, however, the materials relating to the corpus of waqf endowments donated to the shrine of 'Ali provide some clues about the relationship between water management and political and economic power. At Balkh, the core of the waqf endowment of the 'Alid shrine was one of the canals of the Hazhdah Nahr system, the Shahi Canal or Nahr-i Shahi. The story of the management of this waqf is also the story of the management of an irrigation system. The fortunes of the former depended on the efficiency shown in managing the latter. The Hazhdah Nahr irrigation system was the backbone of Balkh's economy. Through the record of the waqf we get a glimpse of the problems and possibilities associated with control of at least a piece of that system.

THE SHRINE OF 'ALI B. ABI TALIB

The establishment of a waqf endowment is usually linked to a specific beneficiary, an object or purpose that the endowment income will sup-

---

[18] *Gaz.* 4:249–50.

port. Here the object was the tomb of 'Ali b. Abi Talib, the son-in-law of the Prophet Muhammad, the fourth successor or caliph in the Sunni-Jama'i tradition of Islam, the first imam in the Imami-Shi'i tradition, and a major archetypal figure in several other Islamic traditions, both literary and folkloric.

The earliest surviving record that 'Ali was buried in the vicinity of Balkh[19] is found in the account left by an Andalusian from Granada, Abu Hamid al-Gharnati, who traveled through Central Asia in the middle of the twelfth century.[20] The account appears at the very end of his book, *Tuhfat al-Albab*, and concerns events that had taken place at Balkh only a few years before his visit between 1153 and 1155.[21]

> We conclude this book with some wonderful stories about the Commander of the Faithful, 'Ali b. Abi Talib—May God honor him! One of the most wonderful stories concerns the tomb of his—on him be peace—and its appearance in the year 530 [A.H./A.D. 1135–1136] in the vicinity of Balkh in a large village called al-Khayr. A number of the village's leading citizens saw the Prophet— on him be peace—in a dream in which he said to them "My uncle's son, 'Ali b. Abi Talib, is [buried] in this place." And he pointed out a spot near the village. The dream recurred and the number of people who experienced it increased until more than four hundred people, all of them leading citizens of al-Khayr and another place, had seen it.
>
> So they went to Qumaj, the ruler of Balkh during the time of Sanjar,[22] and related to him what they had witnessed and heard from the Prophet—God's peace and prayers be upon him. He convened the 'ulama [scholars] and told them what [the villagers] had said and what they had witnessed. The 'ulama responded, "The Prophet—on him be peace—said, 'Whoever sees me, truly sees me, for Satan cannot take my form.' " Then one of the lawyers among them said, "Amir, this is absurd and the Messenger of God does not say absurd things. 'Ali b. Abi Talib was killed in al-Kufah. People disagree as to where he was buried; some say he was buried in the Friday-mosque of al-Kufah under the minaret, others that he was buried in Kardhadhudah. Still others that he was buried at al-Ghadir and a shrine erected on the site. So how could he have come to Balkh, a distance of a thousand farsakhs and more? This is absurd."
>
> At this the people left. But at midnight, that jurist came out of his house accompanied by his children and associates and crying to be brought to Amir Qumaj. Weeping and appealing for help, he was admitted to the presence of

[19] Although the site of the final interment of 'Ali b. Abi Talib remains controversial, the most widely held view among Sunnis and Shi'is alike is that he was buried at the site of present-day Najaf in Iraq (Veccia-Vaglieri 1960). Ibn Babuyah 1956–57 2:351–52 gives the standard Imami-Shi'i account on the authority of Ja'far al-Sadiq, the sixth imam.

[20] Levi-Provencal 1960.

[21] Certain copies of the late-seventeenth-century work, *TR*, date the Saljuqid discovery to A.H. 530/A.D. 1135–1136 (see Salakhetdinova 1970, 223).

[22] Ibn al-Athir 1867–77, 11:179; Lambton 1957, 372.

Amir Qumaj, who said, "What's the matter with you?" He replied, "Oh, Amir, look at my face and body." They examined him by the light of a candle and saw that his face and body were black and blue from being beaten with a stick. He began to weep and Amir Qumaj said, "Oh, imam and shaykh, who did this to you?" He replied, "I was sleeping at home when a group of 'Alawites appeared bearing signs and tokens and all in white. There were young men, middle-aged, elderly, and children. They said, 'Are you the one who called the Messenger of God—on him be God's prayers and peace—a liar? And you say the Commander of the Faithful is not here?' Then they seized me and dragged me out all the while cursing me until they brought me to an open tomb. There I saw the Commander of the Faithful, 'Ali b. Abi Talib, sitting in the tomb. His hair and beard were white. They said, 'Is this not the Commander of the Faithful?' They then began to kick and hit me until I was sure I was going to die. I turned and said, 'Oh Commander of those who believe in God. Have mercy on me.' At this he gave a sign to them with his hand and they let me go. Then I woke up and all my limbs felt as if they were broken. I begged God's forgiveness and repented of what I had said."

When he heard this, [the amir] arose and with his troops went out to that sacred spot. They dug where the Prophet—God's peace and prayers on him—had directed them to. They discovered a tomb on which were two marble panels and the Commander of the Faithful within. He was completely intact and even his shroud was whole. The amir and all the 'ulama saw him. Beneath his side, they found a piece of red brick on which had been written with a finger: "This is the one who loves [muhibb] the Prophet, 'Ali— May God honor him."

He built a large shrine [mashhad] on the spot, finer and more beautiful than the mashhad at al-Ghadir. The piece of brick was placed in a silk /brocade purse and hung in the mihrab of the shrine. Most of those who had had the dream lived long lives. People visit it from all the cities of Khurasan as well as Balkh and Samarqand. Among the most marvelous of tombs is the tomb of the Commander of the Faithful that appeared in the vicinity of Balkh. And it was not known to anyone until after [the year] 500.[23]

In A.H. 548/A.D. 1153, the Ghuzz Turks captured Balkh from the Saljuqs, and they reportedly destroyed the city two years later.[24] If al-Gharnati's remarks were based on his own observations, then the shrine had apparently been thriving for nearly twenty years until the Ghuzz invasion. Whether the Ghuzz were responsible for its decline and perhaps physical destruction is uncertain. It does seem clear that for the next three hundred years the shrine had only a local significance. The Syrian author and traveler 'Ali b. Abi Bakr al-Harawi al-Mawsili (d. 1215) makes

---

[23] The text of al-Gharnati's work was edited by G. Ferrand in *Journal Asiatique* (1925). The section on the 'Alid tomb is on pp. 145–48. For a more recent appraisal of the date of the discovery, see Golombek 1977.

[24] Ibn al-Athir 1867–77, 11:179; Frye 1960a.

a casual and deprecatory reference to the Balkh shrine in his guidebook to pilgrimage sites.[25] He apparently did not visit Khurasan or Balkh, despite the fact that his name (al-Harawi) indicates some kind of link to Herat, and we may assume therefore that the Balkh tradition was at least known in the west if not treated with much credulity.[26] But after al-Harawi, a curtain of silence descends over the tomb tradition and there is little if any evidence in written sources to indicate its survival. Yaqut al-Hamawi, describing Balkh at the very beginning of the thirteenth century just before the appearance of Chingiz Khan's armies, mentions seventy-four toponyms in the Balkh area without mentioning al-Khayr, the village named by al-Gharnati as the tombsite, or the tomb itself.[27] Later on, none of the well-known historians of the thirteenth and early fourteenth centuries—Juzjani, Juwayni, Rashid al-Din, or Wassaf—seems to have been aware of the tradition. And in the 1340s, when Ibn Battutah arrived in Balkh and was shown the famous tombsites, he was apparently not told of one ascribed to ʿAli or at least was unable to recall it later when he dictated his memoirs.[28] Why the tomb tradition disappeared at this point is very difficult to explain. The convenient explanation of the devastating Mongol conquests in the 1220s loses some of its force in view of the survival of other tomb traditions at Balkh—notably Shaqiq-i Balkhi, Khwajah ʿAkkashah, Sufyan al-Thawri, and Kaʿb al-Ahbar, among others less famous. On the other hand, the economic consequences of the Ghuzz invasions followed within two generations by the Mongol invasions may have contributed to a population decline, a decrease in the region's agricultural activity, and a deterioration of Balkh's control over its hinterland. As the consequences of population and economic decline set in, the twelve miles between Balkh and the village of al-Khayr may have seemed longer and longer. That the city's outlying villages would have been the first to suffer from any recession in the economy seems more than likely. If al-Khayr was abandoned by its inhabitants as the rural economy declined, then the temporary disappearance of the tomb tradition from contemporary written records would not have been surprising. The revival of the tomb story perhaps first required an economic renaissance and a population growth in the agricultural villages around Balkh, like al-Khayr. Another factor that may have contributed to the muting of the tradition during the thirteenth and fourteenth centuries was the intellectual and ideological atmosphere of Balkh and its masters—first the shamanist Mongols (the Chaghatay khans were not firmly converted to Islam until the second quarter of the fourteenth century)

[25] Harawi 1953–57, 77 (Arabic text).

[26] Sourdel-Thomine 1971.

[27] Yaqut al-Hamawi 1886. The references are scattered throughout the six volumes of the work.

[28] Ibn Battutah 1853–58, 3:62–63.

and then the amirid "freebooters," as Barthold styles them (epitomized by Timur, the son of Taraghay and founder of the Timurid Empire), whose religion was a folk Islam centered on the shaman-like figures of the Sufi dervishes. In the realm of intellectual history, however, we are on very shaky ground in trying to find intellectual currents in the late fourteenth and early fifteenth centuries that would have discouraged the revival of the tradition.

The figure of 'Ali is a powerful one in the Islam of the dervishes and the Sufi brotherhoods. Based on what we know of Timur and his ties to such figures as Sayyid Barakah and Baba Sangu,[29] it is more than reasonable to assume that he would not only have recognized but probably have wholeheartedly embraced the 'Alid tomb tradition, had he known of it.

Whatever the reasons for the disappearance of the tradition, it was not until the end of the fifteenth century that written sources record its revival. A small treatise on the rediscovery of the shrine is attributed to 'Abd al-Ghafur Lari (d. 5 Sha'ban 912/21 December 1506), a student of the great Herat scholar, poet, and public figure 'Abd al-Rahman Jami.[30] Indeed there is a qasidah attributed to Jami himself that contains information parallel to that found in Lari's small treatise.[31] What follows is a synopsis of the story as contained in both works.

A descendant of Sultan Bayazid (Abu Yazid) Bastami, a man by the name of Shams al-Din Muhammad, arrived in Balkh from Hindustan in the year 885/1480–1481. He carried a book that told how the tomb of 'Ali b. Abi Talib had been discovered in Balkh during the time of Sultan Sanjar. Lari names the source of the information in the book "Imam 'Abd al-Rahman Maghribi Gharnati" (i.e., the author of the *Tuhfat al-Albab*), whose source "they say" (but on what authority is unclear) was Imam Abu Hafs 'Umar b. Muhammad, the great Samarqand traditionist of the eleventh century. Both Jami and Lari tell the same story that Gharnati related about the nocturnal visitations, the skeptical jurist, and the details of the excavation. There is little question that their source is the *Tuhfat*. Jami's qasidah then blames Chingiz Khan's depredations for the disappearance of the tomb for "356 years." When the Bastami sayyid arrived in Balkh and showed his book to the governor, Mirza Bayqara Sultan (Mu'izz al-Din Bayqara, according to Lari), that official gathered the city's leading citizens together and led them out to the village of Khwajah Khayran as indicated in the book. There the tomb was rediscovered (in 886/1481–1482, according to Jami). Lari, in order to counter the general view that Najaf was the actual tombsite of 'Ali b. Abi Talib, adds that his own research in chronicles that he found in Herat turned up the story of

---

[29] Barthold 1963, 19–20.

[30] Lari 1971.

[31] *TMS*, 32–34. The editor, Hafiz Nur Muhammad, doubts that the qasidah is actually by Jami.

how the fifth Shi'i imam, Muhammad Baqir, charged Abu Muslim with the task of transporting the body of 'Ali to Khurasan to protect it from desecration by the Umayyads.[32]

Apparently using Lari's treatise, Mu'in al-Din Muhammad Zamji Isfizari included an account of the rediscovery in his history of Herat, the *Rawdat al-Jannat fi awsaf madinat Harat*, which he wrote in 1491–1492.[33] Isfizari adds to Lari's version the fact that the book brought by Shams al-Din Muhammad was from the library of a certain Radi al-Din Muhammad, a shaykh from the "province of Afghanistan." The standard and most comprehensive account of the rediscovery of the tombsite and the first to mention the waqf endowment was written by Khwandamir thirty years after Isfizari. He first recorded the story in the seventh volume of the *Rawdat al-Safa*, which he completed for his grandfather, Mir Khwand, who died in 1498. Later he included it in his own work, finished in 1523, *Habib al-Siyar*.[34] The following abbreviated translation is based on a comparison of the rather poorly edited editions of both works.

> In 885 [A.H./A.D. 1480–1481] when Mirza Bayqara was governing at Balkh something extremely marvelous happened. In brief it was this. A certain holy man named Shams al-Din Muhammad, a descendant of Abu Yazid Bastami, came from Kabul and Ghaznin to Balkh in that year. He waited upon Mirza Bayqara and showed him a chronicle that had been written during the time of Sultan Sanjar the son of Malik Shah Saljuqi.
>
> In that book it was written that the tomb of . . . the Lion of God, the Commander of the Faithful, 'Ali b. Abi Talib, was at a certain spot in the village of Khwajah Khayran. Consequently, Mirza Bayqara gathered the sayyids, qadis, worthies, and notables of Balkh; consulted them; and then repaired to the abovementioned village, which was three farsakhs from Balkh. There at the place the book indicated he saw a dome [*gunbadh*] in which there was a tomb. He ordered the tomb excavated and when they had dug for a little while suddenly a white stone tablet was discovered on which was inscribed "This is the tomb of the Victorious Lion of God, the Brother of the Messenger of God, 'Ali, the Friend of God."[35]
>
> A great shout was raised by those present and all pressed their faces to the ground in devotion. Alms and gifts were distributed to the deserving. When

---

[32] Lari 1971, 19–21.

[33] Isfizari 1959–60, 1:160–61.

[34] On Khwandamir's contribution to the *Rawdat al-Safa*, see Storey 1927–84, 1:93; Storey and Bregel' 1972, 1:361, 379; and Browne 1902–24, 3:432–33. The editions used here are the 1883 Lucknow edition of the *Rawdat* and the undated four-volume Tehran edition of *Habib al-Siyar*. The tomb discovery story is Khwandamir 1883, 32–33 and Khwandamir n.d., 4:171–73.

[35] Golombek 1977, 343 dates the stone preserved in the Mazar-i Sharif museum to the twelfth century on stylistic grounds and concludes that the stone discovered in 1480 was probably engraved after the Saljuq discovery.

news of the discovery spread, the sick turned the face of hope toward this threshold. It is reported that many were cured of their illnesses and returned home with their dreams fulfilled. Inevitably, unimaginably large throngs of people came to the spot and brought votive offerings of gold and jewels of an amount that passes all comprehension. When matters had reached this state, Mirza Bayqara hurried off to Herat as fast as he could and there related the event to the throne.

The Great Khaqan [Sultan Husayn Bayqara] was astonished when he heard of the discovery and decided to make a pilgrimage there with a contingent of his personal amirs. After he arrived, he paid his respects and ordered a large dome built over that holy spot with *iwans* and adjacent buildings. In the village he had a bazaar with shops and a bath constructed and he endowed the shrine with one of the canals of Balkh, which is now known as Nahr-i Shahi. He appointed Sayyid Taj al-Din Andkhudi as *naqib*. He was related to Sayyid Barakah and was a person of high status. He named the *shaykhzadah* [descendant] of Bastami [Shams al-Din Muhammad] as *shaykh* [of the shrine] and appointed reliable officials ['amalah-yi amin] to supervise the votive and waqf income.

Then the sovereign returned to his capital, Herat, where he lavished favors on his subjects. In short, because of the appearance of the shrine and the sultan's visit, everyone who was able headed for the shrine so that annually a sum of about 100 Kapaki[36] tumans [a unit of 10,000 dinars] worth of cash and valuables was brought there as votive gifts. The shaykh, naqib, and the officials of the shrine spent the money on people visiting the shrine and for maintaining the buildings. The village of Khwajah Khayran became like a capital city as a result of the number of buildings and of the pilgrimage activity. In a short time an indescribably large number of people had come to the vicinity of that sacred place.

A few more details of the "domed building" commissioned by Sultan Husayn appear in a work of the mid-seventeenth century, the *'Aja'ib al-tabaqat*, although the attribution of the building should be treated with some skepticism:[37]

In 886, [Mawlana Banna'i][38] along with his father constructed a sublime building. And he did it without paying any heed to the fundamental principles of

---

[36] The eponym of the term *kapaki* is Kebek Khan (r. 1318–26), "the first Central Asian Mongol khan to strike money in his own name for the whole of the state" (Barthold 1968, 8). As a unit of account, the kapaki dinar lasted at least through the fifteenth century in Central Asia.

[37] Muhammad Tahir Balkhi, p. 86.

[38] The author is referring to the famous late-fifteenth- early-sixteenth-century poet, Kamal al-Din Banna'i (on whom see Naficy 1960; Mirzoev 1976). According to Babur 1922, 286, his father was called Mawlana Sabz, *banna* whence came the poet's pen-name "Banna'i." The *Tuhfah-i Sami*, written by the Safawid prince Sam Mirza (d. 1576–77), refers to his father as "*mi'mar*" (builder, engineer, architect, mason) (cited by Mirzoev 1976, 45).

building construction concerning strength. He laid brick directly on the ground. And from that time until the present, which is 172 years later [i.e., 1058/1648], absolutely no change has appeared. [The author may have had in mind the antiseismic foundation construction used in his day to protect large buildings against earthquake damage.]³⁹

In the accounts mentioned so far waqf is at best an incidental matter. Far more central and here deserving some discussion are the currents of contemporary religion that come to light with the rediscovery of the tomb. The modern observer is burdened with received ideas about Islam and about the features of so-called Sunni Islam and Shiʿi Islam. It is not uncommon for twentieth-century historians and other observers of the Muslim world to assign values to such religious manifestations as the ʿAlid tomb rediscovery without much reflection on the intellectual context of the period. Given modern preconceptions, we should not be surprised that observers label the shrine as "Shiʿi" despite the profound historical and intellectual connection of Central Asia with Sunni-Jamaʿi Islam. The intellectual history of Muslim Central Asia before and after 885/1480–1481 is far too broad and complex a subject to even attempt to sketch here. But certain prominent and well-known features should at least be kept in mind by the reader before rushing to attach such a vague and undefined label as "Shiʿi" to the events surrounding the rediscovery of the ʿAlid tomb. Central Asia, specifically the cities of Balkh, Bukhara, and Samarqand, had a proud history as the cradle of Hanafi scholarship in the eleventh and twelfth centuries. It is probably no exaggeration to say that the legal work of the "shaykhs of Balkh and Bukhara" and such individuals as Abuʾl-Layth al-Samarqandi, al-Sarakhsi, the Mahbubis, al-Nasafi, al-Marghinani, and numerous others created the corpus of Hanafi jurisprudence to which all later Hanafis would refer. In the Sharʿi courts of Central Asia, as elsewhere, the works of these scholars maintained their authority into the twentieth century.

At the same time, however, there was and is the phenomenon of popular or folk religious practice and belief, which does not reject the legal tradition but goes in other directions in search of meaning. In present-day writing this aspect of Islam is often subsumed under the heading "Sufi Islam" or "dervish Islam" after one of its more visible manifestations. But again popular religious belief and practice both encompassed and transcended the somewhat limited phenomenon of the dervish brotherhoods. If one wishes to apply a label to the kind of religious manifestation represented by the tomb rediscovery that is more informative than "Shiʿi" or "dervish," and more specifically Islamic than "folk" or "populist," perhaps the most suitable would be *"ahl al-baytism,"* the spe-

³⁹ Vorotin 1950.

cial reverence for the immediate family of the Prophet Muhammad. This veneration of the Prophet, his daughter Fatimah, her husband 'Ali, and their sons Hasan and Husayn is a nearly universal phenomenon in the popular religious beliefs and practices in Central Asia and Iran, not to mention the Arabic- and Turkish-speaking lands to the west, at least in the Middle Ages. The phenomenon is often labeled "Shi'i," but the deep devotion it inspires in people who would identify themselves, from a legal standpoint, as Hanafi or Shafi'i points up how misleading the term "Shi'i" is here, especially if one has in mind historical Shi'ism in its Zaydi, Ithna 'Ashari, and Fatimi/Sab'i/Isma'ili forms. Devotion to the Family of the Prophet and belief in the efficacy of saintly intercession can coexist quite easily with adherence to a Sunni-Jama'i legal doctrine and with Shi'i historicism. The imams as descendants of the Family of the Prophet have spiritual importance for all people, without regard to such intellectual issues as the absence of sin ('ismah) or successor-designation (nass). For people who in times of political confrontation could identify themselves as defenders of the caliphal rights of Abu Bakr, 'Umar, and 'Uthman and the reputation of 'A'ishah, there was no contradiction in pilgrimage to the shrines of the eighth imam at Mashhad or of 'Ali at Balkh. Political issues required political responses, spiritual questions spiritual responses. The Family of the Prophet represented intercession, hope of salvation, a rallying point for public opinion, and consistently the most visible icon in the daily religion of the great bulk of the population.

But even this view is too broad and ignores the class, economic, regional, ethnic, and family loyalties that shaped the individual's world view and thus his choice of spiritual traditions and perspectives. For instance, the place of the Sufi brotherhoods at this time reflects a broad range of social division. The Naqshbandi order at Herat, to which many if not most of the city's leading figures belonged, did not reach very deep into society for its membership, at least at this time. Naqshbandism was a social framework for intellectual discussions in the salons of Herat presided over by men like 'Ali Shir Nawa'i and 'Abd al-Rahman Jami.[40] But the Naqshbandis were not the only brotherhood in town. As we will see shortly, the lower classes had their organizations, too. In fact, it should be noted that the Naqshbandi order was only by chance a club for high government officials and leading intellectuals. In Samarqand and Bukhara, where it was more closely identified with 'Ubayd Allah Ahrar, it

---

[40] Barthold 1962, 33–34. Other prominent Naqshbandi figures in Sultan Husayn's government were Khwajah Qutb al-Din Ta'us Simnani, auditor (mushrif) of the diwan; Khwajah Sayf al-Din Muzaffar Shabankarah, a wazir; and Mawlana Qutb Muhammad Khwafi, a sadr. See 'Abd al-Razzaq Samarqandi 1941–44, 1370; Khwandamir n.d., 4:328; most recently Maria Eva Subtelny in several articles, especially 1983, 1984, and 1988b, has analyzed the cultural scene of the Timurids.

had a more lumpen reputation.[41] But even to depict the Herat branch as upper class tends to mislead. The publication of Jami's correspondence shows how intricate and pervasive were his contacts with all levels of society and how diligent he was in offering his help and mediation to the less well-placed.[42] Other leaders probably felt similar responsibilities. That there were social tensions and economic exploitation in Timurid society hardly needs be said. What does need to be stated is that, in the pursuit of the mediation and resolution of conflict, a common heritage or set of symbols was appealed to. Here the shrine rediscovery, the role of "ahl al-baytism" in society, and the part played by the Sufi brotherhoods is crucial.

When Mirza Bayqara reported to his brother, Sultan Husayn Bayqara, the rediscovery of the tombsite of 'Ali b. Abi Talib in the village of Khwajah Khayran (formerly al-Khayr), the news was greeted not with indifference or hostility but with an outburst of genuine fervor. That Sultan Husayn's enthusiasm also had a political tinge to it is of course understandable. Much has been made of his apparent flirtation with some kind of political declaration of adherence to Twelver Shi'ism (one must remember this precedes the rise of the Safawid state and the redefinition of the political meaning of Twelver Shi'ism) and the widespread resistance to that public commitment.[43] His immediate recognition of the 'Alid tomb site at Balkh and his appropriation of funds for its development and waqf endowment fit the public perception of what was appropriate and, judging by the literary response of 'Abd al-Ghafur Lari and 'Abd al-Rahman Jami, the tomb rediscovery was an opportunity for reaffirming devotion to the ahl al-bayt within a politically and socially acceptable framework.

There is plenty of evidence that such an event could be politically unacceptable. Khwandamir records, as a kind of instructive contrast, a similar event in Herat very soon after the Balkh discovery. A teamster in the city declared that an apparition of four horsemen had pointed out to him the true burial place of 'Ali near the tomb of Shams al-Din Sangtarrash (the stone cutter) outside the city.[44] Writing forty years later, Khwandamir could afford to dispose of the moment as a minor incident of spiritual charlatanry. But the episode was treated far more seriously by the Herat authorities. The tombsite very shortly became a rallying place for spokesmen for the urban lumpenproletariat and, in particular, for what were then considered dangerously radical religious figures. Khwandamir de-

---

[41] Barthold 1963, 168–69; Ivanov 1954, 7–17 examines Ahrar from an economic perspective.

[42] Jami 1982.

[43] 'Abd al-Razzaq Samarqandi 1941–44, 1391–92; Khwandamir n.d., 4:135–36.

[44] Khwandamir n.d., 4:173; Khwandamir 1883, 32–33.

scribes these people as "qalandars and tabarra'iyan." The term *qalandar* seems to have been used as a general term of abuse for the itinerant and visibly unemployed individuals at the fringes of society, the kinds of people who in other ages and places have been called *malamati, runud, ubash,* beatniks, hippies, and gypsies. The term *tabarra'iyan,* however, seems to have been leveled more at a specific group, probably considered dangerous and subversive of contemporary authority. According to the lexicographer 'Ali Akbar Dihkhuda, the name was "given to a group of people who, after the seating of Shah Isma'il [in 1501] and the establishment of the Safawid state, were ordered by the shah to go out into the street and praise 'Ali while execrating [*tabarra' kardan*] the caliphs [Abu Bakr, 'Umar, and 'Uthman] who preceded him. With the succession of Tahmasp [in 1524] . . . the tabarra'iyan disappeared."[45] The term long predates the rise of the Safawids, however. The twelfth-century heresiographer al-Shahrastani used it, for example.[46] In Herat in the late fifteenth century, the term was probably applied to extreme Shi'ite political elements, whose public posturing (vilifying the first three caliphs) was seen to pose a danger to society.

Two weeks after the Herat tomb announcement was made, Kamal al-Din Shaykh Husayn,[47] the *muhtasib* of the city, was instructed by Sultan Husayn Bayqara, with the full support of the city leaders, to put an end to the demonstration.[48] The muhtasib, a police official, immediately arrested a number of the people now headquartered at the tombsite, expelled others from the city, and thus reportedly quelled the movement.

In contrast, the Balkh tombsite was recognized by the political authorities from the outset. The fact that the Balkh discovery involved the political authorities and members of the intelligentsia from the beginning set a pattern for future state-shrine relations. Especially in the seventeenth and eighteenth centuries, the sources indicate a close identification of the shrine and its administration with the policies of the authorities in Balkh. In at least one instance, the administrators of the waqf at the shrine withheld its benefits from pilgrims at the shrine who engaged in activities deemed hostile to the political authorities at Balkh.[49]

---

[45] Dihkhuda 1946– , fascicule 61. C. N. Seddon in his notes to Hasan-i Rumlu 1931–34, 11 calls the tabarra'iyan those who deny the claims of the first three caliphs and ritually curse them.

[46] Shahrastani 1948–49, 1, 18; the Ottoman poet Vaysi, author of *Khwab-namah*, uses the term in connection with the 'Abbasid wazir Mu'ayyid al-Din al-'Alqami, who "had [both] reviled the Rafidites and defamed [tabarra'] the Companions of the Prophet [ashab]" (Vaysi 1977, 75, 160).

[47] Khwandamir n.d., 4:108. Kamal al-Din was first appointed market inspector (*muhtasib*) of Herat by Sultan Sa'id (r. 1459–69). He died in 1483.

[48] Khwandamir 1883, 33; Khwandamir n.d., 4:173.

[49] See chapter 9.

WAQF IN THE FIFTEENTH CENTURY

It is during the fifteenth century, particularly the second half of the fifteenth century, that the transfer of land and other property to waqf appears suddenly to blossom. Large waqf endowments in Central Asia were not unusual before the fifteenth century. The endowments of Sayf al-Din Bakharzi's mausoleum-complex in Bukhara are one well-known example.[50] But the fifteenth century witnessed the foundation of a number of immense endowments, such as those of Ulugh Beg for his madrasahs in Samarqand and Bukhara,[51] those of 'Ubayd Allah Ahrar for madrasahs and mosques in Samarqand and Tashkent,[52] the endowments for the 'Ishrat Khan mausoleum in Samarqand made by Sultan Abu Sa'id's family,[53] and Sultan Husayn Bayqara's endowment for the newly rediscovered tomb of 'Ali. A similar phenomenon of large-scale waqf endowments was taking place in Herat at the same time.[54]

These waqfs, like the large waqf endowments founded in the sixteenth century by politicians in the Shibanid house and by wealthy private individuals like the Juybaris of Bukhara, help illuminate contemporary attitudes toward social and economic problems. Waqf grants also provided a durable vehicle for carrying out public policy in several areas.[55] In the most obvious way, the establishment of a large public waqf was a visible expression of support for a certain religious and intellectual tradition. The mosques, madrasahs, and khanaqahs maintained by waqf income and the staffs and users of these institutions whose salaries and stipends were paid from waqf revenue all perpetuated a cultural tradition. When an individual founded such an endowment, he obviously committed himself to that tradition. But a waqf endowment meant more than this. It could

[50] Chekhovich 1965. The five published documents all pertain to Bakharzi's mausoleum.

[51] A madrasah (probably the one still standing on the Rigistan) and khanaqah built by Ulugh Beg (d. 1449) in Samarqand had waqfs whose income so far exceeded their operating expenses that a separate capital fund was established on which both institutions could draw as necessary (Barthold 1963, 122). The Ulugh Beg Madrasah waqf generated substantial revenues right through the nineteenth century. When the Russian government inspected and inventoried waqf foundations in 1882–84, the Ulugh Beg foundation was producing about six thousand rubles worth of income for the madrasah in Samarqand. (Information provided by A. M. Tashmukhammedov based on research in the Uzbek State Archives [Gosarkhiv Uzbekistana]). In 1916, the Ulugh Beg Madrasah in Bukhara was ranked as one of the seventeen wealthiest madrasahs in the city, with an annual income of sixty thousand tangahs or about nine thousand rubles (Khamraev 1976, 32).

[52] Chekhovich 1974, 72–84, 107–299.

[53] Viatkin 1958.

[54] On Mir 'Ali Shir Nawa'i's Ikhlasiyah complex and its waqf endowment at Herat, for example, see Togan 1950; Allen 1981, 94–97; Golombek and Wilber 1988, 63–65; Subtelny 1990.

[55] See, e.g., McChesney 1981, 1987; Kunt 1979.

also be used to reward community leaders, especially intellectuals, for their past or future support of the donor. A teacher appointed by a waqf donor or the administrator of a waqf whose salary was paid from waqf revenues may not have felt personally and directly obligated to the founder but nonetheless had an interest in the continuation of the waqf and the political and social atmosphere that helped insure its durability. Furthermore, the donor, in exercising his right to determine how the waqf would be administered, in all probability used that power to reward.

From an economic standpoint, waqf endowments offered significant advantages to their founders and managers. In comparison with other forms of property such as leased land or granted land, which had fixed terms of tenure, or private property, which eventually was subject to division under the Shar'i rules of inheritance, waqf had a relatively permanent character. Although every waqf was naturally subject to historical forces, the institution itself was considered permanent and immutable and therefore durable. Because of its durability, waqf property was discovered to be a very useful tool in economic development. By building a commercial establishment, such as a retail market or shopping area, a wholesale distribution center, or a hotel, and then making it the waqf endowment of a mosque or madrasah, the founder insured that the property would not fall prey to the disintegrative effects of the laws of inheritance and would achieve the urban development goal that such commercial projects usually had. Although the explicit purpose expressed in the waqf deed has often been accepted as a sufficient explanation of the object of large-scale waqf grants, the student of Islamicate economic and social history should not ignore the other ends expected of, or achieved by, these waqfs as a consequence of the character of permanence that they had as legal entities.[56]

The durability was real. A substantial number of the Central Asian waqfs originating in the fifteenth century (the Ahrar waqfs and the Ulugh Beg waqfs, for example), were to endure for the next four hundred years, through the tsarist Russian conquests of the nineteenth century. Consequently, we would expect that the economies and politics of the regions in which the waqfs were located were deeply affected. Waqf administrators were as concerned about political stability and the climate for economic growth as any private property owner, and in some ways they had a greater stake. There is little doubt that the managers of the large waqf domains were inclined to support governments that could provide political and economic stability. Waqf linked the interests of the intellectuals to the interests of the politicians. And in Central Asia, as in much of the

[56] See especially Faroqhi 1984, 40–48.

Muslim world, where the political classes, the khanly families and the amirs,[57] had little in common (whether language, cultural background, or ethnic ties) with the intellectuals, the waqf connection was extremely important. Just as the donors apparently hoped to draw support from those who benefited from their philanthropy, so did the waqf administrators and beneficiaries hope to influence government policy when it affected their waqfs. References from time to time in chronicles and other historical records to the political activities of the beneficiaries of waqf endowments are persuasive evidence that a desire to protect and maintain the economic prerogatives provided by waqf required its beneficiaries to play an active political role. A good example of this is the administration of the Juybari waqfs in Bukhara, which were founded in the sixteenth century. Throughout the seventeenth, and eighteenth centuries and well into the nineteenth, the administrators were prominent in the political and social life of Bukhara, as were their Ahrari counterparts in Samarqand and Tashkent.[58]

THE FIRST CORPUS OF WAQF AT THE 'ALID SHRINE

The waqf endowment established by Sultan Husayn Bayqara at Balkh on behalf of the 'Alid shrine fits well into the pattern sketched above. Unfortunately, contrary to the record for other large waqf endowments, no waqf deed appears to have survived from the 1480–1481 period of the tomb rediscovery and the foundation of the waqf. This leads to some confusion over exactly what the original waqf endowment comprised. Khwandamir states that Sultan Husayn Bayqara had a commercial development built in the village of Khwajah Khayran. This development (a bazaar) included shops and a bath. Without stating clearly that this was then made waqf, he goes on to say that the Nahr-i Shahi, the major canal irrigating that district, was given as waqf by the Timurid sovereign. Later, however, he refers to "waqf properties" (mawqufat). It may be reasonably inferred from the context that the commercial development was also part of the original waqf endowment. Mir 'Ali Shir is implicitly credited with a waqf endowment at this time by a seventeenth-century source, the Bahr al-asrar. He is said to have built a ribat or hospice at the shrine, which would probably have entailed a supporting waqf endowment as well.[59]

[57] On the technical meaning of the term *amir* in Central Asia in the Chingizid era, see McChesney 1980a.

[58] For the Juybaris see Ivanov 1954, 55–83; Muhammad Talib; Kashmiri; Muhammad Badi' (Tashkent) fol. 320a; on the Ahraris see Muhammad Badi' (Dushanbe) fols. 248b–249a; Viatkin 1899, 199–201.

[59] *BA* 4: fol. 319a.

The heart of the Timurid endowment was the Shahi Canal. We have to rely on a late-seventeenth-century source for information about the canal and how it came to be made waqf, for neither Khwandamir nor any other contemporary source is very informative. In a document relating to the endowment, Subhan Quli, who governed Balkh during the latter half of the seventeenth century, says that Sultan Husayn reconstructed the canal and brought back into production the lands lying along its course "as it had been in earlier times."[60] The canal was reportedly built by Sultan Sanjar, but both it and the shrine had gone to rack and ruin "as a consequence of the regime of Hulagu Khan" (1256–1265). It is not clear whether the canal had lain unused for two centuries as Subhan Quli believed or whether it may have been newly constructed by Sultan Husayn Bayqara. It is worth noting that Hafiz-i Abru, writing in the early part of the fifteenth century, did not list the canal as part of the Hazhdah Nahr system, although one cannot rule out the possibility that it went by another name at that time.[61]

The Nahr-i Shahi, along with five other trunk canals, originated at the first barrage on the Balkh River, just above the Imam Bakri Bridge several miles south of Balkh City. It branched off at right angles to the river and flowed nearly due east. Its location on the river may have given it certain advantages. Under competent management, the flow of water from the Balkh River into the main canals would have been strictly regulated. Assuming that the distribution of water followed the pattern of the regulation of the Hari Rud at Herat[62] or the Zayandah Rud at Isfahan,[63] then the flow into each canal would have been determined by the water shares of each village dependent on it. In times of incompetent or corrupt management, when the political authority of Balkh was weak, the upstream position of the Shahi Canal's head was advantageous. Unlike the canals farther downstream, there were no barrages upstream to worry about. With no dams higher up the river its water rights could not be so easily infringed upon. When, as we will see, the political authority of Balkh was drastically reduced in the eighteenth century, the Shahi Canal continued to carry water to its dependent villages as other canals were being abandoned.

We have no information on the dimensions of the Shahi Canal earlier than the late nineteenth century, when it is described as twenty feet wide and about three feet deep at its western (upstream) end.[64]

The most detailed information on the villages drawing water from the Nahr-i Shahi comes from the late seventeenth century—from the *Tarikh-*

---

[60] *TMS* 56 (text), 65 (transcription).
[61] Salakhetdinova 1970, 227.
[62] Qasim b. Yusuf Harawi 1968.
[63] Lambton 1938.
[64] *Gaz.* 4:174.

i Raqimi and the *Jaridah*. They both suggest that the Shahi Canal carried its water about twelve to fifteen miles from the Balkh River before it was distributed. In presenting the lists of villages irrigated by each canal, the authors of these books arranged the names of the villages according to their proximity to the juncture of the canal with the Balkh River. Although neither goes so far as to say that this is an inflexible order of listing the villages, it is clear when we compare the toponyms with either the nineteenth-century *Historical and Political Gazetteer of Afghanistan* or the later Survey of India Map Sheet 42S that the authors followed the order in which the villages were situated along the canal beginning with the one nearest the head.[65] The first village mentioned by both sources was the 'Alid shrine itself, the "Sacred Threshold" (Astanah) located about a dozen miles from the source of the Shahi Canal. The picture that emerges from a comparison of other canals, their villages, and locations on the Survey of India map leads to the conclusion that the Shahi Canal was built primarily to water the shrine region, whether first in the time of Sultan Sanjar or not. Moreover its name, the "Shahi" Canal, probably derived from one of the familiar rubrics for 'Ali, the *shah-i mardan*, "ruler of men."

The other canals in the Hazhdah Nahr have villages distributed along their entire lengths. The Shahi Canal, however, begins to distribute water only at the 'Alid shrine and continues only for a relatively short distance, perhaps three miles, thereafter.

In the late seventeenth century, ten locales were watered by the canal: (1) the 'Alid shrine, (2) Altimur Dawlatabad, (3) Bish Yagach, (4) 'Abd Allah Waqf (*sic*), (5) Baba Shahu, (6) Khanabad-i Baba Shahu, (7) Chughzak, (8) Chukur, (9) Arbab, and (10) Nawabad-i Jawum Ataliq.[66] At this time, there is no information available on the villages, if any, existing when Sultan Husayn Bayqara instituted the waqf. Unless a copy of his waqf deed appears, we may never know the details of this first waqf— especially the amount and sources of anticipated income. All that can be said is that the endowment seems to have been adequate to meet the needs of the shrine throughout the sixteenth century.[67]

THE FIRST ADMINISTRATION

Sultan Husayn Bayqara appointed two officials to administer the shrine and its waqf holdings, a naqib and a shaykh. These two offices survived

[65] Ibid., 4:250–51.

[66] Salakhetdinova 1970, 224; Mukhtarov 1980, 102. For the late nineteenth century, *Gaz.* 4:250–51 has a very different list. Of the eighteen locales mentioned not one name corresponds with the names given in *TR* or Muhammad Mu'min.

[67] On the level of construction during the century, see *TMS*, 35–36.

at least well into the second half of the sixteenth century.[68] It is not possible to describe the specific functions of each office from the account given by Khwandamir. He no doubt assumed his readers would know what the titles meant. A much later source has attempted to differentiate the duties and responsibilities of the two officials, especially concerning the waqf properties, but has only succeeded in confusing the issue.[69]

Clues to the official duties of the shaykh and naqib may be found in the administrative procedures of the Timurids in other cities. At Mashhad-i Tus, where the shrine of the eighth imam was also a beneficiary of Timurid waqf endowments, the office of naqib included supervision of the endowments. In 829/1426, Gawhar Shad, the wife of Shah Rukh and a great patron of Islamic culture, set up a waqf endowment for a congregational mosque she had had built in Mashhad, and she gave the naqib of the shrine the responsibility of supervising the waqf, the function called the *tawliyat*.[70]

In the middle of the sixteenth century, during Shah Tahmasp's regime (1524–1576), a separate office of mutawalli, the person who fulfills the office of the tawliyat, was established and control of the waqf endowments was taken out of the hands of the naqib.[71] No such recorded link between the waqf endowments and the office of naqib is yet known for the 'Alid shrine at Balkh. But in the absence of specific information to the contrary, it is not unreasonable to assume the same sort of conditions existed there as at Mashhad. Further, if we assume that the administrative functions of the mutawalli from the late sixteenth century onward were similar to those of the naqib in the preceding century, then we might speculate that the naqib was the principal administrative figure at the shrine. What role the shaykh filled remains to be discovered.

The first appointments at the shrine are significant for the varying "holy man" traditions they tie, at least for the time being, to the rediscovery of the tomb. The first naqib named at the shrine was Sayyid Taj al-Din Andkhudi, from the line of "Andkhud shaykhs" going back at least as far as Sayyid Barakah. Sayyid Barakah was Timur's spiritual advisor and a man of enormous influence. His origins are uncertain but he appears to have been a Meccan official who arrived in Khurasan on business involving the Haramayn waqf, that is, waqf properties whose revenues went to institutions in Mecca and Medina.[72] He stayed to become Ti-

[68] *TR*, fol. 126a.

[69] *TMS*, 36, where the offices of the *niqabat* (office of the naqib) and tawliyat are combined in the same person. But in a note on p. 100, the author assigns the tawliyat to the first shaykh.

[70] Mu'tamin 1969, 225.

[71] Ibid., 226.

[72] Barthold 1963–77, 2 (2):448–50 and Barthold 1963, 19–22 give the most complete description of Sayyid Barakah.

mur's confidant until his death in 1404, a year before his patron's. The two now lie interred side by side in the Gur-i Amir in Samarqand. Sayyid Barakah was an exemplar of the "shaykh-intimate," a sovereign's companion who mediated, intervened, and advised in state affairs but whose special qualifications were a perceived ability to channel divine assistance to the benefit of his patron. After Sayyid Barakah similar figures arise in Central Asian political life: 'Ubayd Allah Ahrar (d. 1490), Khwajagi Ahmad Kasani (the "Makhdum-i A'zam" or Greatest Master) (d. 1542), Muhammad Islam Juybari (Khwajah Islam or Khwajah Juybari) (d. 1563), and Sa'd al-Din Juybari (Khwajah Sa'd or Khwajah Kalan Khwajah) (d. 1589), to name some of the best-known advisors and confidants of Central Asian sovereigns.[73]

At the request of Sayyid Barakah, Timur dedicated the region of Andkhud (present-day Andkhoy) as Haramayn waqf and placed Sayyid Barakah in charge of it. According to Isfizari, officials from Mecca and Medina would come every year to collect the waqf revenue.[74] Sayyid Barakah and his colleagues received a management fee (*haqq al-tawliyah*), which was a stable and permanent emolument. Barthold quotes Ibn 'Arabshah (d. 1450) that descendants of Sayyid Barakah were still managing the endowment in the fifteenth century. The information in Khwandamir places an even later date on the activities of Sayyid Barakah's line.

Andkhud was also the center of another religious tradition. In 1381, Timur, on a campaign to Khurasan, was confronted there by a holy man named Baba Sangu. This figure, dismissed by Barthold as "deranged," threw a piece of raw meat at the amir's feet, a gesture that Timur took as a favorable omen.[75] Whether or not the newly appointed naqib at the Balkh shrine had any sympathy for the paranormal and psychic currents that Baba Sangu epitomized, it is well to keep in mind that the appeal of the Baba Sangus of the Balkh region remained fairly constant in the intellectual and spiritual climate of the area and had its effect on the life of the shrine and its waqf.

The second position filled by Sultan Husayn Bayqara was that of shaykh. This was given to a man named Shams al-Din Muhammad, who represented another potent religious tradition in Khurasan as a descendant of Abu Yazid Bastami (Sultan Bayazid Bastami, d. c. 877), probably

---

[73] *BA* 4: fols. 141a–b lists the mentor-disciple relationships between prominent spiritual figures and Shibanid khans and sultans. One of these figures of the late Timurid era, Khwajah 'Ubayd Allah Ahrar (Khoja Ahrar), has been studied in some detail (Gross 1982).

[74] Isfizari 1959–60, 1:171 (note 31).

[75] Barthold 1963–77, 2(2):44; Barthold 1963, 20. Ivanov 1954, 9 describes property in Andkhud that Timur gave to Sayyid Barakah and on which the holy man's descendants remained for at least two centuries.

the most celebrated figure in Khurasani Sufism. His shrine at Bastam was second only in importance to Mashhad at this time as a spiritual focus for eastern Iran and Mawarannahr.[76]

As recorded by Khwandamir, the appointments at the rediscovered 'Alid shrine are laden with symbolic importance. Is it simply coincidental that these two offices should be filled by representatives of these two traditions? Or was Sultan Husayn Bayqara consciously attempting to link to the shrine those religious currents that carried authority in the public mind and thereby gave to the shrine greater force than it might otherwise have had? In many ways, it was a neat package that the Timurid sovereign is said to have presented to the public, tying the "high church" meaning of Mecca and Medina (Sayyid Barakah as Haramayn waqf official) to the Timurid political tradition (Sayyid Barakah as Timur's advisor) and adding a gesture to the ecstatic Sufi tradition represented by the Bastam connection.[77]

The reader may interpret this as he or she wishes. In terms of the humdrum day-in day-out management of the shrine and its waqf, these two appointments were not of long-range significance. In this regard the most important appointments made by Sultan Husayn Bayqara were not those of naqib or shaykh but rather of the faceless, anonymous officials (called by Khwandamir "reliable stewards"—the 'amalah-i amin) sent from Herat to run the shrine and manage its waqf properties under the direction of the naqib. We are given little insight, unfortunately, into the backgrounds of the individuals included in this group. A seventeenth-century source numbered its members at "one hundred twenty sayyids, scholars (fudala), and lawyers (fuqaha)."[78] An even later author describes the group as "one hundred households of great khwajahs with one hundred freedmen."[79] Neither account has a contemporary counterpart but the type of individual described—a member of the upper middle class, educated, with good family connections—would fit what we know about the pool from which Sultan Husayn made his appointments in Herat. In both of the above descriptions it is noted that the new officials came to Balkh from Herat.

[76] Ritter 1960; Frye 1960b; LeStrange 1905, 365–66.

[77] In Samsam al-Dawlah 1888–91, 3:411, there is other information about appointments at Balkh related to the Timurid tomb rediscovery. According to him, Mir Sharaf al-Din Sabzawari was appointed "chief naqib" (naqib al-nuqaba'), although the text suggests that he was being named chief naqib of Balkh rather than the shrine: "During the time of Sultan Husayn Mirza when the 'threshold' at Balkh, ascribed to the Amir al-Mu'minin ['Ali b. Abi Talib], appeared, Mir Sharaf al-Din [Sabzawari] hastened from Sabzawar to Balkh at the command of that padshah and was appointed to the chief naqib-ship of that region."

[78] TMS, 57 (text), 65 (transcription).

[79] TMS, 37, citing the unpublished Hujjat al-bayda, Tarikh-i akabir al-din, and "other histories."

Though not at all precise, these vague characterizations of the shrine managers are important because of what developed later in the shrine administration. From the middle of the seventeenth century onward, one particular family, the Ansaris, perhaps descended from these first middle-level anonymous appointees, emerges into the full light of history. The writers who mention the origins of this family attribute them to Sultan Husayn's time. That, of course, is not surprising since such an ascription strengthened the family's claim to the tawliyat of the shrine and its waqfs. But the coincidences of the family name and the reference in Khwandamir to "reliable stewards" lend weight to the claim that the Ansaris did indeed arrive in Balkh from Herat in 1480 or 1481.

The name Ansari was a very common one in Herat and is especially associated with the famous Hanbalite mystic, Khwajah 'Abd Allah Ansari, whose gravesite, Gazargah, is one of Herat's most famous sites.[80] A mid-seventeenth-century anthologist labeled Herat "the little garden of Ansaris."[81] As for the Ansaris who came to play such a dominant role at the 'Alid shrine, we have no information about their Herati origins and very little (and what there is is suspect) about their early history at the shrine. We will pick up the thread of the family's history later. Here it is enough to note that out of the group of "reliable stewards" mentioned by Khwandamir may have come the family whose fortunes eventually became completely bound up with the history of the waqf and of the shrine.

By the end of 1481, the shrine proper, its waqf properties, and its administration had generally taken the form in which they were to endure through the following century. The main shrine area, the *rawdah*, with its buildings and landscaping, was being constructed, allegedly by Kamal al-Din Banna'i and his father; the Shahi Canal, the heart of the waqf endowment, had been, or was in the process of being, renovated; and the bipartite administration of the shrine and its waqf, comprised of a shaykh and a naqib assisted by the "reliable stewards" from Herat, had been formed. For the next century and a quarter, this picture does not seem to have changed much. Mawarannahr and Balkh underwent major political changes during that time, but the shrine appears to have been little affected, as far as we can tell.

[80] De Beaurecueil 1960; Saljuqi 1976; Golombek c. 1969.
[81] Qati'i Harawi 1979, 5.

CHAPTER THREE

Waqf in Its Political Setting

BALKH IN THE SIXTEENTH CENTURY

Government officials had a number of specific interests in waqf, especially public waqfs. The final power to appoint or approve waqf administrations resided with the government and was customarily exercised or supervised by the office of the qadi. Both political and moral considerations shaped the way in which politicians viewed waqf generally and specific waqf endowments in particular. From the founding of the ʿAlid shrine and its endowment in 1480–1481 until the late nineteenth century, the political authorities responsible for the region around Balkh showed a consistent sense of obligation for the well-being of the shrine and its waqf properties.

It is to be expected that politicians will support what the public supports and venerate what the public venerates. The popular aphorism "the religion of the king is the religion of the people" applies both ways. But if one focuses exclusively on the political figures at the apex of government, one misses an important element in the relations between government and waqf. Waqf interests had to be taken into account in a state's implementation of tax policy. Each waqf endowment had to be treated individually as a potentially tax-liable entity. The fiscal history of its component parts, that is, the taxability of property that predated the endowment, was a matter of considerable interest to the state bureaucrats responsible for carrying out policy. Taxes might be collected on some waqf properties and not on others. Tax claims by state bureaucrats and exemption claims by waqf administrators meant continual communication and negotiation between state and waqf administration at a level well below the khan or sultan's court. It is rare to find evidence, however, of these bureaucratic relations until a dispute is appealed to the Sharʿi-court or to the royal court for resolution. At that point a documentary trail begins, a trail that leads back to the point of contention and illuminates the nature of waqf-state relations in the process.

It is a reasonable hypothesis that the more highly developed the state bureaucracy, the greater the interaction of government and waqf officials and the closer the governmental supervision of waqf. The Muslim states considered most bureaucratically developed in this period (e.g., the Safwid state in Iran, the Ottoman state in Anatolia and the Arab regions, and the Timurid (Moghul) state south of the Himalayas) all had offices to supervise waqfs.[1]

The situation was somewhat different in Mawarannahr and Balkh, where a philosophy of government encouraging decentralized political authority prevailed for much of the period covered by this study. The political system that evolved within the framework of these expectations cannot be separated from the evolution of the waqfs under its jurisdiction. Politics was more than just a background to the history of the 'Alid shrine's waqfs. The history of the state is an integral part of the development of those endowments and knowledge of how the political context unfolded is essential to understanding how the waqfs evolved.

One dominant element in the political ecology of Mawarannahr has been its position between the vast steppe stretching hundreds of miles to the north and northeast and the citied regions of greater Iran, India, and Mesopotamia to the south and southwest. It has always been the first citied region of the Middle East to feel the effects of gradual in-migrations or sudden military incursions of steppe nomads. Its political environment has been shaped by its ability to absorb the newcomers, adapt to their expectations, and at the same time to transmit to them urban and agrarian values. I will not attempt to give details of the process as it occurred in an intensified way in the latter part of the fifteenth century and the first decade of the sixteenth century, with the incursion of Uzbek tribal groups under the leadership of the Chingizid clan of the Abu'l-Khayrid/Shibanids; instead I will simply sketch the main features of the confrontation of steppe political ideals with the ideals of the citied region and the evolution of the political structure in the sixteenth and seventeenth centuries arising out of that confrontation.

Steppe nomads, especially as warriors, moving south from the steppe into the agrarian settled regions of Mawarannahr, Balkh, and Khurasan, have brought with them notably similar governing institutions, notwithstanding the long span of time encompassing such intrusions.[2] The fact

---

[1] The office of sadr in seventeenth-century Safawid Iran (Minorsky 1943, 42; Mirza Rafi'a n.d., 33), the judicial administration in Ottoman Anatolia and the Levant (Gibb and Bowen 1957 2:173–74), and the office of sadr in Moghul India (Bilgrami, 1984, 88).

[2] Among those who have described this phenomenon are Barthold 1963–77, 1:69–72, 2(1):98ff.; Dickson 1958, 24–37; Dickson 1960, 208–16; Petrushevsky 1970, 148; Togan 1946, 287–93. The interpretation presented in these works is not without its critics. The late Joseph Fletcher of Harvard University found many of the conclusions offered about nomadic institutions to be over-idealized. (For his own lucid interpretation of such fundamental institutions as chieftainship and succession to chieftainship among the Mongols, see Fletcher 1986.) On the other hand, the typology, however schematic, is useful as a point of departure for further discussion. Although the differences between political structures and principles of succession among nomadic (steppe) and settled (urban/agrarian) peoples are probably not as clear-cut as Petrushevsky 1970, 148, for example, would have one believe

that the military organization of such groups was usually based on units related by kinship ties (e.g., clans, tribes, or families) created certain expectations. First, the unit or confederation of units expected to share in the rewards of military success. Second, safeguards had to exist to prevent the involuntary subordination of one segment of the group by another.

The political structures of the steppe organizations that periodically appeared in Mawarannahr were generally somewhat decentralized and followed a system of succession in which clan membership and seniority were operating principles. The bureaucratic apparatus necessary for an imperial fisc was usually absent. These multi-clan groupings (known to history under such rubrics as Oghuz, Turkman, Mongols, and Uzbeks) were temporarily held together by mutual consent and a common purpose.

In those instances—such as occurred at the beginning of the sixteenth century—when a steppe organization succeeded in extending its control over large sections of territory within the citied region of Central Asia, immediate pressures built up to modify this loose formation. The maintenance of the agrarian infrastructure that provided both rewards and the means to defend against internal or external enemies required at least a rudimentary level of bureaucratic supervision. Furthermore, if the drive for empire that led to the conquest of territory in the first place was to be maintained, then a wider bureaucratic network had to develop to consolidate and secure the newly occupied territories. Such bureaucracies were of course already in place, left over from previous regimes. As the new political authorities exploited this resource and came to identify its interests with their own, the steppe ideals of state—decentralization of authority and the preservation of individual clan rights—came under increasing pressure. To operate effectively, a large-scale bureaucracy needed a central authority to guide and protect it. But the ideal of equality that existed between elements of a steppe army and the principle of consultation and consensus through which this equality was made functional were obstacles to bureaucratic efficiency. Often, the attraction of a dynastic (lineal) tradition would soon make itself felt and lead to the emergence of a predominant group that would attempt to establish permanent legitimacy in its own line and revive such latent institutions as primogeniture to accomplish that end.[3] Over time, the steppe ideals of state would be suppressed in the interests of an efficient and more or less

("a centralised feudal state together with a ramifying bureaucratic apparatus [on the one hand] and that of feudal disintegration together with a system of military fiefs [on the other]"), still there do appear to have been qualitative differences that gave the Chingizid successor states in Mawarannahr and Balkh their distinctive character.

[3] Bregel 1982.

centralized state structure, including a royal court and bureaucracy. Such a process was often symbolized by the emerging importance of a capital city. In many cases the process was taken a step further with the intentional destruction of the steppe groupings that had originally been responsible for the establishment of the new state but which later became an obstacle to its bureaucratization.

Within this general framework, the most likely sequence of events that a political force entering the citied region of the Middle East from the Eurasian steppe would face may be traced. Those events are manifestations of the conflict between what have been called the "Turko-Mongol" and "Irano-Islamic" state traditions, that is, between the political ideals of the steppe and those of the agrarian regions. The development of the waqf at Balkh and its administration are closely tied to this conflict. The way in which the struggle evolved in the sixteenth and seventeenth centuries had a substantial impact on the expansion of waqf at the shrine of ʿAli b. Abi Talib and the development of administrative prerogatives there.

THE UZBEK STATE

The period covered by this study may be labeled the "Uzbek" period from the standpoint of its politics. The word *Uzbek* has acquired several meanings, and in order to understand the political situation in Mawarannahr and Balkh after 1500 it is essential to know how the term has been used. Although the origin of the term is not of immediate concern to this study, the modern importance of its origin has generated considerable discussion, which in turn has affected how the term is used in histories dealing with the period of this study. The issue of the origin of the name Uzbek is therefore worth a moment or two of our time. One of the most recent attempts to establish the origin of the word concludes that the popular etymology that the term meant "self-ruler" (*uz* = self, *bek* = ruler) cannot be supported, and neither is it an eponymous name derived from Uzbek Khan, ruler of the Golden Horde from 1312 to 1340. Rather it was a name applied by medieval historians to all the Turko-Mongol tribes of the White Horde (i.e., the peoples given to Orda after the death of Juchi in 1225) and not to those associated with the abovementioned Uzbek Khan.[4]

The Central Asian sources of the sixteenth and seventeenth centuries add yet another dimension to the term. Very rarely, and then only by late-seventeenth- and eighteenth-century Mawarannahrid sources, was the term *Uzbek* used to designate the sovereign line. In almost all cases,

4 Akhmedov 1965, 11–12.

Uzbek, Uzbekan, or *Uzbekiyah* are used to refer to non-Chingizids, members of those Turko-Mongol tribal groupings who served military and administrative functions but were not agnatic descendants of Chingiz Khan.[5] (They may, however, have possessed genealogies to *ascendants* of Chingiz Khan, but this fact seems to have been of little significance in terms of eligibility for the Chingizid khanate.)[6] In one exceptional case, the anonymous *Shajarat al-atrak* gives the word *Uzbek* an Islamic identity. According to a story (transmitted as far as is known only in this work), an heir to the Golden Horde, Uzbek Khan, converted to Islam in the eighth year of his Khanate (i.e., in A.H. 720/A.D. 1320) and "made the entire people [*il*] of Juchi Muslims and gave them the name [*laqab*] *Ozbek.*"[7]

Generally speaking, however, authors of works of the sixteenth and seventeenth centuries writing in the "Uzbek" areas were fully aware of the distinction between the sovereign lines, with their legitimizing Chingizid genealogies reflected in the dynastic names (i.e., Shibanid, Tuqay-Timurid), and the Turko-Mongol military and political supporters of these lines. These military groups, the Uzbeks proper of the sixteenth and seventeenth centuries, also had their own clan and tribal designations. Traditionally, there were "thirty-two" or "ninety-two" Uzbek "tribes" (*ilat*), including such well-known ones as Ming, Yuz, Alchin, Jalayir, Nayman, Durman, Qunghrat, Qataghan, and Mangghit.[8] For writers outside the "Uzbek" regions, especially those with a political point to make, the distinction between Chingizid and Uzbek is blurred. Iranian writers, in particular, applied the label "Uzbek" indiscriminately both to these Turko-Mongol clan and tribal groupings and to the Chingizid dynasts, often in a condescending if not pejorative way. When the Afghans arrived in Balkh in the late eighteenth century, they applied the term to residents of the region in general to distinguish them from Afghans.[9]

C. N. Seddon, in his notes to the *Ahsan al tawarikh*, calls the Uzbeks a political organization rather than a people.[10] Strictly speaking the term should only be applied to non-Chingizid tribal groups, but as the term has been so widely used as Seddon defines it, it is probably too late to

[5] *BA* 4: fols. 52a, 283b. The Moghul source Muhammad Salih Kanbuh 1923–39, 2:436 uses the term correspondingly. Also see Danish 1960, 12–13; Sami 1962; Badakhshi 1959, 2a. A vivid example of how an early-eighteenth-century writer (of Mawarannahrid roots) saw the difference between Chingizid and Uzbek is in Salim, fol. 113a, "the Juchid-born sultans and the Uzbek soldiers [*salatin-i juchi-nizhad wa lashkar-i uzbak*]."

[6] Bregel 1982, 381–85.

[7] Ibid., 370 and note.

[8] Sultanov, 1977.

[9] Note, for instance, the description of the Ansari family, originally from Herat, as Uzbeks, by a nineteenth-century source (*TMS*, 81).

[10] Hasan-i Rumlu 1931–34, 57:5 (notes).

revise its use. Here the term is used both for the political system as a whole and to refer to the tribal groups and factions that provided most of the state's military and administrative manpower in the sixteenth and seventeenth centuries. The usage should be clear from the context.

THE POLITICAL APPARATUS OF THE SHIBANID STATE

The founding of the Uzbek state of the Shibanids by Abu'l-Khayr Khan in the Qipchaq Steppe[11] in the middle of the fifteenth century, its dissolution and subsequent reorganization under his grandson, Muhammad Shibani, and the conquests of Mawarannahr, Balkh, Khwarazm, and Khurasan have been described elsewhere in considerable detail.[12] The starting point for our discussion here is not the military conquest but rather the events that formalized and instituted certain modes of steppe political practice within the conquered territory. The first was the assembly, the *quriltay*, convened by the Abu'l-Khayrid clan, probably in late winter or early spring 1511 at Samarqand following the death of Muhammad Shibani in December 1510,[13] to redistribute the khanate. The selection of a new khan at this quriltay probably occurred, although the information we have about it is confused.[14] A second important moment was another quriltay held in early winter 1512 after the decisive defeat of a combined Timurid-Safawid army at Ghijduwan, north of Bukhara. At this assembly the clan either chose Kuchkunji b. Abu'l-Khayr as khan or reconfirmed him as their choice from the preceding quriltay.[15] Taken together, these two conventions marked the formation of a new system of state in Central Asia and laid the foundation for the region's political history over the next three and one half centuries.

How did this new political order differ from the Timurid state that

[11] In general the term *Dasht-i Qipchaq*, the Qipchaq Steppe, referred to the heartlands of the appanage or "yurtgah" of Juchi b. Chingiz Khan (Dughlat 1895, 30). Roughly, the region was bounded on the east by the Irtysh River, on the north by the Tobol River and Western Siberia, on the west by the Volga, and on the south by the Syr Darya (Jaxartes) and the Aral Sea.

[12] Akhmedov 1965, 32–70, and Bregel 1983 for the formation of the empire of Abu'l-Khayr Khan Shibani; Babur 1922, Khwandamir n.d., and Khunji 1976 are all contemporary sources for varying eyewitness accounts of the Abu'l-Khayrid/Shibanid conquests in Mawarannahr, Balkh, and Khurasan.

[13] The dating of this quriltay is problematic, but the most likely date would seem to be the one proposed by Dughlat 1895, 241 as "the spring following the winter when Shahi Beg [i.e., Muhammad Shibani Khan] was killed," that is, the spring of 1511.

[14] Again, the information on the khan immediately succeeding Shibani Khan is contradictory and uncertain. His uncles Suyunjuk or Kuchkunji, his cousin Jani Beg, or his nephew 'Ubayd Allah are either implicitly or explicitly identified as the khan-designate in 1511 by the sixteenth-century sources.

[15] Tanish I: fols. 34b, 35b; Tanish 1983– , 1:86–87 (33a–b).

preceded it and how did these differences affect the political ideas and expectations of successive generations of politicans? In order to grasp the basis on which assumptions about such fundamental political issues as legitimacy, succession, territorial prerogatives, and local autonomy were made, one really needs to return at least to the thirteenth century, in which the full political effects of Chingiz Khan's conquests were felt. For our understanding of the politics of the sixteenth century and after it is sufficient for now to highlight certain basic elements that entered the corpus of unchallenged political assumptions. One was the ultimate sovereignty was appropriately Chingizid. That is, only an agnatic descendant of Chingiz Khan could legitimately claim the title "khan" and political paramountcy in Central Asia. This, of course, left the field open to many candidates by the end of even the thirteenth century. There were, however, other assumptions limiting the Chingizid qualification still further, a point we will return to later.

Another fundamental premise was that territorial sovereignty was a clan, not an individual, prerogative. Territory was not for consolidation but for distribution. Qualifying clan members had a right to share in the territory over which the clan had jurisdiction. As time passed, a new generation of eligibles had to be satisfied by new distributions. The success and durability of clan rule was linked to a continuing capability to expand the territory over which the clan had sovereignty. A slowdown in territorial growth did not mean a lessened demand for territorial rights. Instead, such demands were met at the expense of weaker clan members less able to defend their share of the distributed territory. Inter-clan conflict inevitably weakened the group as a whole, leaving it vulnerable to extra-clan forces.

By the fifteenth century the vitality of the Chingizid dispensation had been sapped in Central Asia. Political power passed to the amirs, the Turko-Mongol military men who were not of Chingizid descent and were therefore ineligible for the paramount position of khan. The principal amirid figure of this period is the eponymous Amir Timur "Gurgan" ("son-in-law"). The use of this title, far more widely evident in regional histories than modern scholarship would indicate, was a public display of attachment to the Chingizid way. (Timur married daughters of two different Chingizid khans.)[16] In addition, the amir always had a "show" khan under whose nominal authority he ruled. The premise that only a Chingizid had the right to the ultimate title of khan endured even in the face of more than a century of complete Chingizid powerlessness in Central Asia and even, after Timur, in the face of the refusal by other Timurids

[16] Barthold 1963, 24–25.

to keep even a show khan at court as a badge of legitimacy. Along with the disappearance of a real ruling khan in Central Asia, the issue of clan rights also faded.

But the arrival of Muhammad Shibani in Central Asia and the defeat and expulsion of the current representatives of Timur's line gave new life to the Chingizid dispensation. The group of Chingizid clans to which Muhammad Shibani belonged derived its political prominence from the successful military campaigns of his grandfather, Abu'l-Khayr, against the Timurids, among others. We call this grouping "Abu'l-Khayrid" to distinguish it from other Chingizid clans. The Abu'l-Khayrids traced their Chingizid genealogy, a necessary credential for the khanate, through Shiban, a son of Juchi, the eldest son of Chingiz Khan.[17] It is by the rubric Shibanid or Shaybanid[18] that this grouping of clans is generally known to historians. However, that name obscures the continuing process of generational succession and the addition of new legitimizing amendments to the Chingizid dispensation. The introduction of new clan names in the following section mirrors the process of clan division and amalgamation that characterized Mawarannahrid politics under the Chingizid constitution.

What is noteworthy about the beginning of the sixteenth century and the arrival of the Abu'l-Khayrid/Shibanid clans is that, for the first time in more than one hundred and fifty years, the cities of the region were held by Chingizids with the necessary military backing to give their claims substance. That their claims were so readily accepted and so easily rooted in the political soil of Central Asia shows that the political force of the Chingizid dispensation had survived, even though most outward signs of its existence had disappeared.

The first of the two quriltays was convened shortly after the death of Muhammad Shibani Khan in 1510. The territory that Muhammad Shibani had conquered, less the Khurasan regions captured by the Safawids, was distributed among the "neo-eponymous"[19] Abu'l-Khayrid clans. Samarqand and its region were given to the Kuchkunjid clan led by *Kuchkunji* b. Abu'l-Khayr (although Muhammad Shibani's son, Muhammad Timur, inherited his father's rights there for a time as well); the Tashkent region went to the Suyunjukids led by *Suyunj* (or Suyunjuk) b. Abu'l-Khayr; Bukhara, to the Shah Budaqid clan headed by 'Ubayd Allah b. Mahmud b. *Shah Budaq* b. Abu'l-Khayr; and Miyankal, Sughd, and, later, Balkh, to the Jani-Begids led by *Jani Beg* b. Khwajah Muhammad b. Abu'l-Khayr.[20] This quriltay, coupled with the subsequent quriltay of

[17] On Shiban, see Rashid al-Din 1971, 111–12.
[18] On the spelling *Shibanid* instead of *Shaybanid*, see Subtelny 1983, 121 (note).
[19] See Dickson 1960, 209–10 for a discussion of the term, which he coined.
[20] Tanish I: fols. 34b, 35a; Tanish 1983– , 1:86–87 (33a–b).

either late 1512 or early 1513, after the Timurids and Safawids were finally expelled from Mawarannahr, established a pattern of clan rights that was to determine the course of political conflict through much of the sixteenth century.

The second quriltay chose a successor to Muhammad Shibani as reigning khan and established a precedent for future successions.[21] From accounts of that quriltay we also learn the technical nomenclature of Uzbek politics. Hafiz-i Tanish describes the affair: "In accordance with the ancient *yasaq* and *turah*,[22] the sultans gathered together to address the issue of the khanate. Since Kuchkunji Sultan was the senior member, they designated him 'khan.' "[23] A visitor to Bukhara at the beginning of the century, Fadl Allah Ruzbihan Khunji, made similar observations in a book he wrote while he was there.[24] Khunji was an outsider, a Sunni/Jama'i exile fleeing from the excesses of the new Shi'i dynasty in Iran, and he was interested in phenomena that a local observer might have taken for granted. "They call all the important descendants of Chingiz Khan 'sultans,' " he wrote, "and the one who is eldest is designated 'khan.' "[25]

The titles "khan" and "sultan" retained the technical meaning given by Khunji for at least the next two hundred years. This is a point of considerable importance for the organization of political life, the expectations of the governed, and the development of public institutions like waqf. It is particularly important for us today to understand the regional use of these terms, for they carried very different meanings in Iran and India in the same period. In the regions under the sway of the Chingizid dispensation, khans and sultans formed an exclusive group whose members alone were eligible to hold the highest offices.

The grand khan or reigning khan was entitled to certain prerogatives,

[21] Dickson 1958, 29 presents the information from Iranian sources on the question of who succeeded Muhammad Shibani Khan. Barthold 1963–77, 130–45 adds another version from the *Zubdat al-tawarikh*. In that version, the author says that Suyunj(uk) son of Abu'l-Khayr was named khan at Samarqand at a quriltay immediately after Shibani Khan's death in A.D. 1510 (A.H. 144). But then, sometime between that quriltay and the quriltay of 1513, 'Ubayd Allah, the nephew of Shibani Khan, was given the title of khan at Samarqand by the notables of that city after he defeated Babur at the decisive Battle of Kul Malik (p. 140).

[22] The terms *yasa* or *yasaq* (the phrase *yasa wa yusun* is often used in the Persian sources from Mawarannahr and Balkh) and *turah* designate the ordinances attributed to Chingiz Khan. (See Morgan 1986a and 1986b, 96–99 for the most recent discussion of whether or not such a legal code ever existed.) Turah also carried a secondary meaning, that of a Chingizid sultan, perhaps an extension of the meaning from the law itself to the one who represented the law. These terms in the post-1500 period carried much the same weight in the political sphere that the terms *Shari'ah* and *shar'i* did in the Muslim judicial sphere.

[23] Tanish I: fols. 35a–b (Tanish 1983– , 1:86–87).

[24] Khunji 1962, 1976.

[25] Ibid., 42.

including the customary Irano-Islamic ones of "sikkah and khutbah," that is, the placing of his name on coins and medals (sikkah) and the insertion of it into the "invocation of the believers" during the sermon at the Friday service in the congregational mosque.

In addition, he was generally accorded an outward show of respect and loyalty by the sultans and their supporters. It was his prerogative to convene quriltays and to preside over them. His political position was enhanced by the moral authority that accompanied the Chingizid khanate but, as Shibani Khan discovered, it was difficult to translate that position of first among equals into a position of absolute authority. Moreover, the fact that seniority was a qualification for the khanate tended to reduce the ability of the khan to exercise real political power. Kuchkunji Khan, who reigned from 1513 until 1530,[26] is described as "khan and sultan in name only" by one author.[27] Due to the physical demands of military campaigning, seniority was often a liability in an army leader. To compensate, there emerged the informal institution of what later sources would style the "one who mends and rends" (ratiq wa fatiq) in political matters, the "acting khan" in both senses of the term. This role was filled by a younger and more energetic sultan who could not claim nominal leadership under the terms of Uzbek political law, but who clearly wielded decisive authority within the state because of his martial qualities and political acumen. 'Ubayd Allah b. Mahmud, the appanagee at Bukhara, was such a figure during the reign of Kuchkunji Khan. Later in the century, 'Abd Allah b. Iskandar b. Jani Beg would play the same role during the reigns of his uncle, Pir Muhammad Khan, and then his father, Iskandar Khan.

Thus, already quite early in the sixteenth century, important alterations had been introduced into the Chingizid political system. The khan was formally recognized as supreme authority within the state, but often held little effective power beyond the borders of his own appanage. But while the khan found it difficult to govern his fellow Abu'l-Khayrids, they in turn faced even greater obstacles to imposing their authority outside their appanages. In the first place, they all accepted the theoretical equality of appanage holders based on clan membership. Second, they acknowledged that only the khan possessed the moral authority to unite the different neo-eponymous clans in order to achieve some common goal. To acknowledge the preeminence of another, or to seek such recognition for oneself, was, in effect, unconstitutional and violated the yasa as it was understood. But the khans, perhaps because of advanced age, rarely appeared as the initiators of new policies or as active military leaders. Once the appanages had been distributed, most khans seem to have

---

[26] Babur 1922; Dickson 1958, 168.
[27] Barthold 1963–77, 8:140.

been content to stay in their appanages and remain aloof from the kind of military activity that had established the state in the first place and on which the health of the appanage system to a large degree depended.

This chronic contradiction—that the titular authority lacked the personal energy to lead while those with the energy and ambition lacked the moral authority—encouraged regionalism and local policy-making institutions in both the political-military and civil-cultural spheres. Local institutions, whether appanage leaders and their entourages or even such nonpolitical institutions as waqf foundations and their constituents, tended to thrive at least to a point in such an environment. However, there came a time when the inability to invoke the moral authority of leadership curtailed local ambitions. Nowhere is this more evident than in the unsuccessful attempts by 'Ubayd Allah b. Mahmud, the appanage-holder of Bukhara, to expand Shibanid/Uzbek authority into Khurasan in the years before he became khan. Despite his tenacity and military skill, his efforts repeatedly foundered on his inability to force compliance from fellow sultans, who tended to withdraw their support at critical moments.

Not that ambitious politicians were content to sit on their hands until their turn to be khan arrived. There were early and sustained efforts to modify the system. One such modification was the recognition, at least by contemporary observers, of a "mending and rending" khan. In addition there are references to a "khan-apparent," a *qa'alkhan*, although the link between "mending and rending" khan and "khan-apparent" is not clear. Later in the century, a concentrated effort was undertaken to revise the system by establishing direct lineal succession and gathering sovereignty into the hands of a single family. But for the first part of the century, the main response to the requirements of administering an agrarian-based state appeared in the guise of the acting khan, the man with the ability to muster and lead armies of conquest, whether he held the title of khan or not.[28]

It is something of a paradox, but in its own way quite logical, that while the Shibanid/Uzbek state in general appears to have been rather fragile, the individual appanages displayed, on the whole, remarkable durability. The basic distribution was made in 1511. 'Ubayd Allah and the Shah Budaqids received Bukhara; Jani Beg and the Jani-Begids, Miyankal and Sughd; Suyunj(uk) and the Suyunj(uk)ids, Tashkent; and Kuchkunji and

[28] Tanish II: fol. 35b. The title "qa'alkhan" is first bestowed on Suyunjuk and then, when he died, on Jani Beg. Given the pro–Jani-Begid tendencies of the source of this information, it might be interpreted as an attempt at a post facto legitimation of the forcible seizure of the khanate by Jani Beg's sons and grandsons later in the century. Had such an institution actually functioned in the first half of the century, we might expect to find some mention of the qa'alkhan succeeding Jani Beg, who, after all, died before Kuchkunji, the reigning khan.

the Kuchkunjids, Samarqand. This arrangement remained virtually un-changed for nearly half a century and was not completely revised for a quarter of a century beyond that.[29]

Total control of the affairs of each appanage rested in the hands of its holder, who was subject only to pressures from his own neo-eponymous clan and from his Uzbek amirs. The right of dismissal and appointment ('azl wa nasb), one of the yardsticks of appanage autonomy, was the pre-rogative of the appanage-holder, not the khan. Each appanage was sub-divided and distributed to clan members as suyurghal-grants, and they in turn, probably in consultation with other clan members, parceled out their territories to their amirs as iqta'-grants.[30] To give one example, one of the territories of the Jani-Begid appanage was the tuman[31] of Sagharj in the Zarafshan Valley. In 1552, Sagharj was held as suyurghal by a grandson of Jani Beg, Qilij Qara b. Kistan Qara, and Qarshi (Nasaf), which was part of Qilij Qara's territory within the Jani-Begid appanage, was a subinfeudation held by an amir, Khuday Birdi.[32] The entire Jani-Begid appanage was held by Iskandar Sultan, son of Jani Beg, whose son, 'Abd Allah, actually ran it.

Each appanage-holder's military power was provided by the tribal groups, whose leaders were called "amirs" and who bore such titles as "bey" or "beg." By the term tribe nothing more specific is meant here than the non-Chingizid groupings or factions identified by a specific name. The sources I have used actually employ a wide variety of terms for these groups, including qawm, ta'ifah, uymaq, qabilah, batn, buluk, il, ulus, and ahl, with no indication that the terms are distinct or techni-cal. The leaders of these groups, the amirs, derived their authority partly from their status within these organizations—their ability to lead, com-mand, and win compliance from their relatives, associates, and clients—and partly from their association with and loyalty to specific Chingizid clans. For their loyalty and military and political support, the latter re-warded them with grants of land and financial support. They in turn ac-knowledged the sanctity of the Chingizid right to the khanate.

The Uzbek tribal groupings in Central Asia were somewhat compara-ble to the Qizilbash groupings in the contemporary Safawid state. The two states were structurally distinct, however. Whereas the Safawids in-

---

[29] Although each appanage was designated by a place name, vestiges of the Chingizid system of distributing peoples (ulusat) rather than places occasionally crop up. When the Jani-Begids were driven out of Miyankal, they took their tribal followers with them, thereby preserving a degree of appanage authority.

[30] Abduraimov 1970, 103; Ivanov 1954, 26.

[31] The word tuman denoted the administrative subdivisions of Bukhara and Samarqand, among other meanings.

[32] Tanish II: fol. 67b.

herited and then encouraged the development of an experienced and politically powerful bureaucracy of Persophone officials, the Shibanids did
not. The history of the Turkish elements in both regions in the sixteenth
and seventeenth centuries may be viewed in light of this difference in
the structure of the two states. The fact that large numbers of Timurid
bureaucrats appear to have emigrated to India after 1500, combined with
the political ideals of the steppe expressed in the distribution of territory
to more or less autonomous clans, gave the Uzbek amirs both military
and bureacratic functions. Within the appanages, the two most important
amirid offices in the sixteenth and seventeenth centuries were those of
ataliq and *diwanbegi*. The ataliq held a position comparable to the Saljuq
atabeg or the Safawid *lalah*. In the sixteenth and seventeenth centuries,
the ataliq was both advisor to and supervisor of his designated Chingizid
(Shibanid, later Tugay-Timurid) ward on behalf of the reigning khan or
appanage-holding sultan. There was a marked tendency (even as early as
the Qipchaq Steppe state of Abu'l-Khayr Khan) for the appanage-holder
to appoint ataliqs for younger clan members as a way to restrain their
activities. The office thus had the potential to be a vehicle for consolidating and centralizing authority within an appanage.[33] Furthermore, as advisors to the Chingizid clan members, the ataliqs were also in a position
to voice amirid views and to encourage policies that would benefit the
Uzbek tribal organizations.

The duties of the office of diwanbegi are more difficult to define. Despite the obvious implication of the title, there is little evidence in the
sources for the sixteenth and seventeenth centuries that the "lord of the
diwan" was in any way comparable to the grand vezir of the Irano-Islamic
state.[34] Although nothing is said of his duties, the context in which the
diwanbegi operated is clear. Like the ataliq, the diwanbegi is found only
in association with a Chingizid khan or sultan, not at the head of a bureau, and, like the ataliq, seems to have been appointed to that person.
It is not inconceivable that his role may have included supervision of
the appanage finances, or that part of them controlled by his lord. The
appearance of the title "diwanbegi gari khassah" in the seventeenth
century[35] also suggests supervision of the khanly household's finances.[36]
But when the title "diwanbegi" appears in the written record, it is almost
invariably in connection with its holder taking part in a military campaign
or in inter-appanage political maneuverings.[37]

[33] Akhmedov 1965, 100.

[34] Ibid., 100–1; Bregel 1980; Barthold 1968, 229; Minorsky 1943, 114–16.

[35] *BA* 4: fol. 287b.

[36] See Minorsky 1943, 24–25 for a summary of the *khassah* and *mamlakah* question in
Safawid Iran.

[37] See, e.g., Munshi n.d., 1:556 for the activities of Muhammad Baqi, a Qalmaq amir and

There were a number of other titles to which an amir might aspire, but by and large these reflected the protocol of the court, the hunt, or old traditions ascribed to Mongol law (the yasa and yusun) and did not develop the political importance of the offices of ataliq and diwanbegi. Both offices lent themselves to the administrative demands of an agrarian economy, and it is in their development that one sees most clearly the pressures exerted on the steppe ideals of state by the Central Asian urban environment.

But it is equally true that these offices, which offered ambitious Chingizid rulers the means to establish and extend a consolidated political authority, also had inherent features obstructing such an evolution. The officeholders were first and foremost tribal personalities, loyal to one or another of the Uzbek groupings and perhaps more dependent on their status within the group than on khanly patronage. Without the full backing of their own supporters, their personal power was largely symbolic. This is another apparent paradox in the Uzbek system: offices that appear to have offered the opportunity and the means for gradually drawing together the various threads of political authority were held by men whose personal interests mitigated against allowing the process of centralization to proceed very far. Political life revolved around the balance thus established. Forces attempting to tilt the scales in one direction or another immediately posed a challenge to the interests of other groups, who would react to restore the uncertain but durable relationship. Central authority, in any event, seldom reached beyond the court and appanage seat of the Chingizid khan or sultan, leaving local authorities—whether village or tribal elders, the "graybeards" (*rish safids, aqsaqals, arbabs*), or institutional officials, such as madrasah professors, Shari-ah court officers (qadis, muftis), mosque functionaries (imams, khatibs), or waqf managers—with considerable and often decisive power over local matters.

Such circumstances had, of course, the potential for eventual conflict. There was no such thing as a political vacuum for local forces to fill. There were only dormant claims to authority, which the nature and constitution of Uzbek politics encouraged local powers to revive. The level of conflict between claimants ebbed and flowed according to the acknowledging of rights and the mutual understanding of relative strengths. The fact that the Uzbek system did not develop a sophisticated bureaucracy comparable to the bureaucracies in contemporary Iran, Southwest Asia, and India hardly hampered the collection of agricultural, commercial, and manu-

---

diwanbegi under 'Abd Allah Khan; and *BA* 4:171a on Uz Tanim, a Mangghit amir and a diwanbegi, and his participation in a campaign in Badakhshan just before 1603, among many others.

facturing taxes and fees in Mawarannahr. Instead of a unitary hierarchically organized system of revenue collection and appropriation, the Uzbek system favored pluralism and localism. Responsibility for local security and tax collection devolved on local authorities, usually headquartered in a city or town. The appanage-holders and their amirs in turn encouraged local institutions capable of managing finances as well as protecting the agrarian base of the appanage region.

For a supervisor of waqf properties, such conditions were both a challenge and an opportunity. They added to the complexity of his duties but also made it possible for him to acquire considerable personal power. With no evidence that a governmental bureau to supervise waqf existed in the Uzbek system, we may assume that the latitude for independent action by the waqf administrator, the mutawalli, was relatively broad, subject only to the supervision and control of the local appanage-holder, in our particular case the Chingizid who sat at Balkh in the sixteenth and seventeenth centuries, or to the authority he delegated the local qadi.

Keeping this general scheme for understanding the unfolding of Uzbek political history in mind, along with its consequences for an institution like waqf, let us now turn to the main events of the sixteenth and seventeenth centuries that fixed this system in place.

THE PERIOD OF EXPANSION OF THE SHIBANID/UZBEK STATE

As was noted earlier, one of the essential requirements for the proper operation of the Uzbek system was territorial growth. Failure to expand continually the resources (i.e., land) available for distribution strained the integrity of the system. The political history of the sixteenth century is marked by periodic crises that erupted when the neo-eponymous Abu'l-Khayrid/Shibanid clans and their amirid loyalists found themselves cut off from new territory and felt compelled to turn against their fellow clans in order to satisfy their followers.

The first period of Uzbek expansion following the two quriltays of 1511 and 1513 culminated in the conquest of Balkh in the spring of 1526.[38] In this fourteen-year period, all of Mawarannahr and Balkh up to the Hindu Kush mountains was incorporated into the Shibanid/Uzbek state, with the exception of Badakhshan, the absorption of which was to take somewhat longer. For the next two centuries the cis-Oxus territory was to make up the Balkh appanage.

The second period of Uzbek growth was not nearly as dramatic or successful. The inability to acquire and hold new territories in the south and

[38] Dickson 1958, 83; Akhmedov 1982, 75–79 reviews what is known about Balkh's history from the beginning of the century to 1526, when Kistan Qara Sultan took control of it on behalf of the Abu'l-Khayrid/Shibanids.

west in the fourteen years after 1526 placed enormous pressure on the appanage structure. This is not to say that the Uzbeks enjoyed no success at all in their efforts to expand their territory during this time. In 1527, Astarabad, Mashhad, and the territory in between were captured, lost, and retaken from the Safawids.[39] The following year, failing in their attempt to take Herat, the Uzbeks lost control of the region between Herat and Mashhad. But in 1529, both cities fell to 'Ubayd Allah b. Mahmud Sultan, who then prepared for the conquest of all of Iran. But less than ten months later, faced with a Safawid "liberation army" moving on Herat from the west and a rebuff to his request for troops from his fellow Shibanid sultans, 'Ubayd Allah saw his plans for empire crumble. He was forced to abandon his plans for the conquest of the Safawid lands and to surrender as well the recently won cities of Mashhad and Herat.

The standoff that followed between the Shibanid/Uzbek and Safawid/ Qizilbash forces in Khurasan was in effect a defeat for the Uzbeks. The deadlock increased tension between the neo-eponymous clans ('Ubayd Allah Sultan lacked both the title and the moral authority of grand khan and was thought to be simply an opportunist), some of whose leaders no longer saw any benefit to be gained from a united front in Khurasan. Astarabad had produced little in the way of reward and had convinced many of the Abu'l-Khayrid sultans that success strengthened only 'Ubayd Allah Sultan's hand.

A raid against Herat in 1535 by the amir who held the iqta' of Gharjistan (part of the Jani-Begid appanage) marked the beginning of independent appanage-based foreign policy. The raid itself may have been only an attempt to exploit the political conditions in Herat.[40] But the fact that it occurred at all symbolizes the disintegration of 'Ubayd Allah's unified command and suggests a direct challenge to his policies by the appanage-holder at Balkh, the Jani-Begid Kistan Qara Sultan. The raid, though carried out by the amir at Gharjistan, probably had Kistan Qara's blessing. It is unlikely that it would have taken place without his knowledge or at least tacit approval. Gharjistan was a particularly crucial strategic position on Balkh's western borders and probably in close communication with the appanage seat at Balkh City.

The raid against Herat was a minor affair and only of consequence here for what it symbolized—'Ubayd Allah Sultan's loss of control over military policy in the western marches and the development of independent foreign policies by the individual appanages. As such it is a convenient point to mark the end of the second period of Uzbek expansion. For the political system, the fourth decade of the sixteenth century was a critical

[39] Dickson 1958, 98ff. I have followed Dickson's chronology here.
[40] Dickson 1958, 300–301.

time. Conquest and expansion stopped and internal political pressures generated by the expectations of the clans and their followers began to build.

INTER-APPANAGE WARS

With the death of 'Ubayd Allah (grand khan only from 1533) in 1540, a seventeen-year period of inter- and intra-appanage warfare began.[41] Were it not for the course of events in the seventeenth century, one could assert that at this point the appanage system itself disappeared, as the participants in the Uzbek state withdrew their recognition of the rights of fellow sultans and actively began to attack their kinsmen and seize their territory. But as we shall see, this period presents not an end at all to steppe ideals but only an adjustment necessitated by the permanent circumstances and demands of agrarian life and the temporary cessation of territorial expansion.

During this seventeen-year period, the four principal appanages became virtually separate states. The title "khan," legally the prerogative of the senior Abu'l-Khayrid, was claimed as an exclusive right by the sultans forming a loose alliance of convenience among the appanages of Samarqand, Tashkent, and Bukhara as well as by the Jani-Begid counterclaimants in Balkh. In Mawarannahr, the Suyunjukids at first emerged as the leading neo-eponymous clan. Under their leader, Baraq b. Suyunjuk (also known as Nawruz Ahmad), they attacked the Jani-Begid territory of Karminah and Miyankal, midway between Samarqand and Bukhara, in 1552 and forced the Jani-Begid leaders, Iskandar b. Jani-Beg and his son 'Abd Allah, to abandon the region.[42] This incident followed by one year the unsuccessful bid by another Jani-Begid, Pir Muhammad, who had succeeded Kistan Qara as appanage-holder at Balkh, to oust the Shah Budaqids from Bukhara and thus give more luster to his own claim to the khanate.[43] The two events were clearly connected. Pir Muhammad's initiative contravened the understood terms of the "yasa and yusun" and prompted the Suyunjukids and Kuchkunjids to ally against the Jani-Begids. The latter's appanage holdings in Mawarannahr were then attacked and the defeated Jani-Begids forced to leave for Balkh.[44]

At Balkh, the Jani-Begid "mender and render," 'Abd Allah, a man of great military skill, lent his support to Pir Muhammad's khanate candi-

---

[41] Much of Tanish is a record of the inter- and intra-appanage fighting until the Jani-Begid clan established its preeminence (although it continued to face Suyunjukid opposition to the very end of the sixteenth century).

[42] Ibid., fol. 59a.

[43] Ibid.

[44] Tanish II: fols. 59a–60a.

dacy and began to assemble the forces that would be required to vest the claim with some credibility. In this he was eventually successful. Within five years, he had raised the Jani-Begid house from the ignominy of expulsion from Mawarannahr to a position of preeminence in the Shibanid heartlands. 'Abd Allah's seizure of Bukhara from the Shah Budaqid clan in 1557 marks the moment when the Jani-Begid clan achieved the political paramountcy that it would enjoy for four decades.

In the course of these struggles, we see signs of the institutional conflict going on between the adherents of the steppe ideals of state and the forces of the agrarian world in which the conflicts were taking place. The special place that the city, particularly the imperial city or capital city, was coming to occupy in the thinking of Shibanid politicians is one sign of the conflict. When 'Ubayd Allah Khan died in 1540, he was succeeded for six months by the second son of Kuchkunji, 'Abd Allah (not to be confused with 'Abd Allah b. Iskandar). When 'Abd Allah's brief reign ended with his death, another son of Kuchkunji, 'Abd al-Latif, was named khan.[45] 'Ubayd Allah's appanage was Bukhara and for the seven years he was khan, Bukhara had been the capital. But with the Kuchkunjid assumption of the khanate, the capital moved to Samarqand. Then in 1552, when 'Abd al-Latif died, the khanate passed to the Suyunjukid Baraq Khan (Nawruz Ahmad), and he broke tradition by making Samarqand, the Kuchkunjid appanage seat, his capital, rather than Tashkent, his own appanage center.[46] As would continue to be the case in later similar situations, the Suyunjukid had reservations about claiming khanly status from what was considered a lesser city in Mawarannahr.

Although in some eyes the capital was wherever the khan was, Bukhara and Samarqand still possessed a political aura that the Shibanid/Uzbeks were unable to ignore. Baraq Khan's selection of Samarqand as capital in 1552 serves as a convenient symbol of the changes taking place in the political outlook of the Shibanids and their Uzbek supporters and highlights the changing values that mark the early phases of inter-appanage conflict. If control of a fixed geographical point were to be the test of legitimacy, then the procedure of territorial distribution and the pre-

---

[45] Tanish 1983– , 1:156 (fol. 69a); TR, fol. 127b.

[46] Aminova et al. 1967 1:519 says 1551. According to TR, fol. 139b, another Kuchkunjid, Sultan Sa'id, claimed the appanage capital of Samarqand immediately after 'Abd al-Latif's death, but Baraq Khan (Nawruz Ahmad) shortly thereafter had proclaimed the khanate in his name and soon had most of Mawarannahr under his control. Howorth 1876–88, 727 has Nawruz Ahmad taking Samarqand by force in 1554. A late (mid-nineteenth-century) but very detailed work, the anonymous Dhikr-i ta'dad-i padshahan-i Uzbek, fol. 139a, says that Sultan Sa'id handed Samarqand over to Baraq Khan in 1553, then retrieved it after Baraq Khan's death in 1556.

sumption of clan rights over one's own appanage had to be radically modified.

REPUDIATING STEPPE POLITICAL IDEALS

The fourth era in the evolution of the Shibanid/Uzbek state is marked by a wholesale assault on the steppe ideals of state and in particular on the system of khanly succession and territorial distribution. The leading opponent of the status quo was 'Abd Allah b. Iskandar, the Jani-Begid. Beginning with his conquest of Bukhara in 1557, he made an intensive effort to eradicate the clan system in Mawarannahr as a functioning form of government and substitute for it a state modeled on Irano-Islamic lines with a predictable system of succession. The effort to erase the appanage system was a long and sanguinary one for it required the elimination of all rival sultans in the Abu'l-Khayrid line.

Between 1571 and 1583, 'Abd Allah b. Iskandar channeled all his energies into war against the Abu'l-Khayrid clans, including members of his own Jani-Begid clan. In 1571 and again in 1583 he waged war on the Suyunjukids in the east. In the latter year he captured and annexed Tashkent. In 1573, he seized Balkh from a fellow Jani-Begid and in 1578 he ended Kuchkunjid authority over Samarqand.[47]

In order to purge all Abu'l-Khayrids from Mawarannahr and Balkh, he needed the support of the Uzbek amirs, without whom his goal could not be accomplished. Partly to win their support and partly as a means of enhancing his personal prestige in an atmosphere in which military achievement was an indispensable credential, he embarked on a series of major campaigns that reestablished Uzbek authority in Khurasan and won 'Abd Allah b. Iskandar an enduring reputation.

In hindsight, we can state with some assurance that his efforts to establish a system of succession based on patrilineal descent and to eliminate the appanage system of government were spectacular failures. In the first place, no concrete steps were taken to institute a centralized bureaucratic structure to administer the state in place of the appanage governments. In the second, although 'Abd Allah took the symbolic step of designating his son as heir-apparent (qa'al-khan) when he became khan in 1582, the goal of purging rival Abu'l-Khayrid sultans turned out to be an impossible one, given the numbers involved and the tactical difficulties of such an undertaking. Finally, the need to cultivate amirid support in the struggle with the Abu'l-Khayrid sultans served to strengthen the groups most fundamentally opposed to the establishment of a strong centralized bureaucratic apparatus.

---

[47] Tanish, fols. 221b–223a; Tanish 1983–   , 2:218a–219b (Russian translation 206–9).

The effort to eliminate the appanage system and succession based on extended clan rights and seniority produced results quite the opposite of what was intended. Instead of overturning the system, 'Abd Allah only weakened the ruling Chingizid clan (the Abu'l-Khayrid/Shibanids) that the system had sanctioned in Mawarannahr and Balkh. Clan appanage rights, succession based on seniority, quriltay consultation and decision-making, and adherence to the Chingizid dispensation as understood through the yasa and yusun, all these elements remained the moving forces in Uzbek politics in the next century.

When 'Abd Allah Khan died on 2 Rajab A.H. 1006/8 February A.D. 1598,[48] his expectations concerning the routine succession of his son, 'Abd al-Mu'min, were immediately challenged. Within a few weeks of the recognition by Bukharan and Balkh amirs of 'Abd al-Mu'min's khan-ate, the new khan was faced with claims from rival Abu'l-Khayrids in Tashkent, proof that his father's policies had not been completely carried out. Shortly after disposing of the opposition in the east, 'Abd al-Mu'min, following his father's example, tried to rally amirid support by leading a campaign into Khurasan. But at Ura Tipah, before the campaign could get underway, he was assassinated, the victim of an amirid conspiracy. His reign and his father's plan for a stable new dynastic order had lasted all of six months.[49]

The struggle to eliminate Abu'l-Khayrid rivals to the khanate, a policy initiated by 'Abd Allah and carried on for a short time by his son, had strengthened the position of the amirs as the number and standing of the Abu'l-Khayrid sultans declined. Under 'Abd Allah Khan, certain amirs rose to unprecedented prominence, assuming positions that had formerly been the prerogative of Abu'l-Khayrid sultans. One such amir was Qul Baba Kukaltash. At the end of 'Abd Allah Khan's life, Qul Baba Kukaltash held Herat and its surrounding region. His power was a major source of irritation to 'Abd al-Mu'min. In the appanage tradition, he had believed that as appanage-holder at Balkh he was entitled to Herat when that city was captured from the Safawids in 1588. Although his father intended for him to succeed to the khanate in due course, 'Abd al-Mu'min's desire for what he saw as routine appanage autonomy ran counter to his father's

---

[48] TR, fol. 190b; Muhammad Ya'qub b. Danyal Beg, fol. 124b. Munshi n.d., 1:553 dates his death at the end of the Turki year Takhaquy, A.H. 1006. Howorth 1876–88, 738 misin-terprets this as the last day of A.H. 1006 when in fact it was the middle of the year. In any event, a date at the end of A.H. 1006 or in the first week of August 1598 would have been an impossibility since the successful Safawid assault on Herat to reclaim it opened a week later and the campaign itself, according to a consensus among Iranian and Central Asian sources, was initiated in response to news of 'Abd Allah Khan's death. Vambery 1873, 294 misconverts the date to February 1597. Abu'l-Fadl al-'Allami 1897–1939, 3:1099 (and note) dates the khan's death at 14 Bahman, converted by the translator to 24 January 1598.

[49] McChesney 1982.

centralizing policies, which were supposed to insure a predictable succession. When he became khan, 'Abd al-Mu'min vented his anger on his father's amirs, among them Qul Baba Kukaltash, whom he blamed for the constraints he had been under at Balkh. The amirs responded by assassinating him in early August 1598.[50]

With 'Abd al-Mu'min's death, the failure of 'Abd Allah Khan's attempt to replace steppe practices regarding succession and territorial sovereignty became painfully obvious. The Abu'l-Khayrid/Shibanid clans, decimated by his purges, were in complete disarray. Furthermore, no new institutions had been created to take up the functions served by the clan system. At this moment, only the tenacious and collective adherence of the amirs to the supreme authority of the Chingizid dispensation made it possible for a new Chingizid house, the Tuqay-Timurid,[51] to be enthroned in Mawarannahr and Balkh. The year between 'Abd al-Mu'min's death and the convening of the first Tuqay-Timurid quriltay was a critical one for the political history of Mawarannahr. The values and ideals that public opinion traced back to the early thirteenth century and ascribed to Chingiz Khan were once again revived under the aegis of the amirs. A new Chingizid clan was found and installed. How this all came about is of considerable importance to the history of local institutions, especially to the waqf fund at the shrine of 'Ali. Not only did the continuance of the Uzbek system affect the shrine's governance, but the Tuqay-Timurids themselves became patrons and protectors of the shrine and its waqf endowment. But before examining the rise of the Tuqay-Timurids and the renaissance of steppe ideals, a few words should be said about what we know of developments at the shrine and in its waqf properties during the course of the sixteenth century.

WAQF AND THE 'ALID SHRINE, 1526–1601

In 1526, Balkh finally passed out of Timurid control.[52] For the next three-quarters of a century, it was part of the Jani-Begid appanage. For a few days in August 1536, the Timurid ruler of Badakhshan occupied the city in the absence of the Jani-Begid appanage-holder, but this only underscores the generally unbroken control the Jani-Begids had over the city. From 1526 until 1544, Balkh was governed by Kistan Qara Sultan b. Jani Beg. After him, his son Qilij Qara Sultan governed until 1546. He was superseded by an uncle, Pir Muhammad b. Jani Beg, who held sway for nearly twenty years. During his tenure, Balkh was for a time the seat of

---

[50] Ibid.

[51] On the reasons for the use of this eponym rather than Ashtarkhanid or Janid see McChesney 1980a, 70, note 6.

[52] See Akhmedov 1982, 3–14; Akhmedov 1985.

a Jani-Begid khanate, and it became the base from which Pir Muhammad's nephew, 'Abd Allah b. Iskandar, launched his campaign to unite
all of Mawarannahr under the Jani-Begid banner. During Pir Muhammad's two decades, Balkh's authority extended over the Marw oasis to
the northwest and over Tirmidh and Qubadyan on the right bank of the
Amu Darya.

In March 1567 Pir Muhammad died, and one of his sons, Din Muhammad, took his place at the helm of Balkh. Din Muhammad held the city
for about six years. But for the last six years of Pir Muhammad's life and
throughout the regime of Din Muhammad, Balkh was at war with Bukhara, now under the effective control of 'Abd Allah b. Iskandar. Finally,
in the summer of 1573, after a long siege, 'Abd Allah managed to wrest
control of Balkh away from Din Muhammad. From then until the autumn
of 1582, the Balkh appanage was divided among five of 'Abd Allah's
amirs. In September 1582, when he succeeded his father as khan at Bukhara, he named 'Abd al-Mu'min his heir apparent and gave him Balkh.
'Abd al-Mu'min was fifteen years old at the time, and most of the authority to govern was placed in the hands of his ataliq, Jan Kildi Bi, of the
Utarchi uymaq. Balkh remained under 'Abd al-Mu'min and his ataliq until 1598, when the Shibanid state collapsed.

Balkh's history during the sixteenth century reflects the course of political developments affecting the Shibanid/Uzbek state as a whole. As we
narrow our focus from the appanage to the shrine center, however, it
becomes much more difficult to trace developments at the shrine and the
changes its waqf properties underwent during the same period. The few
scraps of information that emerge from reading the materials of this period only serve to emphasize how little we know about it at this point.

The known facts are these. In 1537–1538, Kistan Qara appointed Mir
'Abd Allah Tirmidhi naqib at the shrine.[53] When Kistan Qara died in
1544, he chose to be buried there.[54] Five years later, in the spring and
summer of 1549, Humayun b. Babur, recently restored to the Timurid
(Moghul) throne of northern India, led a disastrous campaign to Balkh,
in the course of which he briefly used the 'Alid shrine as his headquarters.[55]

In 1573, after his conquest of Balkh, 'Abd Allah b. Iskandar made a
pilgrimage to the shrine. There he conferred the posts of *shaykh al-islam*
and shaykh of the shrine and its tawliyat (administration) on a high court
officer and personal confidant, Hasan Khwajah, the naqib of Bukhara. Of
great interest is Hafiz-i Tanish's assertion that the income of the shrine

[53] *TR*, fol. 126b.
[54] *TMS*, 94.
[55] Abu'l-Fadl al-'Allami 1897–1939, 2:543ff; Gulbadan Begam 1902, 43, 44, 188, 191, 194.

was awarded to Hasan Khwajah as his " 'alufah and iqta' " (i.e., as a stipend and salary).[56]

A few years after the annexation of Balkh to Bukhara, in June 1579, the Badakhshani allies of the Moghuls again occupied the shrine for a brief moment. This time they reportedly plundered the village of Khwajah Khayran, although there are no reports of damage to the shrine.[57]

In late summer of 1584, after his victorious campaign against Badakhshan, 'Abd Allah Khan again stopped at the shrine and distributed votive offerings.[58]

Finally, during the fifteen and one-half years in which he was sultan at Balkh, 'Abd al-Mu'min b. 'Abd Allah Khan sponsored the construction of the "outer domed building" (qubbah-i kharij) at the shrine. This addition nearly doubled the size of Banna'i's original structure (if the existing building housing the tomb generally corresponds with the size of the fifteenth-century original, and there is little reason to doubt that it does).[59] According to Mahmud b. Amir Wali, this new structure was called the "Threshold Congregational Mosque" (jami'i astanah), "threshold" being a common synonym for shrine and one of the names by which the whole complex was known.

About the shrine's waqf, the sources reveal almost nothing. In fact, there is hardly any information at all about waqf in Balkh during this period. A.D. Davydov, author of a study of khanly waqf at Balkh in the seventeenth century, mentions finding a sixteenth-century waqf document from Balkh in the Uzbek State Archives in Tashkent. But he gives no further information about it and to date the document has not been published.[60]

---

[56] Tanish I: fol. 198b.

[57] Ibid., fols. 261a–b.

[58] Ibid., fol. 442b.

[59] BA, 4: fol. 318b. The plan of the building published by Golombek and Wilber (1988, 2: plate no. 94) shows two large adjacent and attached domed sections of the building. The authors raise the possibility that these two structures were part of Sultan Husayn Bayqara's original plan (ibid., 1:337). Bernard O'Kane (1987, 256) arrived at the same tentative conclusion, that "the vestibule, and presumably the aivan flanked by two-storey niches which precedes it, are likely to be part of the original building plan. . . ." But the local sources that describe the Timurid sultan's building project refer to a gunbad (a domed mausoleum, or simply a domed building). Had he built a double-domed building, we might reasonably have expected at least one of the accounts to have mentioned it. Further, if we accept the hypothesis that the two domes were part of the original structure, then how do we account for 'Abd al-Mu'min's "outer dome" addition to the original mausoleum? Mahmud b. Amir Wali's name for this addition, the Threshold Congregational Mosque, leaves little doubt that it was a sizeable structure. The large domed hall on the southeast side of the mausoleum would seem to best answer the description. The 1947 work TMS (35) labels the domed structure housing the tomb the "gunbad-i haram" and the adjacent large domed hall the "gunbad-i khanaqah." Golombek and Wilber (1988, 1:337) call it a masjid or ziyarat-khanah.

[60] Davydov 1960, 63.

Although exceedingly slight, the information about the shrine is still suggestive. First there is no question that the shrine, its administration, and therefore, one must assume, its waqf possessions were functioning entities throughout the sixteenth century. It is clear, too, that, at least under Kistan Qara Sultan and 'Abd al-Mu'min, whose combined regimes lasted some thirty-five years, the shrine enjoyed Jani-Begid patronage and protection. One should probably not take such a fact for granted, despite the expected close relations the Shibanid sultans developed with representatives of the Muslim clergy and the support they gave to public institutions. In the first place, the shrine, as encountered by the Shibanid/Uzbek state, was the creation of the Timurids, and in all probability in the period of transition, the shrine administration would have supported the claims of the last Timurid representatives in Balkh as long as seemed expedient. This transition period, too, it should be noted, was quite extended in the case of Balkh. Although the Shibanid/Uzbek forces first received Balkh's surrender in 1505, the region passed back to Timurid hands after Shibani Khan's death in 1510 and was not permanently reannexed until 1526.[61] During this sixteen-year period, while waqf administrators and religious functionaries in Mawarannahr were making their peace with the new sovereigns, Balkh and the shrine remained a Timurid outpost, and at least as late as 1579 the Timurids of Badakhshan were still making pilgrimages to the shrine.[62] In addition, after the Shibanid annexation, Balkh fell more or less out of the mainstream of intellectual life.[63] Bukhara assumed Herat's mantle as intellectual center of Central Asia, while Samarqand and Bukhara were the centers of the three Sufi movements (all Naqshbandi) that would dominate the life of brotherhood devotees and would be the main focus of royal patronage during the century. These orders were the Juybari in Bukhara and the Dahpidi and Ahrari in Samarqand. The main figure in the formation of the first two of these suborders of the Naqshbandiyah was Khwajah Kasani (d. 1549), known to his disciples as "Makhdum-i A'zam" (Supreme Master). Kasani, whose center was at Dahpid near Samarqand, was without question the most prominent Naqshbandi figure of the sixteenth century. One of his disciples was Muhammad Islam from Juybar, a suburb

---

[61] Barthold 1963–77, 8:133, where the date 1505 is given for the first brief Shibanid conquest of Balkh. Babur 1922, 300 dates it to the campaign season of A.H. 912/A.D. 1506, apparently in the autumn. We may assume that the Shibanids would have been interested in the condition of the 'Alid waqf. When Shibani Khan took Samarqand, for example, he ordered a survey of waqfs to find out how well they were being managed (Khunji 1976, 130b–131a [pp. 157–58 of Russian translation]). Khunji himself took part in the survey.

[62] Akhmedov 1982, 63.

[63] From Wasifi 1961 Balkh's isolation from the intellectual mainstream may be inferred. The author, Zayn al-Din Wasifi, a peripatetic scholar and observer of the literary scene (see Subtelny 1984), mentions neither Balkh nor the 'Alid shrine as destinations for scholars.

of Bukhara. Muhammad Islam, called Khwajah Juybari, established his order at Bukhara. The Ahraris were descendants of the noted late-fifteenth-century dervish Khwajah 'Ubayd Allah Ahrar. The Shibanid/Uzbek khans and sultans of the sixteenth and even seventeenth centuries were very closely allied with all three orders through marriage and discipleship.

The 'Alid shrine was somewhat isolated from this developing system of patronage, partly because of the two decades that had elapsed between the first Shibanid conquest of Balkh and its final annexation and partly because of the emergence and development of the Sufi orders in Samarqand and Bukhara. It is not entirely surprising, therefore, that the shrine seems to have played a comparatively minor role in the religious and intellectual life of sixteenth-century Mawarannahr and Balkh.

The information on the appointment of Hasan Khwajah as "shaykh al-islam" and shaykh of the shrine is more puzzling than helpful, existing as it does in isolation and lacking any independent confirmation or explanation. Perhaps the shaykhship of the shrine was purely ceremonial and did not involve physical presence at the shrine. Hasan Khwajah's career strongly suggests he never resided at Balkh. He was a companion of 'Abd Allah Khan and particularly prominent in the latter's military campaigns. Assuming he was the recipient of a stipend from the shrine's revenues, this arrangement ended with his death in mid-1583.[64] It does tend to show the survival of at least one of the original offices associated with the shrine.

But relying exclusively on what the scant sources have to tell us about the shrine during this period is probably unwise. The appanage system itself and, in particular, Balkh's independent political path may also have contributed to our lack of information today. The surviving sixteenth-century chronicles of Central Asian provenance are all Bukharan. Neither Kistan Qara, Pir Muhammad, nor 'Abd al-Mu'min commissioned chronicles for their regimes in Balkh.[65]

That the shrine should scarcely be mentioned in the Bukharan chronicles is perhaps more understandable if we take into account the fact that Kistan Qara and Pir Muhammad followed visibly independent policies vis-à-vis the rest of the Uzbek regions and were frequently in direct conflict with Bukhara, Samarqand, or Tashkent. It is difficult to say to what extent this affected the accounts about the shrine or the relations of the shrine administration with the authorities in Balkh. It does mean, however, that when events in Balkh found their way into the chronicles, the

---

[64] On Hasan Khwajah see Tanish I: fols. 156a, 169b, 172a, 198b, 221b, 236a, 242b, 264b, 266b, 296b, 382a–b.

[65] Pir Muhammad did commission a geographical work, Sultan Muhammad b. Darwish Muhammad al-Balkhi's *Majma' al-ghara'ib* (see Storey 1927–84, 2(1):135–137).

region's leaders and people are often portrayed as hostile to Bukhara. In the seventeenth century, the picture becomes considerably clearer when Balkh and Bukhara became more or less independent of each other and Balkh's rulers employed their own historians.

The most prominent fact of the sixteenth-century history of the shrine and its waqf is that at the century's end, as at its beginning, there flourished a bureaucracy, assessing and collecting fees and taxes from the waqf lands, supervising and maintaining the Shahi Canal, and encouraging royal patronage of the shrine grounds.

Throughout the sixteenth century, the shrine officials, particularly those engaged in day-to-day administration, labored in obscurity as far as the historical record is concerned, no doubt working to increase the shrine's assets, preserve its base of revenues, and thereby root its religious tradition in Balkh's spiritual soil. Although we may never know for certain, these may have been descendants of the "reliable stewards" of Khwandamir's time. Certainly a share of both the shrine's durability and its obscurity, as far as posterity is concerned, can be attributed to the effects of the appanage system and the comparative lack of political supervision of the shrine's economic activities. The absence of a pervasive government administrative network allowed local institutions to develop and flourish in their own way. The duties of the sultans and khans vis-à-vis such institutions included protection and patronage but did not extend, as far as we know, to formal supervision and regulation, a circumstance that might explain in part the unfortunate (for the historian) dearth of records.[66]

The ground rules for the relations between waqf administrators and government representatives, especially representatives of the royal court, become clearer when we examine the information from the seventeenth century. For that period, the written record is much fuller and the outlines of policies and practices much more distinct.

[66] There is some hope that the shrine itself might yet yield the documents that will help illuminate the period. In the early 1970s, a professor of geography at the University of Genoa, Maria Clothilde Giuliani, visited the shrine and was shown fourteenth-century documents from the archives of the shrine that pertained to Italian trade (personal communication from Prof. Robert S. Lopez, Yale University, 6 October 1976). It is reasonable to suppose that, if the shrine administrators had saved such materials, then in all likelihood they have guarded even more closely the records of the shrine's endowments.

CHAPTER FOUR

Balkh, 1599–1647: Appanage Politics and the Growth of the ʿAlid Waqf

IN THE SPRING of 1599, a new Chingizid clan, the Tuqay-Timurid, assembled at Bukhara in quriltay. The clan members elected a new khan and distributed the newly acquired territory. With the distribution and the election of a khan, the fundamental principles of clan appanage rights and succession by seniority were reasserted in Mawarannahr. Although a new Chingizid line was to embody these ideals of state, the quriltay of 1599 was in many ways a reenactment of the quriltays of 1511 and 1513 and, like those earlier assemblies, would set the pattern for political activity for the remainder of the eleventh century A.H. (seventeenth century A.D.). Because the history of this Chingizid clan is little known and the name given it by later historians, Ashtarkhanids or Janids, obscures the principles of legitimacy by which the clan first gained and then held power in Mawarannahr and Balkh, it is worthwhile here to devote a few pages to its appearance and rise.

TUQAY-TIMURID ORIGINS

Both the Shibanids and Tuqay-Timurids were Juchids, that is, descendants of Chingiz Khan's eldest son, Juchi (d. 1227). The Shibanids claimed descent through Shiban, Juchi's fifth son, while the eponym of the Tuqay-Timurids was his thirteenth son, Tuqay (Tuqa, Toqa) Timur.[1] Depending on which account one prefers, Tuqay Timur ruled over a section of the White Horde or the Golden Horde.[2] The seventeenth-century chronicler of the Tuqay-Timurid line, Mahmud b. Amir Wali, calls Tuqay Timur's ulus the "quadripartite ulus" (*ulus-i chaharganah*) because it was made up of sections of four separate peoples—the Ming, Ushun, Tarkhan, and Uyrat.[3] The line from Tuqay Timur to Mangqishlaq, the first of

---

[1] So according to Rashid al-Din 1971, 115. *BA* 4: fol. 3a calls him the fifth son whose mother was the daughter of the chief of the Qunghrat.

[2] *BA* 4: fol. 3a says that Tuqay Timur received the provinces (*wilayat*) of "As" and "Mangqishlaq." Rashid al-Din 1971, 100 writes that when Batu and Orda divided the Juchid appanage, Tuqay Timur accompanied Orda to the White Horde, between the Syr Darya and Ulagh Dagh, where he remained at least as late as 1310.

[3] *BA* 4: fol. 3a.

his descendants to reach Mawarannahr, is described with numerous variants.[4]

In general the story goes as follows: Sometime in the 1520s, Mangqishlaq, the grandfather of the first Tuqay-Timurid khan in Mawarannahr, was driven from his territory—a region, also named Mangqishlaq, on the northeastern shores of the Caspian—reportedly by "the tribe of the Rus" (the *ulus-i urus*).[5] He made his way to Mawarannahr and, after one attempt to regain his former lands, settled with his clan in the Jani-Begid appanage. The clan allied with the Jani-Begids and their relations were formalized by intermarriage.[6] According to Mahmud b. Amir Wali, the two Juchid clans coexisted amiably until the 1580s, when the then-leading Tuqay-Timurid clansman, Din Muhammad, a greatgrandson of Mangqishlaq, and 'Abd al-Mu'min b. 'Abd Allah, the Jani-Begid appanage-holder at Balkh, came into conflict over the conduct of campaigns in Badakhshan and Khurasan.[7]

By the end of the century, the leading Tuqay-Timurids were the clan's eldest representative (Yar Muhammad, the son of Mangqishlaq); his sons (Jani Muhammad, Pir Muhammad, 'Abbas, Tursun Muhammad, Payandah Muhammad, and Rahman Quli); and the sons of Jani Muhammad (Din Muhammad, Baqi Muhammad, and Wali Muhammad). It is the Janid neo-eponymous clan of the Tuqay-Timurid that is of particular interest to the *Bahr al-asrar*, our main source for the rise of this line of Chingizids and for its links to the Jani-Begid/Abu'l-Khayrid/Shibanid house. Its author was commissioned by one of Din Muhammad's sons to write a history of the family, and the emphasis in it on Din Muhammad's political role should be seen in that context. However, other sources,

---

[4] The available genealogies tracing the sixteenth- and seventeenth-century descendants back to Juchi, the eldest son of Chingiz Khan, vary considerably. Four sources trace the line through Tuqay Timur (Tuqa, Toqa) Timur b. Juchi (Suhayla, fols. 12b–13b; BA 4: fols. 3a–4a; Abu'l-Ghazi 1871–74, 1:179, 2:188; Tali', fol. 1a). One (Muhammad Talib, fol. 136a–b) traces descent through Uz Timur (Uzan Timur) b. Juchi (the preceding four works call Uz Timur the son of Tuqay Timur and grandson of Juchi). Two works (Muhammad Yusuf Munshi, fol. 39b [p. 72 of Russian translation]; Salim, fols. 124b–125a) trace descent through Urus b. Juchi, a name given in none of the other sources. There is even more discrepancy in the number of generations said to intervene between Juchi and Yar Muhammad: Salim names seven; Abu'l-Ghazi and 'Abd al-Rahman Tali', twelve; and BA, thirteen.

[5] BA 4: fols. 35b–36a. Spuler 1965 dates the arrival of the clan members in Bukhara to 1556. He may have chosen this date because of the Russian annexation of Astrakhan (Hajji Tarkhan) in the same year. In BA 4: fol. 37a–b, Mangqishlaq is said to have arrived during the reign of Kuchkunji (grand khan from 1513 to 1530). At Samarqand he was given a large contingent of cavalry to help him regain his ancestral lands. When he failed, he then returned permanently to Mawarannahr.

[6] BA 4: fol. 38a.

[7] See ibid., 4: fol. 38bff. and al-Asil, fol. 554b on relations between the Jani-Begids and Tuqay-Timurids.

especially contemporary Iranian accounts, do corroborate Din Muhammad's role as "mender and render" in the Tuqay-Timurid clan.[8] During the Uzbek campaigns in Khurasan in the last decade of the sixteenth century, the Tuqay-Timurid clan emerged as a powerful military force and, because of its genealogy, as a potential political force as well.

In reward for Tuqay-Timurid participation in the Khurasan campaign of 1587–1588, in which Herat was taken from the Safawids,[9] 'Abd Allah Khan gave Din Muhammad and his brothers control over the march areas west of the city, including the towns of Khwaf, Kariz, Ta'ibat, Bakharz, and Khargird. Din Muhammad made Khargird his headquarters.[10] From here he helped lead the successful siege of Mashhad in 1589. After the Shibanid/Uzbek forces occupied the city, Din Muhammad took a Twelver Shi'i woman of Ridawi descent, the daughter of an official at the shrine of the eighth imam, as his wife. The aspect of the marriage that appears to us today to require some comment, the fact that it was a Sunni-Shi'i political marriage, was treated rather matter-of-factly by the reporters of the event. The alliance of Chingizid and Imami genealogies would produce a line of descendants with both khanly and shaykhly legitimacy. For the offspring and posterity of this union, the shaykhship or sayyidship would be placed in a Sunni context, by giving it the label "Husayni" rather than "Ridawi." In seventeenth- and eighteenth-century Mawarannahr, the adjective "Husayni" did not carry a Shi'ite connotation.

As a result of his military accomplishments in Khurasan, Din Muhammad was assigned to Sistan sometime in 1592 or 1593. At the time, Sistan was the most exposed and least secure part of the newly conquered Shibanid territories. 'Abd Allah Khan wanted to strengthen the Uzbek presence there, and Din Muhammad appears to have soon become the dominant figure in the region.[11] Just as he had done in Khurasan, Din Muhammad governed independently of Bukhara, retaining full control over appointments and budgetary matters.

Because of the prominence of the Tuqay-Timurid clan, it was natural that amirid attention should be drawn to these Chingizids after 'Abd al-Mu'min's assassination in 1598. Din Muhammad appears to have had the khanate in mind for some time, and as soon as he heard the news of 'Abd al-Mu'min's murder he convened a quriltay of the clan in Sistan. (His

---

[8] Din Muhammad also appears under the names Yatim Khan (Munshi n.d., indexes), Yalim Khan (Rida Quli Khan Hidayat 1960, 8:310), Tanim Khan (*TR*, 195b), and Tatam Khan (Abu'l-Fadl al-'Allami, 3:1207).

[9] On the siege and capture of Herat, see Burton 1988a.

[10] On his activities in Khurasan, see *BA* 4: fols. 44b–50a and Munshi n.d., 1:549.

[11] On his four years in Sistan, see *BA* 4: fols. 50bff.; Munshi n.d., 485; and Sistani 1965, 363–64.

father, Jani Muhammad, was in Mawarannahr at the time.[12]) With the consent of the other clan members, Din Muhammad stated his intention of proclaiming the khanate in the name of his grandfather Yar Muhammad at Herat and then proceeding on to Mawarannahr to contest the claims of any of the Shibanids left there. The fact that he planned to proclaim the khanate at Herat is indicative of the role of the urban setting in conveying legitimacy to claims of sovereignty.

Din Muhammad had substantial encouragement from the Uzbek amirs, especially those who had grown disenchanted with inter-Shibanid conflicts. At Herat, the amir appointed governor by 'Abd al-Mu'min quickly acknowledged Din Muhammad's authority and opened the city to him. But ironically the military reputation Din Muhammad had earned in the marches of Khurasan and Sistan now proved his undoing. He arrived in Herat just ahead of a large Iranian army led by the Safawid ruler, Shah 'Abbas. Din Muhammad was faced with the choice of withdrawing to Mawarannahr, a course that many of his supporters advocated, or staying and defending Herat against the Iranian army. In many ways, it would have been more prudent to retire to Mawarannahr and there establish the Tuqay-Timurid khanate of Yar Muhammad before attempting to confront the Safawids for control of Khurasan. But Din Muhammad apparently believed that surrender of Herat would have done serious damage to Tuqay-Timurid claims to leadership, and so he decided to stay and fight. Either in the battle that took place on 6 Muharram 1007/9 August 1598, or shortly thereafter, he lost his life. The Uzbek forces were routed and Herat returned to Safawid possession.[13]

Din Muhammad's death set back Tuqay-Timurid ambitions, but only temporarily. His place as "mender and render" was quickly assumed by his brother, Baqi Muhammad. The latter arrived in Mawarannahr at a time when Qazaq (Kazakh) enemies of the Abu'l-Khayrid house had occupied Tashkent, sacked Samarqand, and were threatening to take Bukhara. The newly proclaimed Abu'l-Khayrid/Shibanid khan, Pir Muham-

---

[12] Salim, fol. 156b.

[13] See Munshi n.d., 1:558–74 (Munshi 1978, 1:741–60) for the sequence of events leading up to the Battle of Ribat-i Paryan (Munshi, n.d., 1:570–74; Munshi 1978, 2:755–60). See also Tahir Muhammad, fol. 100b and BA 4: fols. 54a–55a. There are differing versions of Din Muhammad's death. Munshi's source was Mirza Mawlana Ibrahim Mashhadi, a former employee of Mirza Abu Talib Ridawi, Din Muhammad's father-in-law, who then became a secretary to the Uzbek governor of Herat, Qul Baba Kukaltash, and later entered Din Muhammad's service. He saw Din Muhammad wounded at the battle but was sent away and did not witness the place or time of death (Munshi 1978, 2:758). The assumption is that he died of the wound. BA 4: fol. 55a and Salim, fols. 158b–159a have him killed in the battle with the Qizilbash and, according to Salim, buried at Maruchaq. Muhammad Yusuf Munshi, fols. 36a–b has him killed by nomads after escaping from Herat. TR, fols. 195b–196a, which dates the battle to A.H. 1008, says he escaped to Balkh but does not say how he died.

mad b. Sulayman,[14] quickly accepted the offer of help extended by the
the remnants of the Tuqay-Timurid forces and assigned them the defense
of Samarqand. In a few months, over the autumn and winter of 1598,
Baqi Muhammad repelled the Qazaq threat. After securing his position
in Samarqand, he then turned his energies toward increasing his clan's
power. A crisis in Bukhara brought about by Pir Muhammad's attempt to
purge some of the amirs of the Durman tribal organization provided Baqi
Muhammad with a useful pretext. Responding to the amirs' appeal, he
marched against Bukhara in the spring of 1599, defeated and killed Pir
Muhammad, and immediately convened a Tuqay-Timurid quriltay.[15]

The 1599 quriltay, like the quriltays of 1511 and 1513, reestablished
the ground rules and became the political point of reference for the new
Tuqay-Timurid rulers. It reasserted the norms of seniority and clan appanage rights that, at least in theory, had governed correct political behavior throughout the preceding century. Unlike the earlier Shibanids,
however, the Tuqay-Timurids attempted to provide some sort of formal
recognition of the real, as distinct from the nominal, sovereign. In so
doing, they showed the effects of a century of urban influence on the
ideals of the steppe.

In Sistan in the previous year, Din Muhammad had recognized the
khanate of his grandfather, Yar Muhammad, as senior member of the
clan, and when the 1599 quriltay was held, Yar Muhammad presided.
But at this point, he is reported to have relinquished the tokens of nominal authority because of his advanced age and because he wanted to pur-
sue spiritual interests. (The voluntary or semivoluntary relinquishing of
the khanate would be a recurrent theme in Tuqay-Timurid political his-

[14] *BA* 4: fols. 55b–57b; al-Asil, fol. 554a; Munshi n.d., 1:591–92. Muhammad Yusuf Munshi, fol. 37b and 1956, 70, 73–75 says nothing about Pir Muhammad's khanate nor about
the Shibanid and Tuqay-Timurid struggle for the khanate. His largely imaginary account
says that no Shibanid survived 'Abd al-Mu'min and that the "amirs" offered Jani Muhammad the khanly throne, which he, in a dramatic speech, refused to accept. Then when his
eldest son Din Muhammad was killed after the Battle of Herat, the amirs of Bukhara conferred the throne on his second son, Baqi Muhammad. This version, which otherwise
would not be worth mentioning, has tended to be uncritically accepted by later historians
(e.g., Vambery 1873, 306–7; Aminova et al. 1967, 1:550; Spuler 1965; Spuler 1969, 243–44;
Muminov 1969–70 1:261).

[15] The date for this event, a momentous one in the history of the region, appears only as
A.H. 1007/A.D. 1598–99 in *BA* 4: fol. 58a. We can narrow the time considerably, however,
since we know that between the beginning of the year marked by the Battle of Herat on 6
Muharram 1007/9 August 1598, and the convening of the quriltay, the Tuqay-Timurid clan
returned to Mawarannahr, was settled at Samarqand, had at least one major confrontation
with the Qazaq Shibanids, negotiated with the Durman amirs of Bukhara, and finally ousted
Pir Muhammad from Bukhara. If we assume that the battle for Bukhara did not occur until
the end of winter, then we can fix the quriltay sometime in the third quarter of A.H. 1007,
that is, in the spring of A.D. 1599.

tory.) In his place, his eldest son and the next eldest clan member, Jani Muhammad, was elected khan. The first coinage of the new line of khans in Mawarannahr thus bore Jani Muhammad's name, and it is he who may be called the first Tuqay-Timurid grand khan.[16]

The terminology used by the *Bahr al-asrar* to describe Jani Muhammad's position illustrates the way in which the view of the office of khan was evolving. The office that Yar Muhammad relinquished and which was then passed to Jani Muhammad is called the "nominal sultanate" (*saltanat-i suri*), in contrast to the "real sultanate" (*saltanat-i ma'nawi*), which belonged to the most powerful clan member, in this case Baqi Muhammad. The use of such terminology suggests a somewhat formalized recognition of, and response to, an existing state of affairs. In addition, the usage indicates that the position of the informal leader now received some formal acknowledgment from other clan members.

In many ways, the institution of the "real sovereign" addressed the same concerns as the office of "heir-apparent." It provided a sense of predictability and stability in political succession. There was an alternate or secondary focus of loyalty acceptable to the political interests of the amirs. Uncertainty about motives and actions was lessened. The titular khan understood that his fiat was limited but that his formal rights would not be abridged. The "real sovereign" recognized the limitations on his outward gestures, claims, and symbols. He had no formal rights, but his position was acknowledged and his power was extensive. Such status meant that the "real sovereign" had continually to prove his merit. In the face of a long-lived titular khan, it was not uncommon for the "real sovereignty" to pass from one individual to another as the efficiency, military skills, and leadership of one sultan were surpassed by those of another. The process provided flexibility; it allowed for individual initiative and ambition and yet at the same time made for a semblance of continuity and stability in the office of the titular khan.

The effect of such a development was to slow if not impede what might be called a natural process of agrarianate centralization. It was difficult, as the Shibanid 'Abd Allah Khan discovered, to overcome loyalty to the seniority system. Within a somewhat limited frame, biological circumstances would determine who succeeded as head of state. Any inter-appanage bureaucracy formed in the grand khan's region would be disman-

[16] *BA* 4: fol. 61b. For a variety of conflicting accounts of the early Tuqay-Timurids, see *TR*, fol. 196a; Muhammad Yusuf Munshi, fol. 35a; Morley 1854, CLXI and note; Vambery 1873, 306; Howorth 1876–88, 743; Lane-Poole 1882, 70–71; Aminova et al. 1967 2:550; and Hambly 1969, 167. For the most recent discussion of the early Tuqay-Timurids, see Burton 1988b. The question of whether Yar Muhammad, the father of Jani Muhammad, issued coins is a controversial one. See Burton 1988b, 487–88; Lowick 1966, 311–12; and Davidovich 1979, 69–81.

tled as soon as he died. Faith in the appanage system as the appropriate political form in Central Asia was a formidable obstacle to the creation of a bureaucratized state of the Irano-Islamic type. But the appanage system, seniority selection, and the informal institution of the "real sovereign" appear to have been satisfactory instruments of government for the amirs and the sultans both. This form of state flourished throughout the seventeenth century and left its mark on the political expectations and practices of the eighteenth and nineteenth centuries.

THE FIRST TUQAY-TIMURID APPANAGES

Upon his installation as khan, Jani Muhammad presided over the first distribution of appanages. Again, as in 1511, the major appanages were Bukhara and Samarqand, Balkh not yet having been incorporated into the new state. Bukhara, the richest appanage and increasingly the place that symbolized supreme power, went to Baqi Muhammad. The capital (the *takhtgah* or "throne-place"), however, now became Samarqand, Jani Muhammad's appanage seat. The other appanages and their recipients were: Sagharj to Wali Muhammad b. Jani Muhammad; Shahr-i Sabz to 'Abbas b. Yar Muhammad; Khuzar to another of Jani Muhammad's brothers, Rahman Quli; Ura Tipah to Pir Muhammad, another brother; and last, the Miyankal region to Yar Muhammad.[17]

The distribution of iqta's to amirid supporters is not discussed in the accounts of the first Tuqay-Timurid appanages, but from information appearing later it is more than probable that amirs who had formerly served the Shibanids were either confirmed in their old iqta's or given new ones as a reward for their allegiance to the new Chingizid house. These included such men as Allah Yar diwanbegi Qataghan,[18] Razzaq Birdi ataliq Yuz,[19] Shukur Bi ataliq Saray,[20] and Shah Muhammad Qunghrat.[21] Similarly, amirs who had been associated with the Tuqay-Timurids in Khurasan and Sistan were probably offered iqta's at this point.

The parallels with early Shibanid history in Mawarannahr are obvious, striking, and quite in keeping with the expectations of contemporary politicians. Moreover, the development of the Tuqay-Timurid state follows to a large extent the pattern set by the Shibanids, suggesting the similar political circumstances and the similar responses offered to them by both

---

[17] *BA* 4: fol. 62a. On Pir Muhammad, whose name does not appear in the clan lists of *BA* or *TR*, see Samsam al-Dawlah 1888–91 1:436. Also Salim, fol. 163a for information on Yar Muhammad.

[18] *BA* 4: fol. 278a.

[19] Ibid., 4: fol. 279a.

[20] Ibid., 4: fol. 125a.

[21] Ibid., 4: fol. 281a.

groups. First came a period of consolidation and annexation of territory within Mawarannahr and Balkh, the area suggestively labeled "the patrimonial lands" (*mamalik-i mawruthi*). Next there was a period of adjustment, as growth tapered off and surrounding states stopped further expansion of the appanage state.

But the parallels cease when we compare the clan structure of the Chingizid line at the beginning of the sixteenth century with that at the beginning of the seventeenth. The Shibanids (or more appropriately the Abu'l-Khayrid/Shibanids, for there was a second line, the Yadgarid/Shibanids in Khwarazm) consisted of four major clans—Shah Budaqid, Kuchkunjid, Jani-Begid, and Suyunjukid. The history of the first half of the sixteenth century is dominated by their internecine struggles, while the second half of the century witnessed an intra–Jani-Begid conflict. Although it is difficult to arrive at an estimate of the size of these clans, some idea of the expectations and pressures created may be gained by noting the numbers of adult males in the Jani-Begid clan that prevailed in the inter-appanage wars of the sixteenth century. Jani Beg (d. 20 March 1529) had twelve sons, at least nine of whom grew to adulthood and who among them produced at least nineteen male offspring. There are records of thirteen male children of these nineteen Jani-Begids.[22] In all, then, the Jani-Begid line produced some forty-one adult males in the second, third, and fourth generations who would have been eligible for some share in appanage rights, or would have had the basis for a claim to a share. The other three Abu'l-Khayrid/Shibanid clans were hardly as fecund. For Kuchkunji Khan, for instance, the names of only three sons have come down to us, two of whom had a total of five male children. For the Shah Budaqids and Suyunjukids, the figures are about comparable. It is not surprising, perhaps, that the Jani-Begids, under 'Abd Allah b. Iskandar's leadership, should have so dominated the politics of the sixteenth century.

The Tuqay-Timurid situation was quite different. Mangqishlaq, the first Tuqay-Timurid in Mawarannahr, had only three sons, Yar Muhammad, Muhammad, and Mangali Giray. Muhammad and Mangali Giray's lines all but vanish from the historical record.[23] In Yar Muhammad's line, only two sons, Jani Muhammad and Tursun Muhammad (who either was not yet born or too young to participate in the 1599 distribution), produced recorded offspring. Within the dominant of these two lines, the Jani Muhammadid, only three produced male children. And of these only

---

[22] These figures are based mainly on *BA*, but Tanish n.d. and Abu'l-Ghazi 1871–74 provide some additional as well as corroborating information.

[23] Muhammad was fourteen in 997 (*BA* 3: fol. 255a). One of Mangali's grandsons, Tahir b. Baqi b. Mangali, died at Balkh during Nadhr Muhammad's reign (1612–41) (*BA* 4: fol. 42a). Otherwise nothing is known of that line.

four grew to adulthood. Of those four only one produced children who survived infancy.[24]

In contrast to the situation in the sixteenth century, biological factors rather than political campaigns limited the clan members eligible for the khanate and appanage rights during the seventeenth century, and this circumstance in turn had a substantial effect on the course of events. The absence from the historical record of continual inter-appanage struggles (isolated instances did, of course, occur) is one indication of the effect of a small clan population. The manner in which the state evolved, particularly its relatively stable and permanent division into two parts, Bukhara and Balkh, is another symptom of a small clan cohort.

The fact that the Tuqay-Timurids thus avoided the kind of inter-appanage warfare generated by the demands of clan members for a share of the state helped assure the continuance of the steppe system of appanages. The area of Mawarannahr and Balkh was sufficient to satisfy the claims of the small number of eligible Chingizids. However, the limited size of the clan cohort at any given moment in the seventeenth century provided an opportunity for amirs to assume ever greater political power. The political arena in the seventeenth century was first formally divided into two large appanages under the leading Chingizid (Tuqay-Timurid) personalities of the day. But within those great appanages, local authority was gradually taken by Uzbek amirs. Along with the acquisition of local power came a gradual identification with the locale by the amirid iqta'-holder. Although the Tuqay-Timurid appanagee held the right of "dismissal and appointment," it became increasingly common as the century progressed for amirs to view particular areas as their rightful territory (Ming amirs in Shibarghan, Qataqhan in Qunduz, and Alchin in Kahmard, for example) and the *yurtgah* of their fellow tribesmen and their allies from other Uzbek tribal groups.

All of this had a very direct bearing on the development of the 'Alid shrine and its waqf. What follows here is a brief summary of how the Tuqay-Timurid appanage system developed over the course of the seventeenth century and of the concurrent evolution of the waqf and its administration at the 'Alid shrine.

EXPANSION AND READJUSTMENT, 1599–1611

Expansion of the new state's territory commenced almost immediately after the 1599 distribution was complete. The brothers Baqi Muhammad and Wali Muhammad began to extend Tuqay-Timurid authority south of

---

[24] *BA* 4: fol. 72a.

Bukhara, intending eventually to link up with friendly forces in Balkh who were anxious to be rid of the Shibanid authority there.

Political events in Balkh after the death of 'Abd al-Mu'min in August 1598 present a complicated picture, illustrating the antagonisms within the surviving Abu'l-Khayrid clans, hostilities between Shibanids and Tuqay-Timurids, and the opportunistic policies of the Safawid shah, 'Abbas. The latter, by this time firmly established in control of the Qizilbash factions, was beginning to lay down the policies that would mark his relations with Mawarannahr and Balkh for the next decade.

Immediately after 'Abd al-Mu'min's death, Balkh had come under the amirid-backed young Shibanid, 'Abd al-Amin b. 'Ibad Allah Sultan.[25] Very soon, however, 'Abd al-Amin, a nephew of 'Abd Allah Khan, was deposed and killed by Muhammad Ibrahim b. Suyunj Muhammad b. Kapak b. Bubay b. Khwajah Muhammad b. Abu'l-Khayr.[26] This particular branch of the Abu'l-Khayrids was not one of those appanaged early in the sixteenth century. The ancestor, Bubay, was a brother of Jani Beg[27] and perhaps his line was an ally or client of the Jani-Begids during the century. In any event the appearance of such individuals in moments of crisis is indicative of one of two things. If Muhammad Ibrahim was indeed a genuine descendant of Bubay, then the failure of 'Abd Allah Khan's efforts to eliminate rival clans is again confirmed. If he was a pretender, his appearance indicates how strong the Abu'l-Khayrid tradition was and how necessary to the politics of the period. Without a Chingizid, in this case an Abu'l-Khayrid/Chingizid, a faction had no candidate.

A late source, Muhammad Yusuf, attributes Shi'ite beliefs to Muhammad Ibrahim (perhaps because of the Safawid backing) and asserts, quite fantastically (but, given the late-seventeenth-century readers' expectations, quite persuasively), that Muhammad Ibrahim was secretly colluding in the murders of "Muslims" (read "Sunnis") in the streets and back alleys of Balkh.[28] By the beginning of the eighteenth century, when Muhammad Yusuf was writing, Sunni-Shi'i antagonisms were of quite a different order from what they had been at the beginning of the seventeenth century. Name-calling always had a certain usefulness in the

---

[25] Akhmedov 1982, 97. See Lane-Poole 1882, 68 for a coin of the sultan. Also see Davidovich 1953, 37.

[26] Tanish I: margin fol. 35b has the above genealogy. Salim, fol. 155b has him in the Tuqay-Timurid line. Tahir Muhammad, fol. 98b calls him a father's brother's son of 'Abd al-Mu'min. Jalal-i Munajjim, fols. 135a–b makes him the father's sister's son. On the circumstances of Muhammad Ibrahim's coming to the attention of the Safawids and his activities in Balkh see Munshi n.d., 1:557, 595–96; Tahir Muhammad, fol. 98b; and BA 4: fols. 62b–64a. On his coins see Davidovich 1979, 87–89.

[27] Tanish 1983– , 1:87. Also see Bacqué-Grammont 1970, 444–45.

[28] Muhammad Yusuf Munshi b. Khwajah Baqa, fols. 36b–37a; Muhammad Yusuf Munshi 1956, 75.

relations between the Uzbek and Qizilbash states, but one should not necessarily infer that diplomatic relations between Safawid Iran and Chingizid Mawarannahr and Balkh were governed or even much influenced by sectarian considerations. In the late sixteenth and early seventeenth centuries, relations were often belligerent, but not because of the Hanafi-Sunni program of the one or the Imami-Shi'i ideology of the other. Rather, more mundane issues like irredentism, revenue interests, and ethnic politics lay behind the periodic flare-ups.

To the author of *Tarikh-i Muqim Khani*, ideology may have seemed the easiest explanation for the events that led to the Tuqay-Timurid takeover of Balkh, but since it is the only source to see a sectarian motive behind the events, more prosaic causes seem to explain better the ease with which Wali Muhammad took the city. One such was the death of Muhammad Ibrahim sometime before the arrival of the Tuqay-Timurid force in 1601. Another more potent political factor was the state of amirid politics in Balkh, always a crucial element. When Muhammad Ibrahim appeared with Safawid backing, his closest advisor/supporter was a Qunqhrat amir, Khuda Nazar Bi ataliq. The Balkh amirs, already alienated from Shibanid claims by the purges undertaken by the late 'Abd al-Mu'min, reportedly resented both the new embodiment of Shibanid authority and Khuda Nazar Bi, an outsider to Balkh. Their resentment culminated in his assassination.[29] In the meantime, a group of Balkh amirs, looking for a khanly line to replace the Shibanids, had already made contact with the Tuqay-Timurids. The leader of the amirid faction in Balkh was Baruti Bi Ming.[30] It is worth noting that at least a section of the Ming were traditionally one part of the "quadripartite ulus" given Tuqay Timur in the thirteenth century. The fact that the seventeenth-century historian Mahmud b. Amir Wali relates that tradition suggests that it may have still produced vestigial loyalties and may have been influential in Baruti Bi's decision to support the Tuqay-Timurids. Or, conversely, it may simply be that the Ming role in the seventeenth century is being given a retrospective importance.

Upon Wali Muhammad's arrival outside Balkh, the city was surrendered to him by Baruti Bi. Like the Jani-Begid Kistan Qara Sultan, Wali Muhammad received Balkh and then made it his own appanage. Whether the sultan who annexed new territory had an absolute claim or at least a prior claim is not certain, but such a pattern seems to have been common. There is also some evidence that Baqi Muhammad had hoped to prevent his brother from reaching Balkh first. He had ordered Wali Muhammad, who was at the head of an advance force, to wait outside

[29] Munshi n.d., 1:605–6.
[30] *BA* 4: fol. 64a.

Balkh until he could rejoin him from Tirmidh. Together they would then make a ceremonial entry into the city. But Wali Muhammad did not wait. As he neared the city, he received the delegation of amirs and accepted the city on behalf of the new Chingizid order.[31]

The occupation of Balkh was the first major event of the expansionist period of the Tuqay-Timurid state. The southern cities of Mawarannahr—Tirmidh, Qarshi, and Hisar-i Shadman, all governed as iqta's by amirs—quickly offered their allegiance. Along with this rapid extinction of Shibanid authority, Safawid influence was also curtailed in Mawarannahr and Balkh. In A.H. 1011/A.D. 1602, a Qizilbash army attempting to reestablish Shibanid authority in Balkh was thoroughly humiliated,[32] ending actual military intervention by Safawid/Qizilbash forces in the area east of the Murghab. This defeat did not, however, prevent Safawid governments from equipping and encouraging exiled opponents of the new Tuqay-Timurid state.

After 1602, the Tuqay-Timurids moved quickly into the western marches. Although they were never able to retake Herat, they did manage to establish a relatively secure and durable frontier with the Safawids on a line northeast of Herat up to the east bank of the Murghab. Farther east, the Tuqay-Timurids under their "mender and render" pushed into Badakhshan.[33] But Tashkent and other lands east of the Syr Darya, including the Farghanah Valley, proved as troublesome to the Tuqay-Timurids as they had to the later Shibanids. With the collapse of the Abu'l-Khayrid house, the Qazaqs[34] had gained considerable authority around Tashkent. Military pressure from that direction was a recurring problem in the first half of the seventeenth century.

The period of Tuqay-Timurid expansion came to an end about the time of Jani Muhammad's death in 1012/1603. As senior clan member, his father, Yar Muhammad, was again offered the khanate and again refused.

[31] Ibid.

[32] The accounts of the Balkh campaign are found in Munshi n.d., 1:613–14 and 619–26; *BA* 4: fols. 64b–68b; Junabadi, fols. 311a–12b; al-Asil, fols. 557a–b; Muhammad Amin, fol. 93a; Muhammad Yusuf Munshi, fols. 38b–42a; and Abu'l-Fadl al-'Allami 1897–1939, 3:1207–8. Although Munshi n.d., 1:619 seems to date the conclusion of the campaign to 9 Muharram Bars Il (i.e., 1012/19 June 1603), his correlation of Turki to Hijri years is incorrect here (see McChesney 1980b, 62). The year should be 1011, which corresponds with *BA*, al-Asil, and Junabadi. *BA* provides an appropriately partisan chronogram composed by Mawlana Ghulam Husayn on the occasion of the Safawid retreat: *rafidi bi-dil shud* ("The heart was taken out of the 'Refusers' "). That is, the numerical value of the middle letter of "Refusers" (*rafidi*), the *fa'*, which is 80, should be subtracted from the numerical value of the entire word, which is 1,091, thereby producing the date of the battle.

[33] *BA* 4: fols. 68b–71a.

[34] For a study of Qazaq (Kazakh) origins and their sixteenth-century history, see Pishchulina 1977.

In November 1603, the khanate then passed to Baqi Muhammad. But was Baqi Muhammad senior clan member, and, if not, how was the principle of seniority working? In all likelihood, besides Yar Muhammad, there were at least three other clan members older than Baqi Muhammad, the brothers of Jani Muhammad. In Baqi Muhammad's succession we see evidence of the effect of agrarianate rule, of urban influences on the succession process, and of a tendency to narrow the field of candidates by restricting eligibility. There was no absolute guarantee of succession, but the line of the grand khan certainly enjoyed an advantage if it contained a capable candidate, even one without the requisite seniority. In certain cases in which succession passed to a brother or to his descendants, the intensity with which the former khan's son campaigned for the khanate is evidence that Irano-Islamic ideas of kingship and succession were making inroads into the steppe tradition. Lineage was beginning to assert its superiority to age.

But every set of circumstances has its own mitigating factors. If we try to force the view that people acted according to set rules without weighing the factors that worked against the application of these rules at any given time, we miss the often ad hoc nature of decision-making. In the case of Baqi Muhammad's succession, it is necessary to temper the ideological principle of seniority with other factors. More decisive than blind devotion to ideas about legitimacy seem to have been the practical considerations: Were the eligible candidates capable? Was there some way to adhere to the system of seniority without handing authority to an incompetent or to someone without wide public (that is, amirid) support? Maintaining the public posture of upholding what was sanctioned by the yasa was a sine qua non. But the qualifications of a candidate also had to be considered. Sultans with seniority within the ruling clan could be excluded from the khanate by amirid consensus. Sometimes this deselection process ran its course before the need arose to elect a new khan. At other times, the consensus was not at all clear at election time, and we then read of succession crises. Such a crisis occurred with the election of Wali Muhammad Khan in 1605 and, later in the century, after the abdication of Imam Quli Khan. Consensus depended on the general view of a candidate's competence, and competence was both an acquired characteristic and a circumstantial one. Mahmud b. Amir Wali uses the Arabic epigram, *kulla yawmin wa huwa fi sha'nin* ("Every day he is occupied with affairs [of government]") to illustrate what was expected of a khan. Those who could not or did not live up to this expectation were not considered serious candidates.

Not that such credentials necessarily produced outstanding khans. In fact, once chosen, khans seemed to step away from active leadership. After Baqi Muhammad was elected khan in November 1603, his apparent interest in military campaigning waned, in much the same way as 'Ubayd Allah Khan after his election to the khanate in 1533 and 'Abd Allah Khan on his election in 1583 had virtually ceased their military activities.

With Baqi Muhammad's election, the territorial expansion of the Tuqay-Timurid state came to an end and a governmental structure was established that provided the territorial framework for the politics of the entire seventeenth century.

First, the capital, the khan's appanage seat, was once again moved from Samarqand to Bukhara, Baqi Muhammad's appanage since deposing the last Shibanid, Pir Muhammad Khan.[35] Samarqand was at first awarded to two of the late Din Muhammad's sons, Imam Quli and Nadhr Muhammad, but Baqi Muhammad maintained effective control over the fourteen- and twelve-year-old boys by appointing his own amirs as ataliqs and diwanbegis. In the absence of a vigorous sultan to rule it, Samarqand, in effect, became part of the Bukharan appanage. The second most powerful figure in the Jani Muhammadid clan now was Wali Muhammad, who held Balkh.

The seating at Balkh of the next most powerful figure in the ruling clan was the second prominent feature of the seventeenth-century political arena and amounted to the division of the Tuqay-Timurid state into two large appanages—Bukhara and Balkh. Although the original formation dates from the khanate of Baqi Muhammad, it was to achieve its fullest expression during the period 1610—1681. In those seven decades, the two appanages were held for approximately equal periods by two pairs of brothers, Imam Quli and Nadhr Muhammad, and then by 'Abd al-'Aziz and Subhan Quli, sons of Nadhr Muhammad.

Wali Muhammad and the 'Alid Shrine, 1601–1606

With the arrival of the Tuqay-Timurids at Balkh, there is substantially more information about the shrine and its waqf administration. At the very beginning of the century, the shrine received a large endowment of new waqf properties that substantially changed the nature of its waqf holdings. In addition, the shrine area underwent redevelopment, with the construction of new buildings and grounds financed by the regime in Balkh.

Wali Muhammad, the first Tuqay-Timurid at Balkh, was also the first of the new ruling clan to patronize the shrine. It is a reasonable inference to link his patronage to the demands of the appanage system of government and to the opportunities the system presented. As governor of

---

[35] *BA* 4: fols. 72b–73a, according to which Baqi Muhammad's enthronement occurred on 12 Jumada al-Thani 1012/17 November 1603.

Balkh, Wali Muhammad would naturally have sought local political and administrative backing in order to carry out the functions demanded of his government. Tax assessment and collection, regulation and repair of the irrigation system, supervision and regulation of commercial activities, maintenance of public order, defense of the region against foreign enemies—all these were expected of the man who governed Balkh. Conversely, the newly powerful became the focus of expectations of patronage—financial support for scholarship through building and endowing madrasahs, support for the cult by building and endowing mosques, and aid to the economy by building and maintaining water systems, roads, bridges, hostels, warehouses, and retail space. There was a clear quid pro quo by which political support produced certain rewards and those rewards in turn were supposed to be used to generate more political support. Politicians and the public were bound by a web of mutual obligations and loyalties.

Under the appanage system, local backing from intellectuals and other molders of public opinion was especially important for the politician. Patronage of institutions and individuals was one of the most widely used instruments for building popular support. Not that it was always successful, nor, conversely, that unpopular figures could not often maintain their positions without the liberal dispensing of patronage.

When Wali Muhammad made Balkh his appanage in 1601, he recognized in the 'Alid shrine and its administration an important means of communication with the people of the region. That he chose the shrine as the exclusive object (so far as we know) of his patronage is proof of its regional importance. The shrine officials enjoyed an influence in the Balkh region that arose from two sources. First, they were the guardians of a popular religious tradition that had sunk its roots deep into Balkh's spiritual soil over the previous century. Second, the administrators controlled a substantial segment of the agricultural economy of the region through their management of the Shahi Canal and its dependent lands.

Balkh had several shrines of significance at the beginning of the seventeenth century, one of the most important being the shrine of Abu Nasr Parsa. The Parsa'i shaykhs who were its guardians had held the post of shaykh al-islam of Balkh since the days of Ulugh Beg (r. 1447–1449).[36] Other important shrines were those of Khwajah 'Akkashah (or 'Ukkashah), a Companion of the Prophet,[37] and the tomb of Ka'b al-Ahbar,[38]

---

[36] BA 4: fol. 286a.

[37] Mukhtarov 1980, 38, 92. According to A. A. Semenov, editor and translator of the *Tarikh-i Muqim Khani*, no textual evidence has been found linking the khwajah with the Prophet Muhammad (Muhammad Yusuf Munshi 1956, 252). Although the tomb building itself is variously attributed to the Timurid period (Frye 1960a) and to the seventeenth

near which stands a large mosque, the so-called Masjid-i Nuh Gunba-
dhan (Nine-Domed Mosque), whose origins are believed to have been in
the 'Abbasid period.[39] Wali Muhammad's singling out the 'Alid shrine as
the object of his largesse underscores its prominence in the spiritual life
of the people of Balkh in the early seventeenth century.

Aside from the spiritual aspect and the possible advantage the Balkh
ruler might derive from associating himself with it, the shrine administration offered another kind of connecting thread to the people. The
Tuqay-Timurid appanage system was noted for its relatively decentralized administrative apparatus. This probably meant more discretion and
variation in appanage bureaucratic organization. But the decentralized
nature of the state did not mean there was less demand for governmental
oversight of routine business. Regardless of whether land or other real
estate was held as private property, as a conditional grant (iqta', suyurghal, tiyul), as leased state property (mamlakah), or as waqf (likewise
normally leased), records had to be kept, the qadi's court had to adjudi-
cate disputes, sales had to be registered and verified, taxes and rents had
to be collected, and individual rights had to be protected.

But the appanage-holder would have had to rely more on existing local
bureaucracies to perform these administrative functions than would a
governor in a more centralized state. The 'Alid shrine administration is a
case in point. It was a small bureaucracy with considerable experience in
land and revenue administration because of its waqf endowment. And
that expertise was probably exploited by the authorities at Balkh. But the
shrine's dependence on the politicians' desire to maintain good relations
was probably greater than the latter's reliance on the shrine's administrative experience. Although waqf land was theoretically protected from
state revenue officials and subject only to the waqf managers, in practice
disputes over jurisdiction frequently arose and parties on both sides had
to appeal to the political authorities in Balkh.

There were, therefore, mutual needs that linked the men who sat in
power in Balkh with those who controlled the shrine and its properties.
The politicians needed the shrine officials both to help provide certain
essential services and to weigh in with political support when needed.
The shrine managers in turn expected the authorities to defend their administrative prerogatives when challenged.

The shrine's popular appeal, the role of its administration in the regional economy and its bureaucratic expertise, and the possibility of future close relations between it and Balkh obviously appealed to Wali Mu-

---

century (Mukhtarov 1980, 92), the possibility that the tomb site is much older should not
be dismissed out of hand.

[38] Schmitz 1978.

[39] Pugachenkova 1968, 1970; Golombek c. 1969.

hammad. He added to the shrine's stock of buildings and provided it with many new waqfs. Of the four construction projects that he initiated, we know the dates of only two. The following order therefore is based on the assumption that the projects had a logical sequence.

The first project that the Tuqay-Timurid undertook was laying out an avenue (*khiyaban*) between Balkh and the shrine center at Khwajah Khayran, twelve miles to the east.[40] The term *khiyaban* is perhaps best translated as "highway project," for it goes well beyond the simple building of a road. In fact, the road surface was probably one of the least important features of a khiyaban—if indeed the road were surfaced at all. From the surviving descriptions of Wali Muhammad's boulevard, its most striking feature was the double row of flowering shade trees that were planted along it. Although not specifically mentioned in this case, other customary features of a khiyaban were cisterns, small canals, bridges where appropriate, gardens, rest areas, and other facilities for pedestrians. The khiyaban between Balkh and Khwajah Khayran symbolized Wali Muhammad's support for the spiritual tradition represented by the shrine and may have been intended to suggest as well the two-way flow of commitment.

The second, third, and fourth projects were built at the shrine itself. All three projects may have been constructed simultaneously. The second project involved the design and landscaping of a very large *chaharbagh* or park of one hundred jaribs (approximately fifty acres), which included a smaller, more formal set of gardens called "The Eighteen Parterres" (Hazhdah Chaman). This smaller garden was interlaced with a network of water channels.[41]

The chaharbagh as an architectural form has attracted much attention from scholars.[42] Generally of a symmetrical design, often rectangular, the chaharbagh was a form of landscape architecture incorporating buildings (kiosks, small palaces, covered cisterns, small raised platforms called "suffah,"[43] and sometimes even kitchens); waterways; and pedestrian paths. The chaharbagh was usually enclosed by a wall or other distinctive border. The terms *park* and *formal garden*, which are closest in meaning to the sense of chaharbagh, do not wholly capture, in the first case, the formal, planned nature of the chaharbagh and, in the second, its often extensive scale and the incorporation of buildings into the design.

Wali Muhammad's chaharbagh was located beside the sanctuary area

[40] *TMS*, 37; Muhammad Yusuf Munshi, fol. 40b; Muhammad Tahir Balkhi, fol. 17b; Salim, fol. 181b.

[41] *TMS*, 37; Muhammad Tahir Balkhi, fol. 17b; Salim, fol. 181b.

[42] See, for example, Pugachenkova 1951; Ivanov 1954, 133–34; Moynihan 1979, 49–52; and Golombek and Wilber 1988, 1:174–80.

[43] On the suffah see Blair 1984, 69–70.

(rawdah). It may well have been developed on land already held by the shrine, although there is no indication of this in the sources. Wali Muhammad was not at Balkh to see its completion, having been called to Bukhara by news of Baqi Muhammad's death in 1014/1606. According to Hajji Mir Muhammad Salim, who wrote in the early eighteenth century, the construction of the chaharbagh was begun after Wali Muhammad left Balkh to assume the khanate. He had returned to Balkh because of a Safawid-backed effort by certain Shibanid sultans to reestablish Shibanid claims in Balkh. The Shibanid-led Qizilbash force had just been defeated. Wali Muhammad arrived in Balkh on the last day of Rajab 1014 and, after visiting the 'Alid shrine, ordered work begun on the chaharbagh.[44]

A chronogram, *jannat-i thani* ("a second Garden of Paradise"), which yields the date 1014/1605–1606, was devised by a certain Mirza Kijik Juzjanani[45] and inscribed on one of the entrances to the grounds, called the Nazargah Gate.[46] In addition, there is information that Wali Muhammad appointed Mirza Kijik both professor (*mudarris*) and shaykh al-islam at the 'Alid shrine. Mirza Kijik was the brother of Mir Jujuk, a well-known poet in Balkh at the turn of the century. He had held the title "Malik al-Shu'ara" under the Shibanid 'Abd al-Mu'min, and his poetry reportedly had a wide popular appeal, being recited in "Arabic, Persian, Turki, and Hazaragi."[47]

A third project, which is dated to 1015/1606–1607,[48] was the construction of a cistern or reservoir (*hawd*), called Hawd-i Zirik in the twentieth century.[49] The cistern was built on the northern side of the sanctuary area and within the grounds of a chaharbagh attributed to the Saljuq Sultan Sanjar.[50]

Wali Muhammad's fourth project at the shrine was to renovate the main shrine building attributed to Mawlana Banna'i and/or his father, Mawlana Sabz, in the 1480s and, as mentioned earlier, already renovated by 'Abd al-Mu'min in the 1580s or 1590s. According to the author of *'Aja'ib al-tabaqat*, Wali Muhammad "increased the building's height" to thirty *dhar'* (about sixty to seventy-five feet) and expanded its size to cover about a jarib (some 20,000 square feet).[51] Other sources, without

---

[44] Salim, fol. 170b. There are dating problems with this text. Although the date of Rajab 1014 is given, the events that bring Wali Muhammad to Balkh are dated 1016 or to the Turki year Quy Yil (1015–16).

[45] *Risalah*, fol. 164a. A rather peculiar spelling of the poet's name is given here (K-j-j-k); *TMS*, 37 provides the *nisbah*-name "Juzjanani."

[46] *BA* 4: fol. 352b.

[47] Ibid.

[48] Muhammad Tahir Balkhi, fol. 17b.

[49] *TMS*, 37.

[50] Muhammad Tahir Balkhi, fol. 17b; Salim, fol. 181a; *TMS*, 37.

[51] Muhammad Tahir Balkhi, fol. 17b.

specifying the extent of the work, speak of his "embellishing and improving" the domed shrine.[52] Mahmud b. Amir Wali even goes so far as to characterize Wali Muhammad as "builder and architect" (*bani wa mi'mar*) of the shrine.[53] How Wali Muhammad's renovations affected 'Abd al-Mu'min's congregational mosque is not at all clear. Indeed, even the question of whether his work extended to both parts of the building or was limited, as the texts seem to imply, to the original gunbad of Banna'i requires far more research before it can be answered.

Of particular interest are the waqf endowments made by Wali Muhammad during his five-year tenure at Balkh. Until his grants, we have no record that there had been any additions to the original endowment given by Sultan Husayn Bayqara more than a century before. It is certainly possible, indeed likely, that both 'Abd al-Mu'min and his great-uncle before him, Kistan Qara Sultan, set up waqf endowments to maintain the buildings that they had erected at the shrine. Such would have been routine and expected. But no documentary evidence of any such waqfs has yet come to light.

Wali Muhammad is therefore the first Chingizid politician whose waqf grants are a matter of record. Unlike the waqf foundation of Sultan Husayn Bayqara, which was made up of a contiguous piece of real estate, the Shahi Canal, and some commercial property, the waqf donated by Wali Muhammad included eight separate parcels of property, widely scattered over the territory of Balkh. Unfortunately, we do not have the original waqf deed or deeds for these properties, so that we can only surmise that their intent was to maintain the projects that the Tuqay-Timurid sultan himself sponsored at the shrine. The source of information is a confirmation document drawn up in 1079/1668–1669, some sixty years after the waqfs were actually founded. Locating Wali Muhammad's waqf properties on the basis of this later document is also very difficult, first because only the original waqf deed would have had the exact property boundaries, and second because many of the toponyms mentioned in the 1668–1669 document had disappeared by the nineteenth century, when general surveys were taken of towns and villages in the region. Moreover, we do not know the size of the properties or the amounts of revenue they were expected to produce.

Despite these problems, however, there is a great deal to be learned from the brief citation in the 1668–1669 document about the type of waqf grant and what its location may have meant to the shrine. The order given below corresponds to the order in the text of the document:

[52] *BA* 4: fol. 352b; Salim, fol. 181a.
[53] *BA* 4: fol. 352b.

1. "The entirety of the locale of Hunud and Tatar" (*tamami mawdi'-i hunud wa tatar*). It is possible to read the phrase "mawdi'-i hunud wa tatar" as given or as "the village of the Hindus and Tatars." The presence of both Indians (Hindus) and groups claiming Mongol origin and calling themselves Tatars in the Balkh region is well attested.[54] But the context suggests a place name.

The reference in the 1668–1669 document is evidence that the place was both well known and still part of the shrine's waqf more than a half century after it had been included in the endowment. Had its location been in some doubt, we could expect some kind of modifying phrase, making it clear where the property was to be found. No such toponyms are to be found in any of the later geographical material, although a British member of the Afghan Boundary Commission in 1884–1886 noted a village of about one hundred houses called Tatarak in the Balkh plain.[55] Nor does the main geographical source contemporary with this document, Mir Muhammad Sharif Raqim's survey of the Hazhdah Nahr, list this village among the 232 villages it says were watered by the canals of the irrigation system. One might reasonably infer therefore that, if the village was in the Balkh plain, it had no water rights, or more likely that it was somewhere outside the Hazhdah Nahr irrigation network.

How Wali Muhammad acquired ownership of the village in order to make it waqf is not known.

2. "All of Sum Chak" (*hamagi sum chak*). The village of Sum Chak is as obscure as the previous village. The name does not appear in the Salakhetdinova (1970) list of irrigated villages, nor does it appear to have survived into the nineteenth century.

3. "Six parcels of Manqit rice-land" (*shash qit'ah-i zamin-i shali kari manqit*). Again, the name Manqit is not found as a toponym in the available sources. Like the terms *Hunud* and *Tatar*, it might be an ethnonym. As became increasingly common, areas given to different groups, in this case the Uzbek tribal grouping called Mangghit (Mangit, Manghit) or, as here, Manqit, often came to be named after the group. (The most famous case in the Balkh region is Qataghan, the region of western Badakhshan given to the Qataghan tribal group in the seventeenth century as tribal lands or yurtgah.) The Mangghit were one of the preeminent Uzbek groups of the seventeenth and eighteenth centuries. During the reign of Nadhr Muhammad (Wali Muhammad's successor) in Balkh, the governor of Darzab, a district east of Maymanah and some 180 miles by road west south west of Balkh, was a man named Birdi Bi Mangghit. This is circumstantial evidence that the Mangghit were already ensconced in the region

[54] *Gaz.* 4:199; Mukhtarov 1980, 36.
[55] *Gaz.* 4:575.

by the 1620s and that the parcel of land being referred to may have been somewhere in the vicinity of Darzab.[56] Again, as in the case of the two previous villages, no such toponym appears on the list of villages irrigated by the Hazhdah Nahr system.

4. "All of the dry-farmed [land] of Sadmish and Qarni Sa'i" (*hamah-i lalmi kari sadmish wa qarni sa'i*). About fifteen miles south of Balkh on the Balkh River (Balkhab), the stream is joined by the Sa'i Sadmish, a major tributary branching to the southwest. Another ten miles upriver, a much smaller tributary, the Karnai Sai (as its name is given on modern maps), branches off to the southwest.[57] As these are the only places where the above toponyms are found, for the time being at least we will locate the waqf lands in this region.

The term *lalmi* or *lalmiyah* meant lands without water rights, or dry-farmed lands. The term was current in Balkh and Bukhara in the seventeenth century and appears in Afghan usage today.[58] That the lands were located near water or along watercourses is of no importance. What makes the distinction between irrigated and dryfarmed lands significant is the usually higher rate of taxation (and rents) on the former and therefore, one assumes, their higher value.

5. "Chim Tuy." This is probably a variant of the modern-day town Chimtal, the form in which the name is given by Mir Muhammad Sharif Raqim. The Chimtal Canal was part of the Hazhdah Nahr system. It diverged from the Balkh River at the first barrage, which was also the diversion point for the Shahi Canal. The Nahr-i Chimtal was somewhat longer than the Nahr-i Shahi, extending more than twenty miles to the west. It also watered three more villages than did the Nahr-i Shahi. In the seventeenth century, there were two villages bearing the name Chimtal: Chimtal-i Ghulbah and Chimtal-i Sufla,[59] but by the nineteenth century there is only one village with the name.[60] Since Raqim mentions them as the tenth and twelfth villages on the canal, it is possible that they were combined into one entity at some later time.

6. "Badr al-Din." I have been unable to locate this village.

7. "Kaftar Khwani." For this hamlet there are two likely locations. One is the present-day Kaftar Khan, about eighty miles south of Balkh and deep in the Hindu Kush mountains.[61] The second is Kaftar Khanah or Kaftarkhan, as it appears on modern maps,[62] a name borne by two neigh-

[56] *Gaz.* 4:193. On the administrative importance of Darzab, see Akhmedov 1982, 35–36.

[57] See the map section of *Gaz.* 4:IV-7-D.

[58] Davydov 1960, 96; Ivanov 1954, 72. Afghani Nawis under the entry *lalmiyah*.

[59] Salakhetdinova 1970, 226.

[60] *Gaz.* 4:164–65.

[61] Nahid 1951–60, 3:339.

[62] *Gaz.* 4: map section, IV-11-A.

boring villages about thirty miles west of Maymanah and five miles north of the main road to Bala Murghab, where it passes through Qaysar. In either case it is a long way from the shrine.

8. "Dependencies [*ta 'alluqat*] of the Darrah-i Juz, which is part of Khulm." In this, as in the previous instances, one senses that the 1668–1669 document is referring to the original waqf deeds for the particulars on each case. The use of the word *ta'alluqat* appears designed to avoid a tedious enumeration of each individual place. In the waqf deed itself, such ambiguity would not have been admissible. The toponym Darrah-i Juz (or Deragaz and variants) is found in several places. It is the name of the gorge through which the Balkh River empties onto the plain eighteen miles south of the city.[63] The region around this gorge along the northern slopes of the Kuh-i Alburz ridge of the Hindu Kush was also called Darrah-i Juz.[64] The place referred to here lay south of Khulm (Tashqurghan),[65] and thus it may be to the latter Darrah-i Juz that the waqf document refers. If so, then these lands lay some one hundred miles by road from the shrine.

We have no idea how the distance from the shrine affected the management of these properties. It seems doubtful that Wali Muhammad would have made endowments of properties whose income was difficult to collect. In all likelihood, such properties were leased, and negotiations over the leases and rental payments could have taken place at the shrine. But for comparison's sake, it is worth noting that the original waqf endowment made by Sultan Husayn Bayqara in the 1480s was compact and adjacent to the shrine. With the possible exception of Chim Tuy, which was not far from the western end of the Nahr-i Shahi, all the other parcels donated by Wali Muhammad seem to have been both distant and relatively inaccessible. Sadmish, Qarni Sa'i, Kaftar Khwani, and the districts in the Darrah-i Juz were in mountainous and distant regions. Although we know from the cases of the Haramayn waqfs (which supported purposes in Mecca and Medina)[66] and endowments for shrines in Jerusalem and Hebron[67] that it was not uncommon for great distances to separate the endowments and their beneficiaries, the present case, as well as common sense, suggests that the more distant the endowment from the beneficiary, the more difficult it was to administer, especially in times of political uncertainty.

That a person of Wali Muhammad's status was endowing the shrine

[63] Salakhetdinova 1970, 223; *TR*, fol. 126a; Harlan 1939, 26; Akhmedov 1982, 326.
[64] Akhmedov 1982, 36.
[65] Harlan 1939, 26–28.
[66] See Hoexter 1979 on the Haramayn waqf in Algiers.
[67] Winter 1984, 148–49; Cohen 1984, 233; Hutteroth 1977, map 4.

with such remote waqfs is some indication that Balkh's control over the hinterland was thought to be reasonably secure and that there was no cause for apprehension about the shrine's ability to manage these lands.

It should be noted that the properties as listed seem to have been agricultural and involved only land. How and why such distant lands were acquired as private property and then made waqf by a man who had no roots in the region and remained there no more than five years are questions that cannot yet be answered.

What we can say with some assurance is that the shrine, whose existence is barely attested to in the written record of the sixteenth century, had obviously become an institution of considerable importance by the beginning of the seventeenth century. Wali Muhammad's waqf donations, distant as they were from the shrine, indirectly testify to the continued existence and viability of the original waqf corpus and to the administrative competence of the waqf managers.

THE KHANATE OF WALI MUHAMMAD KHAN, 1606–1612

The death of Baqi Muhammad Khan in A.H. 1014/A.D. 1606,[68] followed by Wali Muhammad's election as khan and the redistribution of appanages among the Tuqay-Timurid sultans, began an era of inter-appanage struggles. But the conflicts that occurred between 1606 and 1612 were hardly comparable in intensity to the inter-Shibanid clan struggles of the previous century. In large part this was due to the small size of the Tuqay-Timurid clan and to the fact that only two significant rival branches appear, the "Walids" (Wali Muhammad's line) and the "Dinids" (the two sons of Din Muhammad Sultan, Imam Quli and Nadhr Muhammad).

Baqi Muhammad fell ill at Qarshi sometime in 1606. Perhaps aware of his impending end, he summoned his brother from Balkh. There at Qarshi, immediately after Baqi Muhammad passed away, Wali Muhammad assumed the title "khan" and was enthroned. His nephews, Imam Quli and Nadhr Muhammad, both of whom were just then in Samarqand, did not attend his installation for reasons not explicitly stated by any of the sources. Their absence was taken as a hostile gesture and Wali Muhammad immediately sent out a call for "the armies of Balkh and Badakhshan." With this force assembled, he marched on Samarqand. The show of authority was sufficient to extract expressions of allegiance from the

---

[68] The date of Baqi Muhammad's death is uncertain. Bars Yil (1010–11, Munshi n.d., 633), Luy Yil (1012–1013, al-Asil fol. 559), 1014 (Samsam al-Dawlah 1888–91, 1:436; *TR*, fol. 204a; Muhammad Ya'qub, fol. 125b, and *Tarikh-i Shibani*, fol. 14a), and 1015 (*BA* 4: fol. 76a; Muhammad Talib fol. 154a) are all found. The numismatic evidence seems to point to A.H. 1014 (19 May A.D. 1605–8 May 1606). Davidovich 1964 (coin tables) gives one coin of Baqi Muhammad dated 1013 and the earliest of Wali Muhammad's coins dated 1014.

two Dinid sultans without further confrontation. In their first withholding and then eventually offering recognition, one senses the guiding hands of their respective amirid advisors, Nadr Beg Arlat for Imam Quli and Yalangtush Bi Alchin for Nadhr Muhammad. The two sultans were seventeen and fifteen years old, respectively, and probably susceptible to the persuasiveness of the older, more experienced, and influential amirs. This near-crisis was amicably settled when it became evident to the Samarqand amirs that Wali Muhammad, at least for the moment, held all the cards.

After a "dervish majlis" (Wali Muhammad is remembered by the sources as a patron and practitioner of dervishism), complete with food, drink, music, and dancing, the two sides reached an amiable agreement on the distribution of the Tuqay-Timurid khanate. Wali Muhammad made Bukhara his appanage while keeping control of his former appanage, Balkh, and Imam Quli and his amirs received Samarqand, while Nadhr Muhammad was reconfirmed at Shahr-i Sabz, where he had been for a year or so. But within a year Nadhr Muhammad was sent to Balkh, not as its appanage-holder (perhaps his age did not yet entitle him) but as the representative of Wali Muhammad.

In the months after Wali Muhammad's enthronement, the campaign for the khanate continued at a subdued level. The amirs of Balkh and Mawarannahr in effect had not yet finished marking their ballots, regardless of agreements reached at Samarqand, and had yet to certify the succession that had occurred at Qarshi. The appanage system created a natural constituency of amirs backing individual appanage-holders. Wali Muhammad, for example, while resident at Balkh during Baqi Muhammad's khanate, had rewarded his amirs with territorial grants, and these amirs consequently had a direct and individual interest in the khan's political security. The same held true, to a lesser extent, for Imam Quli in Samarqand. There, as far as we can tell, most of the main amirid appointments had been made by Baqi Muhammad from Bukhara. The death of the khan therefore would create some anxiety among his amirid appointees and disturb the system until the eventual and decisive shift of loyalties from the deceased khan to a new Chingizid khan or claimant was completed. The initiative in this transfer might be taken either by the khan-candidate, who would actively solicit amirid support, or by the amirs themselves, seeking support from other amirs for their particular candidate. A new khan faced two often contradictory pressures. First, there were the demands of his own amirs for better positions now that he was khan, and second, there was the need for him to win the support of the late khan's amirs, so that they would not throw their backing to another khan-candidate. One feature of the appanage system helped mitigate the problem. That was the tendency for a new khan to make his old appanage seat the capital of his khanate. If he did, he could avoid offending his predecessor's amirs by not appearing in the former capital with a new group of amirs wanting grants there. At the same time, he could establish the khanly court and distribute the ceremonial offices associated with it within his own appanage and among his own amirs with a minimum of dislocation. But the increasing attraction of Bukhara as capital, and with it the crystallizing of the idea that, unless one assumed control of Bukhara, one's claim to the khanate was incomplete, aggravated the problem of meeting amirid expectations.

One of the factors leading to Baqi Muhammad's successful seizure of the khanate in 1599 from the last Shibanid khan, Pir Muhammad, was amirid disaffection in Bukhara caused by Pir Muhammad's purge of the Durman amirs when he had made Bukhara his capital. Wali Muhammad, perhaps to satisfy the demands of his Balkh amirs, likewise disaffected many Bukharan amirs by giving their perquisites to his Balkh supporters. To add to the problem for Wali Muhammad, Imam Quli was beginning to show himself to be a "real sultan" in his military campaigns against Qazaq forces in the region between Tashkent and Samarqand. This made him attractive to any dissatisfied amirs. So, although a distribution was made in 1606 and an apparent balance between Dinids and Walids achieved, in fact, beneath the surface, an amirid poll was gradually eroding Wali Muhammad's position and enhancing Imam Quli's.

At Balkh, too, a similar process was underway. After the distribution of 1606, Wali Muhammad sent his other nephew, Nadhr Muhammad, to Balkh. But perhaps because of his nephew's age or because he wanted to protect the interests of his own son, Rustam, Wali Muhammad assigned one of his own amirs as Nadhr Muhammad's ataliq. In Balkh the main problem in 1606 was a recrudesence of Shibanid claims in the person of Jahangir Sultan, a descendant of the brother of Jani Beg (founder of the Jani-Begid line), Bubay Sultan. These Shibanid claims were backed by Safawid/Qizilbash arms and men. Nadhr Muhammad and his amirs' success against Jahangir Sultan soon made him another rallying point for amirid factions antagonized by Wali Muhammad. The process reached a critical stage in 1608, when the Walid ataliq at Balkh was assassinated. This incident marked the beginning of an active effort to overthrow Wali Muhammad's khanate.

The contest was comparatively brief. Imam Quli and Nadhr Muhammad joined forces at Balkh and, with the help of many of the most influential amirs of the time, they were able within three years to expel Wali Muhammad from Mawarannahr and then, when he attempted to reclaim his khanate with the help of an Iranian army, to defeat and kill him.[69]

[69] Munshi 1978, 1054, 1056 has Wali Muhammad killed on 7 Rajab 1020/15 November 1611.

When the struggle had ended, Imam Quli, the eldest member of the Dinid line of the Tuqay-Timurids, became khan and made Mawarannahr, including Bukhara, Samarqand, and Tashkent, his appanage. Nadhr Muhammad received Balkh. The trend toward limiting khanate succession to one patrilineage was accelerating. The Walids were now excluded from power and the Janid "uncles" were given minor appanages. The Dinids held full control, and the amirs who backed them emerged from the struggle with vast iqta'-grants. The small number of Dinid clan members helped make large tracts of territory available for distribution to the amirs and also limited the scale of inter-appanage conflict.

BALKH UNDER NADHR MUHAMMAD, 1611–1641

Throughout the seventeenth century, the appanage of Balkh covered a fairly extensive region. It stretched in an irregularly rectangular form some 600 miles from east to west and 200 miles from north to south. Not surprisingly, its periphery was most vulnerable to jurisdictional changes and was in continual flux. Generally, the borders of Balkh in the west were the Murghab River and a line extending southward from Maruchaq to Ubah. Shibarghan, Andkhud, Maymanah, Faryab, Jijaktu, Jarzuwan, Darzab, Gharjistan, and Juzjan were important march iqta's, fortifying the western regions against Safawid and Qizilbash expansion and providing bases for raids into Khurasan. During the seventeenth century, Herat remained firmly in Safawid hands, although the Tuqay-Timurids continued to think of it as part of the patrimony. Its two eastern march towns, Shafilan and Ubah, were the objects of Uzbek raids but were never incorporated as iqta's under Balkh's control.[70] For the most part, the western marches of Tuqay-Timurid territory were fairly stable and relatively quiet during the seventeenth century. The long struggle for dominance which had characterized Iranian-Mawarannahrid relations in the sixteenth century, with its periodic and intense flare-ups, tapered off and was revived only on the occasions of the demise of the sovereigns on either side.

The southern boundaries of Balkh brought it into contact with the political ambitions of the Moghul state. The Moghuls controlled the region around Kabul and along the southern flanks of the Hindu Kush, where they competed with the Safawids for hegemony. Balkh's authority extended well into the Hindu Kush, what Mahmud b. Amir Wali calls "the mountains of Ghur" (the western Hindu Kush).[71]

Kahmard, a district center some fifty miles north of Bamyan and one

[70] *BA* 4: fols. 197a–198b, 268a.
[71] Ibid., 4: fol. 122b.

hundred and twenty miles northwest of Kabul, but far more isolated than those distances would suggest because of the extremely rugged terrain, was the southernmost permanent outpost of Balkh's authority. Kahmard lies about one hundred miles south of Khulm-Tashqurghan along one of the main routes between Central Asia and the Indian subcontinent. It had been captured from the Moghuls in 1584 by a Shibanid army and had remained under the jurisdiction of Balkh since then, serving as a customs post and staging area for troops on campaigns against Kabul.[72] In the middle of the century, Kahmard was the iqta' headquarters of one of the two most powerful amirs of the time, Yalangtush Bi Alchin. While Nadhr Muhammad was appanage-holder in Balkh, he was its preeminent amir. Mahmud ibn Amir Wali, describing his holdings around Kahmard in A.H. 1045/A.D. 1634, mentions Darrah-i Yusuf (Darrah-i Suf, Darasuf), Malikan, and the tribal regions (yurtgah) of the Tulakji, Saiqanji, Ziragi, Gulgi, Hazarah-i Nikudari, and "the tribal groups [uymaq and ahsham] as far as Ghazni, Qandahar, Zamindawar, Ghur, and Khurasan."[73]

The eastern regions of the Balkh appanage, because of the mountainous nature of the terrain, defy precise definition. All the towns east of Balkh as far as Ishkashm (var. Ishkamish) near the western entrance to the Wakhan Valley were subject to the appanage-holder of Balkh, at least through the first half of the century. As the politics of the appanage system evolved and the Uzbek amirs became increasingly independent, the subordinate status of the eastern regions—Qunduz, Faydabad, Tukharistan, and Khutlan—became more and more pro forma.

To the north, Balkh's jurisdiction extended across the Amu Darya (Oxus) in places to include Tirmidh, Kulab, and Qubadyan.

As an appanage, Balkh evolved in a way similar to the rest of the Tuqay-Timurid state. Two often conflicting forces were at work: amirid political prerogatives and the rights of ruling clan members. Balkh City, including its immediate districts, was the Chingizid sultan's own "yurtgah," whose revenues supported his household and court. Beyond that core, like a protective ring, was a series of amirid iqta's. These iqta's were, in theory, neither permanent nor hereditary. They were part of the appanage and therefore subject to the appanage-holder's right to "dismiss and appoint." During Nadhr Muhammad's three-decade-long tenure as appanage-holder, there were frequent reassignments of amirid iqta's as well as occasional restructuring of them. For amirs assigned to iqta's, there was a natural tendency to develop a constituency, acquire loyal followers through patronage, and generally come to view the territory as one's own. The longer an amir held an iqta', the more intense

[72] Akhmedov 1982, 47–48.
[73] BA 4: fol. 290b.

were such feelings. This was a natural and anticipated consequence, and responsibility for dealing with it lay with the appanage-holder. The amirs knew their tenures were theoretically limited but at the same time could not help but encourage local constituencies and a sense of attachment to the place.

Sooner or later, time brought to the fore another pressure on the limited resources of the state, the right of male clan members to an appanage share. When Nadhr Muhammad's sons, 'Abd al-'Aziz, Bahram, and Khusraw, came of age (that is, the "age of discretion," about seven years old), a number of the amirid iqta's were consolidated into subappanages and given to them. Nadhr Muhammad's eldest son, 'Abd al-'Aziz, on coming of age in 1620, was sent to Khutlan in the care of an Ushun amir, 'Abd al-Rahman, a diwanbegi. The latter was the young sultan's ataliq and, while helping him gain military experience on raids against Qirghiz tribes, he also was required now and then to restrain the youthful and reportedly headstrong sultan, while reporting on all his doings to his father.[74]

A year or so later, Khusraw Sultan was sent to Maymanah in the west, where various amirid iqta's were now regrouped under his (and his ataliq's) authority. In 1630, Nadhr Muhammad ordered the two sultans and their ataliqs to exchange subappanages with each other, and 'Abd al-'Aziz went west while Khusraw Sultan headed east. When 'Abd al-'Aziz arrived in Maymanah, the iqta'-holder there, an influential amir named Uraz Bi Ming (the son of the Ming amir Baruti Bi, who had helped Wali Muhammad take Balkh in 1601), surrendered his iqta' and returned to Balkh. Five years later, he was sent back to Maymanah to replace 'Abd al-Rahman Ushun as 'Abd al-Aziz's ataliq.[75]

Despite the decentralized nature of the appanage, Nadhr Muhammad exercised a firm control over the iqta's and the subappanages by such periodic transfers for most of his thirty years at Balkh. His control was effective as long as it recognized the rights of the amirs to iqta's but did not give them the opportunity to transform those rights into a permanent claim to a particular territory. At the same time, he had to restrain whatever impulse he may have felt to build a bureaucratic apparatus to supervise and administer the appanage territory, something that would have threatened the administrative prerogatives of his amirs. His policy of leaving local administration to local administrators is reflected in the biographical sections of the chronicle of his regime, the *Bahr al-asrar*. Only one-half of a folio is devoted to "wazirs and diwan officials," the

[74] Ibid., 4: fol. 219a.
[75] Ibid., 4: fol. 221a.

civilian clerks and secretaries who staffed the essential fiscal positions.[76] In contrast, twenty-five folios are given over to notices of amirs active in Balkh politics.[77]

Nonetheless there is evidence that a bureaucratic state was indeed developing. In the Tuqay-Timurid case, a number of inconvenient facts keep cropping up that seem to suggest that structures comparable to bureaucracies in the contemporary Safawid and Moghul states were evolving or had formed.

For example, in 1636, territory was retrieved from an amir who had supported the Qazaqs in Shah Rukhiyah, at the entrance to the Farghanah Valley. The land was, as the *Bahr al-asrar* words it, "enrolled in the diwan-i aʿla."[78] In contemporary Safawid usage, the term *diwan-i aʿla* referred to the state fisc, as distinct administratively and budgetarily from the privy purse, the *khassah*.[79] The land in Shah Rukhiyah might then have been given as an iqtaʿ to an amir, but in any case would have not been considered part of the khan's own properties. This conclusion is supported by complementary evidence of a royal purse. When, for example, Imam Quli Khan was given a reception at Balkh in 1049/1639, the 200,000 tangahs spent for the food, drink, and clothing was taken from the household account (*az khassah-i sharifah*) and deposited in the state treasury (*khizanah-i ʿamirah*).[80] There are other references to both the "public" and "private" budgets for this period by Mahmud b. Amir Wali.

But one, I think, can reasonably explain such references without contradicting the hypothesis of a comparatively small central bureaucratic apparatus. At issue here is both the administrative ethic of the Chingizid/ Uzbek politicians and the extent to which this ethic was translated into practice. Here the ground is somewhat firmer. The tenacity with which Shibanid/Uzbek sultans and amirs held to the appanage system could have had no other effect but to limit the growth of a central bureaucracy. The absence of material of the nature of the *Tadhkirat al-muluk* or *A'in-i Akbari* in Central Asian collections[81] and the relative weight given to amirs and intellectuals in contemporary biographies in comparison with secretaries and government officials, as well as the nature of official nomenclature, which favored Chinghizid, yasa-sanctioned court titles in-

[76] Ibid., 4: fols. 304b–305a.

[77] Ibid., 4: fols. 277b–286a, 290b–304b.

[78] Ibid., 4: fol. 108b.

[79] Minorsky 1943, 24–25.

[80] *BA* 4: fol. 268a.

[81] The contents of both the *Dastur al-muluk* of Khwajah Samandar Tirmidhi and Mirza Badiʿ Diwan's *Majmaʿ al-arqam*, two administrative manuals from Mawarannahr, support this contention. The former is a work of ethics in the "mirror for princes" tradition. The latter, some eighty-six folios long, is a manual for officials engaged in revenue collection. Three of its five sections are on mathematics and explanations of how to use *siyaqi* notation.

stead of Irano-Islamic ones, all suggest a relatively limited sphere for the development of a central bureaucracy.

Appanage politics required a delicate balancing of the rights of amirid and Tuqay-Timurid prerogatives. Despite Nadhr Muhammad's best efforts to keep the two in a stable relationship, the hopes and expectations created by the system tended to unbalance and upset his policies. Transfers of amirs, for example, while outwardly straightforward and not intended to disgrace or penalize, at times clearly angered the amirs involved.[82] His sons, when sent to the subappanages, often proved troublesome as well. As noted earlier, the offices of ataliq and diwanbegi were used to restrain if not control the activities of clan members, particularly junior members. Wali Muhammad had appointed one of his amirs as ataliq to guide and presumably manipulate Nadhr Muhammad at Balkh. Nadhr Muhammad, when his turn came, appointed his own amirs as ataliqs and diwanbegis for his sons with exactly the same end in mind.

But again, while the structure and the theoretical way in which it should have worked seemed reasonable and logical, the results were rarely predictable. For example, when Khusraw Sultan was sent to Khutlan in 1630–1631, there ensued a complete breakdown in his relations with his father and consequently between his father and the amir sent as his ataliq.[83] Khusraw Sultan's administration in Khutlan so outraged the local amirs that Nadhr Muhammad felt compelled to dismiss the ataliq, Nadr Bi Qushji, and to censure his son. But Khusraw, we are told, paid no attention, and in the next four years, despite efforts by his new ataliq to restrain him, led armed parties into territory belonging to his father's and his uncle's amirs in Hisar-i Shadman, Tirmidh, Qarshi, and Nakhshab. His uncle, Imam Quli Khan, threatened him with dire consequences if he did not go back to his own territory. According to Mahmud b. Amir Wali, Khusraw Sultan suddenly "awoke from the sleep of negligence," arranged for mediators to placate his father, and returned to Balkh to express his contrition. The next year he was again sent to Khutlan, where he thereafter seems to have behaved himself.

In many ways, his actions and the amirid reactions to transfers were a normal test of the personalities in the system and their relative positions. Such tests were frequent and a part of the system's internal logic. At some point, such a test would disclose the inability of the khan or the sultan at Balkh to act or react effectively, and the transfer of real authority to someone else would begin.

Part of the public dialogue in which the Tuqay-Timurids engaged dealt with succession and the necessary credentials for sovereignty. After 1611,

[82] McChesney 1983, 53–54.
[83] *BA* 4: fols. 228a–229b.

when Wali Muhammad and, soon thereafter, his son Rustam Muhammad, lost their status in the khanate, succession came to be seen as properly restricted to the Dinid line. Although other non-Dinid Tuqay-Timurids remained active in politics, they were ineligible, by a kind of
unspoken consensus, to be included in the succession scenario and so
became dependent on the patronage of the Dinid line. Tursun Sultan, a
son of Yar Muhammad, received Tashkent after one of the numerous
campaigns against the Qazaqs that marked the first half of the seventeenth century. Later, after losing the region to the Qazaqs, Nadhr Muhammad gave him the town of Taluqan, the district center of the Tukharistan region, today on the road between Khanabad and Faydabad in
Badakhshan.[84] About 1630, a grandson of his was given Tashkent after a
successful round of fighting with the Qazaqs, and a son, Muhammad Yar,
was appanaged in Andijan in the Farghanah Valley.[85] Three Tuqay-Timurids who had received appanages in 1599, Pir Muhammad, Rahman
Quli, and ʿAbbas, disappear from the record along with their descendants, the latter two in purges.[86]

After the division of the Tuqay-Timurid state into the two great appanages of Bukhara and Balkh about 1620, only the Dinids play central
roles, and of the Dinids, only the line of Nadhr Muhammad is significant,
primarily because Imam Quli had no surviving issue recorded. (He did
have a son, Iskandar, but he died in infancy when Imam Quli was in his
early twenties.[87])

This process of a consensual limiting of legitimacy to one line may also
be seen in the politics of the sixteenth century. But in the seventeenth
century, the limits of consensus were tightly defined by biological realities. Although the pool of eligible candidates was narrowed dramatically
by an apparently low rate of reproduction, political conflict was by no
means eliminated. Rather, there was less pressure to divide and subdi-
vide the territory, and the result was the emergence of the two great
appanages of Bukhara and Balkh. As time passed, this bipartite form acquired its own meaning and public acceptance, making unification under
a strong khan neither practical nor, in the eyes of the participating political factions, desirable.

These then are the distinctive political realities of the seventeenth-century appanage system: (1) a relatively small ruling clan (the Dinid/Tuqay-
Timurids), (2) the consequently increased importance of the amirs, and

[84] Ibid., 4: fol. 275a.

[85] Ibid., 4: fol. 117a.

[86] A son of Baqi Muhammad Khan, ʿAbd Allah, received Tashkent for a short period in
1628–29 (BA 4: fol. 112a), but no other mention is made of him. Another non-Dinid is Tahir
b. Baqi b. Mangali (the last a brother of Yar Muhammad), who was executed by Nadhr
Muhammad (BA 4: fol. 42a).

[87] Muhammad Yusuf Munshi, fol. 50a.

(3) the more or less formal division of the Dinid territory into the large appanages of Bukhara and Balkh.

THE 'ALID SHRINE DURING NADHR MUHAMMAD'S ERA AT BALKH

Information about the shrine during Nadhr Muhammad's long tenure at Balkh is scanty. His own contributions to the shrine in the form of either buildings or waqfs were negligible, if the record left by Mahmud b. Amir Wali, his own chronicler, is complete. It is possible that in the fifteen or sixteen years between the work's completion and Nadhr Muhammad's death en route to Mecca in 1650[88] endowments and gifts had been made to the shrine. But a record of such has yet to appear. Mahmud b. Amir Wali does provide a sketch of the shrine as it appeared in 1634–1635,[89] which gives us a glimpse of the attachment of the Tuqay-Timurids to the shrine despite the lack of information about any building projects undertaken by them there.

After relating the account of the tomb discovery involving Abu Muslim, Sultan Sanjar, and Sultan Husayn Bayqara, the author tells us that the structure over the sacred spot is the same one erected by Mawlana Banna'i circa 1480. The outer domed sanctum built by 'Abd al-Mu'min, the Jani-Begid, is "today called 'jami'-i astanah' " (the Threshold Congregational Mosque). Surrounding these buildings in the 1630s were numerous graves, including the tomb of Nadhr Muhammad's sister, Ayum Bibi, and one of his wives, unnamed here. His sister's tomb was located just to the right of the road after one entered the southern gate of the haram area (the rawdah). His wife's grave was called " 'Ajab Nazar" and included a *hazirah* enclosure. It stood in the middle of the rawdah between the mashhad (the tombsite of 'Ali) and a mosque called Masjid-i Khwajah Khayran. (Khwajah Khayran was the original name of the village where the tomb discovery was made.) On the eastern side of the rawdah was the grave of one of Baqi Muhammad Khan's sons, 'Ibad Allah Sultan. Outside the southern gate to the rawdah stood a hospice (ribat) ascribed to the Timurid writer and patron of the arts Amir 'Ali Shir Nawa'i. The rawdah area was completely surrounded by the chaharbagh built by Wali Muhammad, which, according to Mahmud b. Amir Wali, was nearly one hundred jaribs in area.[90] In an ambiguous sentence, referring either to Wali Muhammad or to Nadhr Muhammad, the author says that "through the efforts of the employees of that *hadrat*" shade trees were planted all around the periphery of the rawdah. He notes that pilgrims came to the shrine at all times of the year, but in particular during the first ten days of Muharram and on Thursday evenings (Friday eve) during Rajab. He

[88] *Tarikh-i Shibani*, fol. 115a.
[89] *BA* 4: fols. 318a–319a.
[90] Ibid., 4: fol. 319a.

does not mention the spring festival, Gul-i Surkh, which, at least by the early nineteenth century, was one of the major holidays celebrated at the shrine.

One other piece of information relating to Nadhr Muhammad's relations with the shrine is contained in the *Bahr al-Asrar*. In the section given over to biographies of Balkh's amirs, the author writes,

> Another [amir] is the sayyid, Mirza Sanjar. In the sublimity of his status and the loftiness of his ancestry he surpasses the rest of his colleagues. He is a relative of the mother of that hadrat [i.e., Nadhr Muhammad]. He was born in Hind and, coming to these regions in 1034, he was appointed to the office of tawliyat of the shrine of the Hadrat-i Amir—God honor him! [i.e., 'Ali b. Abi Talib]. Today through the auspicious favors of the royal personage, he has been considerably advanced and the threshold of refined architecture is the place to which people with requests and those seeking salvation turn.[91]

Together, these passages suggest, if not concrete projects on behalf of the shrine, at least a strong sense of obligation and a fairly close attachment to it. From Kistan Qara Sultan's time on, burial at the *mazar-i sharif* (the "Noble Shrine") was preferred by the leading personalities of Balkh to interment at any other site. For politicians at Bukhara, the shrine of Baha' al-Din Naqshband some twenty miles outside the city held a similar position. Only the hajj (pilgrimage), performed in anticipation of one's death, exerted a more powerful attraction.

Of more interest, from the standpoint of the waqf, is the information on the appointment of Mirza Sanjar, a relative of Nadhr Muhammad's mother. He is styled a "sayyid," in all probability, a Ridawi sayyid. Mahmud b. Amir Wali provides the first recorded instance of an appointment to the post of mutawalli. Although I will further on discuss the origins of the family, which by the 1660s was firmly established as mutawallis of the shrine and its waqf, it is worth drawing the reader's attention here to the fact that Mirza Sanjar was, quite possibly, an Imami Shi'ite and, perhaps as intriguing, that Mahmud b. Amir Wali classifies him professionally as an "amir." Amirs were to play a significant role in waqf donations later in the century, but the usual parameters of their profession did not generally encompass the office of mutawalli.[92]

NADHR MUHAMMAD'S KHANATE AND THE MOGHUL INVASION OF BALKH, 1641–1651

In 1641, the reigning khan at Bukhara, Imam Quli Khan, abdicated.[93] His eyesight and health were failing and he wanted to make the hajj-pilgrim-

[91] Ibid., 4: fol. 304b.

[92] On amirid career lines in this period, see McChesney 1983, 49–51.

[93] Muhammad Amin, fol. 96a dates the abdication during Muharram 1051/April-May

age and spend whatever time was left to him in the Holy Cities. His departure and the enthronement of his brother, Nadhr Muhammad, touched off a series of political crises, including a coup d'etat in the name of the new khan's eldest son, 'Abd al-'Aziz, foreign intervention, and intense internal maneuvering by the amirs of Balkh and Bukhara.

The decade beginning with Imam Quli's voluntary departure for Mecca and ending with his brother's involuntary departure on the hajj is an extremely complex one from the standpoint of the myriad political strands running through it and deserves a full study of its own. The period gives us an excellent example of the character of political conflict within the Uzbek system—how it arises, its structure and terms of reference, the options for resolution, and the international ramifications of such periods of conflict.

But because our subject is the 'Alid shrine and its waqf, we will only sketch in the salient moments of this decade with emphasis on those that are crucial to the development of the shrine and its waqfs. Of particular importance is the role of the amirs and the corollary issues of territorial prerogatives and local autonomy.

Nadhr Muhammad accepted the khanate in his brother's presence and then moved his appanage seat from Balkh to Bukhara, an indication of the now well-established position of the "capital city" in political thinking.

According to 'Abd al-Hamid Lahuri, who gives the most detailed account of this period, Nadhr Muhammad came to Bukhara without widespread amirid support.[94] His appointments are cited as further irritants among the Bukharan amirs. Samarqand was given to 'Abd al-'Aziz, his eldest son; a Kanikas amir, Beg Ughlan Beg, was appointed ataliq; and a Nayman amir, Khusraw Beg, was named diwanbegi.[95] Beg Ughlan Beg had had previous experience in the region as governor of Ura Tipah and Tashkent.[96] The new khan gave Qunduz and Badakhshan to Khusraw Sultan, who originally had been sent there while Nadhr Muhammad was still at Balkh. Presumably his ataliq and diwanbegi were reconfirmed, for no

---

1641 and the enthronement on 20 Sha'ban/24 November 1641. Lahuri 1867–72, 2:255 has the khutbah read in Nadhr Muhammad's name on Friday 6 Sha'ban 1051/10 November 1641. Salim, fols. 200a, 202a–b makes the enthronement date somewhat later—20 Dhu'l-Hijjah 1051/22 March 1642. The chronogram "mubarak, mubarak, mubarak, mubarak" ("Congratulations, congratulations, congratulations, congratulations"), composed by Akhund Hajji Bahram for the occasion, yields 1052. Kanbuh 1923–39, 2:436 places Nadhr Muhammad on the throne by 1052. Muhammad Yusuf Munshi, fol. 46a says 1055/1645–46, and Spuler 1965, on unknown authority, gives the date as 1053/1643–44. Akhmedov 1982, 109–13 provides one of the few coherent narratives for the period 1641–51.

[94] Lahuri 1867–72, 2:435–36. Salim, fols. 202bff. appears to be an abbreviated and rather confused version of Lahuri.

[95] Lahuri 1867–72, 2:436.

[96] BA 4: fol. 126a.

mention of new appointments is made. Tashkent was given to a third son, Bahram Sultan, and Baqi Bi of the Yuz was appointed ataliq. The khan did not assign a Tuqay-Timurid sultan to Balkh, naming instead Nazar Bi Nayman (the father of Khusraw Beg) as governor on his own behalf. In part, Lahuri says, this was because Nadhr Muhammad did not want to give Balkh up, and in part it was to remove Nazar Bi, formerly ataliq to Imam Quli Khan, from Bukhara. Lahuri asserts that Nazar Bi was one of those opposed to the khanate of Nadhr Muhammad Khan and was an influential voice in the Bukharan military.[97]

In other appanage assignments, the new khan gave Kahmard to Sub-han Quli, taking it out of the hands of the amir Yalangtush Bi Alchin.[98] Hisar-i Shadman was given to another son, Qutluq Muhammad Sultan, and a sixth son, 'Abd al-Rahman, was given Andkhud and Shibarghan. Because of his age, however, 'Abd al-Rahman was not allowed to go to his assigned appanage.[99] For the latter two appanages, Salim mentions no amirid appointees. Two other minor appanages were awarded to a grandson of the new khan (a son of Khusraw Sultan) and to a nephew.

The refusal to assign Balkh to a Tuqay-Timurid sultan is counted by Lahuri as one of Nadhr Muhammad's major political blunders.[100] Because of Nadhr Muhammad's thirty-year reign over the region and the resulting perception of Balkh as an appanage of nearly equal status to Bukhara, 'Abd al-'Aziz and his amirs considered it his due as eldest son. However, that same thirty-year period had bound Nadhr Muhammad and his amirs to Balkh, and he was unwilling to give it to a son who was more or less independent of paternal control at this point. From the standpoint of ap-panage politics as understood in 1641, Nadhr Muhammad's attempt to keep Balkh under his own control by sending a governor rather than a sultan was taken by a large number of influential figures, including his eldest son, as an affront to the system in general and their rights in par-ticular. The situation mirrored in some ways Wali Muhammad's earlier attempt to keep Balkh under his control after taking the throne and mov-ing to Bukhara.

Another mistake related to Nadhr Muhammad's Balkh policy was the partiality he showed his Balkh amirs, especially 'Abd al-Rahman Bi Ushun, his diwanbegi. In the struggle to oust Qirghiz intruders from around Andijan, he sent 'Abd al-Rahman to command the Bukharan troops. And when he later singled out the same 'Abd al-Rahman for hon-

[97] Lahuri 1867–72, 2:436–37.

[98] Ibid., 437.

[99] Salim, fols. 207b–208a.

[100] See Lahuri 1867–72, 2:439–42 for the inventory of "errors" committed by Nadhr Mu-hammad Khan. Salim follows this list item by item. And see most recently, Haider 1975, 167–68.

ors from among all the participants in the campaign against Qalmaq incursions into Tashkent, he reportedly sowed more resentment among the Bukharan amirs.

A third error in political judgment, in Lahuri's view, was committed in late 1642 when the new khan traveled back to Balkh and assigned Subhan Quli to the march district of Kahmard in the mountains to the south. This appointment had two serious consequences. First, it offended the Alchin amir who then held Kahmard as his iqtaʻ, Nadhr Muhammad's former close advisor and leading military figure, Yalangtush Bi ataliq. Although the ataliq returned to his estates in Samarqand, he did so reluctantly.

As a final and perhaps the decisive blunder in the catalog of errors compiled by Lahuri, Nadhr Muhammad appears to have attempted some kind of administrative reform of the system of grants to amirs. He tried to reclaim most of the amirid pasture areas for the use of his own substantial flocks and to compensate the iqtaʻ holders with cash from the state treasury. Whether the affair was actually as portrayed by Lahuri, who nowhere cites his sources, there does seem to have been some kind of attempt at land reform that aggravated the khan's increasingly strained relations with the amirs of Bukhara.

Over the next three years and after a number of false starts, a coalition of amirs in Samarqand and Tashkent encouraged an initially reluctant ʻAbd al-ʻAziz to join their conspiracy to oust Nadhr Muhammad. The leaders of the movement included Baqi Bi Yuz, Yalangtush Bi Alchin, and Beg Ughlan Beg Nayman. The wave crested on 27 April 1645, when the thirty-five-year-old sultan was seated at Bukhara "on the throne of Mawarannahr" and the khutbah was read in his name.[101] Nadhr Muhammad retired to Balkh.

For the deposed khan, the political situation now worsened. He discovered that his other sons who were appanaged in greater Balkh found ʻAbd al-ʻAziz's example worth imitating, and they refused to acknowledge his authority. In response, according to the author of *Tarikh-i Shibani Khan wa . . . Amir Timur*, the ex-khan now turned to an old nemesis, the Moghul emperor, Shah Jahan, for assistance against his sons.[102]

The subsequent Moghul intervention may or may not have been motivated by Nadhr Muhammad's request for military help, if indeed such aid were ever requested.[103] Certainly there were other, more credible, motives. The range of sources that narrate the period of the Moghul occupation offers a variety of reasons why Shah Jahan decided to send an army to Balkh under the command of his son, Sultan Murad Bakhsh. One

---

[101] Lahuri 1867–72, 2:447; Salim, fol. 213b.

[102] *Tarikh-i Shibani*, fol. 113b.

[103] Lahuri does not mention this request. He treats the invasion in detail in 2:512–709.

was the irredentist dream of retrieving Samarqand, the ancient Timurid capital and burial place of the forebears of the Moghul emperors. Another was revenge for the Uzbek invasion and siege of Kabul in 1628, just after Jahangir died and while Shah Jahan was deeply involved in succession politics. Yet another imputed motive was a desire to end the raids against Kabul and Qandahar launched from Kahmard.[104]

After a swift and virtually unopposed march in 1646, the Moghul army arrived at the 'Alid shrine, where Murad Bakhsh briefly stopped. It is clear that the shrine had very little political value at this point, at least from the Moghul perspective.[105] Although it had some symbolic meaning for the invading army, Balkh was the political focus.

Within a few days, Nadhr Muhammad withdrew from Balkh, first to Shibarghan, and then to the protection of Shah 'Abbas II in Iran, and Balkh was occupied by the Moghul force on 17 July 1646.[106] But the ease with which the occupation was carried out proved deceptive. Governing Balkh turned out to be well beyond the capability of the Moghul force. With no bureaucratic apparatus in place and apparently unable to take on the civilian role of fiscal administration, the Moghul army had very little success collecting taxes. In the first year of the occupation, we are told, only one-half of the annual revenues received by Nadhr Muhammad were collected. In the second year revenues were halved again.[107] Under the Uzbek appanage system, the Balkh sovereign had a rather limited tax base to begin with.

The Moghul units sent to the surrounding regions were able to dislodge the local amirs with comparative ease, but those same amirs simply withdrew across the Amu Darya and then raided their former iqta's at will, thus maintaining their own links to the local peasants and depriving the Moghuls of that source of revenues.

The Moghul army was reportedly drained by the peacekeeping and revenue-collecting burdens laid on it, and no effort was made to invade Mawarannahr, which was, after all, the real object of irredentist aspirations. (Samarqand with its tombs of the Timurid ancestors was a political Mecca for the Moghuls.) The right bank of the Oxus became a sanctuary, a new march region, for various Uzbek warbands (collectively designated "Uzbekan and Almanan" by the Moghul chroniclers), which kept up a constant and in the end overwhelming pressure on the occupiers.

---

[104] Samsam al-Dawlah 1888–91, 2:434, 799; 3:442–43.

[105] Kanbuh 1923–39, 2:490; Muhammad Amin, fol. 96b. gives the date 29 Jumada al-Awwal/2 July immediately after citing the chronogram "zaghan," or 1059/1649. Muhammad Yusuf Munshi relies on the same chronogram. Lahuri 1867–72, 2:544 says 2 Jumada al-Thani 1056/17 July 1646.

[106] Lahuri 1867–72, 2:535.

[107] Kanbuh 1923–39, 2:489; Lahuri 1867–72, 2:543.

The city population in Balkh accepted the change of government with some apparent warmth, perhaps in the hope that it would bring peace to the region. But gradually the residents became disaffected as both security and economic conditions deteriorated. A leading indicator of the economy, the price of grain, was reported to have reached what was clearly considered the astronomical level of one thousand rupees per kharwar.[108]

The Moghul intervention disrupted political expectations as well. It revealed Nadhr Muhammad Khan as an ineffectual leader and indirectly placed more responsibility and thus prestige on the shoulders of the amirs who carried on the resistance. Partly due to their role during the occupation, the amirs emerged from the period more assertive and somewhat less deferential toward the Tuqay-Timurid khans.

THE 'ALID SHRINE DURING THE MOGHUL OCCUPATION

For the shrine administration, the Moghul occupation could have been viewed as threatening, promising, or both. From the most optimistic point of view, the shrine was, after all, a Timurid creation, and that should have established an immediate bond with the leaders of the invading force. In addition, the tradition that the shrine administrators safeguarded transcended politics and political legitimacy. In many ways, the military authorities had as much need of the shrine as the shrine had of its erstwhile protectors. The shrine offered an avenue of communication and identification with the general public. When Murad Bakhsh stopped at the shrine in the early summer of 1646, we may assume that the administrators were willing to submit to the power he represented in the hope that he would help guarantee their control of the shrine and its endowments. It should be noted, though, that when Lahuri lists the leading figures of Balkh who assembled in the congregational mosque (the one built by Nadhr Muhammad Khan) to participate in the khutbah ceremony in Shah Jahan's name, there is no obvious reference to a representative from the 'Alid shrine.[109]

In the absence of a documentary record, there are insurmountable problems in tracing the shrine's waqf and the effect on it of the political crises of the 1640s. We must rely for the most part on a document drafted seventeen years after the decade ended, with no conclusive evidence to show whether the extreme conditions it describes originated in the period just prior to the issuing of the document or had roots in an earlier

---

[108] Muhammad Yusuf Munshi, fol. 62a. Kanbuh 1923–39, 2:13 also notes the high cost of foodstuffs, saying, "grain [ghallah] had become so dear that one mann cost ten rupees and straw and firewood were not to be had at all."

[109] Lahuri 1867–72, 2:544.

time, that is, during the Moghul occupation or even earlier. Whether the problems predated, originated in, or arose later than the Moghul occupation we simply cannot say. It is a reasonable conjecture, however, that the Moghul occupation, which produced warfare, shortages, and general economic disruption, did have a harmful effect on the shrine and its waqf holdings.

It is probably safe to assume that the mutawalli at the shrine at first made his peace with Murad Bakhsh and the Moghul army. After all, the collection of the revenues in the shrine budget, which paid for his own salary as well as for the upkeep of the shrine, depended on the tacit backing of the political authorities. The mutawalli at this time had no coercive power, no military arm of his own, as far as we know. In addition, the shrine administrators, in contemplating the future, may have seen a long Moghul occupation as not undesirable. From a scholarly and popular cultural standpoint, if not from a political one, the Punjab, Afghanistan, Khurasan, and Mawarannahr were all one realm. Sufi brotherhoods and scholarly networks tied the separate regions into one undivided region, albeit with regionally distinctive features. Travel from Central Asia to India and vice versa in search of spiritual experience, learning, and work was common during the period.

To underscore the "Indian" or "Hindustani" element in the culture of Balkh, we need look no further than the man who may still have been mutawalli of the shrine in 1646, Mirza Sanjar Ansari, or indeed the author of the *Bahr al-asrar*, Mahmud b. Amir Wali. Mirza Sanjar's parents were from Mashhad in Khurasan, although he appears to have been born in India, where he spent his infancy and youth. In the 1620s he came to Balkh and in 1624 or 1625, Nadhr Muhammad appointed him mutawalli of the 'Alid shrine.[110] It is not unreasonable to speculate that his administration would have found Murad Bakhsh and his courtiers no less congenial than it found the representatives of the Tuqay-Timurid family.

Similarly, Mahmud b. Amir Wali, a native of Balkh, had spent six years in India simply touring and observing the country.[111] Between 1624 and 1630, he traveled from Kabul to Delhi, then on to Ilahabad and down the Ganges to Benares. From there he headed southeast for Puri, where he managed to get into the temple of Jagannath by pretending to be Hindu. He took part in the procession in which the great carts are taken out and witnessed the devotees throwing themselves beneath the wheels. He visited the temples at Konarak and the Muslim cities of Hyderabad and Bijapur. He sailed to Ceylon and then back up the Coromandel coast and

[110] *BA* 4: fol. 304b.

[111] The section of *BA* including the account of the author's travels has been published with a summary translation by Riazul Islam. See Mahmud b. Amir Wali 1980.

then returned to Balkh via Rajasthan, Sind, Qandahar, and Herat. In India he witnessed Sunni-Shi'i riots, visited many of the major Muslim and Hindu shrines, and by and large seems to have acquired a fascination and admiration for the richness of the culture he encountered.

But as relations between the Moghul occupiers and the people of Balkh deteriorated because of increasing problems with the economy and with regional security, any residual goodwill that such men might have felt probably vanished. Mirza Sanjar, the mutawalli of the 'Alid shrine, was probably forced to temper his relations with the Moghul authorities because they were unable to protect his lands. Part of his waqf holdings, some of those given by Wali Muhammad, were far away from the shrine, and, when the Moghuls were unable to extend their control beyond the city limits of Balkh, the mutawalli would have had to establish relations with the local powers, in order to ensure an uninterrupted flow of revenues from those areas. There is no evidence of any of this, unfortunately, and we have no way of knowing whether the mutawalli was even able to continue to collect the waqf revenues during this period. But common sense tells us that Moghul military weakness could not have endeared the occupiers to the mutawalli.

Furthermore, it is more than likely that within the Balkh region itself, where Moghul authority held, waqf lands suffered from the inability of the occupiers to return fiscal conditions to normal. Grain had to be requisitioned to feed the army, and it is difficult to believe that under the circumstances waqf holdings would have enjoyed any special immunity from seizure of this vital commodity.[112]

But, in any event, the Moghul occupation did not last. Confronted by grain shortages, a rebellious population, and the prospect of a second severe winter, Moghul officials decided to abandon Balkh on 13 October 1647.[113] Shah Jahan notified the exiled Nadhr Muhammad that his forces would leave the city and invited him to return.[114]

The twice-ousted Tuqay-Timurid returned from exile in Iran, probably in the spring of 1648, and the third and final political crisis of the decade began. Nadhr Muhammad remained at Balkh for three years, a period for which there is little information. What records there are show that he regained none of his previous authority. He was never reconciled with his sons, the two most active of whom, 'Abd al-'Aziz and Subhan Quli, seem to have worked throughout the period to remove him permanently from the political scene. Within two months of Nadhr Muhammad's re-

---

[112] The grandfather of the anonymous author of *Tarikh-i Shibani Khan wa mu'amalat ba awlad-i Amir Timur* was with the Moghul army during the occupation and may have been his source of information about the difficulty the army had obtaining grain.

[113] Kanbuh 1923–39, 2:14.

[114] *Tarikh-i Shibani*, fols. 114b–115a.

turn, Baqi Bi, a Yuz amir and a leading conspirator in the Bukharan coup that had earlier cost him the khanate, raided Balkh, burned fields that would have been about ready for the spring harvest, and laid siege to the city. [115]

Nadhr Muhammad survived this siege, but not one launched in 1651 by Subhan Quli, reportedly backed by Qalmaq amirs. The man who had sat at Balkh since 1605 or 1606, with two brief interruptions—one of four years when he was khan at Bukhara and the other of two years when he was in Iranian exile—now took final leave of the city. Like his brother before him, he wanted to end his days in the Holy Cities of Mecca and Medina, but on his way there he became mortally ill at Simnan in Khurasan. [116] Subhan Quli, meanwhile, had taken control of Balkh. Although his brother, 'Abd al-'Aziz, in time-honored fashion, soon made an attempt to annex Balkh to Bukhara, he failed, and another long era of relative stability in the Tuqay-Timurid dominions unfolded.

[115] Ibid., fol. 115a.
[116] Ibid.

CHAPTER FIVE

Balkh and the Shrine, 1651–1681

THE POLITICAL formations of the second half of the seventeenth century mirrored in some intriguing ways the structures of the first half of the century. The thirty-year period between A.H. 1061/A.D. 1651 and 1092/ 1681, during which the Tuqay-Timurid brothers 'Abd al-'Aziz Khan and Subhan Quli Sultan independently governed the great appanages of Bukhara and Balkh, provides a parallel to the three decades between 1612 and 1641, when their father, Nadhr Muhammad, and his brother, Imam Quli Khan, ruled the two appanages. During this second thirty-year period, 'Abd al-'Aziz, as senior member of the royal clan, held the title "khan" while Subhan Quli used the lesser title "sultan." (Because Subhan Quli assumed the khanate when 'Abd al-'Aziz abdicated, he is often referred to as "khan" by later writers even when they are referring to the pre-khanate period. But, like his father before him, Subhan Quli adhered to the rules of the appanage system in his relations with the sovereign at Bukhara and, with only temporary deviations, acknowledged in form and practice the higher status of his brother.)

Although there were formal similarities between the two periods of the bipartite khanate, political conditions in Mawarannahr and Balkh were quite different from what they had been in the first half of the century. Consequently, despite nominal adherence to the old patterns of conduct, relations between the two appanages changed in many significant respects. In the first place, there had never been a direct military confrontation between Balkh and Bukhara during the Imam Quli/Nadhr Muhammad years. In 1654, by contrast, 'Abd al-'Aziz sponsored an expeditionary force against Balkh led by his nephew, Qasim Sultan (a son of Qutluq Muhammad). It was launched from Hisar-i Shadman, Qasim Sultan's appanage. The force, in which Durman and Qunghrat amirs played a prominent part, threatened Balkh for a time but was unable to take it. The incident seems to have been downplayed by both sides. The anonymous author of *Shibani*, in fact, cites another incident altogether, a marital dispute, as the cause of the coolness that developed between the two brothers.[1]

In any event, the 1650s, 1660s, and 1670s witnessed recurrent hostilities. These periodic eruptions had the effect of reinforcing the autono-

[1] *Tarikh-i Shibani*, fol. 115b.

mous tendencies of the two appanages. The cooperation in military and foreign policy that had characterized the regimes of Imam Quli and Nadhr Muhammad is missing from the record of the 'Abd al-'Aziz/Subhan Quli era.[2] As time passed, the idea that Balkh was a separate and independent state connected with Mawarannahr only by a shared Chingizid past and by common Chingizid institutions became embedded in political thinking.

THE EMERGENCE OF THE UZBEK AMIRS

The second half of the seventeenth century has been characterized by Soviet historians as one of "feudal fragmenting," a term used to denote the loss of authority at the traditional centers of power and a corresponding growth in local assertion of authority.[3] What was happening during this time was the gradual redistribution of power into non-Chingizid hands and the waning of the idea of the "capital city," a concept that had never been very strong to begin with. The Chingizid constitution, outlining the way things were supposed to be done as understood in sixteenth- and seventeenth-century Mawarannahr and Balkh, provided little place for central authority beyond the vague idea of the khan as first among equals. When the number of Chingizids shrank, as happened under the Tuqay-Timurids, the amirs assumed greater authority. It was a natural process and conformed to contemporary ideas of what was proper. Since the state had by midcentury come to be dominated by two more or less equally powerful appanages, it was at the appanage level that the growth of amirid authority is most evident.

Appanage structure in the first half of the century was typically made up of an appanage center, including an urban site and its immediate environs. In the case of Balkh, the center was Balkh City and its immediate environs, which were defined by the Hazhdah Nahr irrigation system. The appanage center was flanked to the east, west, and south by amirid iqta'-grants:[4] Shibarghan and Maymanah in the west, Kahmard to the south, and Qunduz in the east.

The iqta's provided the chief Uzbek amirs and their followers and allies with an economic and political base. The amirs administered their own grants and appropriated the revenues for their own expenses. The actual government of these iqta's probably varied not at all from that of the appanage center. The same taxes were assessed and collected and the

[2] On the contrary, see, for example, the account of the reported alliance between Subhan Quli and the Khwarazmians *against* 'Abd al-'Aziz (Abu'l-Ghazi 1871–74, 351).

[3] Ivanov 1958, 8, 67–74.

[4] See Akhmedov 1982, 134–40 for a discussion of the use of the term *iqta'* at Balkh during this period.

same local representatives—such as village and tribal heads (*kadkhuda* or *aqsaqal*) and other officials like the garrison commander (*darughah*), the head militiaman (*mirshabb*), and the water administrator (*mirab*)—were deputed to carry out the daily routine of government. The principal difference between an iqta' administration and, for example, a provincial governorship in contemporary Moghul India or Safawid Iran lay mainly in the kinds of responsibilities that tied the Uzbek amirs to the head of state.

In the first half of the century, the iqta's appear to have been free of any formal fiscal obligation to the appanage center, although a percentage (the Shar'i *khums* or 20 percent) of the booty (*ghanimah*) taken in raids seems to have been routinely sent to Balkh. This we know to have been the case for military activity in Khurasan and in eastern Badakhshan, and it was probably true elsewhere as well. In addition, a kind of formalized gift giving also provided for the distribution of wealth to the appanage center as well as a repeated recognition of sovereignty. The ceremony surrounding the giving of gifts by high officials provided both donor and recipient with a means of displaying generosity, humility, fealty, and gratitude according to the circumstances of the exchange and the relative status of giver and receiver. Detailed accounts of gift exchanges occur repeatedly in the seventeenth-century sources.[5]

The fiscal independence of the amirid iqta's was no indication of political independence. The system allowed administrative autonomy but demanded recognition of Chingizid sovereignty. The higher authority of the Chingizid ruler or "turah"[6] was articulated in iqta' politics by the reserved right of appointment, that is, full nominal control by a Tuqay-Timurid (in the seventeenth century at least) of the right to delegate authority. The first half of the seventeenth century was marked by the frequent exercise of this power, as amirs were transferred from one iqta' to another or their iqta's were consolidated into appanages for Chingizid sultans newly of age and thus eligible for an appanage.

But because the Tuqay-Timurid state was primarily an agrarian one, and since the addition of new territories and therefore new sources of revenue had ceased by the middle of the century, if not earlier, a profound change now occurred in the relations between the amirs and their acknowledged lords, the ruling Tuqay-Timurid/Chingizids. As conquest ebbed, there was less territory to distribute as iqta' and less opportunity

[5] Examples of ceremonial gift-giving may be found in *BA* 4: fols. 269b–270b and Salim, fols. 175b, 184b, 195b, 299b.

[6] *Turah* (pl. *turagan*) is used in late-seventeenth- and early-eighteenth-century Mawarannahrid sources only to refer to Chingizids (e.g., Muhammad Amin, fol. 150b; Abu'l-Ghazi 1871–74, 22). It had a second meaning, "custom" or "usage," in contrast to *yasa*, or "legal precept" (Doerfer 1963– , 1:264–65).

for transferring deserving amirs to more prestigious and wealthier lands. Moreover, the longer amirs were established in one place, the more they identified their interests with those of the region and the less willing they were to be transferred elsewhere. The amirs were not absentee iqta'-holders, for the most part, and developed friendships and loyalties they were loath to break. What was true for the official iqta'-holder whose name has been recorded was no less true for his now-forgotten followers and allies.

The gradual evolution in relations between the Tuqay-Timurids and their Uzbek amirs that these circumstances produced begins to be visible in the historical record toward the middle of the century. We have already noted the dismissal of Yalangtush Bi, an Alchin amir, from his long-time iqta' in Kahmard as one of the causes of the coup that ousted Nadhr Muhammad as khan in Bukhara. The Moghul occupation of Balkh exacerbated khan-amirid relations because it temporarily removed Chingizid authority and exposed the military weakness of the Tuqay-Timurid house. After the Tuqay-Timurid regime was restored at Balkh, the chronicles are suddenly filled with incident after incident of inter-iqta' warfare, references to amirs "taking refuge" from Balkh in their own iqta's, the increasing association of specific Uzbek tribal organizations with certain regions, and other phenomena indicating certain territorial rights and prerogatives that specific amirs and their followers claimed over their iqta' lands.

One of the most striking examples of this in Balkh is the rise of the Qataghan tribe under Mahmud Bi in Badakhshan's western region, the center of which was Qunduz. This region had been the iqta' of the Qataghan tribe probably no earlier than the Moghul withdrawal from Balkh in 1647.[7] Within a decade, Mahmud Bi, the leading Qataghan amir, was the principal political figure in western Badakhshan and used his position to increase the wealth and prestige of the Qataghan through frequent raids in the mountainous march lands to the east. In 1658, he succeeded in capturing Yaftal (present-day Faydabad).[8] Qataghan rule proved so harsh for the area's inhabitants that they sought the help of the shaykhs

[7] A more precise pinpointing of the time when the Qataghan tribe came to dominate the region has so far eluded me. Until the early 1640s, the predominant amirs in the region bore such tribal designations as Ushun (*BA* 4: fol. 230b), Buyrak (*BA* 4: fol. 233a), and Qushji (*BA* 4: fol. 228a). There were some Qataghan participants in campaigns in the area during the first half of the seventeenth century (*BA* 4: fols. 171a, 23a), but none had the preeminent position the tribal organization achieved under Mahmud Bi in the second half of the century. Nor is there any mention of iqta's or governorships (hukumat) assigned to Qataghan amirs prior to the Moghul occupation of 1646–47. The most important Qataghan figure of the preoccupation period was Subhan Quli's ataliq, Tardi (Birdi) 'Ali Qataghan, who was stationed, in any event, at Kahmard, not Qunduz (Samsam al-Dawlah 1888–91, 2:799).

[8] Badakhshi 1959, fol. 2a.

at the famous shrine of Khwajah Ahmad Kasani (the "Makhdum-i A'zam") at Dahpid near Samarqand, whose spiritual authority they recognized.[9] With assistance from Dahpid, the people of Yaftal managed to free them- selves for a time from Mahmud Bi's control, but when he returned again and again with raiding parties, the town's leaders turned to Subhan Quli in Balkh. In return for the appointment of one of their own leaders as iqta'-holder of Yaftal, they agreed to accept Tuqay-Timurid authority. Outmaneuvered by the Yaftalis, Mahmud Bi, whose loyalty to Subhan Quli was at this time unquestioned, sent no more raiders into eastern Badakhshan.

For the years between 1658 and 1681, when Subhan Quli left Balkh to assume the khanate throne in Bukhara, we have no information about Mahmud Bi's political activities. But after 1681, he appears in the sources as the dominant amirid figure not only in western Badakhshan but in greater Balkh as well. The foundations of the power of his tribal follow- ing, the Qataghan, were laid during the score of years in which he held absolute control over Qunduz and its dependencies. It was in this period that the amirate of Qataghan began to take shape. Here and elsewhere in the latter half of the century, the iqta' system of the Tuqay-Timurids was gradually being transformed into nascent amirid states, which would eventually be noticed by historians writing in the eighteenth century.

In the western part of Balkh, in Maymanah, Shibarghan, Andkhud, and Jijaktu, the iqta' of the Ming appears as a counterpart to the Qat- aghan iqta'. The identification of the Ming with this region may be traced to Uraz Bi, a Ming ataliq and one of the three most influential amirs of Nadhr Muhammad's era.[10] Following in the footsteps of his famous fa- ther, Baruti Bi, Uraz Bi began his amirid career in the office of royal falconer (qushbegi-gari khassah). He later served as governor of Tirmidh, and when the Tuqay-Timurid sultan, Khusraw, was given the western part of Balkh as his appanage, he was appointed ataliq. Uraz Bi was a leader in the march warfare between the Uzbek and Qizilbash that fol- lowed the death of Shah 'Abbas I in 1629. When Nadhr Muhammad transferred 'Abd al-'Aziz and his ataliq, 'Abd al-Rahman Ushun, to the western marches, Uraz Bi returned to Balkh. In A.H. 1045/A.D. 1635, he was again sent to Maymanah, where he seems to have stayed until his death. Although the history of the Maymanah region in the half century between 1635 and 1681 is not well documented, there are indications that the Ming, like the Qataghan in western Badakhshan, became more and more entrenched there with the passage of time.[11]

Sometime after the Moghul withdrawal from Balkh in 1647, another

---

[9] Ibid., fols. 2a–b.

[10] BA 4: fols. 293a–b.

[11] For a summary of the economic role of the Uzbek tribal groups in Balkh during this period, see Akhmedov 1982, 123–25.

tribal organization appeared on the scene in and around Balkh City. It became especially important in the city's politics later in the century, and therefore in the fate of the ʿAlid shrine and its waqf in the 1690s, but its arrival in Balkh may have been as early as the 1650s or 1660s. It was known as the Quramah. The name does not appear in the extensive list of Uzbek tribes compiled in the sixteenth century in the *Majmaʿ al-ta-warikh*.[12] This is not particularly surprising, for the tribal organization seems to have been a confederation (the name *quramah* itself meaning "patchwork")[13] of small tribal groups. Barthold found a reference as early as 1635 to a group by this name living on the Angren River near Tashkent. In Balkh they do not appear in the written record until the 1690s, when they emerge as a counterweight to the Qataghan under Mahmud Bi.[14] After 1710, the name disappears from the sources on Balkh. Membership in the Quramah does not seem to have been limited to Turkish-speaking tribal elements. Urbanites and Tajik speakers were allied with or included in the Quramah. One such was Muhammad Saʿid Khwajah, a Dahpidi shaykh who held the office of naqib at Balkh. Muhammad Saʿid himself took part in the wars against the Khwarazmians (he fought at the Battle of Kuhak in 1685)[15] and was active in Balkh politics. The naqib was one of the highest-ranking officers in the seventeenth-century appanages. The office differed from its counterpart in the Safawid and Ottoman states, where it was a civilian one, supervising craft organizations in both the Safawid and Ottoman cases.[16] In Mawarannahr and Balkh, the naqib performed a military function, according to a treatise on offices and ranks written in Bukhara in the early eighteenth century. He was a kind of political commissar, responsible for military discipline and order during troop movements.[17]

The effect of tribal politics became more pronounced during Subhan Quli's tenure there. Increasingly, large tribal groups like the Qataghan and Ming identified their interests with the territories of their iqtaʿs. The appearance of the Quramah may have been a response from smaller groups, formerly secure under the Chingizid umbrella, but now concerned with countering the power of the large tribal organizations.

These apparent changes in the political structure at Balkh—the increasing assertiveness of tribal groups and their claims to specific territory—form a new context for the shrine and its waqf endowments and directly affect the next recorded group of endowments.

[12] Sultanov 1977.

[13] Barthold 1981.

[14] Muhammad Yusuf Munshi, fol. 114b; Muhammad Amin, fol. 151b.

[15] Muhammad Amin, fol. 112a.

[16] Minorsky 1943, 81, 83, 148; McChesney 1988, 85.

[17] See Vilʾdanova 1968, 46.

THE AMIRID WAQFS

Although the Tuqay-Timurids continued to play an active part in the supervision of the waqf endowments at the ʿAlid shrine, after Wali Muhammad's time we have no record that any of the Chingizids were actual donors of waqf. For the latter part of the seventeenth century, seven of the eight donors of record were amirs. The eighth donor may also have been an amir, although his name, Khwajah Maʿruf b. Khwajah Siddiq, does not unambiguously point in that direction. The appearance of amirs as shrine patrons is in keeping with the gradual evolution of political life in Mawarannahr and Balkh and the growing prominence of amirs generally.

With increased local authority came greater wealth, and with more wealth, more opportunity to fulfill the role of patron to local institutions. By 1668, there are records of seven new endowments of waqf to the ʿAlid shrine from non-Chingizids. The amirid donors represented at least five Uzbek tribal organizations—the Ming, Qipchaq, Qaraʾi, Qataghan, and Qirghiz, the most prominent tribal groups in Balkh by midcentury. One of the donors, Amir Timur b. Amir Nur, is not identified by tribal affiliation.

The record of the amirid waqf grants is contained in a summary issued in 1668–1669. We do not have the original waqf deeds themselves. Consequently, it is impossible to say for certain when the waqf grants were made. There is little doubt that they were given after, probably long after, Wali Muhammad made his endowments around 1605. The circumstantial evidence we have about the donors also tends to suggest a time toward the middle of the seventeenth century, or even, at least in one case, shortly before the 1668–1669 manshur was released. In that case, the author of the summary, Subhan Quli, the son of Nadhr Muhammad and the Tuqay-Timurid sovereign at Balkh, calls the waqf donor "one of [our] *khwajahsarays*" (see number 4 in the following summary). In the other cases, none of the named donors is referred to as deceased. Although this is not proof that they were still living in 1668, it does tend to suggest it. Furthermore, since these were obviously well-to-do amirs and since Mahmud b. Amir Wali, who was writing in the 1630s, does not include any of them in his catalog of leading amirs at Balkh,[18] it is reasonable to assume that their fame dates more toward the time of the 1668–1669 summary.

Again, because of our not having the waqf deeds themselves, there remains some doubt about the actual number of separate waqf donations. In the manshur, Subhan Quli refers interested parties to the individual

[18] *BA* 4: fols. 277b–286a, 290b–304b.

waqf deeds, which had been consulted in drafting his document and which contained the full details of each endowment.

The division here into seven separate waqfs is based on my reading of the 1668–1669 text. In what follows I have arranged the information in three parts—the name of the donor, the description of the waqf, and a short commentary. The order given here is the order as presented in the manshur. Whether this order follows the chronological order in which the endowments were made cannot now be determined.

1. *Donor*—Muhammad Shukur Bi Ming Ung b. Adinah Bahadur.

Waqf—"an entire third of Qush Ribat in Khulm, which is forty water shares [*chihil ab*] out of a total of one hundred and twenty."

Commentary—The village of Qush Ribat (present-day Khush Ribat)[19] lies about twenty-five miles east of the 'Alid shrine on the main east-west route and six miles northwest of the Khulm/Tashqurghan urban center. The economy of Qush Ribat, as an agricultural suburb of Khulm/Tashqurghan, was mainly dependent upon an irrigation system that, like Balkh's, canalized snowmelt and runoff from the mountains to the south.

Although identification is not absolutely certain, it appears that the waqf donor, Muhammad Shukur Bi Ming, is identical with the Shukur Ming *parvanaji* mentioned in the chronicle sources of the latter half of the seventeenth century.[20] In the 1680s, he was one of the dozen or so leading amirs of Balkh. His father, Adinah, had held the rank of diwanbegi. His uncle (Adinah's brother) was Yar Muhammad Ming, an ataliq and another of the major politicians of the second half of the century. Yar Muhammad's son, Khushhal Bi, figures in the waqf endowments and was also one of the top amirid personalities in Balkh. The term *Ung* (meaning "left-side") following the tribal name Ming denotes the traditional assignment of his branch of the Ming to the left wing of the army (in the classical formation of left wing, right wing, and center). These formations were then reflected in the arrangement of offices and tribal groups at court.[21]

2. *Donor*—Nur Muhammad diwan, son of Shah Muhammad Qara'i.

Waqf—"twenty water shares, also from the aforementioned water [of Qush Ribat]."

Commentary—Combined with the water shares in Muhammad Shukur's endowment, these twenty shares gave the shrine control of one-half of the village's water supply. What this meant in regional terms about the shrine's economic influence is difficult to say, as we do not know the

---

[19] Nahid 1951–60, 2:177.
[20] Muhammad Yusuf Munshi, fol. 79b; Muhammad Amin, fol. 132a.
[21] *BA* 4: fols. 387b–389a. See also McChesney 1983, 39–42.

relative importance of Qush Ribat in the Khulm/Tashqurghan region at this time. In the late nineteenth century, it was described as a "ruined" village, and in the twentieth it is only one of Khulm/Tashqurghan's 139 villages, with a population of less than 500 persons.[22]

To this point, the only information about Nur Muhammad or his father is this single reference. His tribal name Qara'i does not appear exactly this way in the lists of Uzbek tribal groups. It may be a form of Qari[23] or an abbreviated form of a compound name beginning with Qara (e.g., Qara Qalpaq).

3. *Donor*—Khaliq Jawan Bi Ming Ung (son of?)[24] Ghajit ataliq.

Waqf—"all the springs of Sultan Bayazid, one of the districts [*tawabi'*] of Ay Bik [Aybek or Haibek]."

Commentary—Sultan Bayazid is the present-day town of Hadrat Sultan[25] on the west bank of the Tashqurghan or Samangan River some twenty-five miles south of Khulm/Tashqurghan. The "hadrat-i sultan" for whom the town is named is Sultan Abu Yazid (or Bayazid) Bastami (d. 874/7), the celebrated representative of Khurasani mysticism. Although Bastami's shrine in Bastam, western Khurasan, is a major pilgrimage site, the tomb ascribed to him on the Samangan River has for centuries maintained a regional authority. Since 1669, when the manshur was issued, the village has grown in size and importance. Described in the document as one of the districts of Aybek (located about sixteen miles to the northwest of that town), by the second half of the twentieth century it was a subprovince ('*alaqah dari*) of Samangan province and had given its name to a region of more than 425 square miles. The center of the region now is the eponymous village that houses Sultan Bayazid's shrine. It is interesting to note what appears to be a somewhat analogous evolutionary process to that of the 'Alid shrine at Balkh, that is, the development of a shrine center into an urban center with regional administrative and economic functions.

As is clear from the geographical information, Hadrat-i Sultan relied for its water not only on the Samangan/Tashqurghan River but also on a system of springs that provided part of the river's water.[26] In the twentieth century, and perhaps in earlier times as well, river water alone was not adequate to meet the town's agricultural needs. The remaining water came from the five areas called "chashmahsar," literally "full of springs." These were the springs of Gahkarah, Dawlatabad, Khwajah Parishan, Shalktu, and Kukah Bulak. Without the actual waqf deed we have no way

[22] *Gaz.* 4:333, 337.
[23] *BA* 4: 172a–b, 241b.
[24] Hafiz Nur Muhammad, editor of *TMS*, has added the conjunction *and* (*wa*) to the text.
[25] *Gaz.* 4:264–65; Nahid 1951–60 2:101.
[26] *Gaz.* 4:264–65 and map section IV–8–b, IV–8–D.

of knowing for certain whether all of these were included in the waqf endowment made by the Ming amir Khaliq Jawan Bi. If the waqf grant was indeed for "all the springs of Sultan Bayazid," then on paper at least the shrine administrators were given substantial control of the economy of Sultan Bayazid/Hadrat-i Sultan.

The waqf property lay about seventy-five miles by road from the 'Alid shrine and, along with the Darrah-i Juz grant made by Wali Muhammad Khan, was one of the most distant parcels that the mutawallis were called on to manage. Its donor, Khaliq Jawan Bi, is otherwise unknown to us. However, it is worth drawing attention to the fact that the Ming properties (both his and Muhammad Shukur Bi's) donated as waqf were in the Khulm/Tashqurghan region, in the eastern part of Balkh. Generally, the Ming by midcentury are associated with the western part of Balkh—Maymanah, Shibarghan, and Andkhud. One of the features of the political evolution of the latter part of the seventeenth century, as I have said, is a gradual identification of individual Uzbek groups with specific regions, which come to be seen as their own "patrimonial lands." Although it is somewhat speculative at this point, what the waqf grants may reflect is a divestiture by Ming amirs of their eastern holdings as their identification with the western regions becomes stronger and, at the same time, other rival Uzbek groups, such as the Qataghan, begin to assert their rights in the east.

4. *Donor*—Khwajah Farhang, the mirab.

Waqf—"All of Tilakar on the Siyahgird Canal, the water rights of which are thirty shares, as well as all of Nik Bi, whose water rights [*haqqabah*] from the same canal amount to fifty shares. The boundaries of both these places are set forth in the waqf deeds."

Commentary—The Siyahgird (or Siyahjird) Canal was part of Balkh's Hazhdah Nahr irrigation system. Its source was the first barrage on the Balkh River, which was also the point of origin of the Shahi, Quddar, Balkh, Dastjird, and Chimtal Canals. It is important to note that two sources contemporary with Subhan Quli, Muhammad Mu'min[27] and Mir Sayyid Sharif Raqim,[28] both of whom give lists of the villages on the Siyahgird Canal, do not mention the village of Tilakar nor any village whose name remotely resembles it. Nik Bi, on the other hand, does appear in these sources as the sixteenth and penultimate village on the canal. By the end of the nineteenth century, Nik Bi no longer existed and the seventeen villages watered by the canal in the middle of the seventeenth century had been reduced to five.[29] The large village of Siyahgird, which

---

[27] Mukhtarov 1980, 102–3.

[28] Salakhetdinova 1970.

[29] *Gaz.* 4:252–53. By 1969 the Siyahgird Canal watered only Dih-i Qadi Hazar, a village of ninety-five people and 2,146 jaribs of land (Mukhtarov 1980, 103).

was the last one on the canal in the seventeenth century, survives today and is located about fifteen miles north of the 'Alid shrine.

The waqf donor, Khwajah Farhang, is described in the document as "one of our courtiers [perhaps court eunuchs, *yaki az khwajah sarayan-i majid-i ma-ast*]." The title appended to his name tells us that at some point in his career he held the position of water supervisor (mirab), the person responsible for the complex business of allocating water shares. His tenure as supervisor of the water supply probably gave him the opportunity to purchase water rights himself. Some or perhaps all of these he then conveyed to the shrine as waqf. If we assume that a water share (ab) as described for Hadrat-i Sultan or Khulm was more or less equivalent to a water share in Balkh (i.e., a metered amount of water regulated by flow rate and time, sufficient for a specific area of land), then the endowment of eighty shares exceeded the combined waqf grants at Qush Ribat.

The value of the waqf grant on the Siyahgird Canal probably lay not only in its size but also in its proximity to the shrine. From an administrative standpoint, one would think that the conveyance of property rights within the Hazhdah Nahr system would have been more desirable than grants in remote areas, such as the Hadrat-i Sultan grant or the grants made by Wali Muhammad a half century earlier. Yet the fact that places like Qarni Sa'i and Kaftar Khwani were still claimed by the waqf administrators in 1668 is a caveat against either overestimating the significance of distance or underestimating the administrative ability of the mutawallis at the shrine.

5. *Donor*—Kildish Bi, the son of Tekesh Bi Qataghan.

Waqf—"all of Uz[a]lik,[30] whose 'right to drink' [*haqq al-shurb*] from the Faydabad Canal is equal to fifty water shares."

Commentary—The Faydabad Canal was another trunk canal in the Hazhdah Nahr system.[31] It originated at the third barrage on the Balkh River and ran in a northwesterly direction well west of Balkh City. The name Uzalik is not given by the abovementioned contemporary sources in their lists of villages watered by the canal. They do refer to a village named Yuzluk, located on a nearby canal, the Qut Canal. The name Yuzluk might conceivably be a corrupted form of Uzalik or vice versa.[32]

Kildish Bi Qataghan is also otherwise unknown. It is of some interest that a Qataghan amir was divesting himself of property in the western part of Balkh, at approximately the same time Ming amirs were doing the

---

[30] Salakhetdinova 1970, 228 gives the transliteration *Uzalik*.
[31] *Gaz.* 4:256.
[32] Mukhtarov 1980, 103.

same in the east. Again it is a small piece of circumstantial evidence tending to corroborate the political pattern described earlier in this chapter.

6. *Donor*—Nadr Bi *parvanaji*, son of Qirghiz 'Ali Bi, a qushbegi.

Waqf—"all the pastureland [?*charagah*] and bottomland [?*darakzar*] of the abovementioned canal [Faydabad Canal], which is equivalent to fifteen shares of 'cooked' water located in Yali Tipah [which is under the control of] Khushhal Bi, the son of Yar Muhammad Ming, the ataliq."

Commentary—The wording of this section of the waqf summary is exceedingly uncertain, with toponymic, orthographic, and terminological difficulties to contend with. In the lists of places along the Faydabad Canal Yali Tipah does not appear, either in the contemporary material or in later sources. The word for "pastureland" can only be so read if one assumes the not uncommon abbreviation of the long *a*, i.e., charāgāh, instead of charagah. *Darakzar* is assumed to mean "bottomland," both from the combined meanings of its component parts, *darak* ("bottom, depth") and *zar* ("abounding in"), and the context which supports such a meaning.[33] Ab-i pukhtah or "cooked water" probably should be understood to mean brackish saline water unsuitable for crops but adequate for pastureland, probably the runoff from irrigated fields. Since the water is calculated in terms of a set number of shares, it must be water from the irrigation system. If irrigated fields were regularly inundated in order to leach out ground salts, the resulting runoff might correspond to this "cooked water."

The names of the waqf donor and his father, despite the prominence suggested by the titles parvanaji and qushbegi, have not been encountered yet in other sources. Khushhal Bi, the amir with jurisdiction over this region, on the other hand, is quite well known.[34] With this reference to Khushhal Bi Ming, cousin of Muhammad Shukur, another of the amirid waqf donors, the document provides further evidence of the establishment of Ming tribal members in the western section of Balkh.

7. *Donors*—Khwajah Ma'ruf, the son of Khwajah Siddiq, and Amir Timur, son of Amir Nur, each of whom (co-)owned the conveyed property.

Waqf—"all the pastureland [charagah] in Takhtah Pul, one of the villages on the Nahr-i Quddar. [This is] equivalent to 120 water shares, less 6 shares [for] the *ghulbah* of Yar Naqsh Bi Qipchaq, the *amirakhur* of the Royal Household [*sarkar-i khassah*]."

Commentary—The Quddar Canal was one of the six canals originating at the first barrage on the Balkh River. In the late seventeenth century, it watered seventeen villages, the sixth of which was Takhtah Pul, today located about two and one-half miles west of the shrine. (In the

---

[33] Dihkhuda 1946–
[34] Muhammad Yusuf Munshi, fol. 118a; Muhammad Amin, fol. 140a; Bukhari 1876, 204.

middle of the nineteenth century, Takhtah Pul enjoyed a brief moment
of fame when it became interim capital of Afghan Turkestan, after the
Afghans evacuated Balkh and before they made Mazar-i Sharif the provincial capital.) The reference in the document to Yar Naqsh Bi Qipchaq's
water rights suggests some of the complexities of a developed irrigation
system. Obviously the branch canal into which the 120 shares were metered carried Yar Naqsh Bi's share as well. According to the late-nineteenth-century *Historical and Political Gazetteer of Afghanistan*, the
ghulbah (qulbah, kulba) was an area of land roughly thirty acres in size.[35]
The area of measurement was based not on water but on the amount of
land tilled by a pair of oxen with a plow (qulbah) in one season.

If we assume these equivalents had a rough parity with seventeenth-
century conditions and that one water share satisfied about five acres (six
shares being sufficient for one ghulbah), we can reach some, admittedly
uncertain, idea of the amount of agricultural land made subject to the
shrine's control through the amirid waqf grants. Excluding the pastureland and the springs in Sultan Bayazid/Hadrat-i Sultan, 190 water shares
were conveyed in Khulm and Balkh, or water for some 950 acres of agricultural land. If we assume that pastureland required less water, or, to
put it another way, that a water share equivalent in pastureland was
greater than one in cropland, then the 114 water shares for pasture in
Takhtah Pul and the 15 "cooked" shares indicate an area of at least 820
acres of pastureland.

As in some of the other waqf cases, the 1668–1669 document represents all we know about the donors, Khwajah Ma'ruf and Amir Timur.
We have no other information either on the Qipchaq amir and chief eq-
uerry (amirakhur) mentioned here, Yar Naqsh Bi.

. . .

Unlike the endowments that Wali Muhammad had founded circa 1605,
the waqfs given by these non-Chingizids did not underwrite buildings at
the shrine, or, more precisely, were not established to maintain a public
monument to the donor, at least as far as we know. Since we do not have
the waqf deeds themselves, we can only speculate about the purposes for
which the waqfs were made. Commonly, small waqfs would pay for
Qur'an recitations during holy days, stipends for students, teachers' salaries, lighting, floor coverings, or pilgrim expenses, like food, medical
care, and funeral arrangements.

The amirid contributions to the waqf holdings of the shrine were scattered. The Takhtah Pul property was about two and one-half miles from

[35] *Gaz.* 4:263.

the shrine, while the Sultan Bayazid/Hadrat-i Sultan waqf was nearly seventy-five miles away by road. The endowments do not seem to have been intended to expand or round out waqf properties already in the shrine's hands, for only one of the grants (the Takhtah Pul endowment) was contiguous to existing waqf land.

In the absence of details about the dedicated purpose of these waqfs, the circumstances surrounding their enactment, and information about the donors and their motives, what can one say about their significance to the shrine? First, since the 1668–1669 manshur lists them, they must have been sufficiently important to the mutawalli for him to seek official acknowledgment of his rights over them. On the same grounds, it is logical to conclude that the mutawalli considered himself capable of managing these properties, either directly or through the auction of leases.

The waqf grants are important evidence for the trend sketched in the historical texts of the time, that is, that the Uzbek amirs were playing a proportionately greater role in the political and economic life of Balkh.

All of this would have remained unknown to us had not problems in the administration of these lands arisen and the mutawalli of the waqf asked the sultan at Balkh, Subhan Quli, for help in solving them.

CHAPTER SIX

The Evolution of the Shrine and Its Administration

BALKH UNDER SUBHAN QULI, 1651–1681

In the aftermath of the disruption caused by Nadhr Muhammad's efforts to consolidate Bukhara and Balkh and the subsequent Moghul intervention, Subhan Quli, the fifth son[1] of Nadhr Muhammad, ousted his father from Balkh in A.H. 1061/A.D. 1651. The record of the period just prior to 1651, especially of the Moghul incursion, is far more complete than that for the thirty years of Subhan Quli's reign. In fact, the period of his regime in Balkh hardly drew the notice of contemporary chroniclers.[2] Only one of the late-seventeenth- to early-eighteenth-century sources, Hajji Mir Muhammad Salim, devotes any space to the period, and his account is anecdotal and not chronological. Still, it is interesting to recapitulate briefly the episodes that the chroniclers felt needed recording for the period between 1650 and 1680. Generally, the overall effect is to convey the impression of a time of political calm. At the same time, the theme of support for the scholarly community runs through most of the anecdotes, which portray Subhan Quli as a solicitous and deferential patron of the academic world. The flavor as well as the substance of the chronicled anecdotes tells us something about the kind of leader Subhan Quli wished to be remembered as. Here then is what we know of the three decades of his tenure at Balkh.

1. Salim, fols. 267b–268a: "On Monday 22 Ramadan 1061/[9 September 1651], the Turkish Luy Yil,[3] when Venus and Mars were in conjunction 12 degrees into the sign of Cancer," [Subhan Quli] ascends the throne of Balkh. (In accordance with the conventions of history-writing, there follow chronograms commemorating the event.)

2. Fol. 268b: Two khwajahs (of the line of Sayyid Ata, an important

---

[1] If, as Salim, fol. 217b, asserts, Subhan Quli was born in A.H. 1037/A.D. 1627–28, it is odd that he is not mentioned by *BA*, which was written for Subhan Quli's father circa 1635 and includes accounts of three other sons.

[2] This creates obvious problems for present-day historians. For example, Akhmedov 1982, 113–14, whose work is devoted to the history of Balkh from the beginning of the sixteenth century to the middle of the eighteenth century, treats this thirty-year period (while really only dealing with the 1660s) in just three paragraphs.

[3] The Year of the Dragon in the Sino-Turkic twelve-year cycle of years. On this system of dating, see Turan 1941.

Sufi order in Central Asia) from the party that had accompanied the ex-khan Nadhr Muhammad on his ill-fated hajj-pilgrimage return from Sim-nan with the personal effects of the deceased and are received with ex-pressions of gratitude by Subhan Quli.

3. Fols. 268b–269b: An expedition is led against Balkh in 1065/1655 by Subhan Quli's nephew, Qasim Sultan, for which Subhan Quli holds 'Abd al-'Aziz Khan responsible. He feels threatened, but the account portrays him as more worried lest the invading force commit some outrage against the population. He seeks a settlement by sending mediators. After "forty days," a settlement is reached and Subhan Quli agrees to forego his claim to Hisar (-i Shadman), Qubadyan, and Khulm. These areas are given to Qasim Sultan and his amirs. In 1068/1658, another siege of Balkh by the same group results in Qasim Sultan's death in battle. 'Abd al-'Aziz is re-ported preparing an army to exact vengeance, but Subhan Quli dis-patches a negotiator, Khwajah 'Abd al-Ghaffar, who had previously been 'Abd al-'Aziz's spiritual mentor (pir). The pir effects a reconciliation.[4]

4. Fols. 269b—270a: On 15 Sha'ban 1070 [26 April 1660], Subhan Quli holds a cornerstone-laying ceremony for his madrasah in Balkh, which he has built facing the shrine of Abu Nasr Parsa. Khwajah 'Abd al-Ghaffar lays the first brick, Mir Mahmud 'Ulyabadi the second, and Ata Khan 'Azizan the third. Subhan Quli, "because of the purity of his belief," is portrayed in the role of humble dervish apprentice (darwish-nihad), handing bricks and mortar to each of these worthies.

5. Fols. 270a–273b: Subhan Quli becomes a disciple (murid) of Had-rat-i Sayyid Mirza Ahmad Hashim. The bona fides of the master are given. He is linked through his own mentors to the teachings of Ahmad Kasani, the Makhdum-i A'zam (d. 949/1542 or 1543).

Mirza Ahmad Hashim traced his sayyidship to the fourth of the Twelver Shi'i imams, 'Ali b. Husayn "Zayn al-'Abidin." As an adherent of a variety of Sufi orders, he had links both to the "auditory" Naqshbandi tradition of the dhikr-worship ceremony, through Khwajah 'Abd al-Rah-man Kuhistani, and to the "silent" tradition, the tariqah represented in the line through the Makhdum-i A'zam.[5] The account of this shaykh in-cludes the obligatory record of miracles performed and emphasizes his close ties to politicians, again a typical image in the conventionalized por-trait of a spiritual figure found in sixteenth- and seventeenth-century bi-ographical literature.

6. Fols. 281a–283b: Khwajah 'Abd al-Ghaffar, an agnatic descendant of the Makhdum-i A'zam, dies on the first of Jumada al-Thani 1080/27 Oc-

---

[4] Akhmedov 1982, 113–14, relying on Muhammad Yusuf Munshi (in the Semenov trans-lation), gives a somewhat different date (1070/1660) for the second campaign of Qasim Sul-tan.

[5] Thus according to Salim.

tober 1669. By the time of his death, he had become the leading spiritual figure in Balkh and, by virtue of his role as spiritual mentor, an influential mediator between 'Abd al-'Aziz and Subhan Quli.

7. Fols. 283b–286a: Subhan Quli presses for the return of Hisar-i Shadman (see [3] above), "one of Balkh's regions." Military preparations by Subhan Quli are followed by lengthy negotiations, including four exchanges of embassies. On 24 June 1671, the Balkh envoy returns with a Bukharan ambassador, who goes back to Bukhara two months later. There is a brief account of a minor problem in Balkh with a Qunghrat amir, no date given.

This completes the chronicle record for the thirty years that Balkh was in Subhan Quli's hands. The other nearly contemporary works, the *Tarikh-i Muqim Khan* and *Muhit al-tawarikh*, have even less to say about the period and no additional information.

It is worthwhile comparing this brief record with the very detailed description of the three decades of Nadhr Muhammad's tenure at Balkh during the first half of the century. Most of the difference may be explained by the fact that Nadhr Muhammad hired a writer to record his regime, whereas, as far as we know, Subhan Quli did not get around to commissioning a personal history until he became khan at Bukhara in 1681.

From the perspective of waqf and its importance, Salim's record, notwithstanding its relative brevity, is of considerable interest, for not only does it show Subhan Quli's close ties to scholars and religious figures, and the patronage that cemented those relations, but, even more importantly, it stresses that he was both deliberate and enthusiastic about cultivating such ties. In other sources, there is more evidence that he was a wholehearted supporter of intellectual life in Balkh and probably expected in return to be memorialized in scholars' books. For example, a chronogram dating his accession to Balkh's "throne" is found in the preface of Mulla Dilkhun's translation into Persian of the *Mukhtasar al-Wiqayah*, an abridgment (perhaps the Sadr al-Shari'ah al-Asghar's) of Taj al-Shari'ah al-Mahbubi's famous commentary on 'Ali b. Abi Bakr Marghinani's *al-Hidayah*.[6] The chronogram suggests that the work was sponsored by Subhan Quli, who is known to have commissioned a number of scholarly works.[7] No comparable record of patronage exists for his father, whose tenure in Balkh was as long and whose interest in being remem-

---

[6] Salim, fol. 265a.

[7] For example the *Ihya al-tibb al-Subhani* (Tashkent IVAN, Inventory No. 9750, 358 folios, and Inventory No. 2101), the authorship of which is attributed to Subhan Quli himself (Storey 1927–84, 2:265 and Semenov et al. 1952–75, 1:265–66) and *Fatawa Subhaniyah* (Tashkent IVAN, Inventory No. 9476).

bered by posterity was no less great, but who decided that a hired historian was a better way to memorialize himself. Salim's account of how Subhan Quli became a disciple of Mirza Ahmad Hashim and his part in the cornerstone-laying ceremony typify the public image of the benevolent Irano-Muslim scholar-king, rather than the Turko-Mongol warrior-statesman image, which his father had cultivated. In faint outline, we can discern a new sense of political propriety in which greater emphasis is placed on cultivating the loyalty of the intellectuals and popular religious leaders than on strengthening amirid loyalties. Those too, of course, existed, and amirid support was always crucial. But the public image that Subhan Quli seems to have wanted to project was less that of an upholder of the amirid military values of the steppe and more that of a supporter of the Islamic values of the city—of scholarship and social services rather than of statesmanship and war. Part of the reason for this shift may have been the growing power of the amirs and the need to cultivate another constituency.

A part of realizing this public image involved spending money on facilities for scholars and for the public generally. Besides the madrasah in Balkh, Subhan Quli built a walled chaharbagh called Amanabad ("Abode of Peace"), which included a canal and pavilions[8] and a large audience hall with a congregational mosque and an iwan. He also renovated the Balkh citadel.[9]

One of his most interesting projects was the renovation of the tree-lined avenue between Balkh and the 'Alid shrine, which had originally been laid out and planted under Wali Muhammad's auspices in or about 1605.[10] Subhan Quli is said to have replanted all the shade trees along the entire length of the boulevard.

WAQF IN BALKH'S ECONOMY

We get virtually no sense of daily human activity in Balkh from the chronicles. Its economic life, its commercial links with the outside world, and the daily routine of its residents did not exist as far as the chronicle record is concerned. Fortunately some balance is struck thanks to the information found in the waqf materials, which provide later generations with a record of specific economic and social issues—land tenure, tax policy, crop production, manufacturing, regional and international commerce, personal and commodity service facilities, market organization, the money supply, weight and measurement standards, economic planning, and development and investment.

[8] Muhammad Yusuf Munshi, fol. 126b.
[9] Ibid.
[10] Ibid.

For Subhan Quli, there is a literary and archaeological record of his public projects as well as a documentary record of the waqfs that supported them. The documentary record includes both the deeds for his own foundations and the supporting and confirming documents he issued in his capacity as sovereign in Balkh for waqfs of institutions other than his own. To date, waqf deeds for two of Subhan Quli's projects have been discovered and published. In addition, we also have the 1668–1669 manshur or confirmation that he issued in support of the claims of the managers of the 'Alid shrine's waqfs. Each of these documents contains considerable information about economic life in the second half of the seventeenth century in Balkh and Bukhara, and collectively they are far more descriptive of life in the region than are the combined chronicle accounts.

The Bukharan waqf was founded by Subhan Quli jointly with Padshah Bibi Khanum (probably one of Subhan Quli's wives) for the maintenance of a tomb complex.[11] The waqf deed was issued in 1693, when he was khan in Bukhara. The tomb was that of another woman, Qamar Banu Khanum, who may also have been a wife. Besides maintenance costs, the waqf paid for four attendants (two male and two female) for around-the-clock duty, two Qur'an readers to recite a *juz* (one-thirtieth) of the Qur'an daily at the tomb and give holiday recitations; food (rice, sweets, and fruit) for distribution on holidays; an evening meal of bread and soup served every Friday and Monday; and, when the income sufficed, sweets and fruit after Friday and Monday eve prayers.[12] Such appropriations were typical of waqf endowments. Revenues came from agricultural lands located, for the most part, near the tomb complex, and from commercial properties.

In this relatively short (105 lines) document, there is information on salaries (100 tangahs each per annum for the Qur'an reciters, for example), the price of land (costs ranged from 100 to 239 tangahs per tanab, equivalent to about one-half acre), the size of land parcels (18 to 610 tanabs), the current unit of account (the "1.225-*mithqal* silver tangah"), and processing plants (slaughterhouses). There is even a reference, in the mention of tobacco-drying sheds, to the introduction of at least one New World crop to Mawarannahr.

At Balkh, the madrasah built while Subhan Quli was in power there was apparently not endowed with waqf until he became khan at Bukhara. Construction began in the spring of 1660, and the waqf deed, though not itself dated (one of the annexes to it is dated 1694), is believed to have

---

[11] Chekhovich and Vil'danova 1979.
[12] Ibid., 224–25 (text), 230–31 (translation).

originated no earlier than 1686 and no later than 1694.[13] During the sponsor's tenure in Balkh, we assume that the madrasah was supported by similar sources, if not the same ones, mentioned in the waqf deed.

The Balkh madrasah waqf deed, like the Bukharan tomb deed, contains a considerable amount of raw economic data, and since it pertains to Balkh that information will be summarized here. The properties making up the madrasah endowment included four parcels of irrigated agricultural lands (the term used in the document for "parcel" is *qariyah* or "village," but it should be understood to refer to a cultivated area rather than a residential settlement), five parcels of dry-farmed lands (here the term *aradi* ["lands"] is used), a public bath, three shops, and two small warehouses.

The irrigated parcels—that is the villages of Sayyidabad, Shakh Salar, Rahmatabad, and Juti Ribat—adjoined lands of varying ownership. There were private lands, irrigated state lands, unirrigated state pastures, and uncultivable (saline) abandoned, and therefore technically unowned, lands.[14]

The public bath, called the Tall-i Bazargan bath,[15] and the three shops were adjacent to each other within the city limits. The shops included a buttery (*rawghangari*), a greengrocer (*baqqali*), and a tobacconist (*tamaku furushi*). This latter is a clear sign that tobacco was available in Balkh (the 1712 annex to the 1668–1669 manshur confirms this)[16] and that it was being grown for local consumption. Given the Central Asian climate and its proximity to the Russian market, it is reasonable to assume that tobacco was grown for export as well, although we have no direct evidence of this.

The fact that the shops are identified by use rather than simply as "shops" (*dakakin*) indicates that the equipment specific to those uses was probably also owned by the waqf foundation and leased to the tenants. The two small warehouses stood on the land of the madrasah itself.

The endowment had to support a rather substantial institution. The stipulations set down in the waqf deed called for the creation of 24 salaried positions at the madrasah. Besides these, the college had 75 residential rooms (*hujrah*) on each of two floors. To 149 of these 150 rooms a

[13] Davydov 1960, 83.

[14] It has been impossible to locate these parcels with any certainty. A comparison of the toponyms with *TR* (Salakhetdinova 1970), Muhammad Mu'min (Mukhtarov 1980, 103–4), and *Gaz.* 4 produces no clear correspondences. The only village names found in any of these three sources are Sayyidabad and Rahmatabad, both occurring more than once and in various places.

[15] A commercial section of the city in the seventeenth century (Mukhtarov 1980, 70).

[16] *TMS*, 69.

living allowance (*farjah*),[17] usually paid in grain or a grain-equivalent, was assigned. The stipend was presumably adequate for at least one and perhaps two students. (The 150th room was allocated to the mutawalli with no stipend.)

Briefly summarized, the madrasah budget may be broken down as follows. The mutawalli, who was responsible for both the administration of the school and its endowments, had first to appropriate money for repairs and capital expenses related to the college building and to the endowed properties themselves. After those categories were dealt with, he was to budget salaries as follows:

1. The imam, who led the five daily prayers, received the sum or equivalent of fifteen *ushturs* (3,840 kilograms) of grain (specified as *muthallathah* or of three varieties, presumably barley, wheat, and rye) per annum, of which one-third was to be barley (*jow*). (We assume in this and other similar cases [for example, grain allotted for book repairs] that delivery on the grain was not actually taken but was brokered or sold in advance. The actual value to the imam of this income would thus have fluctuated from year to year depending on crop and market conditions.) The imam also was paid a fixed cash salary of two tangahs per diem.[18]

2. The librarian, whose job was to maintain the collection and control circulation (not to exceed fifty books at any one time), received nine ushturs of grain (2,304 kilograms) per annum, one tangah per diem, and a stipend of three farjahs as "bread" allowance (an amount equivalent to six times a student's stipend, if two students shared a farjah). Another three ushturs of grain (768 kilograms) were allocated for book restoration. There was no budget for book purchases in the deed.

3. Provision was made for twelve Qur'an-reciters: four full-time positions to recite one surah each of the Qur'an at each of the five daily worship services, and eight part-time positions (perhaps partly filled by the full-time reciters) to recite the entire Qur'an after Friday communal services. The amount budgeted in the waqf deed was four ushturs of grain (1,024 kilograms) per annum and one tangah per diem for each of the full-time reciters, and a total of three ushturs annually plus ten tangahs per week for the part-time positions. In Bukhara, the comparable salary for Qur'an-reciters at the Qamar Banu tomb was two hundred tangahs per annum (a 354-day year) or 0.56 tangahs a day. But only one complete recitation of the Qur'an a month was required at the tomb.

---

[17] Davydov 1960, 119, note 31.

[18] Ibid., 116–17 (lines 155–59 of the waqfnamah). For comparison, see Davidovich 1983, 281–88 for per-diem salaries in grain and cash in late-sixteenth-century Bukhara.

The total budget for recitation at the madrasah in Balkh was thus fifteen ushturs or 3,840 kilograms of grain or grain-equivalents and 1,980 tangahs cash per 365-day year. (It is assumed here that the sum listed for the part-time positions, i.e., three ushturs annually and ten tangahs per week, is the cumulative amount for all eight positions. Otherwise, the part-time salaries would be nearly equal to or perhaps exceed the full-time ones.)

4. A muezzin was to be paid a salary of six ushturs (1,536 kilograms) of grain per annum and one tangah in cash per diem.

5. A Qur'an reciter, whose job was to teach recitation to children in one of the outbuildings of the madrasah, was allocated four ushturs of grain (1,024 kilograms) per annum.

6. A barber to shave the heads of the residents of the madrasah each week was assigned four ushturs of grain annually.

7. Two janitors were paid five ushturs (1,280 kilograms) each per annum and one tangah per diem.

In the waqf deed the fixed appropriations total seventy ushtur of grain and 3,970 tangahs in cash.[19] But this by no means completes the budget. The rest of the appropriations may be called contingency appropriations, based on foreseeably fluctuating income, and are not expressed in fixed annual amounts. One such appropriation was for student stipends. There are farjah allotments for 149 student rooms and three farjah allotments for the librarian. Although not specified, we assume this was a subsistence stipend, perhaps of one-half to one tangah per day.

At least one nonrecurring or irregularly recurring expense was also unspecified in terms of annual amounts. Repairing and replacing carpeting is listed as one of the necessary appropriations, but no sum of money is allocated for it.

The mutawalli's and the madrasah teachers' salaries were a proportionate share of what remained. It is worth noting that the mutawalli's salary

[19] Davydov 1960, 126, note 42, calculates that the amount of land required to produce the income stipulated for the madrasah would have ranged from 1,260 to 3,000 hectares, depending on the percentage paid by the tenant sharecroppers. There are some problematic assumptions in his calculations. First, he says that the professors (*mudarrisan*) were paid 300 ushturs of grain per annum, but the document itself (line 153) says only, "one-fifth of the income [remaining after already listed disbursements] is to be divided among four professors." It is not clear what the basis of his figure of 300 ushturs per annum is. Second, in calculating the student stipends, he states that there were two students in each of the one hundred and fifty rooms. This is supported by evidence from a contemporary waqf foundation for two madrasahs established by 'Abd al-'Aziz in Bukhara on or about 5 Shawwal 1080/26 February 1670. The foundation charter specifically assigns two students to each room (Tashkent IVAN, Document No. 62, Fond Vakflar). Still the Balkh document itself does not indicate the number of students per room.

was based on productivity rather than being a set annual amount. As he was overall manager of the waqf, it was probably taken for granted that a salary based on the level of revenues would be an incentive to maintain and increase those revenues. The deed specifies that the salaries of the mutawalli and the teachers were to be identical (lines 148–153 of the document). And the teachers were each to be paid "one-fifth of the remainder of the revenues" (after the specified appropriations and necessary maintenance costs were met). Thus each of the four teachers at the Balkh madrasah and the mutawalli divided equally whatever remained of both cash and grain after the fixed allocations were made. We have no idea how much these were but, for the sake of argument, we may assume that their salaries were not less than that of the imam (fifteen ushturs and two tangahs a day).

A comparison of Subhan Quli's Bukharan tomb waqf and the madrasah waqf provides some basis for estimating the size of the endowment. Although we do not know the amount of appropriations for the tomb complex endowed by Subhan Quli in Bukhara, we do know the number of employees and can compare it with the number at Balkh. In addition, we know the amount of agricultural land (1,008.5 tanabs) that made up the tomb's endowment. It is not unreasonable, therefore, to assume, on the basis of the number of employees, that the madrasah's appropriations were at least five and probably closer to ten times those of the tomb's. If the ratio of income-producing commercial property in the two cases was more or less comparable (i.e., as a proportion of the total) then an estimate of 2,500 to 5,000 acres of agricultural land in the endowment seems appropriate, a figure comparable to the 1,260-hectare figure which Davydov arrived at using the rate of taxation as the basis for estimating the land endowment. This amount of land produced a surplus (after operating costs) to provide the salaries and stipends for 16 full-time employees, 8 part-time employees, and up to 298 students. If one assumes that the shrine netted 10 percent of the gross product of the land and one also assumes that the salaries and stipends were not vastly greater overall than what the agricultural laborers earned, then anywhere from 3,000 to 3,500 people may have been directly involved in this single waqf endowment, either as producers or consumers of its wealth.

What such a corpus of waqf land meant in terms of the entire Balkh region cannot be stated with any great assurance, but again a rough idea is possible. In the late nineteenth century, when the area of land under cultivation and the population on it appear to have been relatively diminished (one British observer calculated that the land could support seven times the existing population), an Indian Muslim estimated that in the entire Hazhdah Nahr system only some 8,120 ghulbahs or about 25,000 acres were under cultivation.[20] Under such conditions, Subhan Quli's madrasah endowment would have constituted a substantial part, perhaps from 10 to 20 percent of the cultivated land. Even in the prosperous times of the seventeenth century, the endowment would still have been a significant economic entity. Since the school was in full operation as late as fifty years after it was built,[21] we know the endowment did function and, in the absence of contrary evidence, may conclude that it was performing more or less as expected.

These are the waqfs of Subhan Quli for which we have documentation. His father, Nadhr Muhammad, is also reported to have set up endowments in Balkh on behalf of his own madrasah.[22] But up to now, no waqf deed or similar document for endowments has been discovered. In addition, there was a madrasah, perhaps two, at the Abu Nasr Parsa mausoleum complex opposite Subhan Quli's own madrasah[23] that were in operation in the middle of the seventeenth century and were probably waqf-supported. Going back a little earlier, to the late sixteenth century, we know of at least four madrasahs besides the Parsa'i college in Balkh. These were built by 'Abd Allah Khan Shibani;[24] 'Abd al-Mu'min Khan, his son;[25] Qul Baba Kukaltash, 'Abd Allah Khan's leading amirid advisor;[26] and Khwajah Kamal al-Din Qiniq.[27] For each of these madrasahs there are some waqf references. 'Abd Allah Khan's madrasah can be traced as an operating madrasah until the end of the seventeenth century. There were other seventeenth-century madrasahs besides 'Abd Allah Khan's, Nadhr Muhammad's, and Subhan Quli's. Shah Beg Kukaltash, Wali Muhammad's ataliq in Balkh, built a madrasah circa 1605 that was still operating thirty years later.[28] One of the leading Qataghan amirs, Allah Yar diwanbegi, built a madrasah circa 1610–1615 and endowed it with waqfs. There are references to professors working there in the 1630s.[29] Other similar institutions normally endowed with waqf included the 'Aliyah Khassah Madrasah, whose builder is unknown[30] (perhaps to be identified with the Nadhr Muhammad Madrasah); mosques built by

---

[20] Gaz. 4:264.

[21] Salim, fols. 269b–270a; Tarikh-i Shibani, fol. 119b.

[22] See BA, 4: fol. 214b for a general description of its waqfs.

[23] Ibid., 4: fol. 369b.

[24] Ibid., 4: fols. 348a, 350a–b (the waqf of which BA mentions later, fol. 364b); Salim, fol. 172a.

[25] Munshi n.d., 1: 297.

[26] BA, 4: fols. 349b, 364b, 365a; Salim, fol. 150a.

[27] TR, fol. 135b.

[28] BA, 4: fols. 365b–366a.

[29] Ibid., 4: fols. 278b, 349–350a, 365b.

[30] Ibid., 4: fol. 289a.

an amir, Jan Kildi Bi,[31] and a Sufi shaykh, Khwajah Sa'd b. Khwajah Islam Juybari;[32] a congregational mosque sponsored by Nadhr Muhammad Khan;[33] and a hospice (khanaqah) constructed by Mawlana Khurd 'Azizan-i Akhsikathi early in the century.[34] Finally, of course, there are the waqf endowments of the 'Alid shrine. And these are but the most obvious of the public waqfs. Of private waqfs and smaller public waqfs there is hardly any surviving information.

Waqf was an immensely important economic institution prior to Subhan Quli's tenure in Balkh. And his own inclinations toward the class of people who usually benefited most from waqf foundations—i.e., religious scholars and clerics—encouraged the establishment of more waqf foundations during his three decades in Balkh, as well as the preservation of existing waqfs.

THE 'ALID SHRINE'S WAQFS IN 1668

The above narrative is by way of background to the situation at the 'Alid shrine in the first part of Subhan Quli's era at Balkh. In A.H. 1079/A.D. 1668–1669, the mutawalli of the 'Alid shrine and its waqf, Hajji Mirza Muhammad Ya'qub, gathered up his papers and, accompanied by a party of religious scholars, traveled the few miles to Balkh.

It was common practice for a waqf administrator to assemble his documents and turn either to a qadi-judge or to the political authorities when he needed a resolution or decree setting forth the rights of the waqf administration and prohibiting interference from other competing jurisdictions. The decree thus promulgated, if indeed the sovereign agreed with the mutawalli's petition, had no permanent legal standing but was nevertheless of some value, at least during the lifetime of the politician who issued it. Confirmation decrees were important weapons in the mutawalli's arsenal in the neverending struggle to defend his institution's endowments against a variety of outside forces.

There were at least two routine occasions when a mutawalli was likely to petition the sovereign for a confirmation of his rights. One was when the political administration changed and a new sovereign was seated. The other was when the waqf administration changed and a new mutawalli succeeded to the post. In either case, it seems to have been common practice for the mutawalli to approach the political authorities. There were other extraordinary circumstances, too, that might have brought the waqf administrator to Balkh to get political backing for his jurisdic-

---

[31] Ibid., 4: fol. 306a.
[32] Muhammad Amin, fol. 93a.
[33] Ibid., fol. 94b; Lahuri 1867–72, 2:544.
[34] Muhammad Tahir Balkhi, fol. 18a.

tional prerogatives. Disputes with tax collectors over exemptions or the amount of tax owed by the waqf, conflicts with tenants over rents, and even perhaps cases in which waqf land had been misappropriated were all justifiable pretexts for seeking political intervention and a political solution. What is often difficult to ascertain, however, as we will see shortly, is the extent to which the admonitions in the sovereign's decree against usurpation and illegal manipulation of the waqf properties referred to actual circumstances. Although the documentary record for the half-century after 1669 is not complete, the pattern that survives in the existing documents indicates that it was more often administrative change (whether in Balkh or at the shrine) that prompted the petition for a restatement of rights, rather than actual infringements on the waqf prerogatives of the shrine.

There is corroborative evidence from a contemporary waqf foundation in Samarqand that succession to office was usually the occasion for seeking a confirmatory decree from the political authorities. In the Samarqand City Museum, there is a series of five decrees spanning a period of about one century (c. 1015/1606–1118/1706) that pertain to a waqf endowment supporting a Ni'matullahi khanaqah and paying stipends to descendants of the founder.[35] Although not yet fully analyzed, the documents are more or less identically worded. They confirm the rights of the descendants of the founder and name the contemporary mutawalli. They also warn local officials against unwarranted interference in the operation of the waqf. But the changing names of both the issuer and the recipient of the documents leads to the conclusion that these documents were sought mainly at times of administrative turnover. Document No. 1122 (undated) was issued under the seal of Wali Muhammad Khan (r. 1605–1612) and names Shah Mirak Husayn, brother of the former and by then deceased mutawalli, Shah Abu'l-Wafa, as the administrator. Document No. 1123 (partially dated ____ 7, i.e., 1027, 1037, or 1047 [1618, 1627–1628, or 1637–1638]) is under the seal of Imam Quli Khan (r. 1612–1641) and was issued to Amir Shah 'Alam. No. 1117 bears the seal of 'Abd al-'Aziz Khan (r. 1645–1681). The date and recipient are particularly important here. The document is dated 1055 (the enthronement year of the khan), and the administrator named is " 'Alam Shah," i.e., the same Amir Shah 'Alam mentioned in No. 1123. No. 1120 was issued in 1700–1701 under the seal of Subhan Quli Khan (r. 1681–1702) and is in the name of "Amir Shah Qasim," identified in the next document as "his [i.e., Shah 'Alam's] son." The final document in the series (No. 1121) came out under the name of 'Ubayd Allah Khan (r. 1702–circa 1706) and was granted to Amir Shah Qasim, *apparently* in 1706.

[35] "K.D.," Nos. 1122, 1123, 1117, 1120, 1121.

In the first, second, and fourth cases, it seems fairly clear that a change in the waqf administration is being confirmed by the political authorities. In the third and fifth cases, it is the political administration that has changed. (The fifth case is somewhat problematic as 'Ubayd Allah was in charge well before 1118/1706, but the date itself sits rather isolated on the document and may have been added later.)

In this light one might be predisposed to conclude that, when Mirza Muhammad Ya'qub went to Balkh in 1668–1669 to petition Subhan Quli for a confirmation resolution, it was because of a recent change in the administration of the shrine.

But the manshur that was issued to him makes it clear that there was much more at stake than official approval of a new administration, if indeed that was an issue at all. The document contains unambiguous references to illegally seized lands and a diminishing of the mutawalli's authority under pressure from both private interests and the ruler's own officials. These statements are not the kind of formulaic expressions we find repeated in the series of five documents from Samarqand.

There are, however, certain implicit parallels with the Samarqand documents. All five Samarqand documents refer back to a major decree issued by the Shibanid 'Abd Allah Khan (r. 1583–1598), which has not yet come to light. The proclamations of the later sovereigns simply reconfirm the terms set out in that decree. The confirmation resolution issued by Subhan Quli in 1668–1669 may be analogous to the 'Abd Allah Khan decree in that both addressed major administrative problems and offered solutions that later politicians felt called upon to reconfirm. For more than a century, whatever it was that 'Abd Allah Khan had decided vis-à-vis the Ni'matullahi khanaqah waqf was reaffirmed by his successors. In the case of Balkh, for seventy years after Subhan Quli issued the decree, whenever there was a change in the administration at Balkh, annexes to his 1668–1669 decree would reiterate those terms.

In the manshur, Mirza Muhammad Ya'qub is called a descendant of a man who is styled the "first" mutawalli, Mirza Abu'l-Hasan Ansari, reportedly appointed by Sultan Husayn Bayqara in the 1480s. Mirza Muhammad Ya'qub is further described as "descended by seed [hasab-i sulbi] from Khwajah 'Abd Allah Ansari," the Herati mystic of the eleventh century, and "by womb [nasab-i batni] from Sultan Mawdud-i Chishti," the Khurasani and Indian mystic of the twelfth century. In other words, his father was an Ansari and his mother was a Chishti, all in all a distinguished pedigree.

The mutawalli was accompanied by a group of worthies whose role was to corroborate the evidence contained in the waqf deeds. In the manshur, these people are referred to as "scholars and intellectuals ['ulama wa fudala], sayyids, servants, dervishes, 'corner-sitters' [gushah ni-

shinan], residents, amirs, khans, notables [*'uzama*], and legal experts [*fuqaha*]."

In Hanafi law, there is an interplay of documents and witnesses,[36] and it is well known that the testimony of competent witnesses was part of judicial procedure even where the facts of the case were only known through the documentary record. That the issuance of the manshur was both a political and a legal proceeding is clear. Hanafi law on waqf reserved to the political authorities (through the qadi's office) the final decision in adjudicating waqf disputes and confirming waqf rights (see chapter 1). Often a qadi had adequate authority and could serve as a final arbiter in an appeal. Sometimes, as here, it was necessary to appeal to a higher authority.

Mirza Muhammad Ya'qub, supported by the witnesses he had brought, laid the facts of his case before Subhan Quli. The sovereign, in turn, issued the manshur, basing his findings of fact on the presentation. Since we do not have the testimony of the mutawalli, we have no way of knowing to what extent the decision met his expectations. Our only source of information is the manshur itself, the main focus of which is an effort to restore the mutawalli's full authority over the Shahi Canal district (Sultan Husayn Bayqara's original endowment) and the outlying regions later given as waqf by Wali Muhammad Khan and the various amirs named previously.

A summarized version of the manshur is given below. It excludes the sections discussed earlier pertaining to the mid-seventeenth-century waqf grants.

[Following the invocation][37] . . . Hajji Mirza Muhammad Ya'qub, the mutawalli, and a group of scholars and intellectuals, sayyids, servants, dervishes, "corner-sitters," residents, amirs, khans, notables, and legal experts (from the shrine), petitioned with one voice and in complete unanimity that:

1. The foundation and building of the holy refuge and shrine were due to the greatest of kings, Sultan Sanjar.

2. That sultan established as the waqf of that shrine the entire Shahi Canal of the "Mother of Cities" [Balkh] lengthwise and breadthwise, including all villages and estates, dwellings and farms, boundaries and roads, and all its appurtenances as *darubast* [for that shrine]. Its borders are the Kutal-i Abdu in the east; Dih Dadi and Karamlik on the Quddar Canal and Takhtah Pul on the west; Ranjaktu and Fuladi on the Quddar Canal and the unowned salt lands to the north; and the Khidrabad Canal along the edge of the Shadyan Desert on the south.

3. After Hulagu Khan's conquest, this place and its canal fell into ruins and

---

[36] Wakin 1972.
[37] *TMS*, 50–56 (text), 61–64 (transcription).

remained thus until Sultan Husayn Mirza Bayqara, a descendant of Amir Timur Gurgan, ascended the throne and restored this shrine from the ruins. He rebuilt the canal as in former times and in accordance with [Sanjar's] farman reestablished it as waqf of the shrine, placing it in the capable hands of Mirza Abu'l-Hasan Ansari, who was descended by seed from Khwajah 'Abd Allah Ansari and by womb from Sultan Mawdud-i Chishti. He also appointed 120 sayyids, intellectuals, and competent legal experts to lofty positions at the shrine.

4. After the sultanate of Sultan Zahir al-Din Babur, Muhammad Shibani Khan, our [sic] noble forebear [jidd-i amjad-i bandagan-i ma], and after him the devout Islam-promoting ancestors, one after another, adhered to these rules and were concerned with the well-being of this shrine, confirming the [Shahi] Canal, with all its appurtenances, both land and amenities, as the waqf of this shrine.

5. Now, however, because of turmoil in the world and usurpation by the immoral, out of all the shrine's waqf there only remains under the mutawalli's control a few places and prerogatives: Chughuz, Jighzak [Chughzak], Habash, Dahanah-i 'Abd al-Rahman, Tash Timur, Dilkhak, the ghulbah of Mihtar Rajab, the ghulbah of Mihtar Baqi, Nawbahar, Maydan, Baba Shahu, Yakah Bagh, and the trades and crafts belonging to the holy threshold as well as [such fiscal prerogatives as] the sargalah [tax] and the jarib tax on orchards and on silkworm plantations [jaribanah-i baghat wa filahjat], whether held by government decree or not.

6. All the rest of the villages and farms and related things within the Shahi Canal district have been usurped, in part by those who, following the path of greed and opportunism as disciples of Satan and

Having no shame before God
Nor any modesty before the Prophet and his Family,

have made them their private property. In addition, some of the waqf property has been registered as part of the royal household properties [khalisah-i sarkar] in total ignorance, by those who have not recognized the rights of the waqf.

7. As these worthy men have proven beyond any doubt that these things are waqf and have sought the sultan's favor to restore all the villages, farms, plains, and pastures of the aforementioned canal district, which is certainly and unequivocally the waqf of the shrine, therefore let it be established that:

    a. Whereas sultans and khaqans have no other duty but seeking the favor of the Lord of the Worlds and the approbation of the Lord of all Prophets and the Rightly Guiding Caliphs and,

    b. Whereas the minds of all right-thinking people are directed toward the embellishment of sacred places and the good management of the country and the safeguarding of the waqfs,

8. Therefore, this humble servant of God, seeking forgiveness for his sins and service to God, [hereby affirms that:]

a. All the lands and appurtenances of the aforementioned canal, whether villages, farms, lands, orchards, uncultivated ground, the income from them [*wujuhat*], or things attached thereto, and all that comes under the pen, be it real estate or moveables, in accordance with what was established in previous times, should be removed from the hands of the usurpers and oppressors and forever be restored to the waqf of the blessed shrine.

b. Regarding these restored rights, we make it incumbent upon all future leaders and politicians, be they of our lineage or not, not to allow any interference with or change in any of these prerogatives and to restrain their own and others' hands from them so that on the day of the Gathering, when the just will be feted and the oppressors given cause to wail, the hems of the garments of their acts will not be stained or soiled but rather they will be worthy of divine reward.

9. Likewise for any lands of other settled areas [*diya' wa 'aqqar*] outside the canal district that charity-minded sultans, amirs, and leaders have purchased with their own money and given to the waqf of the shrine or that were given out of their own private property, [here the waqf lands and water rights given by Wali Muhammad Khan and the amirs over the course of the seventeenth century, as previously discussed, are listed] all those properties are attested by waqfnamah and validated by the seals of the waqf donors.

10. After the aforementioned mutawalli presented all the waqfnamahs for our review, the sayyids, scholars, residents, and Qur'an reciters [accompanying him] petitioned for the issuance of a decree affirming and restoring these rights.

11. In accordance with the dictum, "He who does a good deed, receives its like ten times over," we therefore grant and assign to the charge of the aforementioned mutawalli forever and ever all the abovementioned villages and lands, farms, canals, waters, etc., which are the waqf of the blessed shrine in accordance with the waqf deeds of that blessed threshold of the Imam of all Mankind. [This is done] in the spirit of seeking God's favor.

12. And, as has been the case in the past, he [the mutawalli] shall record in his accounts all revenues, income, and benefices, and shall consider one-fifth to be for his own expenses. What remains shall be for the necessary upkeep of the buildings, for lighting and furnishings for the tomb [rawdah] and the khanaqah, and for the salaries of the imam, muezzin, khatibs, residents, and servants and for other requisite expenditures.

13. The heavenly reward for this shall accrue to the sultans and kings and to the waqf donors and will be for them a "nearness [*qurbah*] unto God."

14. Such should be the same forever and ever and should never be set aside.

15. After him, likewise, all the mutawallis of this angel-guarded shrine, gen-

eration after generation, should conduct their affairs accordingly and not violate these terms.

16. Transgressors, interferers, and usurpers will be the objects of divine damnation and prophetic excoriation.

In the year 1079.

. . .

It should be immediately apparent that the authority of the mutawalli over the waqf endowment was in some jeopardy by 1668–1669. His jurisdiction was recognized in only twelve villages, most of which were in the immediate environs of the shrine, and even in those the extent of his fiscal control seems to have been reduced. What the proximate cause of his troubles was is not known, and the identity of "the followers of the path of greed and opportunism" can only be guessed at.

But it might be useful to keep in mind one or two points. The first is that during the Moghul occupation of Balkh in 1646–1647 the shrine had been briefly occupied by the Moghul army. It would have been reasonable for the shrine administrators to have cooperated with the Moghul authorities during the occupation. It is possible that collaboration with the Moghuls might have cost the shrine administration something after the Moghul withdrawal. Another possible cause of the administrative problems that the mutawalli now hoped to redress was the increasing assertiveness of the Uzbek tribal groups, particularly in light of Tuqay-Timurid helplessness against the Moghul army, and the effect of this assertiveness on local authorities like the waqf administrators. Loss of control of the peripheral waqf properties could have stemmed from the turmoil of the Moghul occupation, but the twenty-year period that passed before the Tuqay-Timurid ruler at Balkh could, or would, do anything to restore those lands may have been far more significant. It was during this period that efforts first had to be made to reestablish Tuqay-Timurid authority at Balkh, and only when that was achieved could petitioners such as the mutawalli anticipate any real assistance from the political leadership.

Unfortunately evidence of what was going on is hard to find. The sources offer what they thought were the causes of the political problems faced by the Tuqay-Timurid house, focusing on Nadhr Muhammad's alleged efforts to reorganize the appanage structure of Balkh and his even more controversial attempts to curtail amirid control of territory by offering cash salaries in lieu of fiefs. What the writers do not tell us are the consequences of these policies, how long they took to resolve themselves, and what effect they had on other administrative entities like the 'Alid waqf administration. It is not unreasonable to assume that after the

Moghul occupation, as the Uzbek amirs reestablished themselves in their iqta's, the waqf administrators had no choice but to wait until the air cleared and the amirs and the Balkh sovereign again arrived at a working relationship. Then and only then could a petition conceivably achieve the desired result. It is highly doubtful that a mutawalli would have taken the trouble to assemble his documents, arrange to travel to Balkh in the company of a group of the shrine's worthies, and lay his case before the sultan, had he not been optimistic about obtaining real help. Looked at in another way, the twenty-year period between the Moghul occupation and the issuance of the manshur is indicative of the depth and seriousness of the political problems of the time.

There is another issue raised by the manshur that is somewhat less amenable to explanation, and that is the registering of waqf lands in the royal desmesnes [*khalisah-i sarkar*] (see paragraph 6). On the face of it, such usurpation would seem to have been easily rectified, or at least fore-stalled, by quick appeal to the sultan at Balkh. After all, it was his purse into which the revenues of these lands were being diverted. Subhan Quli had already been sovereign at Balkh for seventeen years or so before the mutawalli solicited the manshur of 1668–1669. Assuming his respect for waqf and for the institutions it supported to have been more than just a passing enthusiasm, this kind of issue should have been easily solved, unlike those cases involving amirid interference. It is difficult to say why it took so long for the mutawalli to ask a man noted for his interest in and respect for religious institutions and the law to restrain his own employ-ees from illegal acts against the waqf. Perhaps collaboration with the Mo-ghuls had angered the Tuqay-Timurid sultan and it had taken this long for his resentment to fade. Or perhaps the royal household had so great a need of the income produced from properties, even those known to be waqf, that it had been unable up to this point to voluntarily relinquish them. Whatever the case, obtaining the manshur was a major step to-ward restoring the waqf rights of the 'Alid shrine.

The manshur generally defines the jurisdictional area of the waqf to be the region bounded by the Abdu Pass in the east, the Khidrabad Canal (or Juy Qizil Ribat, a small branch off the Shahi Canal, and the lands it watered) in the south, and the Quddar Canal (and some of its territories) in the west and north. This is a sizeable area, measuring roughly twenty-one or twenty-two miles along its east-west axis and seven to eight miles along its north-south axis. The amount of productive land (whether agri-cultural or pastoral) within it is not known. Areas called "*shuristan*" (sa-line ground) may have been found throughout the Shahi Canal region, and not just along its northern side as the document states.

When Mirza Muhammad Ya'qub presented his appeal to Subhan Quli in Balkh, his effective control was limited to a handful of villages close to the shrine. They included Chughuz (perhaps identical with Chukur, the eighth village from the source on the Nahr-i Shahi),[38] Chughzak (the seventh village on the canal), Habash (so far unidentified), Dahanah-i 'Abd al-Rahman (unidentified), Tash Timur (the sixteenth village on the Quddar Canal), Dilkhak (the eighth village on the Quddar Canal), the ghulbah (a parcel of land defined by its rights to water) of the village of Mihtar Rajab (unidentified), the ghulbah of Mihtar Baqi (likewise unknown), Nawbahar (one of the three villages watered by the Juy Qizil Ribat) Maydan (the thirteenth village on the 'Abdallah Canal), Baba Shahu (the fifth village on the Shahi Canal), and Yakah Bagh (unidentified). All of the identified locales are within a short distance of the shrine, and we may assume that the others were as well.

The document also describes the few revenue rights that the shrine still controlled in 1668. The first of these was the income from the artisans and craftspeople connected with the shrine. These probably included shrine concessionaires as well as artisans who rented working space within the shrine precincts. The kinds of artisanry likely to be practiced at the shrine might have included calligraphy, bookbinding, weaving, and ceramics, especially tile-making. The shrine may have paid the workers a salary and entered their earnings into the accounts as those of the "trades and crafts" (*asnaf wa muhtarifah*) of the shrine, or perhaps the workers or groups of workers simply paid a percentage of their earnings or a fixed fee to the shrine for the right to work there. We know very little about the organization of crafts in Balkh during this time, although the existence of such a source of revenue makes it clear that at least at the tax level there was some perceived organization.

This particular tax or revenue right is especially interesting for underlining the official view (as distinct from a strictly Shar'i legal one) of what constituted waqf. Here and elsewhere it is made clear that under the rubric of "the waqf of the 'Alid shrine" officials meant all revenue, with the possible exception of votive offerings, that the shrine disposed of, whether it actually came from an endowed object or not. We assume that this was simply a term of convenience, since it was expected, even when such was not the case, that the bulk of the income of the shrine would be derived from the waqf endowment.

The second tax prerogative was the sargalah. The *Historical and Political Gazetteer of Afghanistan* says that in the nineteenth century the sargalah was a tax on livestock. How, or even if, it differed from the zakat is not clear.[39] The tax was probably collected from the owners of livestock raised within the villages still under the mutawalli's control in 1668.

[38] Mukhtarov 1980, 102.

[39] *Gaz.* 4, where both terms are found, with *zakat* appearing more often.

The third revenue right was the per-jarib tax on land that produced fruit and land that produced silkworms, i.e., on fruit orchards and mulberry groves.

These three taxes cover manufacturing, agriculture, and animal husbandry and give some idea of how extensive revenue sources could be for a waqf administration. It is assumed here that the collection of these revenues by the shrines meant that government officials were not entitled to them, a point of continual controversy.

Besides the jurisdictional reach of the waqf administration and the extent to which that had been reduced by 1668, the manshur also addresses the status of the mutawalli, and thus becomes particularly important for the subsequent history of the shrine, for it provides a document to which the Ansari family would henceforward refer in claiming their exclusive rights to the administration-tawliyat of the shrine and its waqf. Up until this point, we have no written evidence that the Ansaris had ever advanced any such claim. Their position, of course, is implied by the recognition given by the Tuqay-Timurid sultan. But the sources contemporary with Sultan Husayn Bayqara's founding (or revival) of the shrine say nothing of an Ansari mutawalli. The existence of Mirza Abu'l-Hasan, the "first mutawalli," is attested to nowhere else. Moreover, as we have seen from the few bits of data surviving from the sixteenth and early seventeenth centuries, those who were named to leadership positions at the shrine, as either shaykhs, shaykh al-islams, or naqibs, were not Ansaris. The manshur thus becomes a kind of "finding of fact" in regard to Ansari rights, and it would serve the family well in later years.

To Subhan Quli, Hajji Mirza Muhammad Ya'qub was evidently more than a simple functionary; he was the current representative of a long line of Ansari mutawallis stretching back to Abu'l-Hasan, whom Subhan Quli understood to have been the first to hold that position at the shrine and who had been appointed by Sultan Husayn Mirza Bayqara in the fifteenth century. (An early-nineteenth-century source would later add an anterior link, see chapter 10.)

Furthermore, in his exhortations to Mirza Muhammad Ya'qub and to his successors, Subhan Quli made it clear that in his eyes the office was the birthright of the Ansaris and that future generations of mutawallis would naturally be the descendants of the man who stood before him. The Tuqay-Timurid was, in effect, putting his seal of approval to the formation of an administrative dynasty. Subhan Quli still retained the right to confirm or reject appointments of mutawallis, but it was nonetheless generally accepted that an Ansari, presumably raised and trained for that position, was the natural choice. Whether the document simply recognized an existing attitude that the Ansari claim was indeed legitimate, which seems most likely, or was a new departure in the way in which the

'Alid shrine administration was viewed, it nonetheless helped define the sphere within which conflict would later occur.

Besides raising the curtain a bit on the Ansari claim to the tawliyat, the 1668–1669 manshur also provides the first information we have about the administrative fee or commission (*haqq al-tawliyah*) collected by the mutawalli. Toward the end of the document (paragraph 12), Subhan Quli decrees that the mutawalli, after accounting for all the revenues, should consider 20 percent to be for his own expenses (*makhsus-i kharj-i khud*).

Compensation equal to 20 percent of gross revenues was fairly high for a mutawalli, by contemporary standards at least, and may have reflected already high administrative costs. In a madrasah waqf deed issued at Bukhara a year after Subhan Quli's manshur, his brother, the reigning khan 'Abd al-'Aziz, set the administrative fee at 10 percent of the income of the waqf.[40] It is quite possible that, in the case of the 'Alid shrine, the loss of lands and revenues before 1668 had forced the mutawalli to take an even larger percentage of the gross revenue to maintain his income and staff needs. The shrine also had another source of income, the votive offerings (*nudhurat*), which were probably, although we may never know for sure, a substantial part of the shrine's income. We do not know whether the nudhurat income was tallied separately from the waqf income at this time, as was done in the late nineteenth century. It is not inconceivable, though, that when the Tuqay-Timurid sultan referred to "all revenues, income, and benefices" he had in mind both the waqf income and the votive offerings.

In the history of the 'Alid shrine and its waqf, the 1668–1669 manshur is a document of primary importance. It not only confirmed and restated the rights of the waqf administration and reprimanded officers of the royal household for having illegally usurped some of the waqf's prerogatives, it also provided a written standard to which any future jurisdictional conflict could be appealed. Beyond this, it linked the honor of the Tuqay-Timurid sovereigns to the well-being of the shrine's waqf and called on future rulers to observe and protect the rights set out in the manshur. As we will see, this was a charge and a responsibility that later rulers would take quite seriously. Protecting the shrine's waqf was one side of the political exchange that would take place whenever the sovereign reconfirmed the waqf rights. By seeking such reconfirmation, the shrine administrators themselves conferred legitimacy on and acknowledged the authority of the sovereign at Balkh.

This theme is a little clearer if we look again at the series of documents pertaining to the Ni'matullahi khanaqah near Samarqand. Perhaps what is most significant in that series of documents is what is missing. From

[40] See, e.g., Tashkent IVAN, Document No. 62 (Fond Vakflar), lines 185–86.

1606 to 1706, every khan at Bukhara but one, Nadhr Muhammad, is represented in the documents. And his khanate was brief (1642–1645) and beset with political problems from the outset. It is not surprising that the waqf administrators in Samarqand hesitated to ask him for a confirmation of their rights. Such a petition was in its way a kind of confirmation—of the rights of the sovereign, of his legitimacy, and of the willingness of the population to abide by his word. When Hajji Muhammad Ya'qub went to Balkh in 1668–1669 to seek political backing for what he saw as his administrative rights, he also implicitly signaled recognition of the authority of Subhan Quli as the head of the appanage government.

CHAPTER SEVEN

The Eclipse of the Appanage System:
Balkh toward the End of the Seventeenth Century

CERTAIN political themes run through Balkh's history in the period covered by this study, many of which stem from a devotion to the idea of a Chingizid or yasa-approved way of doing things. The appanage system with its subdivision of the territory into amirid iqta's was considered one such yasa-sanctioned political form. In general, the idea of what the yasa did or did not sanction had created a predisposition against more centralized and bureaucratic government and was an inertial force restricting any such moves by the khanly family. At the same time, the amirid leaders of the Uzbek tribal groupings, while themselves subscribing to the yasa way of doing things, tended at a local level to replicate the inclination of the khanly family to consolidate, bureaucratize, and thus centralize. Such dynamics kept the system volatile and constantly seeking a new political equilibrium. The distribution of power most favorable to the maintenance of the yasa-sanctioned appanage system occurred when the khanly representative was seen by the amirs to have adequate but not excessive or threatening power—that is, when the khan or sultan could appoint or dismiss but lacked wider, more arbitrary power—and the amirs viewed each other as more or less of equal status—that is, none appeared as a threat to any of the others. It is important to note that two dominant amirid figures of the first half of the seventeenth century, Yalangtush Bi ataliq, an Alchin amir and a person of wealth and power, and Nadr Bi Taghay Arlat, were both members of apparently minor tribal groupings and never, as far as we can tell, emerged as focuses of factional politics. Their positions were based on personal abilities and ties to the khanly family, not on being heads of powerful tribal factions.

The latter half of the century produced a somewhat different kind of amirid figure, one who sought power for himself and only nominally, if at all, acknowledged khanly rights. A prominent example of this type is Mahmud Bi of the Qataghan tribal organization. The transformation of amirid behavior produced rather predictable results. In order to contend with the general disapproval of behavior thought to be contrary to the unwritten yasa, such a figure not only had to have a strong tribal organization behind him, he needed to be able to manipulate and control the symbol of yasa-sanctioned legitimacy, the khan. The rise of such amirid power meant a decline in khanly authority, but at the same time it provoked a reaction from other amirs who sought ways to prevent such an amir from gaining political ascendancy over the khan and to enhance their own status and power by developing a territorial base and constituency.

The apparent equilibrium of the bipartite appanage state in which rival Tuqay-Timurid claims could be satisfied tended to speed up the trend toward greater amirid power. First the Tuqay-Timurid house was weakened vis-à-vis other internal political elements (not to mention its foreign rivals) by the division into two independent parts. When relations were harmonious the system worked reasonably well. For the three decades of Imam Quli Khan's rule at Bukhara and Nadhr Muhammad's at Balkh, cooperation and goodwill generally prevailed. Imam Quli often called on his brother for military aid in his constant struggles with the Qazaqs around Tashkent, and when the Moghuls threatened Balkh, Imam Quli in his turn sent an army to support Nadhr Muhammad.[1] But when the two parts ceased acting in conjunction, the result was a drastic weakening of the whole khanly structure. The thirty years in which Subhan Quli held Balkh and his brother, 'Abd al-'Aziz Khan, held Bukhara were marked by cool relations and the occasional eruption of armed confrontations. Subhan Quli refused, for the most part, to help his brother against the increasingly destructive raids of the Khwarazmian Chingizids, Abu'l-Ghazi Khan and his son Anushah. In fact there were occasions when Subhan Quli encouraged the Khwarazmian attacks, and early in the period, the two Tuqay-Timurid rulers confronted each other directly.[2]

During the period 1650–1680, Balkh was by and large free from external political pressures and was content to let Bukhara fend for itself against the Khwarazmians. It seems clear that 'Abd al-'Aziz and Subhan Quli were well aware of the deleterious consequences of such a division within the Tuqay-Timurid state. Both were sensible men with a good grasp of the political realities. But changing what nearly two centuries had wrought in Mawarannahr and Balkh was another matter. 'Abd al-'Aziz Khan had neither the means to unite the state nor the diplomatic gifts to heal the breach with his brother. Nor, in the end, was Subhan Quli, when he ascended the khanly throne in 1681, any more successful in bringing the two appanages under his dominion, even though he had the advantage of no fraternal rival of any consequence. The result of the long period of bifurcation was a political organism less able to defend

---

[1] Akhmedov 1982, 191.

[2] Ibid., 113ff. provides an excellent survey of the political events of this period. *Tarikh-i Shibani*, fol. 115b introduces the theme of jealousy into the conflict. According to him, 'Abd al-'Aziz had somehow stolen away a cousin (a daughter of Imam Quli Khan) to whom Subhan Quli was reportedly betrothed.

itself from external enemies and more prone to further division from within. The amirs recognized and contributed to the diminished power of the Tuqay-Timurid family by the ways in which they responded to political crises.

On 28 October 1681, Subhan Quli ascended the khanly throne relinquished by 'Abd al-'Aziz.[3] 'Abd al-'Aziz's departure was ironically, if not surprisingly, a replay of 1645, when he had compelled his father to abdicate in favor of him. In both instances, it was dissatisfied amirs who forced the ouster of the reigning khan. The author of *Muhit al-tawarikh* describes the traditional enthronement: "On Monday, at the properly auspicious moment and in accordance with the Chingizi Yasa, they sat him down on a white felt carpet. Four of the great amirs—Khadim Bi, ataliq; Imam Quli, diwanbegi; Khwajah Quli, diwanbegi; and Muhammad Jan Bi, diwanbegi—lifted up the four corners of the carpet and set him on the throne."[4]

The political history of Balkh from this point until the death of Subhan Quli in 1702 is unusually well recorded, in marked contrast to the record of Balkh during Subhan Quli's tenure there. The reason lies, in no small part, in Subhan Quli policies toward Balkh and the reactions these produced.

Because the written material is comparatively rich, it is worth saying a few words here about the historiographic record. One of the problems present-day historians must face when considering the seventeenth-century history of Mawarannahr and Balkh, and especially the story of the second half of the century, is the disproportionate weight given by later writers to the record left by Muhammad Yusuf Munshi, the author of the *Tarikh-i* (or *Tadhkirah-i*) *Muqim Khani*. (Elsewhere I have discussed some of the problems this book creates for students of the early seventeenth century.)[5] Despite its being highly partisan, prone to polemics, and rather cavalier about factual accuracy, the book still remains extremely influential.[6]

Without ignoring Muhammad Yusuf Munshi's work, which is particularly important for understanding the contending factions in the struggle for Balkh in the 1680s and 1690s, the following summary of the period

[3] Muhammad Amin, fol. 106a; *Tarikh-i Shibani*, fol. 116a, perhaps relying on Muhammad Amin, dates the enthronement to "mid-Shawwal 1092." Salim, fol. 297b also has 15 Shawwal 1092 A.H./28 October 1681 A.D. Without clearly indicating his source, Akhmedov 1982, 114 dates the enthronement 1 Muharram 1092/21 January 1681. Apparently the month and day were taken from Muhammad Yusuf Munshi, fol. 72a, although the latter's year date of 1091 is wrong.

[4] Muhammad Amin, fol. 106a.

[5] McChesney 1980a, 71–72.

[6] For examples, see Hambly 1969, chapters 12–13; Vambery 1873, chapters 14–16.

and the attempt to bring out the main issues at stake in Subhan Quli's policies relies on these sources: (1) Mirza Muhammad Amin b. Muhammad Zaman Bukhari Sufyani's *Muhit al-tawarikh*, which was written during Subhan Quli's reign and commissioned by Ibrahim *qushbegi*,[7] one of the top amirid officials in the khanate; (2) Haji Mir Muhammad Salim's untitled work (styled *Silsilat al-salatin* in the Bodleian catalog), composed in A.H. 1123/A.D, 1711–1712; and (3) the untitled and anonymous work (styled *Tarikh-i Shibani Khan wa mu'amalat ba awlad-i Amir Timur* in the Tashkent catalog) written in 1134/1721–1722. The works often overlap but are sufficiently different in detail and emphasis that they may be considered (with Muhammad Yusuf's *Tarikh-i Muqim Khani*) to represent four different perspectives.[8] The *Silsilat* and the *Tarikh-i Shibani* share much, but by no means all, of the same data, while the other two works offer independent narratives. In what follows I make no attempt to prove the accuracy of one source over another or the "reliability" of one over another, but rather try to bring out what they saw as the main issues and the different emphases they chose in delineating those issues.

When Subhan Quli became khan in the fall of 1681, he first turned his attention to the difficult problem of the relations between Bukhara and Balkh. During his two decades as khan, this issue with all its political ramifications elicited one policy after another from him, not one of which proved to have any staying power.

His main aim from the outset was to reduce Balkh's independence. The circumstances of the Tuqay-Timurid clan at this point favored appanage reorganization. There was no one of comparable status within the clan to challenge his policies, and it must have seemed an opportune moment to unite Bukhara and Balkh. (It should be added, however, that his own apparently philogynous nature guaranteed problems for the next generation.)[9]

His efforts fall into three distinct periods: (1) the years 1683–1685, in which he tried to establish as qa'alkhan or vice-khan and heir-apparent at Balkh someone wholly loyal and subordinate to him; (2) the span 1685–1697, during which he tried to dispense with a Chingizid representative entirely and to rely on amirs as governors of Balkh; and (3) the period

---

[7] Salim, fols. 319a–320a lists Ibrahim *qushbegi* as one of the eight leading amirs in the Bukharan government at the time of Subhan Quli's death in 1702.

[8] McChesney 1980a, 72–73.

[9] Subhan Quli had at least nine sons—Iskandar, 'Ibad Allah, Abu'l-Mansur, Siddiq Muhammad, 'Abd al-Ghani, 'Abd al-Qayyum, 'Ubayd Allah, Asad Allah, and Abu'l-Fayd. There is also a reference in Salim, fol. 303a to his releasing the "other princes" from incarceration at Balkh after the deaths of the first six of these. At his death, only two seem to have survived—'Ubayd Allah and Abu'l-Fayd (*Tarikh-i Shibani*, fol. 119a).

from 1697 to 1702, during which a Chingizid, one of his grandsons, was reestablished at Balkh and its independent status reacknowledged.

The effects of these policies show up in the history of the 'Alid shrine and its endowments in the short term and played a major part in determining the way in which the shrine administration developed in the long run.

THE QA'ALKHAN PERIOD, 1683–1685

During the first period, Subhan Quli Khan experimented with what might be called a "subordinate heir-apparent policy." His eldest son, the twenty-nine-year-old Iskandar Sultan, a man characterized as never acting without his father's say-so,[10] was sent to Balkh in early 1683.[11]

Perhaps as early as the beginning of his khanate, or maybe even while he was still at Balkh, Subhan Quli had put his sons and potential Chingizid rivals under house arrest in the citadel or Arg in Balkh's inner city. The sources refer to this euphemistically as the "khalwat-saray" or "khalwat-kadah" (place of retreat or isolation). Why he should have left them there when he was in Bukhara is not at all clear. Perhaps it was more politic to keep them distant from the khanly throne at Bukhara and far removed from possible plots there. In any event, for at least the first five years of his khanate, his sons were in Balkh.

There, during the few years in which the khan tried to maintain a dependent sultan, it became customary for the amirs to "bring out" the new sultan from his incarceration and "seat him on the throne." In one source, the analogy of Joseph being brought out of prison by the Pharoah and placed in a position of high authority is used to emphasize what the writer wanted seen as a dramatic change in fortune for the sultan, one which the observer might even consider divinely ordained.[12]

Iskandar Sultan, Subhan Quli's first choice as his heir-apparent, died of food poisoning. In this case, the "king-poisoned-by-a-trusted-servant" story is used to explain the event. Those sources that point the finger of blame for instigating the act (servants generally are not seen to have sufficient motive themselves for such a crime) single out another son, Abu'l-Mansur Sultan, who happened to be incarcerated in the Arg. Iskandar

---

[10] *Tarikh-i Shibani*, fol. 116a.

[11] Thus ibid. and by inference Salim, fol. 299a, who says his rule lasted 299 days and ended on 1 Dhu'l-Hijjah 1094/21 November 1683. Muhammad Yusuf's typical imprecision is evident here. He states Iskandar Sultan was appointed in Rabi' al-Thani 1090 (*sic*) (May-June 1679) and governed "for three years" (Muhammad Yusuf Munshi 1956, 118). The Royal Asiatic Society manuscript (Morley 1854, No. 161) says "two years" (fol. 75a).

[12] Salim, fol. 300b, referring to Qur'an, Surah 12, verses 50 and following.

Sultan, like several other Balkh sovereigns, was buried at the 'Alid shrine.[13]

The story now becomes very convoluted. By force of circumstances, we are told, Subhan Quli felt compelled to name Abu'l-Mansur the "heir-apparent and deputy khan." But the same source then describes a super-seding yarligh (decree) from Subhan Quli naming another son, 'Ibad Allah Sultan, as qa'alkhan. However, this latter edict somehow fell into the hands of Abu'l-Mansur, who executed his would-be replacement.[14]

Abu'l-Mansur was a prince of a type quite different from Iskandar Sultan. Portrayed as both ambitious and something of a playboy, Abu'l-Mansur attracted immediate opposition. (The reader is clearly expected to find this figure reprehensible.) Haji Mir Muhammad Salim claims, somewhat improbably, that Abu'l-Mansur's profligacy and self-aggran-dizement led Subhan Quli to incite his own sister, Shamsah-i Banu Khanum, the wife of the Parsa'i shaykh 'Abd al-Wali, to concoct an assas-sination plot.[15] In one of the time-honored methods, she invited her nephew to dinner at her house in the Khwajah Parsa Quarter (near the site of the tomb and masjid of Abu Nasr Parsa in the center of present-day Balkh), and there unleashed the assassins on him on 2 May 1684.[16] The slightly later (by about ten years) anonymous author of *Tarikh-i Shi-bani* tones this down somewhat and has Abu'l-Mansur killed at his aunt's house, but places no onus for it on her. Muhammad Yusuf Munshi han-dles the incident in a similar manner.[17] One telling item, introduced without much fanfare by the former source, is that Abu'l-Mansur's mother was a Qalmaq and, as a result, Abu'l-Mansur favored the Qal-maqs over all others, much to the disgruntlement of the "Uzbeks."

The character of his successor, another brother, Siddiq Muhammad Sultan, is even more luridly portrayed. The anonymous author calls him a pederast: "He had Indian and Kafir slave boys to whom he devoted all his attention." One of these was particularly obnoxious, but he was so beloved by Siddiq Muhammad that he had the almond-shaped seal that was the khan's prerogative made for him.[18] If pedophilia were not suffi-ciently damning, Siddiq Muhammad is also portrayed as having an es-pecially sanguinary nature. This kind of depiction, like the one that por-trays Abu'l-Mansur as in thrall to his Qalmaq mother and overly solicitous of Qalmaq interests, is a device that helps rationalize the sub-sequent end.

[13] *Tarikh-i Shibani*, fol. 116a.
[14] Salim, fol. 300b.
[15] Ibid., fols. 300a–b.
[16] Ibid., fol. 299b.
[17] Muhammad Yusuf Munshi 1956, 120–21; *Tarikh-i Shibani*, fol. 116b.
[18] *Tarikh-i Shibani*, fol. 116b.

But the career of Siddiq Muhammad presents other, somewhat more credible, themes. Like Abu'l-Mansur before him, Siddiq Muhammad saw Balkh as an opportunity for political advancement, and with amirid support he began to act the way Balkh sovereigns had historically behaved. As soon as the khanly yarligh arrived anointing him qa'alkhan on 12 October 1684, he began to work to reestablish Balkh's historic independence. As a warning to potential enemies, he hunted down and executed his brother's assassins. The exercise of such political muscle (called by Haji Mir Muhammad Salim "ferocity and violence") was pleasing neither to the amirs nor to Subhan Quli, who still envisioned a dependent, subordinate qa'alkhan in Balkh. The written record suggests that three major Uzbek tribal groupings resisted Siddiq Muhammad when he began to make his intentions clear. They were the Turkman, the Ming, and the Qunghrat. The Ming, long established in the western part of the Balkh appanage, fortified themselves at Shibarghan and declared their independence of Balkh. Siddiq Muhammad immediately marched against them. Meanwhile the Alchin attacked Baba Shahu, seven miles east of Balkh and part of the waqf territories of the 'Alid shrine.[19] The purpose of the attack, we assume, was to oust Siddiq Muhammad. If so, it failed, and Siddiq Muhammad took the unusual step of massacring 400 Alchin— men, women, and children—after bringing them back to Balkh as prisoners.

Again, one needs to step back and place these accounts in the literary context. Iskandar Sultan was too ineffective, too much the pawn of his father; Abu'l-Mansur was a wastrel, a fratricide, and overly protective of the Qalmaq; Siddiq Muhammad was licentious and bloodthirsty, as well as disrespectful toward his religion (he expelled a well-regarded Dahpidi shaykh from Balkh and sacked his house).[20] Readers are thus prepared for the fates of these men well before the writer actually recounts them.

From the standpoint of the political stakes involved in the behavior of these figures, it is more credible to highlight as the cause of their downfall the uncooperative attitude displayed by at least the latter two toward Subhan Quli's unification policy. Add to that the alienation of some of the major tribal confederations at a time when the political power of the Tuqay-Timurid house was somewhat open to challenge, and one need look no further for the reasons for the reaction against them.

Siddiq Muhammad's tenure lasted a little more than a year. Subhan Quli, under pressure from his Uzbek supporters, finally took action to

---

[19] Salim, fol. 301a; Muhammad Yusuf Munshi 1956, 123.

[20] The attack on the Parsa'i shaykh reportedly stemmed from the fact that the shaykh's son, a leader of the tribal grouping called the Quramah, allegedly defamed Siddiq Muhammad before Subhan Quli Khan because of Siddiq Muhammad's refusal to assist the khan in a campaign against the Khwarazmians (Muhammad Amin, fol. 113b).

restore Balkh's dependent status. After a brief siege of the city, Siddiq Muhammad negotiated a surrender, but was then arrested and executed the same day (22 December 1685), along with his principal amirid supporters.[21] Only Muhammad Yusuf Munshi suggests (although the allusion may be merely metaphorical) that Siddiq Muhammad died of natural causes, from a "serious illness" that proved resistant to even the "best efforts of the physicians."[22]

THE ERA OF GOVERNORS, 1685–1697

Subhan Quli Khan now changed his Balkh policy. Rather than hope for a dutiful son to carry out his orders, he decided instead to remove the Chingizid element entirely from the city and diminish its symbolic value as the seat of the historically independent heir-apparent to the Bukharan khanly throne. So he collected the princes still incarcerated in the Arg and appointed an Uzbek amir to govern the city. The sources disagree on who the designated amir was. In the chronological order in which the various chronicles were composed, we find that the appointed governor was either Muhammad (Yar) Jan Bi Yuz,[23] Muhammad Khan Haji ataliq Yuz,[24] Mahmud Bi b. Beg Murad b. Shah Murad Qataghan,[25] or Imam Quli ataliq Kilchi, who died shortly thereafter and was succeeded by Khadim ataliq Ming, who was in turn succeeded by the above Muhammad (Yar) Jan Bi Yuz (but not until 1100, five years after Siddiq Muhammad's deposal).[26] Given the otherwise parallel treatment of events, the ascription of the governorship to such a disparate group—representing rival tribal groups (the Yuz, Qataghan, and Ming—suggests an adaptation of history to meet certain contemporary needs. It is difficult at this point to go beyond pointing out the discrepancies and suggesting their importance for understanding the historiography if not the history of the period.

As far as Subhan Quli's policies toward Balkh are concerned, the appointment of an Uzbek amir indicates a major departure from what was considered politically proper. Balkh, as everyone knew, was consecrated by history as a separate appanage, the seat not only of one of the Tuqay-Timurid sultans but also of the one expected to succeed in due course to the Bukharan khanate. It was therefore something of a sacred cow in Uzbek politics, and Subhan Quli's decision to reduce it to a mere governorship as the iqta' of one of his amirs was bound to have repercussions.

---

[21] Salim, fols. 302b–303a; Muhammad Amin, fols. 116b–121a. For a more detailed account, see Akhmedov 1982, 116–17.

[22] Muhammad Yusuf Munshi, fol. 84b; Muhammad Yusuf Munshi 1956, 128–29.

[23] Samandar Tirmidhi 1977, 121.

[24] Muhammad Yusuf Munshi, fol. 88a; Muhammad Yusuf Munshi 1956, 130.

[25] Salim, fol. 303a.

[26] *Tarikh-i Shibani*, fols. 117a–b.

For one thing, removing the Chingizid presence from Balkh intensified the phenomenon mentioned earlier of increasing Uzbek tribal identification with a particular area (e.g., the Qataghan with Badakhshan and the eastern parts of Balkh, the Ming with Shibarghan and the west, and the Alchin with the southern areas). Up to this point, the Tuqay-Timurid at Balkh had served to mediate and arbitrate the inevitable conflicts that arose over territorial rights as the process of territorial identification continued. This was especially true when that sultan by length of tenure had become adroit at mediating disputes. The recognition of Tuqay-Timurid paramountcy by the amirs was an essential ingredient of political stability at Balkh. With the appointment of an amir as final authority there, subordinate only to the khan in Bukhara, the situation was completely changed. If Balkh were to be converted from appanage to iqta', then it behooved every amir, or at least those with both ambition and adequate power, to try to be the one who held it.

Assuming that the discrepancies concerning the first amirid governor of Balkh implicitly reflect the inter-amirid struggles, then we understand better why the narrative accounts of the period 1686–1697 are so diverse. Although each of the sources on its own seems to tell a clear and straightforward story, when taken together the narrative is confused and in many ways impenetrable. In the notes, I have set out in brief the way in which each chronicle account presents the twelve-year period and the struggle for control of Balkh.[27] There are three related trends, however, that are

[27] The sources diverge considerably in reporting the decade beginning with the appointment of the amir Muhammad Yuz ataliq in 1686, and ending with Muhammad Muqim's appointment in 1697. According to Muhammad Yusuf Munshi, fols. 84a–112b, the chronology would be: Muharram 1097/January 1686: deposal of Siddiq Muhammad and appointment of Muhammad Haji Yuz ataliq in his place. 1098/1687?: the death of Khadim Bi and the appointment of Mahmud Bi Qataghan as governor of Balkh. Then a series of undated events—Subhan Quli Khan refuses a request for a Chingizid turah; the rise of the Quramah faction; Mahmud Bi Qataghan puts the Parsa'i shaykh (and a Chingizid through the maternal line) Salih Khwajah on the throne of Balkh; Salih Khwajah rules two and one-half years and is deposed; coup against Mahmud Bi Qataghan; and finally in 1697 the appointment of Muhammad Muqim.

Muhammad Amin, fols. 114a–161a, 169a–170b has the following chronology: 24 Muharram 1097/21 December 1685: Siddiq (Muhammad) Sultan is deposed (no successor mentioned). Rajab 1099/May 1688: Subhan Quli makes a second trip to Balkh, where he stays until 10 Dhu'l-Qa'dah 1099/6 September 1688 (again no Balkh ruler is mentioned, although an order to raise an army is addressed to Muhammad Sa'id Khwajah, the naqib). 23 Jumada al-Awwal 1104/29 January 1693: Subhan Quli Khan makes his third trip to Balkh (Mahmud Bi is in Qunduz) and appoints Yar Muhammad Ming as diwanbegi at Balkh before returning to Bukhara. 30 Rabi' al-Awwal 1105/5 December 1693: he appoints Mahmud Bi to govern Balkh. 1107/1695: the first appearance of the Quramah faction; their request for a Chingizid turah is turned down by Subhan Quli. 24 Shawwal 1107/27 May 1696: Mahmud Bi names Salih Khwajah as turah of Balkh. 27 Rabi' al-Thani 1107 (sic), i.e., 1108/24 December 1696: a Bukharan force led by Subhan Quli is unable to dislodge Mahmud Bi and Salih Khwajah and returns to Mawarannahr. 3 Rabi' al-Thani 1109/19 October 1697: Subhan Quli accedes to amirid requests and names Muhammad Muqim turah of Balkh.

discernible in the welter of contradictory data. One is the effort made by stronger amirs to increase the territorial range of their tribal group at the expense of weaker groups. The second trend (much more problematic because it is very uncertainly understood at this point) was the emergence of an alliance of smaller tribal groups under the name "Quramah" in confederation with non-Uzbek urban groups, perhaps Persian-speaking artisans and members of the Sufi orders like the Parsa'i.[28] The third trend, likewise a product of the aggressive behavior of the strongest tribal groups, was a growing sentiment that Balkh had to have a Chingizid "turah" or sovereign. This latter sentiment seems to have been held even by the most powerful amirs, such as Mahmud Beg Qataghan and Yar Muhammad Ming, who knew that the legitimacy issue could not otherwise be resolved.

THE ERA OF THE INDEPENDENT CHINGIZID TURAH, 1697–1702

Sometime in late 1696, Salih Khwajah, a nephew of the Bukharan khan, was placed in the nominal position of Chingizid turah of Balkh. It is not clear whether he was the choice of Mahmud Bi Qataghan or of Subhan Quli, for the sources all take very different approaches to him. His antecedents are of some interest in the context of Chingizid politics and no less so in the context of the political role of the Sufi orders in Balkh. He was a direct agnatic descendant of Khwajah Abu Nasr Parsa, a cult figure

---

Tarikh-i Shibani, fols. 117a–118b offers the following sequence: 1097/28 November 1685–16 November 1686: Subhan Quli appoints Imam Quli Kilchi ataliq as governor of Balkh; he soon dies and is replaced by Khadim Ming ataliq. 1099/7 November 1687–25 October 1688: Subhan Quli comes to Balkh, stays one year, and then returns to Bukhara. 1100/26 October 1688–14 October 1689: Khadim Ming ataliq dies and Balkh is awarded to Muhammad Jan Yuz ataliq. At the end of 1104/12 September 1692–1 September 1693 Muhammad Jan ataliq goes blind; Mahmud Bi, a parvanaji and the son of Beg Murad Beg Qataghan, is promoted to ataliq and given Balkh ("with the concurrence of the *nuyans*"). Mahmud Bi participates in the Khwarazmian campaign (circa 1105/2 September 1693–21 August 1694). 1106/22 August 1694–11 August 1695: he travels from Bukhara to Balkh. At the end of 1107/12 August 1695–30 July 1696, Mahmud Bi "on behalf of the turah" (here the term turah seems to point to its second meaning, Chingizid customary law) sacks the Inner City of Balkh and sets Salih Khwajah (Parsa'i) on the throne. 1108/31 July 1696–19 July 1697: Subhan Quli campaigns against Balkh with "200,000 horsemen"; he besieges Balkh and then returns to Bukhara after agreeing to send an heir-apparent or vice-khan (qa'alkhan). He then names Muhammad Muqim the turah and sends 'Adil Bi Ming as his ataliq from Bukhara; Mahmud Bi Qataghan withdraws from Balkh with Salih Khwajah, who goes into exile in India.

Salim, fols. 314b–317b has an abbreviated version: After Siddiq Muhammad appoints Mahmud Bi (in 1097), other amirs appeal to Subhan Quli, who comes to Balkh (at an unspecified date) and installs Salih Khwajah on the throne. Mahmud Bi, then in Qunduz, returns to Balkh, seizes the citadel, and sets himself up as Salih Khwajah's protector. He later exiles Salih Khwajah to India, and on 1 Jumada al-Thani 1109/15 December 1697 Subhan Quli appoints Muhammad Muqim as turah at Balkh.

28 Barthold 1981.

of great importance in Balkh. Some indication of the force of his cult over time is the survival of his tombsite (built in the fifteenth and rebuilt in the sixteenth century) when virtually every other major monument in Balkh succumbed to the ravages of time and deurbanization. The family itself had held the office of naqib of Balkh for more than two centuries.

Salih Khwajah's father had married Shamsah-i Banu Khanum, Subhan Quli's sister, whence came the purported Chingizid connection. Shamsah-i Banu Khanum was a prominent player in the politics of the era. It was at her house and perhaps with her connivance, as one source asserts, that an earlier Tuqay-Timurid sultan, Abu'l-Mansur, had been assassinated. And in this instance she may have been actively promoting the candidacy of her son.

The appointment of the Parsa'i scion as the Chingizid representative, no matter who or what lay behind it, indicates a compromise between Subhan Quli's desire to change Balkh's status as an appanage and the amirs' demands for a Chingizid sovereign. Chingizid political ideology, however, generally did not admit the legitimacy of cognatic descent, and Salih Khwajah's elevation was not widely recognized. To us it is important mainly as a symbol of the struggle going on over Balkh's status. The episode also reveals how closely the shaykhly families were involved with political issues.

In 1697, Subhan Quli finally acceded to amirid demands and named a grandson, Muhammad Muqim, a son of Iskandar Sultan, the first of the ill-fated successors to Subhan Quli in Balkh, as Chingizid turah. Although the khan passed over two of his sons, 'Ubayd Allah and Abu'l-Fayd, and still may have been trying to salvage something from his now-discredited policy of making Balkh an amirid governorate, in fact the appointment of Muhammad Muqim was a reversion to long-standing practice. Balkh once more had a genuine Chingizid turah and, as was to be expected, he quickly reverted to type in his relations with the khan at Bukhara.

It is not overly simplistic to see in Subhan Quli's appointment of Muhammad Muqim an abandonment of the hope of consolidating and centralizing the Tuqay-Timurid territories. Such policies ran counter to what was considered by the amirs to be yasa-approved and eventually foundered on their opposition.

It is difficult to assess the effect on events after the khan's death in 1702 of this return to what was yasa-sanctioned in Balkh. There is little basis for assuming that supplanting the Chingizid tradition and substantially modifying the yasa sanction would have precluded the political struggles of the first decade of the eighteenth century. Much of the drama of the last decade of the seventeenth century would be replayed in the decade after Subhan Quli's death. Amirid power, a weakened Tuqay-Timurid family, and the continuing adherence to the yasa and what it approved, all shaped politics after Subhan Quli's death as they had before.

What was different about the latter part of the seventeenth century and very first part of the eighteenth century was the lack of the kind of political balance that had existed during much of the previous century. If one looks back as far as the early Shibanid period, when the Jani-Begid Kistan Qara held Balkh as his appanage, and traces the history of the region to the beginning of the eighteenth century, what strikes one are the long periods of tenure by strong sultans in Balkh contemporary with the rule of equally strong khans in Bukhara. After Subhan Quli ascended the Bukharan khanly throne, no comparably powerful Tuqay-Timurid figure ever again emerged in Balkh. As a consequence, power was increasingly assumed by amirid figures who, in the absence of a powerful arbiter, had to resort to military contests to settle conflicts.

All this impinged on the operation of the 'Alid shrine and its waqf and has a direct bearing on the institutions that were developed to protect shrine and waqf prerogatives. In Balkh the position of Muhammad Muqim was considerably bolstered by a temporary resolution of the decade-long conflict between the Qataghan amir, Mahmud Bi, on one side and the Quramah confederation and the Ming amirs on the other. The conflict more or less represented the breakup of the Balkh appanage into three distinct polities—the Qataghan territory in the east, the Ming in the west, and Balkh proper in the center, alternately dominated by Yuz, Quramah, Qataghan, and Ming. Balkh was the prize for the now more or less autonomous regions centered on Shibarghan in the west and Qunduz in the east. Just as Bukhara had long been the symbol of ultimate authority in Mawarannahr, Balkh too had come to be seen as the capital city, control of which was the goal for anyone with political ambitions. When Muhammad Muqim arrived in Balkh from Bukhara in the autumn of 1697, Mahmud Bi retired to Qunduz. The principal amirid parties at Balkh were now made up of the Ming ('Adil Bi Ming was Muhammad Muqim's first ataliq)[29] and the Quramah (Shah Niyaz Bi was the first diwanbegi).[30]

Within a year Mahmud Bi attempted to reestablish his influence in Balkh. Before dealing with this, it is again worth reminding ourselves of the tendentious nature of the chronicle sources we have. Muhammad Yusuf Munshi wrote for Muhammad Muqim and tells his story accordingly. In contrast, the anonymous author of *Tarikh-i Shibani Khan*—who had a very low opinion of Muhammad Muqim, calling him "a man void of courage, inclined to foolish behavior, lewd with women, and addicted to drink"—saw things somewhat differently.[31] When the issue of Muham-

[29] Muhammad Amin, fol. 169b.
[30] Ibid.
[31] *Tarikh-i Shibani*, fol. 118b.

mad Muqim's rights arise, the two works usually adopt diametrically opposed views. What we do find in them, even though the accuracy of their facts is often open to doubt, is a sense of what the conflicts were about as well as the claims on either side.

Mahmud Bi's efforts to bring Balkh back under Qataghan dominion were aided by problems in the Quramah-Ming coalition. Two other tribal groups, the Durman and the Qipchaq, the latter a new and growing power in the area, are depicted as resenting the power the coalition had over Muhammad Muqim, and so declared their support for Mahmud Bi. Just then Shah Niyaz Bi, the diwanbegi and a leader of the Quramah, died, and, for reasons that are not particularly clear, his colleague, the Ming amir and ataliq to Muhammad Muqim, left Balkh for his iqta' in Shibarghan.[32]

Without having to face a military test, Mahmud Bi returned to Balkh and set himself up as Muhammad Muqim's protector. Not long after (the chronology here is still not established), Subhan Quli Khan died. The seating of Muhammad Muqim at Balkh, the conflict between the Quramah-Ming coalition and the Qipchaq and Durman, the death of Shah Niyaz and the consequent collapse of the coalition, Mahmud Bi's return to Balkh, and Subhan Quli's death all took place within a period of about five years (between October 1697 and October 1702) and in that order, but the intervals between these events are unknown.[33]

RIVAL KHANATES

The death of the khan ended an era. Subhan Quli was the last Bukharan ruler to have served an apprenticeship at Balkh, and his own efforts to

[32] Muhammad Yusuf Munshi, fols. 115a, 118b. Muhammad Ya'qub, writing in 1240/1824–1825, says Muhammad Muqim was "vexed by 'Adil Bi and sent him to Shibarghan."

[33] According to Muhammad Yusuf Munshi, fol. 120a, he died on 1 Rabi' al-Thani 1114/25 August 1702. But Semenov, in a note to his translation of Muhammad Amin's 'Ubayd Allah Namah, p. 46, says that Muhammad Yusuf Munshi, in Tarikh-i Muqim Khani (which he also translated), gives a date of 21 Rabi' al-Thani 1114/14 September 1702. Complicating this is the information in the translation of the 'Ubayd Allah Namah itself (also p. 46) that 'Ubayd Allah, son and successor to Subhan Quli, had already taken the throne at Bukhara and was planning to campaign against Balkh at the very beginning of 1114/c. May-June 1702. Salim, fol. 318a also dates the death at 1 Rabi' al-Thani 1114/25 August 1702. Tarikh-i Shibani, fol. 118b says Subhan Quli died in 1113, but this does not seem likely. I have accepted the date as Sunday, 24 Jumada al-Awwal 1114/16 October 1702 following Muhammad Ya'qub. In the margin of Muhammad Ya'qub, fol. 132a is this attestation (perhaps by the author): "I have seen it written in the hand of Hadrat-i Mawla-yi Sharif [a contemporary of Subhan Quli, for whom see Tarikh-i Shibani, fol. 119a] that Subhan Quli Khan died in 1114 on Sunday, the 24th of Jumada al-Awwal and on Monday he was buried in the furaq [or quruq?] of the Mazar-i Fayd Anwar [i.e., the shrine of Baha al-Din Naqshband east of Bukhara, site of the tomb of one of his wives, among other relatives]."

reduce Balkh's status as an appanage center were largely responsible. Partly as a result, none of his successors had much opportunity to acquire political experience before being thrust into the khanate. As amirid power became more and more decisive in the choice and policies of the khans, that trend continued.

On 17 October 1702, 'Ubayd Allah b. Subhan Quli was named khan at Bukhara.[34] His enthronement, like that of his father's, was carried out "in accordance with the code of Chingiz Khan and according to the custom of Oguz Khan."[35] He sat on a piece of white felt and four amirs from four of the leading Uzbek tribes lifted him up and placed him on the throne.[36] One day later, at Balkh, Muhammad Muqim Sultan was also "seated on the khanly throne,"[37] and for the first time in the 103-year history of the Tuqay-Timurid state, Balkh and Bukhara were now the seats of rival claimants to the Chingizid khanate, a reflection of the divisions within the khanly house and among its diverse and increasingly interventionist amirs.

'Ubayd Allah and his backers justified his assumption of the khanate on the grounds that he was the eldest surviving son of Subhan Quli. Muhammad Muqim, on the other hand, also appears to have laid claim to the khanate on the basis of seniority in the ruling clan. He was the son of Subhan Quli's eldest son, Iskandar Sultan, and it is quite possible that he indeed was older than 'Ubayd Allah.[38] The issue of the old appanage rights now also reappeared when Asad Allah Sultan, a brother of 'Ubayd Allah, reportedly demanded of the new Bukharan khan that he divide the state as it had been divided under the two brothers 'Abd al-'Aziz and Subhan Quli. He claimed the appanage of Balkh and half the treasury as his fair share "to accord with the Shari'ah."[39]

Muhammad Muqim, or his chronicler, also tries to inject a Shari'ah issue by declaring that it was Subhan Quli's *wasiyah* (testament) that he, Muhammad Muqim, as eldest Tuqay-Timurid and therefore legitimate

[34] According to every manuscript of the *'Ubayd Allah Namah* seen by Semenov, the date of the enthronement was 25 Jumada al-Awwal 1116/25 September 1704. But he believes that the text should be read 1114 rather than 1116.

[35] Muhammad Amin 1957, 23. The Persian text is unavailable to me, but there is some likelihood that Semenov's "ulozhenie i obychai" is a translation of the Persian "yasa wa yusun."

[36] Muhammad Amin does not identify the amirs or their tribal groups.

[37] Muhammad Yusuf Munshi, fol. 132a.

[38] Muhammad Yusuf Munshi is a very tendentious source, but there is other evidence that 'Ubayd Allah might not have been the senior clan member. *Tarikh-i Shibani*, for example, written in early 1722 (fol. 123a says, "today is 1 Jumada al-Thani 1134[/17 February 1722]") never mentions 'Ubayd Allah's name, despite the detail that it provides concerning the Balkh amirs' requests for a Chingizid ruler there.

[39] Muhammad Amin 1957, 29.

successor, was to be the new khan and 'Ubayd Allah was only to act as caretaker until Muhammad Muqim could arrive from Balkh. The likelihood that this was only propaganda is suggested by the fact that Muhammad Muqim made no recorded effort to go to Bukhara.

In any event it was 'Ubayd Allah and his amirs who took the first step to eliminate the rival khanate. Mir Muhammad Amin Bukhari, the author of the *'Ubayd Allah Namah*, depicts 'Ubayd Allah facing numerous objections from his amirs against going to war with Muhammad Muqim but shrewdly manipulating them into consenting to participate in a campaign against Balkh.[40] Perhaps this was indeed the case. But certainly the amirs of Mawarannahr had as much, if not more, to lose by a strong unchallenged khanate in Balkh. The most direct threat was Mahmud Bi Qataghan, a man of undisputed political and military skill who had made himself the principle amirid force since succeeding the Ming-Quramah coalition in Balkh. Since the establishment of the khanate of Muhammad Muqim, his protégé, Mahmud Bi Qataghan had been successfully establishing Balkh's authority on the north bank, the Bukharan side, of the Amu Darya. He had made noticeable progress in obtaining the support of the Qunghrat around Tirmidh, the coalition called the "Ung wa Sul" (right and left wing)[41] Uzbeks near Shahr-i Sabz and along the right (north) bank of the Amu Darya, the Durman at Qubadyan, and certain Yuz groups in the vicinity of Hisar-i Shadman. Such activity was a threat to at least some of the amirs of Mawarannahr.

MAHMUD BI QATAGHAN'S CHALLENGE TO THE CHINGIZID SYSTEM

Circumstances changed completely when Muhammad Muqim, Mahmud Bi's pretext for exercising power, was killed in early 1707[42] and the nature

[40] Ibid., pp. 44ff., 59ff., 87ff., 113ff.

[41] Semenov (Muhammad Amin 1957, 49, note) explains the name "ung wa sul" Uzbeks as follows: "It is well known that Uzbeks were divided into two groups: the tribes of the so-called 'left side' [sul] had the most privileged place of power, for the heart is on man's left side. The tribes of the 'right side' [ung] held second place. At this time the center of these tribes [the "ung and sul" presumably] was the Shahr-i Sabz region." The use of the term *ung wa sul*—which was traditionally used in reference to the right and left wings of an army in battle formation (Doerfer 1963, 2:165–66, 3:302–3) and then, by extension, to those tribes associated in some way with one or the other wing—does not appear in Mawarannahrid sources until the early eighteenth century as a name for certain tribal groups in specific regions. It is interesting to note that two of the Ming amirs who made waqfs for the 'Alid shrine were designated "Ming Ung" (Ming of the Right Wing)—whether to indicate the traditional Ming position or to imply the existence of Ming in the left wing is not clear.

[42] Muhammad Amin 1957, 101–2. Muhammad Yusuf Munshi, fol. 168b ends his narrative on 27 Sha'ban 1116 (Christmas Day 1704), so the main source for the death of Muhammad Muqim becomes the equally partisan (but on 'Ubayd Allah's behalf) Mir Muhammad Amin. He in turn lays the blame for Muhammad Muqim's murder at the feet of Mahmud Bi (as

of the Balkh-Bukhara contest was altered. 'Ubayd Allah became the only significant member of the Tuqay-Timurid house (Abu'l-Fayd, his brother, was only twelve years old and under khanly and amirid watch in Bukhara). Resistance to 'Ubayd Allah's khanly rights by Mahmud Bi could not be justified under the yasa sanction. So when Mahmud Bi refused to acknowledge the Bukharan khan's sovereignty after his protégé's death, and even, we are told, took the unprecedented and anti-yasa step of calling himself Mahmud Bahadur Khan,[43] many of the Uzbek supporters of Muhammad Muqim, who had accepted Mahmud Bi's leading role during the sultan's lifetime, now offered 'Ubayd Allah Khan their assistance against Balkh. Or so 'Ubayd Allah's court chronicler tells us.[44]

Mahmud Bi was driven from Balkh in May 1707, not long after the murder of Muhammad Muqim. To some extent, the death of the Chingizid and the fall of Mahmud Bi marked the end of the relationship of equality and rivalry that had existed between Balkh and Bukhara for more than a century. Administrative control of Balkh was at first established at Bukhara.[45] The supporters of Mahmud Bi were purged and the appanage was distributed among amirs loyal to 'Ubayd Allah. But the divisible territory was not the same as the appanage of the seventeenth century. 'Ubayd Allah had no influence either in the eastern part of the former appanage, Mahmud Bi's Qataghan stronghold, or in the Ming territory in the west. Moreover, the nature of the tiger now ridden by 'Ubayd Allah Khan precluded any possibility of centralizing administrative authority at Bukhara. The amirs who disposed of real political power still saw the appanage system, the yasa-sanctioned state, as viable and renewable.

There are obvious parallels between political conditions in Mawarannahr and Balkh at the end of the sixteenth century and those at the beginning of the eighteenth. In both periods persistent attacks on the appanage system had weakened the ruling Chingizid clan. But unlike conditions at the end of the sixteenth century, there were two new and decisive factors in the politics of the early eighteenth century. In the first place, there was no new dynamic Chingizid house ready to lay claim to the khaniyat and to prove its worthiness. In the second place, the latter part of the seventeenth century had seen the emergence of what were in

---

does Muhammad Ya'qub, fol. 132a), without offering a motive. The hostility between 'Ubayd Allah Khan and Muhammad Muqim must have abated at times, at least for official reasons, for one of the confirmation decrees issued on behalf of the 'Alid shrine's waqfs bears the seals and names of both men, with both having the suffixed title "Bahadur Khan" (*TMS*, 51 [text], 68 [transcription]).

[43] *Tarikh-i Shibani*, fol. 119b; Muhammad Ya'qub, fol. 132a.
[44] Muhammad Amin 1957, 109.
[45] Ibid., 143.

reality small independent amirid states. Their sovereigns may have believed they were part of a greater appanage based on loyalty to the khan, but in fact circumstances had made them territorially distinct, administratively autonomous, and subject to tribal succession. The Ming in Shibarghan, the Mangghit in Khujand, the Qataghan in Qunduz, and the Alchin in Kahmard had all by the early eighteenth century acquired a very different sense than their grandfathers and great-grandfathers had had of what their territory meant.

These new conditions—the absence of a dynamic new Chingizid house waiting in the wings as the Tuqay-Timurids had waited in Khurasan and Sistan, and the de facto subdivision of Balkh and Mawarannahr into amirid principalities—made the political situation far less susceptible to internal reorganization.

At Balkh, 'Ubayd Allah Khan's efforts to annex the region to Bukhara were stymied.[46] Mahmud Bi Qataghan, muting any claims to the khanate for the time being, had recovered sufficiently within two years to pose a direct military threat to the Ming amirs who were preeminent at Balkh after the 1707 conquest. The Quramah coalition, now led by Muhammad Sa'id Khwajah naqib, the Parsa'i shaykh, had made overtures to Mahmud Bi, its former enemy. Even the Ming under 'Adil Bi ataliq, who held Balkh in the name of 'Ubayd Allah Khan, showed increasing independence in the face of the popular antipathy felt toward Bukharans. An incident that happened to a Bukharan bureaucrat, a khwajah appointed to the post of market inspector (ra'is) in Balkh, illustrates the depth of the popular sentiment with which politicians had to contend.

The Bukharan khwajah rode into Balkh and asked to be directed to the headquarters of 'Adil Bi Ming. Outside the house, "a group of impudent and cheeky youths" dragged the khwajah off his horse, tore his saddle apart, and showered him with abuse. He then made his way back to Bukhara and complained to the khan, who demanded, but did not get, satisfaction from 'Adil Bi.[47] Over the strenuous objections of his amirs, 'Ubayd Allah tried to organize a punitive campaign against Balkh for this insult. Instead a conspiracy led to his assassination and the enthronement of his sixteen-year-old brother, Abu'l-Fayd, in March 1711.[48]

The next few decades witnessed the substantial growth of amirid power. The presence of a Chingizid on the khanly throne remained essential to the conduct of yasa-sanctioned politics, and the amirs went to great lengths to insure that such a condition was fulfilled. It is not partic-

[46] The politics of city and appanage are detailed by Muhammad Amin 1957, 191ff. for the period after 'Ubayd Allah Khan's return to Bukhara.

[47] Ibid., 199–200.

[48] Ibid., 250; Tarikh-i Shibani, fol. 120a has 1122/2 March 1710–18 February 1711; Muhammad Ya'qub, 132b says 1123/19 February 1711–8 February 1712.

ularly illuminating to refer to the men they installed as mere figureheads, although in some cases they may have been no more than that. Being khan always presented an opportunity for acquiring real political power. But with amirid ideas of what constituted their proper political role gradually changing from one of existence within the framework of loyalty to the person of the khan to one of territorial associations, in which the rights of the tribal organization to a particular piece of land came first and the khan became a legitimizing symbol of those rights, it became more and more difficult for a khan to exercise power. What constituted the exercise of power was embodied, from a literary standpoint, in the phrase "removing and appointing" ('azl wa nasb). A khan who could "remove and appoint" by definition exercised political power. The more extensive the ability and the greater the discretionary right, the greater the power. But in the early eighteenth century, exercising the removal and appointment powers meant negotiating first with the considerable power of the Uzbek amirs. Abu'l-Fayd is described by a contemporary living in India as "a person of capability, courage, and learning, struggling against the tyranny of the Uzbeks."[49] In that sentence both the opportunities for and the obstacles to a Chingizid sovereign are revealed.

THE REAFFIRMATION OF THE CHINGIZID WAY, 1711–1738

The presence of a Chingizid khan was essential to the idea of what constituted yasa-sanctioned government. In Balkh we see just how far, literally, the amirs would go to assure the presence of a Chingizid. Soon after the death of 'Ubayd Allah Khan, the amirs of Balkh, led by the Ming amir, 'Adil Bi ataliq, sought to find another Chingizid turah who could be "raised up." The only ones to be found, or more precisely, the only ones available with the necessary qualifications, were living in Herat. They were descendants of Wali Muhammad Khan (d. 1610), whose son, Rustam, after unsuccessfully trying to reestablish the Walid line as khans of Mawarannahr and Balkh in the second decade of the seventeenth century, had retired to exile in Herat. After negotiating with the Safawid shah, a number of amirs went from Balkh to escort 'Ibad Allah Sultan and his two sons Jahangir and Sanjar back to their "patrimonial lands" after an absence of "101 years."[50] They reached Balkh sometime in 1711.

'Ibad Allah is praised for trying to make life easy for the people of Balkh. Neither he nor his first son, Jahangir (who succeeded him), lasted very long. In 1713, after 'Ibad Allah had served for seventeen months and his son apparently only a few days, Sanjar Sultan took the Balkh

---

[49] *Tarikh-i Shibani*, fol. 120b.

[50] The story of the reestablishment of the Walid line of the Tuqay-Timurids in Balkh is found in *Tarikh-i Shibani*, fols. 120b–122a and Muhammad Ya'qub, fol. 132b.

throne. During his five years in office, one of the most powerful political figures of the time, Mahmud Bi Qataghan, died in Ishkashm, Badakhshan, when a house he was staying in collapsed during an earthquake in A.H. 1126/A.D. 1714. It was an appropriate end for the man who had produced such upheaval in Balkh's politics since the late 1690s.

Sanjar Sultan is characterized as "a debauchee and a voluptuary," and as a result, "the Uzbeks [i.e., the amirs] had all affairs under their control."[51] In 1129/1717, after returning from hunting in the Darrah-i Juz, he was murdered by one of his own officials (a diwan named Mirza Kulli), who was reportedly enraged by his wife's liaison with the Chingizid.[52]

The death of Sanjar left Balkh with no Chingizid, and again a delegation went to Herat, where, "after much effort," they managed to find and bring back another Walid, Muhammad Sultan, who was placed on the throne in 1130/1717–1718. What little light is shed on amirid politics in Balkh at this time shows that the leading tribal groups were the Qipchaq around Balkh and the Qataghan and Ming in the east and west, respectively. In the *Tarikh-i Shibani Khan*'s account of Muhammad Sultan's efforts to revive Chingizid power, the Qipchaq are cited as the main obstacle. Other groups whom he reportedly was compelled to suppress were the Qanqli and Qa'at, both of whom are described as allies of the Qipchaq and opponents of the Ming.

The problems created by Muhammad Sultan led to his deposal by the Qipchaq, who then placed 'Arab Muhammad Sultan on the throne. Although he was presumably a Chingizid, his lineage is actually unknown. Neither in the chronicle nor on his signet ring is his patronymic given, which is somewhat unusual. His enthronement took place in June-July 1720. As a result of it, "the Uzbeks fought with the Qanqli ulus, were defeated, and were thrown out of the court. They then settled in Aybek."[53] The "Uzbeks" referred to here are probably the Qataghan.

'Arab Muhammad is the last of the Chingizid sultans for whom the chronicles give any information. The waqf reviews, on the other hand, show that 'Arab Muhammad, who was still in power in Balkh as late as 1730–1731, was succeeded by two more Chingizids, perhaps Tuqay-Timurids. The first was Chingiz Muhammad, whose review of the waqf is dated 1736–1737, and the second, Abu'l-Hasan, who reviewed the waqf in 1737–1738.[54]

All of these men were styled "khan" (more precisely "Bahadur Khan") on their signet rings, and certainly from 1710 or so onward Balkh was considered by all parties as an autonomous region, fully independent of

[51] *Tarikh-i Shibani*, fol. 121a.
[52] Ibid.
[53] Ibid.
[54] *TMS*, 53–54 (text), 70–71 (transcription).

Bukhara. Virtually no diplomatic correspondence between the two regions nor evidence of mutual policies survives after 'Ubayd Allah Khan.

A new order had now emerged in the politics of Mawarannahr and Balkh. By the early eighteenth century, the khanate as a forceful institution had vanished, but its shell remained as a symbol of political ideals. Independent amirid political organizations centered in small cities and towns now emerged to exercise real authority while the great appanage organism of Balkh disappeared.

For the 'Alid shrine, these developments were to have an enormous and visible impact. Hardly any information at all exists about the shrine itself for the period after Subhan Quli left Balkh for Bukhara (i.e., after 1681), and we have to extract whatever data there are from the waqf material. But the waqf documents are mostly of an administrative character. About the shrine grounds and buildings we have only one piece of data, but it is of special interest not only for the information it offers but for the way in which it is presented and what it is meant to convey to the reader. Near the end of Muhammad Yusuf Munshi's work, there is a four-page chapter on Muhammad Muqim's rebuilding of the khanaqah attributed to Sultan Husayn Mirza Bayqara at the shrine. The khanaqah's main dome had collapsed in an earthquake, and in 1704–1705 Muhammad Muqim decided to rebuild it. The project was assigned to Khwajah Faqir diwanbegi and completed "in a short time."[55] So much for the "hard" information contained in the four pages. The rest comprises Qur'anic quotations, poetry, and the traditional long modifying phrases prefixed and suffixed to the names of both Muhammad Muqim, the patron, and the saintly figure for whom the shrine had been built, 'Ali b. Abi Talib. Phrases like

> his holiness, monarch of the saints, proof of the pious, embodiment of the pith of the Qur'anic verse "Has there come on man a while of time when he was a thing unremembered" [76:1] and the precise meaning of the expression "There is no hero . . ." [i.e., "There is no hero other than 'Ali and no sword but Zul-fiqar"]

> VERSES
> "Sun of the saints, pearl of the sea of the expression
> " 'There is no hero . . .' "

> Glory of the family of the Chosen One, corresponding precisely to the exact sense of "has there come on man a while of time . . . commander of the faithful, imam of the devout, the victorious lion of God, 'Ali b. Abi Talib—May God ennoble his face! . . ."

---

[55] Muhammad Yusuf Munshi, fols. 165a–b; Muhammad Yusuf Munshi, 1956, 225–29.

all serve to set off the object, like a Persian miniature in which a sumptuous palace or a richly figured carpet provides the appropriate setting for a king.

Work on the khanaqah gave Muhammad Muqim two opportunities for self-promotion. One was the actual building itself, whereby he placed himself squarely in the approved role of ruler-patron or politician-builder. (This is the only recorded instance of monument-building by him.) The second opportunity it presented was the literary one: to mount, display, and preserve the act in a way that would carry to its readers a sense of his fidelity to the 'Alid cult and thus by extension to the Family of the Prophet, the personifications of the true religion.

Rebuilding the khanaqah probably had other levels of meaning as well. It was a gesture to the shrine administrators and it was a monument to posterity, besides which it provided work for the local building trades.

The reconstruction of its dome was the last building done at the shrine by Tuqay-Timurids, as far as we know. It would be another century and a half before major new donations of capital for construction at the shrine would be made by the authorities at Balkh.

CHAPTER EIGHT

The Waqf Administration, 1668–1738

POLITICAL AND JUDICIAL REVIEW

During the seventy years after Subhan Quli issued his manshur-decree on the rights of the waqf administration, officials at Balkh periodically reviewed the waqf decree. The reviews were generally of two types. In one, the reviewing official simply stamped his seal on the document, either below or beside the place where Subhan Quli had affixed his seal. There are some one hundred and twenty seal impressions in addition to the Chingizid seals visible on the facsimile published by Hafiz Nur Muhammad, of which he deciphered eighteen.

Some of these imprints were probably made by witnesses at the time Subhan Quli sealed the document. For the rest, we assume that, at times of administrative change or at other moments when the mutawalli felt such an act was worthwhile, he would have gone to the official he believed was the appropriate authority and sought by seal a reconfirmation of the waqf rights set out in the manshur and, later, in its annexes.

The second type of review was the annex issued by a new ruler at Balkh. The annexes not only help us follow changes to the waqf, as new prerogatives are mentioned and new mutawallis appear, but they also corroborate or revise information found in other sources or provide entirely new information about political changes in Balkh. As was stated earlier, it was usual for the mutawalli to solicit a restatement of his rights from the political authorities soon after a new political administration was installed. The annexes shed new light on who was recognized as supreme political authority in Balkh and when changes actually occurred.

Seal evidence shows that the waqf came under review within a few years of the issuance of the manshur. Two qadi-judges, 'Abd al-Latif b. Khwajah 'Abd Allah and Muhammad 'Iwad b. Muhammad Yusuf, whose official seals both bore the date A.H. 1082/A.D. 1671–1672, reviewed, and affirmed the terms of the manshur.[1] The date on their seals establishes the *terminus a quo* for the review. Whether the seal date represented the year in which the officeholder was appointed, the year in which the seal was cast, or the year in which the document received the imprint (which would signify, somewhat improbably, a new seal every year) is not certain. These, of course, are not necessarily mutually exclusive con-

---

[1] Muhammad Amin, fol. 167a; Muhammad Amin 1957, 301. Both mention a Qadi 'Abd Allah, who had studied in Balkh under Qadi Abu Nasr.

ditions. The Tuqay-Timurid reviews of the waqf that took place in the eighteenth century have seal dates that are especially difficult to explain. We will leave the discussion of some of those difficulties until later, but draw attention here only to one particularly problematic seal date, that of Chingiz Muhammad Bahadur Khan, the penultimate Tuqay-Timurid to review the waqf. The review itself is legibly dated 1149 (six years after the previous review) and the seal date is read by the editor of *TMS* as 1142.[2] (That date cannot be read from the published facsimile of the document, however.) If the review of his predecessor, dated 1143, tells us that 'Arab Muhammad Bahadur Khan was then the Balkh sovereign, what does the date 1142 mean on a seal that calls Chingiz Muhammad "Bahadur Khan"? The most reasonable explanation would seem to be that the editor misread the seal date. But there may be a completely different reason for which we have no information at all. In any case, concerning the seal dates of the qadi reviews, it is probably only safe to say that a seal of a certain date was applied to a document no earlier than that date.[3]

What were some of the conditions under which the qadi would have put his seal to the document? One might have been when witnessing the document on behalf of its author. One undated seal, that of Qadi Abu Nasr b. Mawlana Hasan, was probably just that. He was a man known to have lived in Balkh and to have held the office of qadi while Subhan Quli reigned there.[4]

Another case in which a qadi's attestation might have been sought would be if a dispute arose over the terms of the waqf. In such a case one would expect the dispute and its resolution or postponement to have been registered by iqrar in a court register. A separate copy would then have been taken by the affected parties. Obviously, a dispute of any complexity could not be noted on the manshur. Nor would it have been procedurally correct to do so. But the qadi's seal there and on the accompanying iqrar might have testified that the two documents were related. Finally, occasions when the qadiship changed hands might well have been a time to bring the documents in for review and the seal of the new qadi.

About twenty years after its original issuance, in 1107/1695–1696 (the seal date), the manshur was again submitted to a qadi, in this case the chief qadi (*aqda al-qudat, qadi al-qudat*), Mir Sayyid Sharif b. Qadi 'Abd al-Fattah al-'Alawi, and he too put his seal to the document. It is worth noting that this period was one of considerable political upheaval in Balkh

[2] *TMS*, 55 (text), 71 (transcription).

[3] *TMS*, 67–68 (transcription). The quality of the photoreproduction is too poor to read the seal impressions. Neither Deny 1913–36; Allan 1978; Busse 1959, 47–58; Minorsky 1943, 197–203; nor Rabino 1945 offer an answer to the problem. In what follows I have used the dates only as a means of showing the relative times of the reviews.

[4] Muhammad Amin, fol. 167a; Muhammad Amin 1957, 301.

(see chapter 7) involving Subhan Quli's unsuccessful attempt to make Balkh a governorate. But as we have no way of knowing how long after 1107 the qadi reviewed the manshur, it is difficult to link the review directly to political conditions.

Qadi review of the waqf is a part of normal legal procedure, and therefore finding evidence of it does not surprise us. Somewhat unexpected and therefore more interesting is the seal evidence for non-qadi reviews. Of the eighteen seals that Hafiz Nur Muhammad managed to decipher, three were those of diwanbegis, one belonged to an ataliq, and one simply bore the title bi. These seals raise a number of questions about de jure and de facto jurisdiction in cases of waqf review and about the relations between the waqf administrators and the officials of the state. For instance, was review by an Uzbek amir part of the normal judicial process of review or does it reflect a temporary state of affairs? Were qadis consulted simply as a pro forma gesture or does the presence of their seal impressions testify to the regulatory power of the office at the time the seal was affixed?

The seals cover a period of more than one hundred years, assuming the dates have been correctly read. The earliest date is 1082/1671–1672, while the latest decipherable seal date is 1191/1777–1778. There is no pattern visible here that hints of a shift from qadi-court review to amirid review. The two latest seals are those of Qadi Ghulam Mirza Shah b. Qadi Mirza Kalan (1181/1767–1768) and Muhammad Shah ataliq b. Muhammad Aman Bi (1191/1777–1778).

It may well have been the case that a cautious mutawalli sought confirmation by seal from whoever appeared to be in a position to affect the waqf prerogatives of the shrine. As representative of the law, the qadi was of course a party to the document's attestation. But at the same time, it was apparently prudent to solicit approval from the leading amirs as well. Without deciphering the full complement of seals, it cannot be said with absolute certainty that those amirs who set their seals to the manshur were the leading political figures of their time. In one case, and one case only, can we identify the seal of a top politician, that of Khushhal Bi diwanbegi, the son of Muhammad (Yar) ataliq Ming, who is also mentioned in the manshur itself as holder of Yali Tapah, a village in which part of the shrine's waqf properties were located. During 'Ubayd Allah's khanate (1702–1711), he was a leader of the Ming in control of Balkh.[5]

The deciphered seals also yield enough sociological information to make one wish even more that the rest had been read and transcribed. Four of the eighteen deciphered seals belonged to two lineages. As mentioned previously, Qadi Abu Nasr b. Mawlana Hasan, a contemporary of

[5] Muhammad Amin 1957, 204–5.

Subhan Quli while he was in Balkh, sealed the document. Sometime later, his son, Qadi Mirza Khan b. Qadi Abu Nasr b. Mawlana Hasan, also stamped the document. In the second case of fathers and sons sealing the manshur, we have the seal of the chief qadi, Mir Sayyid Sharif b. Qadi Khwajah 'Abd al-Fattah al-'Alawi, dated 1107. Later his son, Muhammad b. Sayyid (Sharif) b. Qadi Khwajah 'Abd al-Fattah[6] al-'Alawi, also a chief qadi, pressed his signet on the document. In the first case, the office of qadi came into the family in the second generation. In the second case, at least three generations were qadis, although the grandfather, 'Abd al-Fattah, was not apparently appointed to a chief qadiship.

The general issue of seal procedures, and in particular those procedures and their evolution in Balkh, demands more scrutiny than can be given here. The actual manshur document rather than the published photograph of it needs to be examined and a further attempt made at reading the undeciphered seals. It might then be possible to describe the protocol of sealing a document with more certainty. At this point, it is probably safe to say that the seals played some role in providing certain assurances about the state's responsibility to safeguard the waqf, a point that would have been a concern of the waqf administration, especially in politically uncertain times. The dates of the deciphered seals suggest that, for the most part, the seals represented a review that stood independent of the Tuqay-Timurid reviews and reconfirmations. In every case where a seal date is legible, it is well removed (in the latter two cited cases by thirty and forty years, respectively) from the dates of the reviews, indicating that it was not simply a contemporary attestation of the Chingizid sovereign's review.

TUQAY-TIMURID REVIEW: THE SEVEN ANNEXES, 1121/1709–1710 TO 1150/1737–1738

For the history of the shrine's waqf prerogatives and its administration, the annexes to the manshur of 1668–1669 are invaluable. Here we see, in some small but significant way, the evolution of the waqf administration over three decades, the problems it faced, and how it sought to resolve them. The resolutions take the form of officially worded texts penned in the margins of the manshur. There are seven of these, some exceedingly brief and simply confirming in a general way the existing terms, others very detailed, specifying the fiscal prerogatives that pertain to the waqf administrators. In the latter, the impression is given that these specific rights have been compromised or usurped by state officials

---

[6] The transcriber, Hafiz Nur Muhammad, has produced the (seemingly) impossible form Abu'l-Fattah.

and that by means of the annex, the reigning monarch is attempting to end such violations.

The annexes, like the manshur itself, are aimed primarily at a contemporary audience, one familiar with the terms of reference and the syntax of such official statements. For the present-day reader, both terminological meaning and syntactic meaning (i.e., which technical terms are compound, which stand alone) are not always evident. In the remainder of this chapter, the annex will first be translated, then each of the terms in it will be discussed, and finally a general commentary about its particular context and meaning to the history of the waqf will be provided.

The Annex of 1121/1709–1710

This annex was issued under the names and *tughra*-seals of "Abu'l-Muzaffar wa'l-Mansur Sayyid 'Ubayd Allah Bahadur Khan—we say" and "Abu'l-Muzaffar wa'l-Mansur Sayyid Muhammad Muqim Bahadur Khan—we say":[7]

> It is the sovereign order that: just as the Paradise-dwelling one [Subhan Quli Khan] issued an order by way of affirming [*az qarar*] the stipulations of the written waqf record [*waqfnamah-i marqumah*] concerning the waqfs of the Holy Threshold, so we too decree likewise that all the waqfs, permanently and forever, should be thus affirmed and that no one should alter and change them. Whatever has been at the disposal of the mutawalli, the revenues of that should be spent for the stipulated expenses.
>
> In the year 1121 [1709–1710]

The document poses one major historical puzzle—why the names of both 'Ubayd Allah and Muhammad Muqim should appear on it and both with the title "khan." As far as we know from the chronicle record, Muhammad Muqim, 'Ubayd Allah's fraternal nephew, and 'Ubayd Allah were outspoken rival claimants for the khanate from the moment of Subhan Quli Khan's death in 1702 (see chapter 7). Nor is there any evidence at all in the chronicles that the two ever met, in either Balkh or Bukhara, after Subhan Quli's demise. Perhaps the most difficult problem of all is the date of the annex, 1121, three years after the commonly agreed-upon date when Muhammad Muqim was reportedly assassinated.

Another related problem, one that might perhaps be laid at the editor's door, is the transcription of the seals affixed to the annex. In the facsimile their legends are not decipherable. Hafiz Nur Muhammad has transcribed them as "Sayyid 'Ubayd Allah Khan b. Sayyid Subhan Quli Khan

---

[7] The Turkish phrase "we say" or "our word" (*sozumuz*) appears at the beginning of all the annexes.

Bahadur" and "Sultan Sayyid Muhammad Muqim b. Sayyid Subhan Quli Khan Bahadur." Two points stand out in this transcription. The first is that the seal of Muhammad Muqim, according to Hafiz Nur Muhammad's reading, bears the title "sultan" rather than "khan," a very significant difference from the standpoint of the information in our sources for the period and from the annex itself. The second is the fact that Muhammad Muqim is styled "son" of Subhan Quli, when all the textual and circumstantial evidence has him as the son of Iskandar Sultan and the grandson of Subhan Quli Khan.

At this point, given the nature and extent of the available material, all one can do is point out the problems raised by the annex. There is no misreading the date on the annex, which is quite clear in the facsimile reproduction and, to all appearances, unaltered by later hands.

The brevity and nonspecificity of the text would seem to indicate that the mutawalli may have been seeking confirmation from a newly established authority rather than looking for a resolution to a particular problem. Although the mutawalli is not mentioned by name, it was probably either Haji Mirza Muhammad Ya'qub Ansari (although some forty years had passed since his obtaining the manshur from Subhan Quli Khan) or his son Qadi Mirza Muhammad Amin Ansari, who would be mentioned by name in the next annex, issued in 1123/1711–1712.

To what extent the shrine administration and its waqf economy had been affected by the political events of the early eighteenth century is difficult to say. If the conciseness of the 1709–1710 annex is taken to mean that no specific infringements of waqf prerogatives were at issue, then perhaps one could conclude that during the first decade of the eighteenth century, despite the struggles between Uzbek tribal groups for preeminence in Balkh politics and the repeated efforts by Bukharan authorities to bring Balkh under their administration, the mutawalli of the shrine maintained his control over revenue assessments and collections in the Shahi Canal district.

There is at least one recorded incident, however, that suggests that the mutawalli, like other administrative figures, was vulnerable to political pressures. In 1707, not long after 'Ubayd Allah took Balkh by force from Mahmud Bi Qataghan, there appears to have been a direct challenge to Ansari control of the shrine and its tawliyat-administration. In that year, as part of his general reorganization of Balkh's administration, 'Ubayd Allah Khan, we are told, appointed a man named Baba Khwajah, his chief page (*chuhrah-aqasi-bashi*)[8] "guardian and manager [of the affairs] of the shaykhs of . . . the Threshold of 'Ali."[9] The appointment (or its report)

---

[8] Akhmedov 1982, 170.
[9] Muhammad Amin 1957, 543.

is a fairly unambiguous sign that 'Ubayd Allah intended to revamp the waqf administration at this time and end the long hold that the Ansari family had on the tawliyat.

We have no information about the fate of Baba Khwajah, or whether he even set foot on the grounds of the shrine. The 1709–1710 annex is silent on the name of the current mutawalli as well as Baba Khwajah. This seems significant, for one assumes that, when 'Ubayd Allah or his attorney drafted the annex, some effort would have been made to connect Baba Khwajah's name with the tawliyat. In other annexes, the mutawalli is almost always mentioned.

In light of the next annex (1123/1711–1712), it is clear that Baba Khwajah's appointment had no long-term effect on Ansari control of the shrine. Given the absence of his name from the 1709–1710 annex, it may not have even had a short-term effect.

A challenge to the mutawalli's position would have been difficult for the Bukharan khan to mount, in light of both the historic independence of Balkh from Bukhara and the fact that 'Ubayd Allah's own father, Subhan Quli, had stipulated an Ansari tawliyat "generation after generation." When 'Ubayd Allah sealed the annex of 1709–1710, he gave his tacit approval to that condition of the waqf. Moreover, the mutawalli enjoyed some influence over the hundreds of people either employed at the shrine itself, benefiting from waqf income, or working the waqf lands. He therefore could bring to bear a considerable amount of persuasive power in his dealings with the state. Making it even more difficult for 'Ubayd Allah Khan was the fact that the power of the Tuqay-Timurid khan, such as it was, was exercised only through negotiation. Real coercive power lay in the hands of those who controlled production and revenues; these included the amirs on their iqta's as well as less politically visible figures like the administrators of large waqfs. 'Ubayd Allah's relations with his own amirs were never very good and were even worse with the amirs of Balkh. As long as he left them alone they caused him no trouble, but his efforts to buttress his own position by administrative expansion threatened amirid authority and finally led to his assassination.

It is not unlikely that the Ansari mutawallis used the Balkh-Bukharan antagonisms, especially the antipathy of the amirs of Balkh toward 'Ubayd Allah and his attempts at centralization, to derail Baba Khwajah's appointment to the 'Alid shrine administration.

The annexes are in a way a result of the increased flow of power into amirid hands. But they also reflect the fact that the amirs themselves continued to cling to the old ideology of Chingizid supremacy. The fact that the annexes were only issued by Chingizids and that when Tuqay-Timurid suzerainty ended in Balkh no more annexes appeared tells us something of the special role assigned to the Tuqay-Timurid khans, even when they had lost all effective political control. All evidence indicates that what these apparently nominal figureheads decreed in the annexes was taken as fully incumbent upon the amirs. The presence of amirid seals does suggest, however, some role for this class in the appeals process, solicited either by the mutawallis or by the khans.

The Annex of 1123/1711–1712

This annex was issued under the name of "Abu'l-Muzaffar wa'l-Mansur Sayyid 'Ibad Allah Muhammad Bahadur Khan—we say":

> It is the sovereign order that: from olden times to now, in the times of the reigns of our fathers and forefathers, the sum and entirety of the Shahi Canal [district] has been the waqf of the shining Holy Threshold, the throne of the Hadrat ['Ali b. Abi Talib]. We too decree in affirmation of the farmans of previous sultans: that all the per-*zawj* revenues from cereal grains [*hasilat-i kabud bari wa safid bari azwaji*], the fee on artisanal organizations [*bilgu-yi asnaf*], the zakat-tax on sheep and cows by tale, the plow [*malah*] tax on the residents and inhabitants of the abovementioned canal [district], the tax on silk cocoons [*filahjat*], and all [other] royal levies, whether established by a governmental decree or not [*kull takalif-i padshahi hukmi wa ghayr-i hukmi*], should neither be demanded nor extracted. They should know all these to be outside state tax jurisdiction [*marfu' al-qalam*]. The darughahs and mirabs of the Hazhdah Nahr region should not meddle [in the Shahi Canal district] and should allow the present mutawalli, the refuge of sayyidship and the culmination of his illustrious family, Qadi Mir Muhammad Amin, the mutawalli and son of the late mutawalli Haji Mirza [Muhammad] Ya'qub, to disburse [these] revenues for the appropriate expenses. Should anyone extend the hand of oppression, it will be his downfall in this world and the next.
>
> In the year 1123 [1711–1712]

This annex is our first detailed look at the fiscal prerogatives that the waqf administrators were granted over the Shahi Canal district. In the 1668–1669 manshur, only those prerogatives still exercised by the mutawalli are mentioned. Subhan Quli's main concern had been to restore the regions over which the mutawalli had lost control rather than reinstate specific usurped prerogatives. But here we are given details of the presumptive claims made by the mutawalli about fiscal dues he was entitled to and which he was not obliged to pay to state officials. Because of the specific nature of these taxes and what they tell us about administrative fiscal policy, it is worth saying a word or two about each one.

1. "The per-zawj revenues from cereal grains [*hasilat-i kabud bari wa safid bari azwaji*]." The term "kabud bari wa safid bari" (literally, "blue-

bearing and white-bearing"—in reference to leaf color?) was used in Bukhara at this time to refer to tax payments made in kind.[10] The term
distinguishes winter crops (*safid bari*) from spring crops (*kabud bari*).[11]
The unit of measurement for assessment was the "zawj" (pl. azwaj) or
"pair," in reference to the ancient concept of the area that a team of oxen
might plow in a fixed period. In Bukhara, the term more commonly encountered at this time is *juft* or *juft-i gaw*, for a yoke or team of oxen. In
the eighteenth century, the juft-i gaw was equivalent to about fifty
tanab.[12] The tanab, also called the jarib, was about 50–60 percent of an
acre.[13] Fifty tanabs thus represented something between twenty-five and
thirty acres of land.[14]

The use of the word *azwaji* (from zawj) to qualify the type of tax is
important. The generic term for the tax on productive land is *kharaj*, but
it was generally assessed not by acreage but by yield (i.e., as a percentage
of the harvest based on whether the land was irrigated or dry-farmed and
who supplied seed, labor, and tools, among other negotiable issues). The
term *azwaji* points rather unambiguously to a method of assessment more
commonly linked to sericulture, viticulture, and horticulture, i.e., taxation by acreage (or jarib/tanab). It is somewhat unusual to find cereal
grain lands assessed by area rather than by yield; whether this was indeed intended in either of the annexes in which the kabud bari and safid
bari taxes are mentioned is not clear.

2. The craft organization fees (*bilgu-yi asnaf*). A late-seventeenth-century Bukharan work, the *Majma' al-arqam*, says that the word *bilgu* indicates "a document that gives to its holder the right to receive a specified sum of money or grain from the kharaj collections."[15] In the more or
less contemporary Safawid administrative manuals *Tadhkirat al-muluk*
and *Dastur al-muluk*, there are full descriptions of the way in which the
craft fees were assessed and levied.[16]

3. "The zakat on sheep and cattle by tale." The zakat is a form of compulsory wealth-based alms-giving, with specified classes of recipients

[10] Abduraimov 1970, 25.

[11] See Dihkhuda 1946– under "safid bari," another name for autumn. Dihkhuda has no
entry for "kabud bari." The taxes on the winter crop (safid bari) were collected in the middle
of the summer. Those on the spring or summer crop (kabud bari) were taken at the end of
autumn (Abduraimov 1970, 161).

[12] Abduraimov 1970, 43, note.

[13] See Davidovich et al. 1976 for a detailed discussion of the tanab in the sixteenth
through the nineteenth centuries in Central Asia. The tanab was an area sixty by sixty gaz.

[14] The juft-i gaw or zawj thus had a rough parity with the ghulbah (qulbah, kulbah). Ivanov, using nineteenth-century sources, equates fifty tanabs to eight to nine hectares or
twenty to twenty-two acres (Ivanov 1954, 10, note).

[15] Mirza Badi' Diwan 1981, 16–17 and 102, note 12.

[16] Minorsky 1943, 81–82, 148; Rafi'a n.d., 121.

prescribed by the Qur'an.[17] But in the eastern Islamic world, at least, by the late Middle Ages, the term had come to designate taxes levied on livestock. As far as I know, in practice, the zakat in Balkh was simply the name for a particular government revenue, unencumbered by claims from any class or classes of recipients.[18]

4. "The plow tax on the residents and inhabitants of the abovementioned canal." In modern usage, the term *malah* refers to an instrument more akin to the harrow than the plow, a device for leveling and smoothing, rather than breaking and turning, the soil.[19]

5. "The tax on silk cocoons [*filahjat*]." From this and the reference in the 1668–1669 manshur, it appears that, although cocoons were raised on the waqf lands, no processing went on there, for we find no terms for manufacturing facilities or for finished (spooled, dyed, woven) silk. The only mention of a textile factory of any kind on the waqf territories[20] dates to the nineteenth century, and the factory referred to was probably built at that time. But the possibility cannot be ruled out that among the crafts operating on shrine territory were silk processors and silk weavers. Taxes levied on them would probably have been classified as bilgu-yi asnaf, that is, taxes on the groups of craftsmen rather than directly on their products.

6. "All [other] royal levies, whether established by a governmental decree or not [*kull takalif-i padshahi hukmi wa ghayr-i hukmi*]." The phrase "hukmi wa ghayr-i hukmi" may be simply taken as a merism to cover all other revenue possibilities or may in fact refer to different procedures for enacting fees.

This annex presents a minor historiographical problem. In transcribing the date of the document, Hafiz Nur Muhammad gives it as 1133 rather than 1123. However, according to the *Tarikh-i Shibani Khan*, the most thorough source on the reigning figures at Balkh after Muhammad Muqim, 'Ibad Allah Khan and his two sons, Jahangir and Sanjar, were brought to Balkh early in 1123/1711 and 'Ibad Allah died seventeen months later. Even the *Gulshan al-muluk*, which asserts that 'Ibad Allah reigned at Balkh for "five years," would place his demise well before

[17] Al-Ghazzali 1966, 5–15, 55–59.

[18] Ivanov 1954, 38; Abduraimov 1970, 81. According to Mirza Badi' 1981, zakat revenues along with 'ushr and khums income were theoretically deposited in a special account (*bayt al-mal*), the proceeds of which went to the poor. This, of course is simply the classical legal formulation of zakat collections and disbursements. Vil'danova, the editor of Mirza Badi's work, characterizes the theory as "far from the actual practice" (p. 18), which also appears to have been the case with Balkh.

[19] Afghani Nawis 1961, 527 defines it as "a board hitched behind an ox and dragged over (already) plowed ground." See also Rakhimi and Uspenskoi 1954, 232.

[20] Moorcroft and Trebeck 1841, 2:491.

1133. In examining the facsimile of the annex, it becomes clear that part of the last digit intersects with the next-to-last digit in such a way as to make the 2 appear like a 3. Presumably this misled the editor.

The contrast between the general nature of the annex issued jointly by 'Ubayd Allah Khan and Muhammad Muqim and the more specific one issued two years later by 'Ibad Allah Khan is striking. It is quite possible that in the political uncertainty of the intervening two years, during which Balkh was without a Chingizid sovereign, unknown parties made serious inroads on the tax privileges of the waqf administration.

The Annex of Muharram 1124/February-March 1712

This annex was issued under the name of "Abu'l-Muzaffar wa'l-Mansur Sayyid Sanjar Muhammad Bahadur Khan—we say":

> The order to be heeded is: Since the Nahr-i Shahi, during the times of the padshahs now abiding in eternity, has been waqf in its entirety and has enjoyed tax immunity [bi-tariqah-i darubast], so we, the royal personage, also decree that it belongs to the shrine of . . . the Hadrat, the Commander of the Faithful, the Victorious Lion of God. Let the governors [hukkam], fiscal agents ['um-mal], and village elders [arbaban] of Balkh, the Mother of Cities, know that [the following] revenues are outside their fiscal jurisdiction: the safid bari-ka-bud bari revenues; water fees; the tax on grinding stones in grist mills; the assessments (muqarrari) on market laborers; the zakat on live-stock; the reve-nues from the "light bale" of silk cocoons; the jarib tax on tobacco; the jarib tax on orchards; the castellan's tax; the plow tax; the garrison tax; the night-watch-man tax; the citadel tax; the revenues from brick kiln fuel; the straw tax; the grass tax; the suqum ataliq [amaliq?] tax; the bond paid to the agents of ambas-sadors, the sultan's umbrella-holders, and the sultan's advance men; the fee for the irrigation supervisor; the [levies] for the "comings and goings," in particu-lar, of the chief of the royal hunt, the head huntsman, and the crane hunters; the fees from ruby, lapis lazuli, and gold miners; and all other sultanic levies.
>
> Should anyone extend the hand of oppression to the affairs of the aforemen-tioned canal [district] and its inhabitants, it will lead to his downfall in this world and the next. He will deserve damnation and eternal vituperation. On the Day of the Gathering-in, the Hadrat, the Sayyid of Prophets, his Family, and his Companions will all be his enemies and he will be consigned to Hell's fire along with the rest of the damned and accursed.
>
> Those [on the other hand] whose prayers God hears should allow that mu-tawalli, the noble one who enjoys the sublime status of sayyid and sharif, the one from whom the rays of the Shari'ah radiate, Qadi Mirza Muhammad Amin, the son of the late Hajji Mirza Ya'qub, to disburse the appropriations of the Blessed Shrine in accord with the set terms of the waqfnamah, especially the

necessary expenditures on the buildings and employees, and [thus] to invoke blessings on behalf of the Paradise-dwelling padshahs and forebears as well as on behalf of this humble supplicant.

In Muharram 1124 [February-March 1712]

Of the seven annexes, the ones issued in 1711 and 1712 are the only two to specify fiscal rights and, incidentally, the only two to limit their inclusiveness to the Shahi Canal district. Because of the specific nature of these two annexes, they are particularly informative about the economy of the shrine and about the understood meaning of its "waqf" rights. The 1712 annex repeats a few of the fiscal rights that the waqf administration was entitled to by virtue of the documentary evidence (subsumed here under the term *waqfnamah*). In the succeeding discussion, I have grouped similar kinds of levies under a single heading (such as the various levies that royal officials collected) where the syntax of the annex seemed to require it.

But before beginning an item-by-item examination of the fiscal prerogatives, it is necessary first to deal with the word *darubast*, which appears in the introduction, where Sanjar Muhammad characterizes the Shahi Canal district as waqf enjoying tax immunity (*bi-tariqah-i darubast*).

Sanjar Muhammad attributes the status to earlier rulers, and indeed the term is found in the manshur of 1668–1669 in the same context and characterizing the lands of the Shahi canal district only. The word has been noted and explained in a variety of ways by a number of scholars. A. A. Semenov translated it as "something transferred or turned over to someone else."[21] P. P. Ivanov said the word referred to granted lands and was equivalent in meaning to suyurghal or iqta', "the right of a particular individual to dispose of the income of a particular place." As an example he cites the case of a khwajah in Sayram who was given the water rights of an irrigation canal as darubast.[22] M. A. Abduraimov added another shade of meaning to the definition of the term. "Darbast [*sic*]," he wrote, ". . . is a form of conditional land tenure and conveys the right to complete tax immunity."[23]

Given the entire context of the manshur and the 1712 annex, it appears that it was this latter meaning that both Subhan Quli and Sanjar Muhammad had in mind. This seems particularly true in the latter case, in which Sanjar Muhammad carefully spells out the actual taxes from which the Shahi Canal district was exempt. Tax immunity was not a natural adjunct of waqf tenure, in Mawarannahr and Balkh at least, and not even particularly common. An article entitled "Waqfs in Tashkent" that

---

[21] Cited by Abduraimov 1970, 124.

[22] Ivanov 1954, 28.

[23] Abduraimov 1970, 130.

appeared in the newspaper *Turkestanskie Vedomosti* in 1884 noted that, although some of the waqfs in Tashkent were exempt from taxes, most of the large ones were not. The waqfs that were administered by the descendants of the fifteenth-century religious figure Khwajah 'Ubayd Allah Ahrar paid two-thirds of their net income in taxes, whether kharaj (the land tax based on a percentage of the harvest) or "tanap," i.e., *tanabanah* (the tax on orchards and gardens assessed by area rather than yield). The remaining one-third went to the institutions being maintained by the waqfs. (In this particular case, the net income was about 20% of gross revenues.)[24]

Other indications that taxable real estate maintained its tax liability after conversion to waqf are found in the legal maneuvers that prospective waqf donors went through to make their real estate tax-exempt before transferring it to waqf. Legal treatises, too, devote space to explaining how tax money could be raised if the mutawalli was faced with a revenue shortfall at tax time.[25] Scholars of other regions subject to Islamic law have also discussed the tax liability of waqfs.[26] At Balkh the clearest evidence that tax exemption was the exception rather than the rule is found in the repeated admonitions to the tax collectors that the Shahi Canal district was darubast, and "outside their jurisdiction."

Although Subhan Quli had also described the Shahi Canal as tax-immune, it appears that Sanjar Muhammad felt obliged at this point to state precisely what that meant so that there would be no future misunderstandings. In doing so, he gives us an unusually detailed look at the kinds of economic activities that were taxed in Balkh in the early eighteenth century:

1. The kabud-bari and safid-bari revenues from cereals. These were discussed previously. I would only draw attention here to the omission of the qualifier *azwaji* (assessment per-zawj), which appears in the 'Ibad Allah annex.

2. "Water fees" (*pul-i ab*). This particular term is somewhat problematic. The text in all three places spells the word *pul* "p-l" with no lengthened vowel. That spelling can mean either "bridge" (*hasilat-i pul-i ab* might then perhaps mean "the bridge tolls") or low embankment (*pal*), especially that used to demarcate a cultivated field (for water retention) (in which case the phrase might mean "revenues from paddies"). However, in combination with two other words, *qal'ah* (fortress) and *margh*

---

[24] *Turkestanskie Vedomosti* 1884, 10:32.
[25] Al-Tarabulusi 1952, 57.
[26] Lambton 1969, 234, note 4; Spuler 1969, 241; Papazian 1968, 482–83.

(grass), neither of these latter two are possible. In all three cases I am assuming the author simply used a variant spelling of pul (money).

The tax in question here is probably that on revenues raised from the sale of water. Specific amounts raised by this and other taxes are not available for Balkh in this period, but we get an idea of the importance of such revenues in other comparable settings. Isfahan at about the same time raised some 4,000 tuman in water taxes from the region dependent on the Zayandah Rud.[27] In fifteenth-century Herat, where water distribution was based on a *buluk* system (each trunk canal from the Hari Rud and the land it watered comprising a single buluk), the buluk of Sabqar paid an annual water tax of 5,000 Tabrizi dinars.[28]

3. The (mill)stone tax (*maliyah-i kull tawahin-i da'irah*). By and large, the grist mills in Balkh were water-driven, although some reference has been found to windmills operating in this period.[29] Here we assume, however, that what is at issue are the mills that were driven by the water of the Shahi Canal. The fact that this tax is listed third may indicate its relative fiscal importance. In fifteenth-century Herat, for comparison, it was not a trivial tax. There the amount levied per stone depended on the location of the mill along the canal. In the Anjil buluk, for example, mills nearer the head (*az a'la*) of the canal, presumably where the flow was more predictable and stronger, paid 500 Tabrizi dinars per stone. Mills in the middle were assessed 300 Tabrizi dinars per stone, while the ones farthest downstream paid 150 Tabrizi dinars.[30] In the buluks of Alanjan and Kadhrah, however, there was only one rate of assessment.[31] The mills were not only a source of tax revenue, they could also be used as a standard of flow. In sixteenth-century Isfahan, the amount of water distributed to the various districts was regulated according to a standard based on the time it took to grind one mann of flour.[32]

4. The fixed assessment on market laborers (*muqarrari kasabah-i bazar*). A mid-eighteenth-century Iranian source describing conditions in Balkh draws a distinction between the occasional laborers (*kasib*, pl. *kasabah*) and the permanent craftsmen or tradesmen (*ahl al-muhtarifah*).[33] In the early eighteenth century, the muqarrari assessment may have applied as well to those who brought produce or goods into the market to

[27] Minorsky 1943, 180.
[28] Qasim b. Yusuf Harawi 1968, 61.
[29] Mukhtarov 1980, 25.
[30] Qasim b. Yusuf Harawi 1968, 20.
[31] Ibid., 24, 34.
[32] Lambton 1938, 669.
[33] Muhammad Kazim 1962–66, 2:104a: "*kasabah wa ahl al-muhtarifah farigh-i bal wa marfah-i ahwal bi dukkan wa bazar nishastah . . .*"

sell on market days, equivalent to the nineteenth-century "place tax" (tah-ja'i) at the shrine.[34]

5. The zakat on livestock (*zakat-i mawashi*). This tax has been already been treated in conjunction with the 1711 annex and needs no further discussion here.

6. The tax on the "light bale" (or load) of silk cocoons (*bar-i sabuki filahjat*). The tax on silk here differs from the one mentioned in the 1711 annex. There the syntax suggested jaribanah-i filahjat, i.e., a tax assessed per jarib on the orchards of mulberry trees that supported sericulture. Here, the tax is clearly on the yield of cocoons, measured in the so-called light bale.

7. The jarib tax on tobacco (*jaribanah-yi tamaku*). Tobacco was grown, dried, consumed, and probably exported at both Bukhara and Balkh. Tobacco was a New World crop and unknown in the Eastern Hemisphere before the Spanish and English explorations of the sixteenth and early seventeenth centuries. It made its way to Europe by the middle of the sixteenth century[35] and spread from there. The earliest reference I have found to it at Balkh is in Subhan Quli Khan's waqfnamah for his madrasah in Balkh, dated between 1686 and 1693.[36] In that deed, the Bukharan khan endows as waqf "a bath in Tall-i Bazargan [Balkh] as well as three adjoining shops—a buttery, a greengrocer, and a tobacconist [*rawghan-gari, baqqali, wa tamaku-furushi*]."[37] In 1693, the same khan set up a trust in Bukhara to support a relative's tomb, among the endowments of which was a tobacco barn (*qawalah-i tamaku*).[38]

The two earlier references indicate that there were both processing facilities and retail outlets for tobacco by the end of the seventeenth century. The 1712 annex provides the additional evidence, which we can only assume for the period thirty years earlier, that tobacco was not only processed and sold but also grown in the region.

The dates suggest that Balkh and Bukhara were very much part of the world tobacco market. When the crop was first introduced to Mawaran-

---

[34] *TMS*, 73 (text), 77 (transcription). The term *muqarrari* was common in Safawid fiscal documents. See Schimkoreit 1982, 538, where muqarrari appears as a kind of fixed stipend. Here it would appear to be a fixed assessment.

[35] Braudel 1981, 262. Tobacco was cultivated in Spain in 1558. From there it spread quickly to France and Britain. By 1588 it had made its way back across the Atlantic to Virginia, where production boomed after 1612. See also Masefield 1967, 293–95.

[36] Davydov 1960, 114 (line 73 of document). Other more or less contemporary references in neighboring regions are Sipinta 1969, 84 (a tobacco shop in Isfahan) and Bafiqi 1967, 444 (a Yazd poet of the late seventeenth century who sold tobacco).

[37] Davydov 1960, 114 (line 73).

[38] Chekhovich and Vil'danova 1979, 223 (text), 230 (translation). In a long note on the term *qawalah*, the authors conclude that it meant a processing plant for tobacco. Perhaps they had in mind a drying shed or barn for tobacco leaf.

nahr and Balkh is uncertain. Nor do we know whether it came via the Russian or Syrian markets. But it must have arrived not long after it was first brought to Europe and the Middle East. Its introduction in Central Asia certainly predated the boom in the tobacco market engendered by the demand for snuff, which caused imports to Europe to soar between 1700 and 1750, when it became particularly fashionable.[39] But Balkh and Mawarannahr had already been producing the noxious weed for some years before this.

8. The jarib tax on orchards and gardens (*baghat*). I have already discussed the nature of the jarib tax and the size of the jarib (equivalent to the tanab and approximately one-half acre). Vil'danova, in her notes to the late-eighteenth-century manual of Bukharan administration, the *Majma' al-arqam*, draws a distinction between the terms charbagh (charharbagh) and bagh (pl. baghat). In late-eighteenth- and early-nineteenth-century usage, she believes, the former term was used for orchards, whereas the latter was used for vineyards.[40] However, she cites no particular source for such a distinction. Without getting into a discussion of the meaning of the two terms and what distinguished them, if anything, I would here only offer the general impression that the term *jaribanah-i baghat* covered vineyards, orchards, and vegetable and flower gardens.

9. The various police levies for the *kutwal*, darughah, and mirshabb. All three of these titles designated officials whose duties overlapped to some degree through the centuries. In the early eighteenth century, the offices seem to have been differentiated as follows: the darughah was the commandant of the military garrison[41] and the tax levied in his name supported it; the kutwal was in charge of the city fortifications (walls, bastions, and gates) and the mirshabb was responsible for the curfew—for insuring that the city's shops were locked after dark and that people were off the bazaar streets.[42] Generally, the official responsible for maintaining public order during the seventeenth and eighteenth centuries in both Balkh and Bukhara was the darughah.[43] By the late nineteenth century in Afghanistan, the kutwal appears as the principal police officer, over-

[39] Braudel 1981, 262; see also the *Encyclopaedia Americana* article "Tobacco," in which there is information that between 1700 and 1750, for example, European demand raised Virginian exports from eighteen to forty million pounds annually.

[40] Mirza Badi' 1981, 103.

[41] Although Vil'danova defines the term *darughah* in the late eighteenth century as meaning "military commandant of the city" (Mirza Badi' 1981, 113), elsewhere she translates it somewhat differently: "On him [the ataliq] also lies the responsibility of being mirab [water superintendent] of the Rud-i Shahr [the main waterway through Bukhara] and darughah, night guard, within the rabad [suburbs] of Bukhara, excluding the functions of *shihnah* and *uydachi*" (Mirza Badi' 1981, 95).

[42] Ibid., 99. For a more general discussion, see Bosworth 1980.

[43] Abduraimov 1970, 2:184–85.

seeing market inspection, night patrols, and the maintenance of civil order.[44] In Isfahan in the period roughly contemporary with this annex, the mirshabb served as assistant to the darughah and supervised the night guards and the paid informers.[45]

10. The fee on plows (malah gari). This was discussed previously.

11. The fees for maintaining the walls (pul-i qal'ah). In Balkh at this time the term qal'ah was used to refer to the walls of both the Shahr-i Darun (the Inner City) and the Shahr-i Birun (the Outer City). The citadel, which stood in the southeastern part of the Inner City, was called the Arg. The pul-i qal'ah probably was a regular cash levy distinct from the periodic corvée (bigar or hashar) for maintenance of the fortifications.[46]

12. The tax on the thorn wood used as fuel in brick kilns (khar-i khumdan). In the Lughat-namah, a passage taken from the Anis al-talibin—a late-fourteenth-century book on the life, works, and miracles of the Bukharan shaykh, Baha al-Din Naqshband—speaks of the use of thorns as fuel for brick kilns: "They say that Baha al-Din had a son, a robust healthy lad. It was a time when fuel was needed for the kilns but there was no one around to gather the firewood. At that time the fuel in use was thorn wood [khar-i mughilan] and [his son said,] 'I carried that thornwood on my bare back to the kilns and would give thanks [for the opportunity].' "[47]

13. The straw or stubble fee (kah-i dasturi). Mayil Harawi, editor of a fifteenth-century handbook of water administration from Herat, defines dastur as a license. (In the particular case with which he is dealing it was a license or permit for millstones.)[48] In Balkh, the kah-i dasturi seems to have been a fee paid for the right to collect or harvest the vegetation that grew on canal banks or in the canal beds when the canals were drained.[49] The reserved public space (harim) of the canal, like the right-of-way of a public road, was land in the public domain and under government control. Land of a canal could be owned, but access to the water for drinking only was a public right. The extent of the reserved spaces is discussed in the early kharaj works of Abu Yusuf and Qudamah b. Ja'far, although those sources say nothing about ownership of plants that grow on those public spaces.[50] Here it is clear that the tax officials from Balkh consid-

[44] Martin 1907, 47, 142.
[45] Minorsky 1943, 83, 149.
[46] Abduraimov 1970, 2:184–85.
[47] Dihkhuda 1946– ; on the khumdan generally, see now Pugachenkova and Rtveladze 1986, 324a.
[48] Qasim b. Yusuf Harawi 1968, 44, note 2.
[49] Lambton 1938, 669.
[50] Abu Yusuf 1969, 123–26; Qudamah b. Ja'far 1965, 63–64.

ered such products of the harim to be under their jurisdiction, perhaps regardless of waqf rights to the canal water. Such a gray area of the law (the canal right-of-way could not legally be private property, hence it could not be conveyed into waqf) obviously caused jurisdictional disputes between the waqf administrators and the government tax collectors.

14. The fee for grass (*pul-i margh*). It is worth noting that, both in this document and in the water regulations published by Lambton on the Zayandah River in Isfahan, the straw and grass fees are mentioned together. The distinction between margh and kah, or margh and *shush* in the Isfahan case, would seem to be that between grass harvested while green, in the first case, and dry dead vegetation, in the second. Both were gathered from the same places, the canal banks.

15. The suqum ataliq (or amaliq?). I have so far been unable to find a satisfactory meaning for this phrase. In a conversation in 1976 with Bori Akhmedov of the Institute of Orientalism in Tashkent, he suggested that it may have referred to fat-tailed sheep. Hafiz Nur Muhammad transcribes the last word *amaliq* but the text, though unclear, seems to be *ataliq*.

16. Surety for the agents (*gurumanah-i 'amaldaran*) of ambassadors (*il-chi*), the sultan's umbrella-holders (*shukurchi haqq allah*), and the sultan's advance men (*yurchi*).[51] The term *gurumanah* signifies the levy on villages or settlements lying along major routes as surety that they would offer food and shelter to official parties traveling those roads. What form such exactions took, i.e., the holding of some collateral or even hostages, or simply assessing each village a fixed amount each year, is not known. Unlike the preceding revenues, the *gurumanah* was a matter of geography rather than productivity. I remain very uncertain about the second of the three officials whose agents can claim the bond. The phrase *haqq Allah* (God's right or claim) after umbrella-holder (shukurchi) is particularly confusing.

17. The levies for the chief of the royal hunt (*qushbegi*),[52] head huntsman (*mir-i shikar*), and crane hunters (*sayyadan-i kalang*). These levies probably meant supplying food, shelter, and manpower for royal hunts. The *Majma' al-arqam* calls the *qushbegi* the "chief of the royal hunt" and one of the people closest to the sovereign person.[53] Y. Bregel, however, in his analysis of the origin and use of the term *qushbegi* in Central Asian sources, is skeptical of the hunting attribution.[54] But, the fact that this

[51] Akhmedov 1982, 177.
[52] Ibid., 164.
[53] Mirza Badi' 1981, 91.
[54] Bregel 1980.

annex groups the three titles together indicates at least some connection of the qushbegi with the hunt.

18. The fee for the irrigation supervisor (*mirabanah*). The mirabanah appears well down the list and so, we assume, low in the order of importance of the taxes and revenues. If so, it is surprising, given the importance of the office elsewhere. According to the early-eighteenth-century *Tadhkirat al-muluk*, "The duty of the mirab of the capital, Isfahan, is to appoint the supervisors of the irrigation canals, to clean the canals and rills, to conduct the surplus water of the [Zayanda] river to the whole of the district of Isfahan irrigated from the river according to the rights of each place."[55] Chardin, who composed his description of Iran toward the end of the seventeenth century, estimated the mirab's income at a very high, perhaps exaggeratedly so, figure of 4,000 tuman per annum.[56] In Herat in the fifteenth century, the mirab and his assistants (the *dahyakah* or "ten percenters," from their reported share in the harvest,[57] and the *bandbanan*, those who regulated the flow of water into the fields or branch canals) received varying incomes, depending on where they worked. In the buluk of Anjil on the Shah Juy, one of the two main canals in the buluk, irrigating about 3,000 acres (6,000 jaribs), the mirabanah, dahyak, and bandbani taxes amounted to 60 mann of mixed grain[58] (*ghallah-i munasifah*) and 5 mann of cotton bolls per *nafar* (there were 299.5 nafar on the Shah Juy).[59] The mann was a unit of weight of widely varying proportions.[60] Its range could be from 2 to 26 kilograms. The amount represented by these levies could therefore have been as little as some 36,000 kilograms or as much as 467,000 kilograms of grain and from 3,000 to almost 39,000 kilograms of cotton.

19. The fees levied on ruby, lapis lazuli, and gold miners (*arandagan-i la'al wa gil-i lajurd wa tilajat*). It is somewhat unexpected to find reference to exploitable quantities of minerals associated with the Shahi Canal district in this period. In the early 1970s, an Italian scholar visiting the 'Alid shrine was shown a document from 1372 reporting purchases of silk and gems by the Genoese merchant Gentile Adorno.[61] Badakhshan to the east was far more famous as a source of rubies and lapis[62] and in the eighteenth century it still had rich resources. When Nadir Shah Afshar

[55] Minorsky 1943, 83.
[56] Cited in Minorsky 1943.
[57] Qasim b. Yusuf Harawi 1968, 158.
[58] Grain of varying quality was often mixed or averaged for bookkeeping purposes. See Davidovich 1983, note 406.
[59] Qasim b. Yusuf Harawi 1968, 20.
[60] Hinz 1970, 25–33; Davidovich 1970, 85–94.
[61] See chapter 3, note 66.
[62] Barthold et al. 1960, 851–52.

invaded Balkh and Badakhshan, he is said to have seized one hundred thousand tumans worth of rubies from the mines of Badakhshan.[63] But in the Shahi Canal district itself, there is little evidence that in 1712 either gold, rubies, or lapis lazuli were anything more than incidental elements of the area's economy.

20. All miscellaneous sultanic levies (*kull takalif-i sultani*) (see the previous discussion).

Both the 1711 and the 1712 annexes raise the issue of the status of the peripheral waqf lands, those land and water rights donated during the seventeenth century that lay outside the Shahi Canal district. In his manshur, Subhan Quli took great care to distinguish between the Nahr-i Shahi (the Shahi Canal district), which made up the original waqf endowment and was its core, and the waqfs given to the shrine by seventeenth-century donors. All the other annexes except 'Ibad Allah's and Sanjar Muhammad's are couched in sufficiently general terms to encompass both the peripheral and the core waqfs of the Shahi Canal district. But these two, by explicitly limiting their annexes to the Nahr-i Shahi, raise the question of what happened to the rest of the waqf fund, the lands and water rights of Darrah-i Juz, Qush Ribat, Sum Chak, Sadmish and Qarni Sa'i, Kaftar Khwani, and Sultan Bayazid. It strains credulity to think that either khan, let alone both men, was unaware of those endowments. The annexes, after all, were written in the right-hand margin of the 1668–1669 manshur. Why then was there no mention of those lands?

There may be a number of explanations or at least partial explanations. The first is simply that the mutawalli, Qadi Mir Muhammad Amin, was having no problems with the administration of those areas and thus had no need of a restatement of his rights when he obtained the documents from the two Chingizids. What makes this answer less than wholly satisfactory is that the reason for seeking such an official confirmation of rights was not just to correct existing abuses but to obtain from a new political authority his seal of approval and support for the mutawalli's rights. The date of the annex and the date of 'Ibad Allah's accession to the throne of Balkh correspond, and so we might reasonably conclude that the annex was a routine one. Likewise in Sanjar Muhammad's case, we have a comparably neat fit between annex and accession dates. He ascended the throne of Balkh apparently at the very beginning of 1124 and the annex is dated to Muharram of that year. Thus one would have expected a general comprehensive reaffirmation of waqf rights rather than the highly specific listing given in both annexes.

A second explanation, and one somewhat related to the first, is that these peripheral waqfs, some of them quite far from the shrine, were not

[63] Muhammad Kazim 1962–66, 3:179a.

within the jurisdiction of the Tuqay-Timurid sovereign at Balkh, and thus his decree would have been irrelevant. Moreover, if the mutawalli negotiated separately with the amirid authorities (notably the Qataghan and Ming amirs) in those areas where he had waqf properties, he might have thought it impolitic to seek the protection of the Chingizid at Balkh at the same time.

There may be some justification for such an assumption in light of the intense inter-tribal, inter-iqta' struggles that mark this period. And had no reference ever again been made in the annex record to these peripheral waqf lands, then perhaps we could attribute the omission to the Tuqay-Timurid's loss of jurisdiction. But the fact that they are again mentioned within a few years in another annex would suggest that the Tuqay-Timurids had not, in fact, lost their hold.

The omission of the peripheral waqf properties may be most closely linked to what seems to be the main focus of these two annexes: the special tax position, i.e., general immunity, of the Shahi Canal. None of the other annexes address the question of tax status, and yet all include explicitly or implicitly both the core waqf lands of the Shahi Canal and the peripheral territories. If such is the case, then the main reason for omitting any mention of the peripheral waqf lands is not because they were not within either the mutawalli's or the Tuqay-Timurid sovereign's jurisdiction, but because they had no tax immunity. This conclusion fits well with the kind of property found in the areas outside the Shahi Canal district.

It is worth recalling that the district itself appears to have been as much a creation of history as of a particular act of waqf-making. Although no waqf deed of the original corpus exists, nor is there any direct reference to one, there was nonetheless a general consensus that the canal had been made waqf for the shrine by Sultan Husayn Mirza Bayqara in the 1480s. Moreover, it was certainly the mutawalli's opinion in the early 1700s, at least, that the original grant was all-inclusive. All the net revenue of the Shahi Canal district was to be considered waqf and no one but the shrine administrators had any claim on its revenues. By inference, the officials who collected taxes held a somewhat narrower view of the shrine administration's rights. Their actions (reflected in the 1668–1669 manshur and subsequent annexes) show that, while the Shahi Canal district may have been waqf, like other forms of land tenure and like other waqfs, these officials believed it had certain tax obligations to the state. Some of these were direct assessments for services provided by the state (police and security, for example), while others were the customary taxes on productivity and the means of production. These conflicting views on jurisdictions required periodic resolution by the ultimate arbiter, the sultan or khan at Balkh. Constant conflict was characteristic of waqf endowments created out of government-controlled or -administered properties, in no small part because the revenues at stake were part of the tax base. In these disputes, public sentiment and the inertial force of the historical development of the waqf weighed heavily on the side of waqf administrators when they sought political backing for their claims.

The character of the peripheral waqf properties, on the other hand, was quite different from the comprehensive character of the Shahi Canal district. As defined in the manshur, the waqf parcels were precise units of property (so many water shares in such and such a place, for example) whose tax liability was probably taken for granted. There was no need for a sultan to overrule his tax officials because the waqf administrators had no disagreement with them. The mutawalli, or more likely the tenant, paid the appropriate taxes and that was that. But where the issue was ambiguous, disputes arose. And the annexes that have survived, especially those issued in 1711 and 1712, provide material evidence of the consequences of the perceived ambiguities.

Besides the issue of the omission of the peripheral waqf territories, Sanjar Muhammad's annex also presents a minor historiographical problem involving an editorial error. Having misread the date of the 'Ibad Allah annex as 1133 rather than 1123, Hafiz Nur Muhammad was more or less obliged to read the Sanjar Muhammad annex as 1134. The date visible on the facsimile could be read either way. But the chronicles again encourage us to correct the date to 1124. However, this still leaves us with a slight problem. 'Ibad Allah was brought to the throne in 1123 and then reigned "one year and five months,"[64] which would put his death well into 1124. However, the annex issued by Sanjar, his second successor (his elder son Jahangir apparently took the throne and then quickly died), is dated Muharram 1124, the first month of the year. Nevertheless, the choice of 1124 as the date of the annex seems by far the best. If we follow the editor's reading of 1134, we are confronted with insurmountable difficulties in explaining the dates of subsequent annexes in light of the regnal dates of their authors as given in other sources.

The annexes of 1123 and 1124 give the most detailed and comprehensive view of the economic base of the Nahr-i Shahi waqf that we find until the materials of the late nineteenth century. They show an economy heavily dependent on agricultural income, with irrigation playing a central role. In fact, the waqf economy at the 'Alid shrine was not merely irrigation-based, the heart of the endowment was the irrigation system. The annexes also tell us of other economic activities, not agricultural, that the waqf administrators oversaw. Skilled and unskilled labor in the mar-

[64] *Tarikh-i Shibani*, fol. 121a.

ketplace, the extraction of precious metals and gems, livestock breeding, grain processing, and the export trade in silk and tobacco were areas of the economy in which the waqf administrators had an interest. Managing a large and diverse waqf was not unlike managing a small state: it involved territorial security and defense, diplomatic relations with one's more powerful neighbors, an organized system of extracting the economic surplus, and maintenance of the fabric of the economy by repairs and new capital investment. The scale was smaller than that of neighboring states, but the problems were similar to what the ruler of Balkh, for example, faced in his day-to-day supervision of the government.

The Annex of Ramadan 1131(?) (July–August 1719)

This annex was issued under the name of "Abu'l-Muzaffar wa'l-Mansur Muhammad Bahadur Khan—we say":

> The world-obeying order of the one the world obeys is: Illustrious khaqans and worthy sultans have attested the terms of former waqfnamahs and in particular have confirmed the waqfnamah for the Nahr-i Shahi and some of the locales along other canals of Balkh and [in] dependent provinces like Darrah-i Juz and Khulm and others that belong to the Angel-guarded Threshhold of the Hadrat, the Commander of the Faithful and the Imam of the Pious. We too declare that no one of God's creatures should have any claim or recourse [dukhl wa ruju'] to the waqf of the bright Holy Threshold whose status is like God's throne. If anyone in any way should interfere in the waqf by as much as one iota [hub-bah], one dinar, or one hair, may he be eternally damned. Governors and fiscal agents of the Mother of Cities, Balkh, should allow the present mutawalli, the servant of the poor, friend to scholars, the soul of generosity and the kernel of nobility, Qadi Mir Muhammad Amin the mutawalli, successor to Hajji Mirza Ya'qub mutawalli, to disburse money for the expenses related to the employees and others at the Illustrious Threshold.
>
> In the month of Ramadan 1131[65] [July–August 1719]

Muhammad Bahadur Khan, the signer of this annex, was the second scion of the Walid line from Herat to be recruited to the Chingizid throne at Balkh. He succeeded Sanjar Muhammad, who died in 1717. Shortly after Muhammad Bahadur's accession, the mutawalli, who was still Qadi Mirza Muhammad Amin, petitioned him for another annex to the manshur issued by Subhan Quli. The one he was given is quite different from the ones Sanjar Muhammad and his father had given seven and eight

---

[65] Hafiz Nur Muhammad reads the date (mistakenly, I believe) as 1141 (TMS, 70). The photoreproduction is so poor that it can be read either way. He read the khan's seal date as 1131, but perhaps because of the dates he had already assigned to the previous two annexes he could not date this one to 1131.

years earlier, respectively. Although omitting any reference to specific tax issues, the annex does restore to the historical record some mention of the peripheral waqf areas: the property rights on canals other than the Shahi Canal and in places "like Darrah-i Juz and Khulm." The general designation applies both to the lands donated by Wali Muhammad around 1606 (e.g., Darrah-i Juz) and to the water rights given by the amirs (in and around Khulm as well as on the Siyahgird Canal, another of Balkh's eighteen canals).

The Annex of Rabiʿ al-Awwal 1133 (January 1721)

This annex was issued under the name "Abu'l-Muzaffar wa'l-Mansur ʿArab Muhammad Bahadur Khan":

> The sublime farman is issued: In accord with the decrees of former padshahs we too ordain that from ancient times until now the Nahr-i Shahi and some locations on the canals and dependent districts like Darrah-i Juz, Khulm, and other districts of the Mother of Cities, Balkh, as established by the waqfnamah, belong to the economy [sarkar] of the one of abundant good works, the Commander of the Faithful, the Victorious Lion of God, the Hadrat. Likewise, during the reigns of the Paradise-dwelling former padshahs, especially during the time of the [after extended honorifics] . . . khaqan son of the khaqan son of the khaqan [i.e., Subhan Quli?], the waqf of this Angel-guarded threshhold was reestablished as it had been during the time of the Saljuqi, Chingizi, and Chaghatay padshahs.
>
> Some amirs and governors, ignorant of God, following selfish whim, and unafraid of His inquisition on the Day of Reckoning, have violated this waqfnamah.
>
> No one would base the keys of the gates of sovereignty and world rule and the affairs of might and world conquest, according to the dictum "You give sovereignty to whom you will," just on grasping the hilt of capability and volition, nor put on the bright glorious diadem and the brilliant royal crown [just] in accord with the saying "Your Lord creates what he wills and what he chooses." This is a matter of the *dawlat*, as long as the world turns.
>
> Since the Sublime and Almighty has joined the demands of this world to the horizon of the desires and will of the venerable servants and noble servitors, in accordance with that which is intended and that which is obtained, and the goals of the next world and the aims of success and achieving victory are made easy by what the heart's desire dictates; therefore the Noble Hadrat now dwelling in Heaven, having planted the seed of love for the family of the [Prophet's] cloak and the lord of the saints [ʿAli] in the pure space of his sincere heart, he twice [*du barah*] revived this waqf, took it out of the oppressive hands of those ignorant of God and as of old handed it over to the summa of the family of

cognition, the one to whom the masters of integrity defer, the servitor of the people of veracity and rectitude, Qadi Mirza Muhammad Amin, son of the late Hajji Mirza Muhammad Ya'qub, the mutawalli, in accordance with the waqfna-mah of the Hadrat, the Paradise-Dwelling [Subhan Quli].

Since, during the time of the Hadrat, Lord of the Conjunction [sahib-i qiran], one of the forebears [az ajdad) of Hajji Mirza Muhammad Ya'qub, the ra'is of Islam, revealer of the secrets, the one of rectitude, Mirza Sanjar Ansari, was elevated to the tawliyat of the shrine,

Now, therefore, in accordance with the noble decree, no governor nor fiscal agent of the Mother of Cities, Balkh, should expect even one seed or one hair from the aforementioned canal district or the locales or other things belonging to the waqfnamah. Should anyone do so, then he will be the object of eternal damnation."

Dated Rabi' al-Awwal 1133 [January 1721]

Hafiz Nur Muhammad, editor of the *Tarikh-i Mazar-i Sharif*, read the date on the document as 1143, again perhaps prompted to do so by reading the date of the previous annex as 1134 instead of 1124. The misreading is not quite as obvious as it was in the earlier cases. First, the facsimile itself can be read either way. The penultimate digit is not clearly a 3 or a 4. In addition, the chronicles disagree on their dates for 'Arab Muhammad. He came to the throne of Balkh, such as it was at this point, in either 1130/1718 or 1131/1719.[66] But Tali' has him settling under Ming tutelage at Shibarghan at some unspecified time.[67] We have no terminal regnal date for him, so either 1133 or 1143 is possible. The main reason for selecting the earlier date as more probable has to do with the rapid turnover of Chingizid turahs by this time. In contrast with Subhan Quli's three decades as sovereign in the city, the years of his successors' tenures could be counted on the fingers of one hand. The Herat recruits for the post lasted, in order, a year to a year and a half ('Ibad Allah), a few days (Jahangir), three years or five years, depending on the source (Sanjar Muhammad), and two years (Muhammad Bahadur). Politics at Balkh had become so highly tribalized and the struggle for territorial control so endemic that as tribal fortunes rose and fell so too did the Tuqay-Timurid khans under whose aegis the struggles went on. It is more likely than not, given the political situation, that 'Arab Muhammad did not reign at Balkh for the minimum thirteen or fourteen years that an 1143

---

[66] *Tarikh-i Shibani*, fol. 121b calls him "Muhammad Bahadur" and dates his enthronement at Balkh to 1130/5 December 1717–23 November 1718. Muhammad Ya'qub, fol. 132b, referring to him as Muhammad Sultan, dates his arrival from Herat to 1131/24 November 1718–13 November 1719. Tali', fol. 38b seems to date his being brought to prominence to 1130.

[67] Tali', fol. 39a.

annex date would require. Another reason for choosing 1133 over 1143 as the proper annex date is the pattern to which the mutawallis seemed to adhere of petitioning a khan early in his reign, if not at the very outset.

The contents of the annex are extremely interesting and seem to be addressing a conflict over the Ansari right to the tawliyat. It is the one concrete issue raised in the annex, aside from veiled references to people who had violated the waqfnamah.

The annex speaks of deceased padshahs only by their necronyms, a style that leaves us with some question as to exactly who is intended. Generally speaking, the necronym "Heaven-Dwelling" (jannat makan) is used in Mawarannahrid literature in the period after 1114 (but for how long is not entirely clear) to refer to Subhan Quli Khan. However the "Heaven Dweller" of the annex is not Subhan Quli, since he had no dealings with Qadi Mir Muhammad Amin. Subhan Quli's father, Nadhr Muhammad, is often referred to at about the same time as "Firdaws Makan" (Paradise-Dwelling) while his brother, 'Abd al-'Aziz Khan, was most often known as "the Haji Khan" (the Pilgrim Khan) for his abdication and hajj-pilgrimage in 1682. The quintessential "Sahib-i Qiran" (Lord of the Conjunction) in Mawarannahrid historiography is usually Timur (Tamerlane). Here we assume that by the honorific "Hadrat Sahib-i Qiran" Nadhr Muhammad Khan is meant, for we know from BA that it was he who appointed Mirza Sanjar Ansari to the tawliyat in the 1630s.[68]

Several questions are raised by the annex. What does the author of the annex mean by the phrase "he [the person is unnamed] twice revived this waqf . . . and . . . handed it over to . . . Qadi Mirza Muhammad Amin"? There is no record, here at least, that any of the Tuqay-Timurid sovereigns had issued more than one decree to Qadi Mir Muhammad Amin. Is the word twice used because the qadi's name appears in two previous annexes? Why was it necessary to refer to the earlier appointment of Mirza Sanjar? If this was to validate the Ansari family claim to the tawliyat, why does 'Arab Muhammad make no mention of Abu'l-Hasan Ansari, whom Subhan Quli, in the manshur itself, had called the first Ansari mutawalli? The wording of the annex raises these questions but offers no help in answering them.

The Annex of Rajab 1149/November 1736

This annex was issued under the name of "Abu'l-Muzaffar wa'l-Mansur Chingiz Muhammad Bahadur Khan—we say":

In accordance with the farman of the Paradise-dwelling padshahs and the noble forebears, we too decree that the waqfnamah is true and sound in accordance

[68] BA 4: fol. 304b.

with previous ordinances [*bi-dastur-i sabiq*]. No one should violate it or deviate from it.

Dated Rajab 1149 [November 1736]

The Annex of Shawwal 1150/January–February 1738

This annex was issued under the name of "Abu'l-Muzaffar wa'l-Mansur Sayyid Abu'l-Hasan Bahadur Khan—we say":

> In accordance with those obedience-requiring farmans of our illustrious forebears, we too decree that the waqfnamah is true and sound in accordance with previous ordinances. No one should violate it or deviate from it lest he be the object of eternal damnation.
>
> Dated Shawwal 1150 [January–February 1738]

The last two annexes are the kind of confirmation a new sovereign would give. They are general, comprehensive, and suggest no specific problems.

These two annexes are, as far as I know, the only sources for the names of the last Chingizid sovereigns at Balkh. Hafiz Nur Muhammad says that the seal of Chingiz Muhammad Khan was dated 1142, and one might take this as the terminus a quo for his reign. But the editor also gives the seal date of Abu'l-Hasan as 1143, which presents a problem of interpretation given the date of his predecessor's annex (1149). Tali' offers a hint as to what Chingizid sovereignty probably meant by this point in Balkh when he states that 'Arab Muhammad Bahadur Khan established himself (or was established) at Shibarghan with the Ming.[69] The Chingizids who put their names and seals to the annexes were by now little more than tokens in the inter-amirid conflicts. It is by no means unthinkable that Chingiz Muhammad and Abu'l-Hasan may have been nominal simultaneous sovereigns sponsored by rival tribes—by the Ming, Qipchaq, Qanqli, Qa'at, or even the Qataghan.

There is one final point about the last of the Chingizids at Balkh. Muhammad Bahadur is the last sovereign whose origins are given as Tuqay-Timurid (of Wali Muhammad's line). His next two successors, 'Arab Muhammad and Chingiz Muhammad, may have been Walid, but there is no evidence of it. The very last Chingizid, Abu'l-Hasan, has the title "sayyid" before his name. The three immediately preceding him do not, although the two preceding Walids, Sanjar Muhammad and his father 'Ibad Allah, do. The term, as used in Khurasan, Mawarannahr, and Balkh, meant a descendant (through either the male or female line) of the Prophet Muhammad. The first Tuqay-Timurid to adopt the title was

[69] Tali', fol. 39a.

Nadhr Muhammad. His mother, Shah Bibi Shahr Banu Begum, was the daughter of a Ridawi sayyid from Mashhad. Nadhr Muhammad's sons (most prominently 'Abd al-'Aziz, Subhan Quli) and Subhan Quli's sons and grandsons carried on the title. The fact that neither 'Arab Muhammad nor Chingiz Muhammad included it in their titulature strongly suggests that they were neither of Subhan Quli's line nor of the Herat Walid line represented by 'Ibad Allah and Sanjar Muhammad. (Although Wali Muhammad himself was not a "sayyid," eligibility for the title was probably acquired maritally by his descendants while in exile in Herat.) It is reasonable to assume that 'Arab Muhammad and Chingiz Muhammad were Chingizids and more than likely Tuqay-Timurid Chingizids. But of what line is at this point impossible to say. Abu'l-Hasan, on the other hand, might have been from any one of several Tuqay-Timurid families.

. . .

The annexes, which would be preserved (and presumably used) for the next two centuries by the waqf administrators, are invaluable for the light they shed on the workings of the shrine administration over some seventy years. They tell us a good deal about the kind of economy that the waqf comprised and reveal the procedures by which the mutawalli periodically petitioned for formal (and routine) acknowledgment of the terms of the waqf and his rights. There are indications that the same procedures were often followed in dealing with extraordinary circumstances, when the fiscal prerogatives of the shrine or the administrative rights of the mutawalli were being challenged or usurped. The information in the annexes shows above all else the tenacity, adaptibility, and durability of the waqf and its administrators. In doing so it gives us a picture of how an essentially local institution maintained itself over a long period of time and in the face of forces that seem at times to have been quite hostile to the longevity of any independent economic institution.

CHAPTER NINE

The Nadirid Occupation of Balkh, 1737–1747

THE ADMINISTRATIVE REPERCUSSIONS

From 1668 to 1737, the waqf properties and waqf prerogatives dominate the recorded history of the shrine. During the last seven decades of the Chingizid era, the shrine's property rights had been periodically reviewed. The outcome of these reviews established precedents to which succeeding generations of administrators continually referred. But after the fall of the Chingizids, the political context within which the shrine administration functioned changed radically. And with these changes came changes in the ways in which the shrine administrators responded to the political authorities at Balkh. Moreover, the jurisdictional horizons of those responsible for the shrine and its waqf gradually expanded as they moved to meet economic and social needs that ceased to be served by Balkh. In the process, the shrine became increasingly political, in the sense that it became more and more the final arbiter of disputes within its own territory. Disputes and conflicts that the mutawallis might earlier have taken to Balkh for resolution came to be settled at the shrine itself.

The Chingizid era, which had lasted in one dynastic form or another for half a millennium in Balkh, was brought suddenly and finally to an end in the summer of 1737.[1] That spring, Rida Quli Mirza, the son of the recently crowned monarch of Iran, Nadir Shah Afshar, marched to Balkh from Mashhad, forcibly expelled the Ming ataliq, Sayyid Khan,[2] and de-

---

[1] The dating of the Nadirid conquest of Balkh presents a problem. Muhammad Kazim 1962–66, 2:98b dates the beginning of the campaign against the city to 1199 (sic), i.e., 1149, but gives no information on its conclusion. The only date for the actual surrender of Balkh is in Astarabadi 1848, 287, which uses the mixed Turki-Hijri system of dating. The fall of the city is included under the events of the Year of the Serpent (Yilan Yil), "corresponding to 1149 Hijri." Yilan Yil actually began quite late in 1149 (in the eleventh month, Dhu'l-Qa'dah), that is, in March 1737. Astarabadi 1848, 295 says that the final battle for Balkh began on 3 Rabi' al-Awwal (1150 not 1149), or 1 July 1737, and the city capitulated soon after. The problem with the date arises from the fact that in Shawwal 1150/January-February 1738, the Chingizid ruler of Balkh—the same person who is reported to have surrendered the city and been sent to Qandahar—issued an annex to the waqf. For the time being, there is no way to explain this apparent anomaly satisfactorily.

[2] Muhammad Kazim 1962–66, 2:102bff. consistently styles Sayyid Khan "Qipchaq." Equally consistent is the work of a later hand in the manuscript (the Moscow facsimile edition), perhaps the author's own, which has carefully placed the word *Ming* above the word *Qipchaq* wherever it appears after Sayyid Khan's name. Astarabadi does not mention the ataliq's name in either of his works.

posed Abu'l-Hasan Khan.[3] Abu'l-Hasan was required to present himself before Nadir Shah, who was then in Qandahar. There he was given leave to make the hajj-pilgrimage. He never returned, and the Chingizid age in Balkh was over.

It was a significant moment in Balkh's political history. The political dispensation that had survived some five centuries in the region had breathed its last, although signs of its failing health had been evident for some time. In the half century since Subhan Quli's regime at Balkh, the power of the sultan or khan there had steadily deteriorated while the strength of the Uzbek amirs had grown. Nevertheless, the Chingizid line still retained its exclusive legitimacy—more symbolic than effective by the end, but for the amirs still an important means of legitimizing their own authority and enhancing their standing with their peers. With the Chingizid mandate now at an end, new ideas of what constituted legitimate authority had to be instilled more or less from scratch. Up to this point, the status of individuals within the Uzbek tribal groupings—the Ming, Yuz, Qipchaq, Qataghan, Qunqhrat, Qanqli, et al.—had depended to no small extent on the place of a Chingizid line at the pinnacle of authority and on the functioning of the Chingizid code, the yasa, or yasa and yusun, of which it was guardian and nominal upholder and on which political activity was thought to depend. The political terminology in which "khan" and "amir" carried clear connotations when it came to political action likewise was a phenomenon of the Chingizid system. Politicians saw the world contained within a Chingizid framework, expressed their aspirations in Chingizid terms, and had their horizons of the possible bounded by the Chingizid legacy as they knew it.

For a time, the Iranian occupation forces, which were acting in the name of a different tradition, obscured the great void left by their excising the constitutional basis of politics in Balkh and Mawarannahr.

From an administrative standpoint, the Iranian conquest meant radical changes for Balkh and its dependent territories.[4] The Nadirid occupiers brought their own administrators and style of government. Iranian governors (hukkam) and fiscal agents ('ummal) were assigned to each town, bringing with them requisitions (hawalahjat) issued by the central diwan.

---

[3] Lockhart erred in calling this man a "governor" (his translation of wali) and lumping him with 'Ali Mardan Khan Afshar as governors who had "rebelled" (Lockhart 1938, 102, 163). Abu'l-Hasan was the last Tuqay-Timurid khan at Balkh, and there is no evidence of any ties between Nadir Shah and him prior to the conquest of Balkh.

[4] It is clear that the term Balkh in 1737 still covered a wide area, one nearly as large as the appanage ruled by Nadhr Muhammad in the first half of the seventeenth century. Muhammad Kazim 1962–66, 2:23b (margin) speaks of Jijaktu and Maymanah as "districts of Balkh." Astarabadi 1848, 273 describes Andkhud as "one of the tax districts [a'mal]" of Balkh. Qunduz to the east and the trans-Oxus towns of Tirmidh and Kulab were similarly still counted as dependencies of Balkh (Muhammad Kazim 1962–66, 2:107a).

The fiscal agents, backed by the military forces under the governors, collected the revenues stipulated in the requisitions and remitted them to Balkh, whence they were forwarded to the Iranian state treasury.[5] The decentralized administration favored by the Chingizids and their amirid supporters, in which revenues were remitted and then in large part appropriated locally, gave way to a closely supervised and centralized budgetary system. Balkh, which had been an autonomous city and the administrative and cultural focal point for the towns of its region for a century and a half, was reduced to the status of a minor provincial town within the imperial state of Nadir Shah.

THE ECONOMIC REPERCUSSIONS

The conquest had a very disruptive effect on the local economy. Whether the effects were any more severe or long-lasting than might be reasonably expected from any military occupation cannot be said. Balkh's economy was agrarian, its export earnings at this time coming mainly from fruit, horses, silk, and tobacco.[6] But the main product of Balkh was cereal grains, as may be inferred from the primary position in the annexes given to taxes on grain. Along with manufactured articles, grain formed the basis of regional trade between village and town and between herders and farmers. The herders in turn sold their wool, meat, horses, and milk products to the townsmen, who exported the surplus to India and Central Asia.

On the eve of the Iranian occupation, there were some signs that local economies were prospering, or at least were thought to be. One indication was the large capital investment made at Qunduz to build a new bazaar complex in the center of the city. This wholesale and retail center was designed to include shops and storage facilities and the workshops of some thirty different crafts.[7] Although we have no comparable information for Balkh during the same period, the economies of the two adjacent regions (Qunduz is 120 miles east of Balkh) were no doubt affected by the same regional and international forces and for now at least we may assume that an atmosphere conducive to capital investment in the one reflected a similar climate in the other. In addition, there was still a more or less unified monetary system, the currency of exchange and account throughout the entire region of the former appanage of greater Balkh, from Badakhshan in the east to Maymanah in the west, being the Subhan Quli tangah.[8]

[5] Muhammad Kazim 1962–66, 3:167b.

[6] Arunova and Ashrafi 1958, 245.

[7] Muhammad Kazim 1962–66, 2:124b.

[8] Badakhshi 1959, 10a–b. Monetary information, indeed economic information of any

The Nadirid occupation stripped away the basis of the local market economy. Besides having to support the garrisoned Iranian troops and officials, the farmers of Balkh were also required to help underwrite the costs of imperial expansion. Huge quantities of grain were requisitioned for Iranian troops in the field, much of it taken under the administrative rubric of "irregular levies [sursat]." Animals were likewise appropriated, to transport the grain. In 1742, as the Iranian army in Khurasan prepared to invade Khwarazm, Balkh was forced to ship four thousand kharwars[9] (about one thousand tons) of grain to the army staging area at Chahar Juy on the banks of the Oxus. The fact that the Iranian governor, Niyaz Khan, found it impossible to send more than three thousand kharwars gives some sign of the extent to which local stocks must have been depleted. One assumes that seed grains were also seized in an effort to meet the army's needs. If so, the effects on subsequent harvests and the ripple effects through the entire local economy would have been enormous. The fact that Niyaz Khan's inability to fulfill the requisition cost him his job strongly suggests that before admitting failure he would have left no silo untouched.[10]

The effect of the requisitions of grain was, not unexpectedly, a phenomenal rise in its price. According to the Iranian chronicler, Muhammad Kazim, whose point of view may have led him to downplay the dire economic consequences, the price of grain, when grain was available at all, reached two tuman per (Tabrizi) mann.[11] Fifty years earlier, we are told that the price of grain at Balkh was forty tangahs per kharwar.[12]

Given the present state of knowledge, it is impossible to compare these data with any hope of accuracy. Still, some idea of the range of magnitude of the increase in prices is perhaps possible. The kharwar used by Muhammad Yusuf Munshi equaled ten Bukharan mann (256 kilograms), one Bukharan mann being, we believe, the equivalent of ten Tabrizi mann of the time.[13] The equivalent value of the currencies is highly problematic. According to an early-eighteenth-century source in

---

kind, is very scarce for this period. The reference here is actually to a time two decades before the Nadirid invasion but is the most recent we have prior to the conquest. In 1782, the Subhan Quli tangah was still the unit of currency and account in Central Asian towns (Mukhtarov 1963, 43).

[9] Since the reference here is from an Iranian source, I assume that the kharwar in question is the one hundred mann-i Tabrizi unit of weight (Lambton 1969, 406–7), equivalent to some three hundred kilograms. This sursat levy would have amounted to something less than one million kilograms. The comparable Central Asian weight is probably the shuturwar (ushturwar, 256 kilograms) (Davidovich et al. 1976, 161).

[10] Muhammad Kazim 1962–66, 3:174a.

[11] Ibid., 202b.

[12] Muhammad Yusuf Munshi, fol. 106a.

[13] Davidovich et al. 1976, 161.

which the exchange ratios of Indian, Central Asian, and Iranian currencies are given, one " 'Iraqi" (i.e., Iranian) tuman was equivalent to about
143 Bukharan tangahs.[14] If Muhammad Kazim was reckoning in the 'Iraqi
tuman, which I assume he was, the price of grain might have risen as
much as 700 times as a result of the requisitions. If his tuman were simply a tuman of Bukharan (copper) dinars (40–50 to the tangah), then the
price had been increased five times. In either case, such prices had not
been experienced in Balkh for almost a century, since the Moghul occupation of the city in 1646–1647.

EFFECTS ON THE 'ALID WAQF

We have no direct information of the effect of the occupation on the waqf
properties. Obviously, if Balkh's economy was suffering under the Nadirid requisitions, it would be difficult to assume that the waqf lands were
not equally affected. Besides the grain requisitions, which must have
been made on the waqf lands as well, other waqf properties would have
felt the pinch of economic hard times. With no grain trade, the level of
personal income must have declined and reduced revenues for shopkeep-
ers and artisans. These in turn would have been more hard-pressed to
meet the rent payments on their shops, a major source of waqf income.
Perhaps the fighting in Khwarazm and the separation of Balkh from Mawarannahr by the Nadirid occupation created havoc with exports to Central Asia and Russia, although such problems tended to be temporary and
often balanced by the opportunities for profiteering created during times
of war.

The evidence we do have for relations between the shrine and the Iranian authorities suggests that the waqf administrators, even though seriously and negatively affected by the occupation, were at least attempting
to forestall or alleviate future problems by forging friendly ties with the
occupiers. The shrine administration, whose relations with the authorities at Balkh had been fairly routine and predictable for about a century,
had to come to grips quickly with the Iranian presence, the possibility of
its permanence, and the need in that case to insure the security of the
waqf properties. In developing a policy to deal with the Iranians, it would
have been difficult for the shrine administration to see in the present
situation an analogy with the Mughal period, in which the foreign occu-

[14] Haji Mir Muhammad Salim, fol. 225b, in reporting the cost of the Moghul invasion of
Balkh in 1646–1647, equates 20 crores of tangahs to 14 laks of Iraqi tumans to 4 crores of
Indian rupees. This gives a nominal relationship of 1 tuman to 142.86 tangahs. (A crore is a
unit of ten million, a lak a unit of one hundred thousand.) Whether his rates of exchange
were based on those current at the time he was writing or at the time about which he was
writing (eighty-five years earlier) is uncertain.

pier was soon faced with popular resistance and quickly forced to withdraw. There was nothing to tell the mutawalli and his staff that the Nadirids would not be in power for the foreseeable future nor that accommodation was not the best policy.

It is clear that the administration had to make certain choices at this time. Should the shrine cooperate with the Iranian governor, despite the heavy financial burden placed on the waqf economy, in the hope that cooperation would lead to some relief, or should it resist, either passively or actively, and give aid to any local forces that emerged to challenge Iranian authority? From the information available now, this appears to have been a decision the mutawalli had to make. Whether deliberate or not, as soon as local resistance to the Iranian occupation emerged, the shrine authorities were forced to choose one course or the other.

LOCAL RESISTANCE AND THE ROLE OF THE SHRINE

There is some evidence that the waqf administration made its peace with the Nadirids soon after the conquest had been completed in the summer of 1737. Despite the influx of Iranian officials to administer the territory,[15] there was no apparent attempt to replace the shrine administration. The mutawalli, Khwajah Ni'mat,[16] who seems to have been both successor to and son of Qadi Mir Muhammad Amin, continued the Ansari line at the shrine and held the post throughout the Nadirid decade. Conspicuously missing from our trail of documentation, though, is any form of confirmation of the mutawalli's position, something one would have expected in light of the practice of the previous century. It is possible that there was such a record, but that it was later suppressed when the unpopular Iranians eventually withdrew in the face of strong opposition. As far as we can tell, however, at the outset of the occupation the mutawalli gave the Iranian governor, Niyaz Khan, no cause to worry that the waqf or any other resources of the shrine would be used to support anti-Nadirid forces.

What little we know of the relations between the Iranian occupiers and the shrine comes from the account of a popular uprising with strong messianic overtones, which at first threatened to turn the shrine into a haven of popular religious resistance to the Nadirid authorities. The movement offers us the sole opportunity to see what the shrine administration was

---

[15] Muhammad Kazim 1962–66, 2:283b; 3:167b.

[16] Astarabadi 1848, 30 gives the name as Khwajah Ni'mat. A nineteenth-century document renders it as Ni'mat Khan (*TMS*, 74 [text], 81 [transcription]). Muhammad Kazim offers the most complete account of his activities but does not mention his name. Nor does his name appear in the defective list of Ansari mutawallis compiled by Hafiz Nur Muhammad (*TMS*, 100, note), even though it appears elsewhere in his book (Ibid., 74, 81).

doing during this period, although the references are only tangential to the account's main concern with the form and ideology of the religious movement that appeared.

As an aside, it is worth injecting here a note about the durability and popularity of Abu Muslim's role in Khurasan. People in Khurasan, including the Balkh area, had no more forgotten the symbolism of Abu Muslim, the fighter for Khurasani rights against the Arab tribal aristocracy in Damascus and Iraq in the early eighth century, than had Shi'ites forgotten the role of Shimr at Karbala. Abu Muslim, an archetypal hero of the oppressed, was connected in popular lore with the foundation of the 'Alid shrine. According to one version of that legend, the Shi'ite imam Ja'far al-Sadiq (d. 765), after refusing Abu Muslim's offer of backing should he make a bid for the caliphate, assigned the general the mission of removing the Caliph 'Ali's body from a secret hiding place in Najaf and transporting it to Balkh. In this story, Ja'far al-Sadiq actually wanted the caliphate and needed Abu Muslim's support, but first wished to test his loyalty. The removal of the holy relic was to serve a number of purposes: first, to test Abu Muslim's devotion to the 'Alid cause; second, to provide a rallying point for the "party of 'Ali" in Khurasan; and third, to forestall Umayyad or Kharijite desecration of the holy corpse.

All of the cited sources for this legend were written after the sixteenth century.[17] We are not interested here in the origin of the story but rather in its vitality in such a comparatively late period. It offers a glimpse of what shaped the world view of the inhabitants of this region, of their salvationist instincts, and of the place of the 'Alid shrine in popular religious thought. The association of Abu Muslim's name with the shrine and his role as savior in times of injustice have particular significance for the Nadirid period, for it was during the decade-long occupation of Balkh by Iranian troops that there appeared one of the largest and most powerful religious movements seen in Balkh since the days of Abu Muslim.

At the time that Nadir Shah's army moved east into what is now Afghanistan, a man whom our sources rather provocatively call "Rasul" ("Messenger"—the epithet of the Prophet Muhammad)[18] lived in the region of Ubah and Shafilan, a mountainous district east of Herat. He had

---

[17] Muhammad Murid 1319. *TMS*, 112 also cites other unpublished sources: the anonymous *Tarikh-i Akabir al-Din* written about 1824–25; the *Tadhkirah-i Haftad Mashayikh-i Balkh* of Muhammad Salih Badawani Warsaji, written in 1594–95 for the then-ruler of Balkh, 'Abd al-Mu'min b. 'Abd Allah Khan (on this work, see Mukhtarov 1980, 14); and an untitled work by Muhammad Mu'min b. 'Iwad Baqi Balkhi (probably the *Jaridah* described by Mukhtarov 1980, 9–12). *BA* 4: fols. 318a–b also has a version of the Abu Muslim story.

[18] The narrative that follows is derived mainly from Muhammad Kazim 1962–66, 3:91b–100a. Astarabadi 1848, 379–80 has a very brief reference, while Astarabadi 1876 and Rida Quli Khan Hidayat 1960 do not mention the movement at all.

tried to make his living at a number of different occupations without success. As one work says, "he was always getting into scrapes and tight spots because of ill fortune."[19] He led a transient's life and fell in with local "hermits, yogis and qalandars,"[20] generic names by which the writer was trying to convey an idea of counterculturalists or street people.

The towns of Ubah and Shafilan were in a region that had for a long time been the border between the political jurisdictions of Iran, Central Asia, and Hindustan. As such it was a conduit as well as a refuge for people and ideas persecuted in their native lands by their more conservative co-religionists.

Apparently, Rasul found his association with these qalandars and yogis useful but not necessarily inspiring. Inspiration and spiritual direction came one day when he traveled down from the mountains to Herat. There, the story goes, he came across a street dervish who was extremely ill and in need of help. Rasul was reportedly moved by the man's plight, took him under his wing and in three months nursed him back to health. The dervish happened to be a skilled geomancer and numerologist[21] and, in gratitude for Rasul's help, offered to teach him all he knew. A three-year apprenticeship followed, and when it ended Rasul struck out on his own.

The structure used by the narrator of this tale is one that would resonate even more in his time than it does today. The themes of alienation, selflessness and reward, and the imparting of esoterica are carefully crafted here to provide a context within which the "real" events could be credibly told.

Rasul (perhaps we should say "the rasul") now left Herat for Ghazni, a flourishing town midway between Qandahar and Kabul (though one far reduced from its glory days in the eleventh century). In Ghazni he found an audience of "crowds of the common folk and tribal peoples"[22] for whom his numerological systems and the prophecies that sprang from them provided meaning and insight into life's mysteries when more conventional religion could not. The crowds found enough evidence in his predictions and miraculous works to convince them of his saintliness. When his successes in Ghazni had run their course, a follower suggested he take his message to Turkistan. Not long afterwards, sometime in the late summer or early fall of 1741, Rasul left Ghazni for Andkhud. Whether his route took him more or less directly though the Hindu Kush via his former residence in the western part of the mountain range is difficult to say. If we accept the assertion that he was accompanied by

[19] Muhammad Kazim 1962–66, 3:91b.
[20] Ibid.
[21] Ibid., 92a.
[22] Ibid., 92b.

fifty thousand disciples, it seems likely that the Nadirid authorities would have preferred to keep him clear of the cities. Nor do we know why he chose Andkhud as his destination, although the fact that it was a shrine center with a peculiarly populist history may have had something to do with his choice.

In any event, as this large body of people approached the town, Rasul instructed them, according to Muhammad Kazim, to tie palm fronds to their clothes, put on green turbans, and carry sticks in their hands.[23] The messianic message of rebirth and regeneration could hardly have been more overtly signaled. Rasul camped just outside Andkhud and was soon besieged by the city's poor and sick, who expected miracles from him. Word spread that he could turn the palm fronds into food, and, when he reportedly restored a man's sight by rubbing his saliva on the man's eyes, onlookers tore the cured man's clothing to shreds in the hope of acquiring some of Rasul's divine grace. News of the miracle worker quickly spread throughout the region.

The potential danger of Rasul's movement as a focus for rallying anti-Iranian feelings was not lost on the Nadirid governor of Andkhud. Apparently intending to debunk the rapidly growing legend and to defuse the volatile undercurrents, the governor went out to visit the holy man at his camp. But when he challenged Rasul on his reported miracles, the latter performed a number of wonders (karamat)[24] in which he conjured up trays of sweets and caused a small stream of water to flow. This made a convert of the Iranian governor, and he gave Rasul gold, silver, food, and cloth.

In the meantime, the holy man was now being referred to as "Hadrat-i Ishan," a term of respect reserved for the most highly regarded spiritual figures. In Andkhud, one such famous "hadrat-i ishan" had been the fourteenth century Baba Sangu, whom we have already encountered. Another, and perhaps the most famous of the "hadrat-i ishans" of Central Asia, was 'Ubayd Allah Ahrar.

Not long after convincing the governor of Andkhud that his powers were genuine, Rasul, the Hadrat-i Ishan, received word from some unnamed religious personages in Balkh that his presence there would be welcome. On hearing this, he immediately left Andkhud and, accompanied by some "three or four thousand rough-and-ready types" (ajamirah wa ubash) according to Muhammad Kazim, moved on to Balkh.[25] Perhaps the author, knowing what was to come and not unsympathetic to

---

[23] Ibid.

[24] Jami 1957, 21 gives a useful definition of the distinction between "unusual feats" (karamat) and "miracles" (mu'jizat).

[25] Muhammad Kazim 1962–66, 3:94b.

the holy man, wanted to shift blame for subsequent events away from the Hadrat-i Ishan and so identified a group of likely culprits.

When the Hadrat-i Ishan reached the outskirts of Balkh, he found an audience that was extremely receptive to the egalitarian and oppression-minded themes of his preaching. His appeal, as in Ghazni and Andkhud, was to the poor, the sick, and the pastoralist tribes whose presence was increasingly visible around Balkh. In the latter part of the Tuqay-Timurid period, these tribal groups, particularly the more recent arrivals, had actively injected themselves into the political process.

Now, as a consequence of the Nadirid invasions, their economic and political positions had been threatened. Nadirid economic policies were especially crippling to agriculturalists and pastoralists. Squeezed on the one hand by the sursat, the extraordinary wartime levies that took not only the peasant's grain but also the herder's animals to transport it, the tribal groups were further tyrannized by the impressment of their members as farm laborers in Khurasan. While Rida Quli Khan Mirza was still at Balkh, Nadir Shah ordered him to send off certain "Khurasani tribes" to cultivate the land around Marw and free the presumably more trustworthy Marwis for the proposed invasion of Khwarazm. On 5 December 1737, a Marwi contingent left Balkh for home, taking under escort unspecified "Khurasani tribes" as forced laborers.[26]

The preeminent tribal grouping at Balkh, at least in terms of the number of references to it, was the Qipchaq. In the latter part of the seventeenth century, as the identifications of specific tribal groups with certain territories emerged, the Qipchaq were to be found around Salu Charyak (or San u Charyak), an ancient administrative center between Darrah-i Juz (Darrah-i Gaz) and Bamyan.[27] It was a mountainous region and offered summer pastures for the tribe that controlled it. By the time of the Nadirid conquest, the Qipchaq were ensconced on the plain around Balkh (perhaps what had become their winter pasture) and are one of the two tribal groups (the Ming being the other) mentioned as resisting the Nadirid army.[28] When the Ming ataliq escaped to the east, his tribesmen appear to have accompanied him, for it is only the Qipchaq who remain as named opponents of the Iranian forces and who later are cited as the dominant tribal group around Balkh. By the end of 1741, when the Hadrat-i Ishan reached Balkh, the Qipchaq were well under the Nadirid thumb. But the resentment caused by the impressments of livestock and labor ran deep.

The Hadrat-i Ishan was greeted outside Balkh by a crowd estimated at

[26] Ibid., 2:126a. The Nadirids viewed Balkh as part of Khurasan (p. 28b), and people from Balkh were likely therefore to be called "Khurasani."

[27] Akhmedov 1982, 48–49; Muhammad Yusuf Munshi, fol. 116a.

[28] Muhammad Kazim 1962–66, 2:102a.

some fifty or sixty thousand people. The messianic elements of his movement are first voiced, or first recorded, here, the crowd addressing him as the "Apostle of the Age" (*rasul-i muddati*) and "True Imam" (*imam bi-haqq*).

With these cries resounding in his ears, the Hadrat-i Ishan decided not to enter Balkh City itself but to make his headquarters at a more appropriate place, the tombsite of ʿAli b. Abi Talib, the archetypal imam of his time. The irony of this may not have escaped the Jaʿfari/Shiʿite governors in Balkh City.

When the holy man reached the shrine, a room was prepared for him next to the inner sanctum containing the holy relics. There he began to receive, we are told, an influx of sick and maimed visitors who hoped for miraculous healing. Although there are reports of unhappiness at the lack of efficacy of his cures, his reputation continued to spread, and reached its zenith when he revived two decapitated men before the no doubt incredulous eyes of the Nadirid governor of Balkh, Niyaz Khan, and the mutawalli of the shrine, Khwajah Niʿmat Ansari.[29]

The political consequences of his spiritual feats were far-reaching. At this point, we are told, a Qipchaq leader, ʿIsmat Allah Beg, decided to exploit the passions aroused by the Hadrat-i Ishan. (A caveat about the way in which this tribal figure is portrayed by Muhammad Kazim: since the author clearly has feelings of sympathy for the holy man, he tended to cast those around him as the villains in the piece.)

ʿIsmat Allah Beg represented the Qipchaq before the Nadirid authorities. His title, apparently an official one, was Master of Tribe and Clan (*sahib-i ayl wa ulus*), and he held sway over "ten thousand households." He now placed himself and his people at the Hadrat-i Ishan's disposal, perhaps seeing, as the account alleges, an opportunity to rally anti-Nadirid elements in Balkh. His followers were accepted as disciples by the Hadrat-i Ishan, and ʿIsmat Allah began militarizing the holy man's heretofore somewhat loose and undisciplined following. Open conflict erupted between this movement and the Iranian authorities when the Qipchaq leader demanded that the Nadirid governor pay homage to the Hadrat-i Ishan. When the Iranian refused, an armed insurrection broke out.

Throughout these preliminaries, the mutawalli of the shrine and its waqf, Khwajah Niʿmat, plays a shadowy part. The sudden arrival of the Hadrat-i Ishan with a large band of followers at the shrine must have caused him some apprehension. As mutawalli, he seems to have been obligated at this time to provide food, shelter, clothing, medicine, and, if need be, shrouds to anyone who visited the shrine. (Although we do

---

[29] Ibid., 3:95a.

not have the original waqfnamahs, either from Sultan Husayn Bayqara or the seventeenth-century amirid and khanly donors, such provisions were quite common and, at least for the nineteenth century, can be documented at the 'Alid shrine.)

Still, one guesses that the numbers involved here and the circumstances surrounding this manifestation of religious fervor would have burdened the shrine and could hardly have been welcome. And when the Qipchaq appeared on the scene and began to use the shrine as the base for anti-Nadirid activity, the mutawalli's anxiety probably deepened. The specter of political conflict with its associated and inevitable tribal violence would not have been a particularly pleasant prospect for a man charged with the efficient operation of an extensive and vulnerable economy. In 1741 it was the Nadirid administration in Balkh, Niyaz Khan to be specific, that protected waqf rights and provided the regional security within which the mutawalli could best function. It is not surprising, therefore, to find that, in the infrequent references to the mutawalli, he is generally depicted as aligned with and at the right hand of the Iranian governor.

On the other hand, protection of the waqf rights required a certain ability to trim sails when necessary, and it is clear that the mutawalli never staked everything on the Iranians. When Niyaz Khan visited the shrine to confront and test the Hadrat-i Ishan, Khwajah Ni'mat was at the governor's side as host and probably ally as well. But when the power of the holy man proved more potent than he had anticipated and the hadrat and his followers became the source of an anti-Nadirid rebellion, the mutawalli appears to have quietly disassociated himself from Niyaz Khan and faded into the background.

The Qipchaq rising in the fall of 1741 was at first very effective. The Iranians came out of Balkh with a small force but were defeated in open battle and forced to take up siege positions inside the inner city of Balkh. Lacking supplies, the Iranians were only able to maintain their position for ten days, after which time they tried to flee to the west. But a Qipchaq force, reportedly numbering sixty thousand men, cut off their escape route and forced Niyaz Khan and his men back into the citadel.

The tables soon turned, however. In the skirmish in which the Iranians were prevented from making good their escape, 'Ismat Allah Beg, the Qipchaq leader, sustained a serious wound. Undaunted, his followers carried him back to the 'Alid shrine, convinced that the Hadrat-i Ishan would restore him to health. But unfortunately for the hadrat, 'Ismat Allah Beg died, and the Qipchaq, our source tells us, promptly withdrew their support from the Hadrat-i Ishan. On or about 19 December 1741, the holy man from Herat, for a brief time the most powerful man in Balkh, found himself abandoned and virtually alone at the 'Alid shrine.

Khwajah Niʿmat had stayed out of the fray while the Qipchaq had the Iranians under siege in Balkh. But now, with the desertion of the Hadrat-i Ishan and the restoration of Iranian authority imminent, he took steps to retrieve his standing as a staunch supporter of the Nadirid administration. One source says that Khwajah Niʿmat, accompanied by a band of ghazis took the holy man into custody and marched him off to Niyaz Khan in Balkh.[30] Another source, however, casts the mutawalli in a more cautious role. According to Muhammad Kazim, when the mutawalli saw the hadrat abandoned by his followers, he sent Niyaz Khan a message that the Hadrat-i Ishan was defenceless and that a force of two hundred men would be enough to take him prisoner. The mutawalli then moved to prevent the hadrat from leaving the shrine until the Iranian forces could arrive.[31]

The Hadrat-i Ishan, the "Apostle of the Age" and "True Imam," was martyred and severe reprisals taken against his followers by a special relief force sent by Nadir Shah to Balkh. This contingent made its headquarters well west of the city,[32] staying clear of the shrine and its properties. After erecting a fortification, the Iranians began violent retaliations against the Qipchaq living around Balkh, the campaign reportedly leading to the death and enslavement of thousands.[33] Six thousand five hundred Qipchaq prisoners were chosen to die by lot. In a fashion familiar to the region, their heads were piled in a tower fifteen cubits (*dharʿ*) high and seven dharʿ in diameter. Rubble was used to create some structural rigidity, and to Muhammad Kazim, who was an eyewitness, it looked like a "boxed wall" (*sanduqah-i diwar*)[34] in which heads were substituted for bricks.[35] At the top of this grisly tower, one of the Hadrat-i Ishan's closest disciples, a man who had announced his arrival in villages along his way as "Lord of the Age and the Time" was entombed alive, and his screams reportedly could be heard for days until he died.[36]

Fascinating as all this is, what concerns us here is the course followed by the mutawalli, Khwajah Niʿmat Ansari, for the episode provides one of the rare glimpses we have of a shrine administrator caught up in a political crisis. Generally, the shrine and its waqf operated outside the sphere of interest of those who chronicled the events of khans and amirs, so that when some information is provided it takes on added significance.

[30] Astarabadi 1848, 380.
[31] Muhammad Kazim 1962–66, 3:96b–97a. The size of the force required to arrest the dervish suggests that he had not been totally forsaken.
[32] Ibid., 98a.
[33] Ibid., 99a–b.
[34] Dihkhuda, 1946–
[35] Muhammad Kazim 1962–66, 3:99b.
[36] Ibid. 99b–100a.

In tracing the mutawalli's behavior throughout the series of events that culminated in the complete suppression of the Qipchaq uprising, what is striking is the administrator's apparently unalloyed concern for the security and economic welfare of the shrine and the corresponding lack of recorded interest in the spiritual and moral tradition that the shrine represented. The figure of 'Ali b. Abi Talib represents courage, deliverance from oppression, defense of the weak, and, through the holy site where he was buried, intercession with the Almighty. His tombsite, as the sacred "threshold" between the world of wickedness and sin and the divine world of grace and redemption, was a focus of hope for people with grievances against those they saw as their political and economic oppressors. But the apparent contradiction between the conservative and defensive postures of the mutawalli in the face of forces seeking to use the shrine to rally the sentiment of the oppressed is only that. His concerns were more mundane, pragmatic, and ultimately more geared to protecting the shrine against politicization and a possible loss of its economic prerogatives—prerogatives in which by now he and his family also had a personal stake.

It is worth raising the possibility here that neither the shrine nor the Ansari family of administrators had any apparent reputation for scholarship or scholarly patronage. It would probably be incorrect to say that the 'Alid shrine was isolated, geographically anyway, from the intellectual life of Mawarannahr. Yet the fact that no reference has yet been found to famous scholars who lived and worked at the shrine or to any noteworthy scholarship by the mutawallis or their kin strongly suggests that the shrine played no major role in perpetuating Muslim intellectual life. The men who supervised the shrine were businessmen and bureaucrats whose interests were probably entirely engaged by their account books and their political relations. The titles of "qadi," "mirza," and "khwajah" that are prefixed to the names of the mutawalli suggest middle-level learning.

Certainly not conclusive, but still suggestive, is the list of scholars, "the Iranian, Afghan, and Mawarannahr 'ulama" present at Najaf for the ecumenical council convened by Nadir Shah in December of 1743. Despite the fact that the Ansari mutawalli had cooperated, if not collaborated, with the Iranian authorities and despite the obviously compatible symbolism that the 'Alid shrine at Balkh represented, not one of the fourteen "Afghan" or "Mawarannahrid" scholars had any apparent connection with either the shrine or even Balkh itself.[37] (Perhaps it would have been

---

[37] al-Suwaydi 1905–06, 18–19. That the shrine was not represented at the conclave would tend to support the hypothesis that it was not an intellectual center of any note and that its administration lacked scholarly credentials. What would have been more appropriate, after all, as a symbol of unifying elements in Sunni-Jama'i and Imami-Shi'i Islam than to have

overstepping the already strained limits of what the Shi'ite scholars of Najaf, Qum, and Karbala could tolerate by inviting to Najaf the protectors of a Central Asian shrine that purported to be the true burial place of 'Ali b. Abi Talib.)

None of this is to state unequivocally that the mutawallis lacked both spiritual and scholarly credentials. There is simply no proof for such an assertion. However, from what we do know, it is reasonably safe to conclude that the suitability of acknowledging the Hadrat-i Ishan as the personification of the ideals attributed to 'Ali b. Abi Talib, let alone publicly recognizing the popular perception that he was the Apostle of the Age, would probably never have occurred to Khwajah Ni'mat Ansari. Instead he seems to have been preoccupied with thoughts of unanticipated expenses, possible alienation of the Iranian authorities, and the consequences of both to the secure operation of the shrine's economy. His attendance at the governor's side at the sessions at which the holy man restored two men to life and later his part in the arrest and execution of the Hadrat-i Ishan, despite having to violate the sanctuary tradition to do so, indicate that when it was judicious he would cooperate with the Nadirid administration in Balkh, even if this meant contravening the moral principles that the shrine symbolized—the struggle against oppression, sanctuary from injustice, and courage in the face of overwhelming odds.

Khwajah Ni'mat took a pragmatic approach in fulfilling his responsibility for the shrine's welfare. He had no apparent brief for the Nadirid cause, either. While it was in power and no alternative was visible on the political horizon, the Iranian authorities offered the best guarantee of stability and thus security for the economic operations of the shrine and the protection of its waqf holdings. As long as he believed it was in the best interests of the shrine, he supported the Nadirids. When, however, it appeared that the Iranians might be forced to abandon Balkh in the face of the Qipchaq uprising, Khwajah Ni'mat backed away and waited to see what turn events would take. When the special force dispatched by Nadir Shah arrived on the scene to quell the disturbance and, at the same time, the Hadrat-i Ishan lost a substantial part of his Qipchaq following, Khwajah Ni'mat did not hesitate to put himself forward as a loyal friend and supporter of the Iranian authorities.

It is easy in this to assign only economic motives and opportunism to the mutawalli's behavior, to see in his maneuvering only a desire to protect the economy of the shrine and his position in it. But one should not overlook the element of the shrine's own history and tradition in his pol-

had in attendance representatives of the Central Asian tradition of the burial place of 'Ali b. Abi Talib? (I am grateful to Prof. Michel Mazzaoui for drawing my attention to the list of scholars at the Najaf conclave.)

icy. For reference he had available to him at least the documents we have today and probably much more material, in which his ancestors' relations with the political authorities at Balkh were recorded. The shrine and its waqf properties had survived a quarter of a millenium by Khwajah Niʿmat's time, and this too must have gone through his mind as he pondered what step to take next in handling the crisis posed by the advent of the Hadrat-i Ishan. He could also look around him and, with some sense of satisfaction, compare the longevity of the ʿAlid waqf properties with the longevity, or lack thereof, of the waqfs founded to support other large institutions in the region: the waqfs established a century earlier endowing Nadhr Muhammad's madrasah, for instance, or the endowments dedicated to maintaining the madrasah of Subhan Quli later in the seventeenth century.[38] Neither had survived the intervening years very well and both could have been an object lesson to any mutawalli, but especially to one with such an extensive waqf inventory to manage.

Both considerations, the economic and the historical, must have shaped Khwajah Niʿmat's policies in political and religious matters. His first responsibility was the survival and prosperity of the shrine. He followed his predecessors in shunning political partisanship unless the security of the waqf properties was at stake, and then in backing the authority he judged would best serve the needs of the shrine.

In light of the political conditions that his forefathers had faced, this "bandwagon" approach to the authorities at Balkh had been an effective policy. Whether it would remain so depended in large part on the shape of politics in the Balkh region in the post-Nadirid period.

THE NADIRID LEGACY

The years between 1741 and 1747 were marked by parallel developments in the political life of the formerly great appanage of Balkh. One development was the erosion and eventual disappearance of a strong political center and with it the decline of Balkh City as an economic and political focus. Simultaneously, regional urban centers—Andkhud and Maymanah in the west and Khulm and Qunduz in the east—were growing up. Although the force of tribalism remained strong throughout the former appanage territory, these regional units appear to have had a stronger geographic than tribal identity. Qunduz, headquarters of the Qataghan tribe, was an exception. In the post-Nadirid period, tribal connections are seldom given when mention is made of a local politician, again with the exception of the Qataghan in Qunduz.

The defeat of the Qipchaq in 1741 was the high-water mark for Nadirid

---

[38] *BA* 4: fols. 214a–b.

authority in Balkh. There was no sudden loss of power nor even a perceptible erosion of authority prior to their withdrawal. On the eve of their abandoning Balkh in 1747, the Iranian forces were still strong enough to smash with ease an assault by local rebels.[39] But the period after 1741 is marked by a steady revival and display of Uzbek power, largely as a result of Nadirid policies. As Nadir Shah's forces spread into India, Khwarazm, Mawarannahr, Iraq, and the Persian Gulf, his demands for troops and supplies grew. Conquered regions like Balkh began to use locally recruited soldiers to do the policing necessary to maintain a steady flow of revenue and supplies to the imperial center, that is, wherever the war front happened to be. In the campaign into Badakhshan in 1745–1746 to suppress a taxpayers' revolt, the Nadirid governor of Balkh had to rely entirely on a force of Ming, Yuz, Qipchaq, Qunghrat, "and other Uzbek *uruqat*" to defeat the rebels of Kulab and Badakhshan.[40] The consequence of this process was the rebuilding of the military power of the tribes of Balkh and their reemergence as a political force. As a result, certain prominent amirid figures began to challenge Nadirid paramountcy.

One of these was Hazarah Khan,[41] a Qataghan amir and descendant of Mahmud Bi.[42] He ruled Qunduz when the Nadirids conquered Balkh and, despite his having given sanctuary to the Ming ataliq of Balkh, Sayyid Khan, he nonetheless made his peace with the Iranians and was instrumental in carrying out their economic policies in the eastern part of Balkh. But after the Badakhshan events of 1745–1746, when it became clear to Hazarah Khan that without his support the Nadirids could not remain, he adopted an increasingly independent stance.

The death of Nadir Shah on 19 June 1747[43] persuaded the Iranians, who were under pressure from townsmen as well as tribesmen,[44] to evacuate Balkh. From 'Abd al-Karim's untitled history of Bukhara, we get a flavor of the kind of (possibly desperate) negotiations that the Iranian administrators were forced into in order to detach themselves without loss

---

[39] Muhammad Kazim 1962–66, 3:206a.

[40] Ibid., 177b–178b.

[41] The use of the title "khan" suffixed to the names of non-Chingizids is symptomatic of both the reinterpretation of the yasa sanction and the inability of Iranian historians to recognize its specific meaning in the Central Asian context. In Iran, the title had long been used by Qizilbash (i.e., non-Safawid) amirs.

[42] According to Kushkaki 1924, 14, Hazarah was the son of Muhammad Yusuf Bi b. Midrab Bi b. Suhrab "Khan" b. Mahmud Bi. Kushkaki, who nowhere mentions his sources, is in fundamental disagreement with the chronology of Muhammad Kazim. According to the latter, Hazarah was ruling at Qunduz in 1737. Kushkaki says that Hazarah did not come to govern Qunduz until the death of Muhammad Yusuf Bi in 1747.

[43] Lockhart 1938, 262.

[44] Muhammad Kazim 1962–66, 3:201b.

of life.[45] The pullout in Balkh took place at the end of the summer, and as soon as it was accomplished various Uzbek factions rushed in to pick up the pieces.

The Ming were the first to take control of Balkh. They were led either by Musa Khwajah "Uzbek" (the absence of a tribal name is probably due to lack of sophistication on the part of the source), a man reputed to be of great wealth,[46] or "Haji Khan."[47] The Ming amir was soon unseated by Hazarah Khan, the Qataghan from Qunduz, who was then forced to contend with an embattled group of Iranians trying to withdraw from Mawarannahr. Unable to find food in Balkh, this group of Iranians hurried west in early October 1747.[48]

After a decade in the region, the last Iranian troops left Balkh's soil. The main effect of the occupation was felt in the area of Chingizid politics. The Chingizid dispensation, in which political legitimacy and nominal authority were attributed to the descendants of Chingiz Khan, had been under challenge for at least the previous generation. The rise of the amirid ataliqs and the increasing exercise of real power not by the Chingizids but by their Uzbek amirs had eroded popular acceptance of Chingizid prerogatives. In the last few years before the Nadirid occupation, the city's leaders had been obliged to go abroad to find Chingizid khan-candidates. But it was the occupation itself that tolled the death knell for the Chingizids in Balkh. The failure to reestablish a Balkh line coupled with the inability of the Chingizid khan and his supporters to defend the polity against the Iranians ended all Chingizid pretensions to political authority, and, more importantly, dissuaded the Uzbek amirs from continuing on the Chingizid course. Henceforth, or at least until the arrival of the bearers of a new political mandate, the politics of the region was to be defined solely in terms of local amirid rights and prerogatives. For changing the course of local politics and political expectations, the Nadirids were in no small measure responsible.

In the wake of the Nadirid withdrawal, the city of Balkh became the focus of political ambition and the arena in which contests took place. For a time, Balkh City retained its special attractiveness despite the severe economic effects that the occupation had had on it. For the amirid factions that immediately emerged once the Nadirids had left, possession of Balkh was seen to bestow special status. The city was still thought of as the center of the entire cis-Oxine region, from the Murghab in the west to Badakhshan in the east. As the seat of Chingizid power for two centu-

[45] Bukhari 1876, 112–113 (translation).

[46] Muhammad Kazim 1962–66, 3:204b.

[47] Bukhari 1876, 262. C. Schefer, the editor and translator, cites Rida Quli Khan, *Fihrist al-tawarikh*, as Bukhari's source.

[48] Muhammad Kazim 1962–66, 3:205b–206a.

ries, it retained a charismatic appeal, which, if the desire for control of
the city is any indication, still exerted a powerful pull long after the Chingizids themselves were gone.

But what clearly emerges from the amirid campaigns for control of
Balkh is the inescapable fact that possession of the city really meant very
little. Without a broader political base and more substantial economic
means, jurisdiction over the entire Balkh region—the former appanage
area with the city as its center and comprising the Hazhdah Nahr irrigation system—was impossible. Rather than enhancing a regional amir's
prestige, control of Balkh tended instead to weaken his authority in his
home district, an important factor in the rise of the political influence of
the shrine and in the ongoing subdivision of the former appanage into
petty amirid states.

CHAPTER TEN

The Consequences of Autonomy: The Emergence of a Shrine-State in the Century after 1747

POLITICS TO 1797

Although individual events rarely prove as important as they are portrayed to be by authors close to them, and "turning points" in history are more often than not just devices by means of which a historian may organize his or her material, the withdrawal of Nadirid forces from Balkh after Nadir Shah's death may be an exception to this rule. It does not stretch credulity to see in the end of the Nadirid period a decisive break with the Chingizid political past. The Nadirid period had also introduced a number of major, albeit temporary, economic changes. Balkh was briefly colonized, and its output appropriated by the Iranian empire of Nadir Shah. For the decade of its occupation, Balkh was little more than a supplier of foodstuffs for the Nadirid state's military forces. This role ran counter to what the region had been accustomed to in the previous quarter-millennium, when it enjoyed autonomy in both political and economic matters within a larger state structure organized on appanage principles.

In the autumn of 1747, when what was to be the last Nadirid force in Balkh performed a farewell pilgrimage to the 'Alid shrine,[1] Balkh returned, at least outwardly, to its erstwhile position of relative political autonomy. But the economic context in 1747 was markedly different from what it had been even as late as the end of the seventeenth century, when Balkh was still exchanging delegations with Moscow to negotiate trade agreements.[2] Central Asia had long since moved from the center to the edge of the stage on which world trade was transacted. World economic trends were no longer so visible in the inland areas of Asia but now were determined around its periphery. The edges of the Mediterranean, the Persian Gulf, and the western Indian Ocean had become magnets attracting the agents of world production and consumption away from the center of the Asian land mass.

Balkh's distance from the areas of greatest economic activity inevitably made its political importance equally peripheral. The region was not completely isolated from worldwide trends, and certain of its products,

---

[1] Muhammad Kazim 1962–66, 3:205b.
[2] Akhmedov 1982, 211ff.

notably horses, remained in demand until the twentieth century. Indeed, the fact that silk and tobacco, with their specialized production facilities, were important commodities as late as 1721 indicates Balkh's inclusion, on however limited a scale, in the world market. It is worth noting, though, that another worldwide commodity, coffee, which with all its related cultural paraphernalia had swept through Iran in the late seventeenth century, appears not to have touched Balkh in any significant way.

If true, this supposition perhaps indicates the region's relative inability to finance luxury imports by this time. Certainly the material on which we base such conclusions is depressingly scant, a circumstance that in and of itself may be significant. But if we use references to foreign goods and trade as crude indicators of Balkh's role in the world economy and the influence of the rest of the world on local economic decisions, then we arrive at the inescapable conclusion that, in comparison with the second half of the seventeenth century, the latter half of the eighteenth was one of virtual economic seclusion. Missing from the few chronicle sources are references to not only the direct evidence of the exchange of goods but also the indirect evidence of a world economy at work in the accounts of international travel that inevitably accompanied trade flows. For example, we do not find information on intellectuals traveling to and from India or Iran in the second half of the eighteenth century in anywhere near the numbers or with the kind of mobility found in the previous century.

The Nadirid occupation of the 1730s and 1740s appears to have left deep scars on the regional economy. That economy remained, as always, agrarian, and export commodities (dried fruits, horses, tobacco, silk) were possible only when the region was self-sufficient in food production. The draconian Nadirid requisitions of foodstuffs for export may have destroyed Balkh's ability to compete on the world market. It is not at all unlikely that the agricultural policies of the occupying forces caused the conversion of dry-farmed areas to pasturage and led to a deterioration of the irrigated areas as well when revenues were siphoned off for imperial needs. Although in the absence of hard evidence this conclusion is largely speculative, it fits with conventional interpretations and would help explain why Balkh ceased to be considered of major political importance after the middle of the eighteenth century. Perhaps someday numismatic evidence and the discovery of local archives will provide a clearer picture of economic conditions during this time and help explain the course that politics inevitably followed.

There is no question that interest in governing the region or controlling its surplus production was minimal, judging by the policies of the major regional states that arose from the ashes of Nadir Shah's imperial apparatus, notably the Saduza'i/Durrani Afghan empire and the Mangghit Uzbek state of Bukhara.

Reconstructing the political history of Balkh in the period between 1747 and 1849, when it was permanently annexed by the Afghan state, is as problematic as analyzing economic conditions during the time. Contrary to what might be supposed, there is a fairly extensive literature that covers Balkh during this period, although none of it can be said to focus on the Balkh region alone.[3] What makes the reconstruction difficult is the rather widely variant stories we are told in these works. Nonetheless, it is possible to unravel the threads of two general political themes during this period. The first is the on-again–off-again attempts by the newly emergent Mangghit authorities in Bukhara (the Uzbek amirid successors to the last of the Tuqay-Timurid Chingizid khans) and the Durrani Afghans in Qandahar and Kabul to establish at least nominal authority over Balkh. These efforts are viewed against the background of the continual contests that went on for real local control among the tribal amirs scattered over the former Chingizid appanage. Underlying both policies was some recognition of the still politically evocative force of the Chingizid mandate. To the Mangghits, of course, it was taken for granted. But even the Durrani Afghans, though coming from a completely different environment, show signs of having acknowledged the power of Chingizid legitimacy.

The jockeying for influence by Bukhara, Qandahar, or Kabul was occasionally violent, but more often took the form of verbal backing for one or another of the local amirid contestants. It was the second current, the struggle among Uzbek amirid factions claiming some form of Chingizid legitimacy to expand or maintain their positions, that was most crucial in the politics and economy of the Balkh region. Under the influence of these two themes, the 'Alid shrine administration took on a rather dramatic new role. For the administrators who were used to dealing with one authority at Balkh, the rise of independent Uzbek factions presented a serious challenge. They responded pragmatically, adopting measures that we can interpret as those thought necessary to preserve the shrine and its waqf properties. But the consequences of their response, and the gradual assumption by them of functions typically associated with a state apparatus, appear, if not unique in waqf history, still quite unusual. Relying on their administrative expertise, the shrine administrators began to take on the role hitherto played by the politicians at Balkh. Eventually this led to the emergence of what was, to all intents and purposes, a small

---

[3] The Persian sources are: Mahmud al-Husayni 1974; Sultan Mahmud Khan Durrani 1881; Gulistanah 1965; Bukhari 1876; Badakhshi 1959; Husayn b. 'Ali 1961; Rida Quli Khan Hidayat 1960, vol. 9; Fayd Muhammad Katib 1913–15, vols. 1–2; Kushkaki 1924.

shrine state. The shrine administrators gradually created a small army to defend the waqf properties, their economic resource; they expanded the shrine's bureaucracy; they laid claim to legitimacy as protectors of the 'Alid tradition, and they created a capital city out of the "mazar-i sharif" (the "noble shrine").

Before we examine the transformation of the administration and some of the consequences of that transformation, an effort should be made here to flesh out the political context within which the transformation took place and to understand the interplay of local Uzbek amirid struggles with the policies of the two regional powers, the Afghans in Qandahar and Kabul and the Mangghit Uzbeks in Bukhara.

In a process that predated the Nadirid occupation and, in retrospect, appears to have been a logical consequence of the appanage system, the former mamlakah of Balkh had over time been carved up into Uzbek amirates centered on the major towns of the region. One of these amirates was Maymanah or Maymanah and Shibarghan (at times the two were united, at times independent). Maymanah had been an amirate under the control of the Ming since the 1630s. In 1747, the man who governed Maymanah was Haji Bi Ming.[4]

Haji Bi seems to have been the first major political figure to claim Balkh in the wake of the Nadirid retreat. The chronicler of Ahmad Shah Durrani has the latter awarding Balkh to Haji Bi, probably in 1750, shortly after his own conquest of Herat, sending along with him a contingent of "Kabul, Afghan, and Qizilbash" troops to help him suppress local opposition. But the circumstances suggest that the Ming amir already had control of Balkh and that the Afghan ruler was simply acknowledging the fact while positioning himself to intervene more directly if conditions allowed.

There is evidence that Ahmad Shah Durrani and Haji Bi Ming were once comrades-in-arms while both were in service to Nadir Shah.[5] But what is most intriguing about the account concerning Ahmad Shah's recognition or appointment of Haji Bi as governor of Balkh is that it says that the Afghan leader gave the Ming amir the title "khan," the style by which Haji Bi Ming is known in all the other accounts. Mahmud al-Husayni, author of Tarikh-i Ahmad Shahi, understood the Chingizid significance of the term, and we must assume that Ahmad Shah was probably also aware of its resonance.[6]

He writes that the first Durranid contingent, made up of Qizilbash (Shi'i) and Afghan (Sunni) elements, succeeded in bringing the region

---

[4] Mahmud al-Husayni 1974, 1: fol. 126b; Bukhari 1876, 262 gives no tribal identification; Adamec 1975, 162 (apparently based on Rida Quli Khan or a common source).

[5] Adamec 1975, 162–63.

[6] Mahmud al-Husayni 1974, 1: fol. 128b.

south of the Amu Darya, already known to the southerners as Turkistan, under control. But tensions between the Qizilbash and Afghan corps soon led to fighting (after the Qizilbash tried to enlist the support of Ilbars Khan of Urganj), and the Afghans drove the Qizilbash from Balkh.[7] In 1752, Qunduz, the now-traditional homeland of the Qataghan Uzbeks, erupted against control by the Balkh-Afghan coalition. The old Ming-Qataghan rivalry was reignited by the presence of Afghan forces, and as a result, the Durrani state was drawn deeper into the political problems of Balkh. In a fight on 25 July 1753, an Afghan army defeated a Qataghan force under Midrab Bi, who had just succeeded his father at Qunduz.[8] The struggles between contending amirid forces, in particular the Qataghan-Ming duel for Turkistan, proved an irresistible lure to the Afghans. Ahmad Shah's policy was to intervene with military assistance but not to attempt annexation and incorporation of the region into his empire. His representative in Turkistan was called *sardar*, and although we have one reference to the appointment by the shah of a bureaucratic overseer of financial affairs, there is little other evidence of efforts to administer the region from Kabul or Qandahar.[9]

Sometime about 1755 or 1756, Haji Khan Ming journeyed to Kabul and there asked that the sardarship of Turkistan be conferred on him. Ahmad Shah agreed, thereby formalizing his support for the Ming against the Qataghan. The result was "oppression and extortion" on the part of the Ming amir and the appointment of an Afghan military ombudsman (*darughah-i 'adalat*) who was supposed to check Haji Khan's ambitions.[10] But an uprising in Shibarghan showed just how precarious the Afghan position was, and it appears that from 1756 until 1761 there was considerable jockeying for power between the main Qataghan and Ming factions and their clients. Ahmad Shah's representatives meanwhile struggled to find trustworthy allies likely to survive the intra-regional struggles.

In 1761, the Bukharan state entered the fray. A force allied with an amir ousted from Aqchah, who apparently had sought Bukharan support in the struggle for supremacy in Balkh, crossed the Amu Darya and reoccupied the town, which was west of Balkh City. But according to the somewhat partisan Afghan source, a coalition led by Ahmad Shah's sardar in Turkistan, Nawwab Khan Alikuza'i, who had replaced Haji Khan

[7] Ibid., 1: fol. 167a; Fayd Muhammad Katib 1913–15, 1:16; Sultan Mahmud Khan Durrani 1881, 144, where Badakhshan is mentioned as well. But from Badakhshi 1959, 33b–43b (covering the years 1750–1752), there is no indication of an Afghan Durrani incursion into Badakhshan at this time.

[8] Mahmud al-Husayni 1974, 1: fol. 292b.

[9] Ibid., 1: fol. 128b

[10] Ibid., 2: fol. 353b–354a.

Ming, ultimately prevailed over the Bukharans.[11] This confrontation between Afghan and Bukharan forces concluded with the Bukharan ruler,
Shah Murad Bi (also known as Mir Ma'sum), accepting Ahmad Shah's
claim to sovereignty over Balkh.

Ahmad Shah, who had heard that a piece of the Prophet Muhammad's
cloak, the *khirqah*, was in the possession of the Bukharan amir, asked for
and received the holy relic as a token of his victory. The story of the
khirqah and its transfer symbolizes the shift of dominant political and
economic, and ultimately cultural, influence from north of the Amu
Darya to south of the Hindu Kush, from Chingizid/Uzbek to Afghan.

Shah Murad Bi, ruler of the ancient city that had been the seedbed
and nursery of Hanafi Sunnism, surrendered both his claim and his responsibilities as defender of Hanafi-Sunni Islam in Balkh to the new ad-
vocates of Hanafi Sunnism in the cis-Oxine region, the Durrani Afghans.
This transfer was enacted in the passing, or in the story of the passing, of
the khirqah from the Uzbeks to the Afghans. The story also gives some
insight into the temper of popular religious sentiment, with its emphasis
on the intercessory efficacy of saints, especially the ahl al-bayt, and tomb
and relic worship.

THE KHIRQAH TRADITION IN BALKH AND BADAKHSHAN, 1640–1762

In a rather intriguing section that is somewhat uncharacteristic of the rest
of his work, Fayd Muhammad Katib, the author of *Siraj al-tawarikh*,
presents a scholarly attestation of the khirqah tradition in Afghanistan.
He bases his proof on both written and architectural evidence, but in so
doing raises the suspicion that there was always public skepticism about
the khirqah's authenticity. Perhaps it would be fairer to say that the need
to prove the authenticity of any religious relic was, and still is, a conventional aspect of relic worship, and this was what he was about.

After describing the way in which the relic of the Prophet's cloak came
from the north to Qandahar during Ahmad Shah's time, Fayd Muhammad projects the story to the present and tells of a tour around the country made by his patron, Amir Habib Allah Khan, in A.H. 1325/A.D. 1907,
which included a stop at Qandahar, site of the relic's shrine. Habib Allah,
portrayed as somewhat skeptical, not of the existence of the cloak but of
some of the details of Ahmad Shah's intent with regard to it, inspected
the domed tomb of Ahmad Shah, which it was widely believed had been
constructed to house the khirqah as well. According to Fayd Muhammad,
the amir immediately recognized the truth of the story from the design
of the tomb. The sepulcher of Ahmad Shah was placed off-center in the

[11] Ibid., 2: fol. 514a–515b.

mausoleum, leaving room, as the amir and others believed, for the sacred relic to be housed in the center, directly beneath the dome. The cloak was never placed in the mausoleum, however, because of a fatwa-decree issued by the 'ulama of Qandahar. They ruled that it should not be subject to the whims of politicians and moved from place to place. Instead it ought to remain in what had been originally intended as only a temporary resting place in Qandahar, a place the author does not identify.

Fayd Muhammad further records that the amir then commissioned him to research the whole question of the cloak's presence in Afghanistan. He found his answer in a collection of fatwas issued by Miyan Faqir Allah Shikarpuri, a shaykh of the Naqshbandi order. The seventy-fourth of the collected fatwas outlines the basic facts of the cloak's odyssey. The shaykh's response to the question posed in the fatwa, without directly authenticating the khirqah's presence in Afghanistan, does assert its existence by quoting the fifteenth-century Egyptian scholar, al-Suyuti, and the well-known commentator on al-Bukhari's *al-Sahih*, al-Qastallani. Fayd Muhammad's presentation of the fatwa leaves the reader with ambivalent feelings. Did he mean to imply that the Naqshbandi shaykh from Shikarpur was refusing to give his imprimatur to the Afghan tradition, offering only a learned verification of the existence of the relic?

It is possible to trace the khirqah tradition at Balkh at least as far back as 1049/1640. In that year, Nadhr Muhammad, the Tuqay-Timurid sovereign at Balkh, sent his son, later khan, 'Abd al-'Aziz Sultan, at the head of a reconnaissance force toward Kabul in order to assess the military objectives of Shah Jahan, who had recently marched from the Punjab to Kabul. It was Nadhr Muhammad's fear, justified as it turned out, that the Timurid-Moghul ruler had designs on Balkh. En route, as 'Abd al-'Aziz's force marched along the Kahmard road to Bamyan and eventually Kabul, arrangements were made for the cloak of the Prophet, which had been handed down through the family of a certain Langar Muhammad Sadiq Shaykh, to be brought to 'Abd al-'Aziz so that he could bless his troops with it.[12] Although the account does not say where the shaykh and the cloak resided, one assumes, in light of other information and the proximity to the army's route, that it was either in Badakhshan or perhaps Balkh.

If the cloak was already in Balkh or Badakhshan by 1640, then the query section of Miyan Faqir Allah's fatwa, despite its apparent precision, needs to be treated with caution. There the story, in brief, is given as follows: After the death of the Prophet, 'Ali entrusted his cloak to Uways-i Qarani in accordance with the former's wishes; Uways wore it and then, after his death, it was brought to Mecca and placed in the

---

[12] *BA* 4: fol. 263a.

Ghar-i Harah, where it remained "for many years." Thereupon a certain Shaykh Dust Muhammad discovered it and, proclaiming it as the true cloak of the Prophet, brought it to Baghdad, whence his descendants eventually carried it to Bukhara. There it stayed for eighty years, after which two shaykhs, Agha Muhammad and Nazir Muhammad, took it to Balkh, where it remained another thirty-five years. Finally, on 24 Muharram 1109/12 August 1697, it was carried to a khanaqah in Juzun in Badakhshan, where it remained until Ahmad Shah's wazir, Shah Wali Khan Bamiza'i, carried it off in 1768.

If we take the fatwa at face value, the cloak would have been in Bukhara from 1586 to 1663, in Balkh from 1663 to 1697, and then in Badakhshan from 1697 to 1768. But according to Mahmud b. Amir Wali, writing this section of his work in 1645, the khirqah was already either in Balkh or Badakhshan by 1640.

Badakhshi, whose chronology begins in 1658, tells a significantly different story of the cloak's arrival in Badakhshan, one that closely corresponds to the history of the region as related in his book. In this version, the khirqah had been in Samarqand and was being carried from that city to India by three Dahpidi shaykhs. (The Dahpidi family was descended from the mid-sixteenth century Naqshbandi figure, the "Makhdum-i A'zam" (Greatest Master), Khwajah Ahmad Kasani, and remained for the entire seventeenth century one of the two most prominent families of Samarqand.) The Dahpidi shaykhs were intercepted in the rugged mountainous region along the Badakhshan-Chitral border by the forces of Amir Yari Beg, himself a Dahpidi who had come earlier to Badakhshan and was now a prominent politician. He refused to allow the shaykhs to continue on to India with the cloak. Apparently unwilling to surrender it, the shaykhs agreed to settle at Juzun, Amir Yari Beg's headquarters and the site of his new citadel. They were given houses and lands and a shrine was built for the cloak.[13] In both this and Fayd Muhammad's account, the town of Juzun (Juzgun, Juzgan) received the soubriquet *Faydabad* (Abode of God's Bounty) because of the presence of the cloak.

Badakhshi adds some rather provocative information, that the three shaykhs were given the titles of "shaykh, mutawalli, and sahib al-da'wat" and that their descendants continued to hold those titles, at least down to 1768, when the cloak was taken away. The first two titles are familiar ones, the former probably designating the head of the shrine, the latter the man in charge of the waqf endowments. The third title, however, is what provokes interest. It is a title associated not with Hanafi Islam, of which the Dahpidi family were ardent adherents, at least in Samarqand, but rather with Isma'ili Shi'ism. Badakhshan had been a bastion of Nizari Isma'ilism since the eleventh century. The title may reflect a process of

---

[13] Badakhshi 1959, 6a–7a.

assimilation of a Sunni tradition into an Isma'ili one, though Badakhshi, a Hanafi Muslim, frequently refers to Hanafi-Isma'ili conflict. Or perhaps it is simply the Hanafi adoption of Isma'ili terminology (the Hanafis may have felt it was they who needed to be missionaries to the Isma'ilis of Badakhshan).

Fayd Muhammad, adapting Mahmud al-Husayni's and Sultan Mahmud Khan Durrani's accounts, offers the clearest version of how the khirqah found its way to Qandahar. In 1768, Ahmad Shah sent a force (referred to previously) under the command of his wazir, Shah Wali Khan Bamiza'i, "to put down the seditious activities of troublemakers in Balkh and Badakhshan." This move was countered by Shah Murad Bi, the amir of Bukhara, whose mobilization in turn prompted Ahmad Shah himself to reinforce his wazir. Once in Balkh, Ahmad Shah made a major show of force by sending Shah Wali Khan to Badakhshan while he himself marched north toward Shah Murad.[14] But because of his devotion to Islam, we are told, Ahmad Shah agreed to negotiate with the Bukharan shah. In the discussions that followed, the two men concurred that from that point on the Amu Darya would separate the jurisdictions of the two powers. In addition, the Bukharan ruler sent the Prophet's cloak to Ahmad Shah as a mark of esteem. Fayd Muhammad may have doubted the authenticity of the sources he used,[15] for he juxtaposes this narrative with a section beginning "the most reliable and correct account concerning the Prophet's cloak," in which he quotes a story told by his patron, Amir Habib Allah Khan. Or perhaps his patron required him to include his own version, and Fayd Muhammad's juxtaposition of Mahmud al-Husayni's and Sultan Mahmud's accounts implies doubt about Habib Allah Khan's story.

In any case, Habib Allah Khan's story fills in pieces missing from the account found in Badakhshi, which begins with the arrival of the Samarqandi shaykhs in Badakhshan. Here is the Afghan amir's narrative as told to Fayd Muhammad:

> Of all the stories I have heard about the khirqah, the one I believe to be true is that Amir Timur[16] brought the sacred cloak of the Prophet and its guardians

[14] Mahmud al-Husayni 1974, 2: fol. 601a has Ahmad Shah only going as far as Charikar on the road from Kabul to Turkistan and credits Shah Wali Khan Bamiza'i with the defeat of the pro-Bukharan forces, the capture of Badakhshan, and the acquisition of the khirqah.

[15] Fayd Muhammad Katib used Sultan Mahmud Khan Durrani and perhaps Mahmud al-Husayni (see vol. 1, p. 3, where the *Tarikh-i Sultani* and a *Tarikh-i Ahmad Shahi* are listed among the written sources he consulted). There are other books with titles similar to Mahmud al-Husayni's, such as 'Abd al-Karim 'Alawi's *Tarikh-i Ahmad* and Nizam al-Din " 'Ishrat" Siyalkuti's *Shah-namah-i Ahmadi* (see Storey and Bregel' 1972, 2:1231, 1219), to either of which Fayd Muhammad could have been referring.

[16] Timur Gurgan (1335–1405), "world-conqueror" and founder of the Timurid dynasty of amirs in Central Asia.

from 'Iraq-i 'Arab to Mawarannahr, built a structure to house it in Samarqand, and appointed sayyids of authentic lineage to supervise the shrine. He also made the village of Dahpid a waqf endowment, the income of which would pay the salaries of those charged with responsibility for the sacred garment. That domed building is now called Khwajah Khidr and is in a thriving and sound state. In 1297,[17] I saw it with my own eyes and can attest to its prosperity. It is possible that after the death of Amir Timur . . . the cloak was moved to Bukhara along with its guardians. Similarly, it was later moved to Juzun by a descendant of Amir Timur. The chief guardian [mutawalli-bashi] at that time was Shah Beg Khan Wali.[18] A domed building was constructed outside the walls of Juzun and, because of God's bounty [fayd], which that cloak brought to the city, it came to be called Faydabad [Abode of God's Bounty].[19] Until Ahmad Shah brought the cloak to Qandahar, it had remained in Faydabad.

The khirqah story is important for the study of the 'Alid shrine because its mass appeal and the fervent demonstrations that it aroused mirrored those which the shrine, especially during the spring festival called Gul-i Surkh (the Red Rose), also inspired. When Ahmad Shah returned to the south with the cloak in hand, he did so in as ceremonious a fashion as possible. At every stopping place along the way, he would have a sadaqah, or alms, deed drafted, fasten it around the neck of the camel that had transported the cloak that day, and release the camel. Whoever found the animal could then claim it, the sadaqah deed providing the new owner with legal title. When the shah approached Kabul, he was forced to stay several days at each stopping place to accommodate the throngs of people coming to perform a ziyarat pilgrimage to the cloak. Once in the Kabul valley, the cloak remained nine months at 'Aliabad so that all who wanted could see it. Habib Allah, in the account recorded by Fayd Muhammad, adds that each place along the route from the north at which the shah stopped to display the cloak came to be called "the place where the Lord of Men set foot" (qadamgah-i Shah-i Mardan).

For Ahmad Shah, the khirqah story may be taken as an indication of his interest in Balkh and the surrounding region. As a repository of a sacred tradition, the place exerted considerable attraction on the founder of a new and by no means legitimized state. With at least part of that sacred tradition in hand and removed to more familiar and friendlier ter-

[17] In 1297/1879–80, Habib Allah was still in exile in Samarqand along with his brother, Nasr Allah Khan, and other family members and retainers. His father, 'Abd al-Rahman Khan, had returned to Afghanistan early that year intent on getting control of the Afghan throne.

[18] A name rather close to that of Ahmad Shah's general, Shah Wali Khan Bamiza'i, who is linked to the arrival of the khirqah in Afghanistan.

[19] See Dupree 1976 for a recent report on interpretations of the sacred lore relating to Faydabad (with no mention of the khirqah tradition, however).

ritory, Ahmad Shah's political aspirations in Balkh seem to have been satisfied. Such also seems to have been the case for his Saduza'i successors, at least. For more than three-quarters of a century, the actions taken by Afghan governments vis-á-vis Balkh suggest that they felt that the region had some obligation (nominal allegiance involving tribute payments of some kind) to the Afghan kingdom. In addition, the Afghan interest encouraged local aspiring politicians to appeal for Afghan help when it might further their own careers. But the Afghans seemed unwilling during that time to take the next logical step of establishing direct rule over Balkh.[20] The region north of the Hindu Kush continued to be thought of and dealt with as if it were still part of Mawarannahr.

With the withdrawal of the Afghans, relic in hand, the region returned to its political status of being just outside the jurisdictions of Bukhara and Kabul but within the areas deemed of strategic interest by both. Regional politics reverted to the pattern set at the end of the Tuqay-Timurid period earlier in the century, and the second of the two trends mentioned earlier, local factionalism, now flowered. For about fifty years after the Bukhara-Kabul rapprochement, Balkh divided up into a handful of petty amirates. The towns of Maymanah, Andkhud, Shibarghan, Aqchah, Balkh, Qunduz, Faydabad, and Mazar-i Sharif all enjoyed self-rule at one time or another during this half century. Various Uzbek chieftains—the leaders of the Ming, Qataghan, and Qipchaq, among others—were to marshal the resources of these towns and forge political units out of them. The power of these amirates ebbed and flowed as more or less capable amirs rose to lead them and power and authority were continually tested by colleagues in neighboring amirates. In this contest for regional preeminence, a number of individuals achieved sufficient notoriety to be recorded for posterity or had the foresight to hire someone to insure that history remembered them.

One such politician to emerge in this post-appanage landscape was Qubad Khan.[21] His tribal affiliation does not appear in the sources we have but, given his roots in Qunduz, it is more than likely that he was a Qataghan amir.[22] Qubad first comes to the attention of historians as a fighter of the Qalmaq nomads pressing on Qunduz from the east. Chi-

---

[20] Fayd Muhammad Katib 1913–15, 1:16 writes that "Afghan and Uzbek governors" were appointed throughout the region. Fayd Muhammad, who bases his account almost exclusively on Sultan Mahmud Khan Durrani here, appears to be taking a few liberties with his source. There is no other evidence to suggest that the Afghans established any formal control over the region at this time.

[21] Voloshina, editor of Husayn b. 'Ali, vocalizes the name as Kabad throughout. What Qubad's relationship was to Hazarah "Khan," who was another prominent Qataghan figure at Qunduz in the immediate post-Nadirid period (see the end of chapter 9), is not known.

[22] Badakhshi 1959, 54b.

nese military activity in Kashghar, the pasturelands of the Qalmaq in the middle of the eighteenth century, had driven some Qalmaq groups and their Dahpidi (or Makhdum-i A'zami) khwajah leaders[23] out of Kashghar toward the southwest. They entered Badakhshan circa 1747[24] and Qubad Khan sent a force against them. (It seems reasonable to assume some link between the Dahpidi leaders of the Qalmaq and the Dahpidi caretakers of the khirqah shrine in Faydabad.) Qubad's campaign against the Qalmaq enjoyed a certain success, and, either because of this or because of his dabbling in the dynastic politics of Faydabad, he acquired some influence in the Badakhshan capital. He is said to have backed an out-of-power faction of the ruling family and then, when the group managed to depose the ruling amir with his help, to have withdrawn his support and taken advantage of the weakening of both factions to install one of his own subordinates as governor at Faydabad. But controlling Faydabad from Qunduz proved beyond his capabilities, and within a short time his man at Faydabad was forced to return Badakhshan to its own politicians.[25]

Qubad's dabbling in Balkh politics is a matter of some controversy in the sources.[26] According to Husayn b. 'Ali, Qubad rose to a preeminent position in Balkh politics about two decades after becoming governor of Qunduz, that is sometime early in the reign of the second Afghan shah, Timur Shah b. Ahmad Shah (r. 1773–1793). Therefore, he could be accused by a pro-Afghan source of "rebelling" against Timur Shah, behavior probably involving the withholding of a customary or expected sum of tribute or perhaps failing to insert the shah's name into the appropriate section of the Friday service. If this did occur early in Timur Shah's reign, it would explain the latter's action, which was to send an army under one of his generals, Jahan Khan, to extract the nominal recognition expected of Balkh's ruler. As the successor of a legendarily successful conqueror-ruler but with no particular achievements of his own, Timur Shah may have been overly sensitive to any gesture, however insignificant, that could be interpreted as contemptuous of his authority. The outcome of the Afghan campaign was, however, far less satisfactory than the consequences of ignoring Qubad Khan would have been. The Qunduz force defeated the Afghan army and took many prisoners.

---

[23] Fletcher 1978, 74–75, 87–90.

[24] Fufalza'i 1967, 1:167.

[25] Badakhshi 1959, 61b–62b.

[26] Husayn b. 'Ali 1961, 17b–18b; Gulistanah 1965, 124–25; Badakhshi 1959, 64a–b. Voloshina's remark (Husayn b. 'Ali, 8) that *Zib al-tarikh-ha* is a unique source for Qubad is obviously incorrect. Husayn b. 'Ali and Gulistanah both locate the events in "Balkh," that is the region not the city. No dates are given. Badakhshi 1959, 63b dates the conclusion of the Afghan-Uzbek conflict over Qunduz and Badakhshan to 1184 (1770–71). Fufalza'i 1967, 1:163–66 summarizes the Gulistanah, Badakhshi, and Bukhari narratives.

But success is often a prelude to disaster. According to Husayn b. 'Ali, Qubad's victory cost him his life. Another Uzbek amir, a certain Khuda Nazar, who is described as a supporter of the Afghans, assassinated Qubad and took control of Balkh. But instead of freeing the Afghan prisoners, Khuda Nazar kept them detained, thereby proclaiming his own independence of Afghan influence. When Timur Shah was informed of the turn events had taken, he sent another force, this one led by a Bamiza'i sardar, Barkhurdar, who arrested Khuda Nazar, freed the prisoners, and established Afghan control over Balkh. Barkhurdar then stayed at Balkh until his death and was succeeded by another Afghan governor sent by Timur Shah.

Gulistanah offers a somewhat different version. Without suggesting a motive, he tells us that Timur Shah, at some unspecified time, sent an army under Barkhurdar to deal with Qubad (not Khuda Nazar). In the ensuing confrontation, the Afghan force was defeated by Qubad and Barkhurdar retreated to Kabul. In the meantime, an unnamed enemy of Qubad Khan assassinated him and provoked another Afghan expedition to Balkh under Barkhurdar. This time, the Afghan leader managed to take the city and capture a rather unprepossessing quantity of booty, including "some Balkhi horses and 300 Qalmaq slaves," all of which he sent back to Kabul.[27] (The writer notes that the Qalmaq had only recently arrived in numbers in the region, coming from Kashghar under the leadership of the Dahpidi khwajahs.)

Badakhshi gives the most radically different version. He links Qubad's downfall not to the politics of Balkh but to affairs in Qunduz and Badakhshan, and he credits the Afghans with only a minor part in these events. He also dates Qubad's downfall and death to 1771, two years before Timur Shah came to the throne. In this version of the Qubad affair, the amir was governing Qunduz when an Afghan force with orders to conquer the town approached. Anticipating their arrival, Qubad imprisoned Khuda Nazar, presumably—although nothing is said of this—because of his known pro-Afghan sympathies. Persuaded that the least dangerous course was to get rid of Khuda Nazar, Qubad ordered a group of men to take him out of the city and execute him. But the Afghan army arrived in the nick of time, rescued Khuda Nazar, and sent him to safety in Faydabad. Although the text is vague here, it appears that Khuda Nazar then returned to Qunduz with an armed force, took Qubad prisoner, and turned him over to the son of a Badakhshani amir whom Qubad had killed during his brief intervention in Badakhshan politics.[28]

It is impossible to reconcile these three accounts at this point even if

[27] Gulistanah 1965, 125.
[28] Badakhshi 1959, 63b–65a.

it were necessary to do so. The elements that matter in all the stories are fairly clear. Besides the cultural ones of revenge and disloyalty and its consequences, the sources agree on certain political themes—an Afghan military commitment, inter-Uzbek struggles for local power, and Balkh's historic right, as perceived by its military and political leaders, to a measure of autonomy, a view harking back to its appanage status during the Chingizid era. One other lesser but symbolically noteworthy point is the application of the title "khan" to Qubad. In the Chingizid context, such a usage verged on political blasphemy. To Iranians and their political heirs in Kabul, the term was far less loaded and had long been used as a title of high rank for political and military leaders outside the royal family. When Ahmad Shah bestowed the title "khan" on Haji Bi Ming, it seems likely that he was aware of its meaning in the Chingizid context but was more familiar with it in his own environment, where it was a common title without any particular political overtones.

The combination of political rhetoric and the outline of events, however muddied the underlying causes appear, suggests a period in which ideas of what was tolerable, appropriate, or desirable in the political arena were changing. Kabul and the Afghans were new players in the game of politics in Balkh, and an old participant, Bukhara, was fading from the scene but had not yet foresworn its historic rights in the region.

Both Bukhara and Kabul, despite the agreement between Ahmad Shah and Shah Murad in 1768, continued to spar for influence in Balkh. A Bukharan military expedition to Balkh, testing the waters after Ahmad Shah's death, prompted an immediate Afghan counter campaign led by Timur Shah himself.[29] When Timur Shah passed from the scene in 1793, another Bukharan force crossed the Amu Darya to unknown effect. Late-eighteenth-century Afghan sources considered Balkh, by which name was still meant the entire former Chingizid appanage, an administrative division of the Afghan state. But in 1797–1798 at least, the amirs of the region not only were sending no revenue to the Afghan treasury but were being paid subsidies out of Afghan revenues collected elsewhere, reportedly because of a severely depressed economy in Balkh.[30]

The significance of the historical evidence in all its varied forms is, of course, predicated on the meaning attached to it by the historian. To later Afghan chroniclers, the Afghan campaigns of the eighteenth century

---

[29] Fayd Muhammad Katib 1913–15, 1:41 and Sultan Mahmud Khan Durrani 1881, 156 suggest a date for this confrontation early in Timur Shah's reign, although they do not actually offer one. Bukhari 1876, 22–23, which says that no battle was actually fought, dates the confrontation to 1792, the year before Timur Shah's death. Elphinstone 1815, 562 says the events occurred in 1789 according to a document that "is in many people's hands in Caubul."

[30] Fayd Muhammad Katib 1913–15, 1:57.

were of little political significance. The early-twentieth century *Siraj al-tawarikh*, the official Muhammadza'i (the Durrani branch beginning with Dust Muhammad Khan) history of Afghanistan, which reported the earlier expeditions, dates the "first conquest" of "Lesser Turkistan" (i.e., the region between the Oxus River and the Hindu Kush Mountains) to 1849,[31] and credits Dust Muhammad.

It is probably fair to conclude that for most of the century after the Nadirid withdrawal, irrespective of the assertions made in the court records of Kabul and Bukhara about the fixing of borders and respective sovereign rights, no significant political intervention from either Bukhara or Kabul occurred in the former appanage of Balkh. Instead small autonomous regions, usually comprising a major town and its adjacent agricultural lands, developed under the control of local Uzbek groups.

BALKH POLITICS, 1797–1849

If one can characterize the story of politics in Balkh during the second half of the eighteenth century as shaped by the theme of a Bukharan-Kabul rivalry, the politics of the first half of the nineteenth century may be as justifiably portrayed as a dance to the tune of local political melodies.

The relatively intense maneuvering of Bukhara and Kabul for control of the old Balkh appanage had faded for a variety of reasons. The political energy of the Afghan state was drawn increasingly toward India, especially the Punjab, as its hold over the territories conquered by Ahmad Shah began to weaken. For the time being, Turkistan, or Lesser Turkistan, as Afghan writers labeled the Balkh appanage, became a low priority. Once the threat of Afghan intervention disappeared, Bukhara's interest also diminished. The region remained linked to the city beyond the Amu Darya by cultural and economic ties, an arrangement that apparently satisfied the Mangghit rulers, who in any event had political challenges nearer home with which to concern themselves.

As a result, the amir-ruled towns and villages assumed a more visible place, at least in the descriptions of the period. Between about 1800 and 1826, the main protagonists were the petty amirates or begates of Khulm (Tashqurghan) and Qunduz. Their political goals were modest: dominance of their amirid colleagues in the handful of more or less autonomous amirate/begates in the region between Badakhshan in the east and Balkh City in the west, including Aybak (south of Khulm), Darrah-i Suf or Darrah-i Yusuf, Darrah-i Juz (Darrah-i Gaz), Ghuri, Sar-i Pul, Mazar (the shrine), and Balkh City. (The more western amirates, like May-

[31] Ibid., 1:206.

manah, Andkhud, Shibarghan, and even Aqchah, were generally beyond the reach of the powers in the east.)

The first of a number of amirid figures who rose to the top in this environment was Qilij 'Ali Beg, who extended his authority over all of the region between Balkh and Qunduz during the first decade of the nineteenth century. Mountstuart Elphinstone, whose information, though not firsthand, is the earliest and most detailed, wrote that Qilij 'Ali's "abilities . . . [i.e., before 1814] soon enabled him, first to reduce his rebellious subjects, and afterwards to annex the petty states of Eibuk, Ghoree, Mozaur, Derra Guz, etc. which lay in his territory."[32] Perhaps reflecting the declining status of Balkh City in contemporary political thought, Qilij 'Ali, unlike Qubad Khan a half-century earlier, was content to exercise control from Khulm, where he had built a brand new fortress and carried out a major revision of the urban plan.[33] The period of his regime was relatively peaceful and prosperous, in contrast to the time after his death in 1817.

Disputes among Qilij 'Ali's sons provided an opportunity for a Qataghan amir from Qunduz, Murad Beg or Mir Murad Beg. The sons, Mir Baba and Mir Wali, fought for control of Khulm/Tashqurghan after their father's death. Mir Wali expelled his brother, who then turned to Murad Beg for help. Mir Baba was reinstated, we are told, but then Mir Wali again forced him off the seat of power. Once more Murad Beg intervened, but ultimately, impressed by Mir Wali's abilities, he arranged for the latter to retain Tashqurghan, while Mir Baba was placed at Aybak. Thus did Murad Beg establish his influence in Tashqurghan and Aybak.[34]

Murad Beg's image in the history books is quite different from Qilij 'Ali's. The latter is depicted as an adroit diplomat, maintaining his influence in Balkh by deftly manipulating different amirid factions. Murad Beg, on the other hand, is shown in a much more unpleasant light. Lieutenant John Wood, traveling through Qunduz in 1836 on a surveying mission, gives this description of how Murad Beg exercised power: "Not the least remarkable trait in the character of this man is the contrast afforded by his well-ordered domestic government and the uninterrupted course of rapine which forms the occupation of himself and his subjects, whose 'chuppaws' or plundering expeditions embrace the whole of the upper waters of the Oxus, from the frontiers of China on the east to the river that runs through Balk [sic] . . ."[35] An earlier visitor, William Moorcroft, described another coercive technique used by Murad Beg, the transportation of populations: "The people of Tash Kurghan had been threatened the year before with compulsory removal to Kunduz, to which Murad

[32] Elphinstone 1815, 474.
[33] Gaz. 4:566–67, 571–72.
[34] Ibid., 4:572–73.
[35] Wood 1841, 217.

Beg occasionally transplants whole villages or towns. Last year [1823] he had carried thither the population of Sarbagh and Khulm. . . ."[36]

One has to treat the accounts of these European writers with a good deal of caution. We know nothing of their sources and little of the circumstances in which they were working, and can only guess at their willingness to retail rumor and gossip. But other evidence suggests that Murad Beg enjoyed none of the consensual support his predecessor had had. Late in the fall of 1824, a coalition of amirs of the Balkh region assembled eight thousand men to overthrow him. When he countered with a twenty-thousand-man display, the opposition evaporated.[37] Murad Beg passed from the scene about 1841 and his regional leadership was assumed by Mir Wali, ruling from Khulm.[38]

It is not clear who governed Balkh after the regime of Qilij 'Ali. Probably as a consequence of the struggle between his sons, there is a report that, about 1820, a man named Ishan Naqib became governor of Balkh. The name (really a title) is provocative and suggests a member of one of the Naqshbandi Sufi branch orders—the Salihiyah, the Parsa'i, or perhaps the Dahpidi. The titles "ishan" and "naqib" were almost never associated with Uzbek amirs. It is quite probable that representatives of the local religious leadership took political control in Balkh following the death of Qilij 'Ali. Such had happened before.[39]

Ishan Naqib held Balkh under Murad Beg's aegis until 1840, when the Mangghit amir of Bukhara, Nasr Allah, reasserted Bukharan interest in the cis-Oxine region, crossed the river, and deposed Ishan Naqib. Ishan Naqib was taken away to Bukhara, but soon after, his son, Ishan Uraq, retook Balkh. His power grew in the decade during which he held the city and toward the end of his reign he came into conflict with Mir Wali of Tashqurghan.[40] As best as can be determined, this collision of local interests, coupled with Kabul's defeat of the British army of occupation and the prestige and influence this brought Dust Muhammad and his sons, reintroduced the Afghan element in a finally decisive way to the former Balkh appanage.

At the time of what proved to be the decisive invasion and occupation in 1849, the series of events that Fayd Muhammad styles the first conquest, the major political figures in the Balkh region were Mir Wali, the son of Qilij 'Ali, and Ishan Uraq. The former ruled from the family amirate of Khulm/Tashqurghan, with significant influence in Qunduz and Aybak, while the latter governed from Balkh City.

The manifestations of political activity, of the incessant jockeying for

[36] Moorcroft and Trebeck 1841, 2:453–54.
[37] Ibid., 2:444.
[38] *Gaz.* 4:586–90.
[39] See chapter 7.
[40] *Gaz.* 4:586–90.

regional power, are far more dramatic and easily defined than are the economic currents. It is possible, however, to find here and there in the written sources clues to the direction in which these currents were running. One current, probably as strong then as it had been earlier in the eighteenth century, was that of pastoralism, perhaps at the expense of agriculture, although direct evidence of a decline in agricultural production is hard to find.

It is generally accepted, though the thesis has not yet been examined in depth, that the degree of penetration by pastoralists into the Balkh basin, especially the Hazhdah Nahr irrigation region, increased from the late seventeenth century onward. This may have been partly due to the apparently increasing importance of the equine trade with India and China in comparison with other export products. If there was an increase in stockbreeding, we might infer that the claims on agricultural resources shifted during the century from crop cultivation to pasturage. That is, marginal dry-farmed lands, for example, would have been taken out of grain production and been used as pasturelands. That the shift away from agriculture to animal husbandry may have been significant is suggested by such observations as the one cited previously of the depressed state of the economy from which state revenues came, i.e., the agricultural sector. But was it shifting economic patterns, i.e., a proportionately larger demand for horses, that led to a change in production, encouraging the expansion of pastoralism and at the same time the abandonment of irrigated lands, the migration of the rural population, and a decline in the urban share of the rural surplus, leading to a weakened political center? Or did the political structure, weakened by prolonged struggles for control of Balkh, unwittingly permit an influx of pastoralists, who forced a transformation of the local economy by occupying agricultural lands? For each proposition evidence can be found. Whether the pastoralist pressures shifted crop land to pasturage or whether the pastoralists simply moved in as lands were vacated because of other economic circumstances is very difficult to say. Nor does it much matter. The result, an increase in pastoral activity, would have been the same in either case.

Whatever the factors behind the transformation, the eighteenth century was a period of considerable political uncertainty, necessitating increased vigilance on the part of people entrusted with administering agricultural lands and with revenue assessment and collection.

POLITICAL CONDITIONS AND SHRINE MILITARIZATION

The 'Alid shrine town was in no way isolated from the overall political and economic currents of the region. Indeed, because of its unusual circumstances and its historical dependence on outside political protection, it was if anything more vulnerable to the changes going on around it.

The mutawalli performed many of the same functions as a state bureaucrat when it came to the assessment and collection of revenue. But, unlike the apparatus of the state bureaucrat, there was no enforcement arm within his jurisdiction and disputes had to be appealed to the political authorities. With the growth of the pastoral sector of the economy and the concomitant subsidence of a strong political center, the mutawalli of the shrine's waqf must have faced increasing erosion of his revenue base. The waqf material makes clear how large a percentage of waqf income was derived from the agricultural surplus. Our early-eighteenth-century material, in particular the annexes to the decree issued by Subhan Quli Sultan, mentions revenues collected from stockbreeders, but it is clear that these were incidental to the income from rents and other agricultural levies. As the local economy became increasingly affected by the pastoral sector and the relative decline in agricultural revenues weakened the political structure on which the shrine had customarily relied for protection, the mutawalli appears to have taken steps to guarantee himself the security of the waqf properties and thus of the shrine's income. Although both the Mangghit dynasty in Bukhara and the Durranis in Kabul periodically voiced a claim to Balkh, two generations would pass before either one could provide the necessary military force to give the claim legitimacy and extend at least a minimal level of security to the region.

When Khwajah Niʿmat, the Ansari mutawalli of the ʿAlid shrine, watched the Nadirid troops depart the shrine in 1747, he found himself face to face with a very uncertain future. The political authority with which the shrine had been allied was withdrawing in some ignominy, leaving the political status of Balkh very much in doubt. Certainly anyone as attuned to politics as the mutawalli would not have been unprepared for this turn of events. But encumbered as he was by extensive property holdings, Khwajah Niʿmat was far more vulnerable to political chaos than a man of lesser responsibilities would have been. Questions about maintaining revenue collections, resisting outside encroachments, and protecting the historic prerogatives of the shrine must have been uppermost in his mind as he viewed the departure of the Iranian army.

But despite the vulnerability of his position, Khwajah Niʿmat began the post-Nadirid period with certain advantages. For one thing, the long tradition of Ansari shrine administration, periodically reconfirmed by rulers at Balkh, made his position as mutawalli nearly unassailable. His status was rooted not only in the past but also in the continuing dependent relationships created through management of an extensive economy. Through his staff, the mutawalli had a decisive hand in the economic fortunes of all those who worked the shrine's lands, operated its mills, depended on its water resources, produced goods in its workshops, and rented its retail space. Economic pressure was always available as a means to encourage compliance with administrative decisions. The mutawalli could refuse to renew a lease or could make the terms of a new lease unacceptable to a tenant he wished to evict. Beyond the power that the administration held over those who used its facilities for production, the shrine administration also could command at least some degree of loyalty from the beneficiaries of shrine patronage. To some extent—although we should not overlook the ability of human beings to act contrary to what appears from a distance to be their objective economic interests—the scholars, holy men, and other shrine regulars who resided there or received some kind of a stipend were beholden to the administration. And beyond the tangible economic power lay a less easily definable but no less real ability to invoke spiritual loyalties. As guardians of a holy site whose power to intercede with God on behalf of one seeking a miraculous remedy for disease, poverty, or barrenness was universally recognized, the administrators had another tool at hand with which to fend off those opposed to their authority.

But the most tangible asset in the mutawalli's portfolio and the one on which he most directly relied was the bureaucracy that had evolved over the life of the shrine and perhaps taken its most decisive shape in the first half of the eighteenth century as Khwajah Ni'mat's predecessors, Haji Mirza Muhammad Ya'qub Ansari and his son and successor, Qadi Mir Muhammad Amin, obtained ever wider administrative powers from the politicians at Balkh. We have no specific information on the size of the shrine bureaucracy in the eighteenth century. As a point of reference, however, in 1889, long after many of the revenue-collecting functions and all of the police duties had been taken over by the Afghan state, the shrine administration included 109 officials.[41] In addition, by the 1890s, the amount of property designated as waqf had decreased enormously, a circumstance that may or may not have had the effect of reducing the size of the shrine's bureaucracy. It may be argued then that, at a time when the amount of land under shrine control was at or near its height and when all the revenue collections, water management, and market policing were in the hands of the mutawalli, the size of his bureaucracy would have far exceeded the 109 officials counted in 1889.

In the bureaucratic apparatus, Khwajah Ni'mat had all the elements of a police force. The shrine may have already performed some police functions on its own territory. Because of the administrative need for routine collection of revenues due the shrine—e.g., tax-rents, water fees, and

[41] *TMS*, 75 (text), 82–83 (transcription).

fees on such transactions as trades and sales of livestock—various types of coercive means had undoubtedly been developed to insure proper fiscal accounting. As security decreased in the region and the implicit backing of the authorities at Balkh disappeared with it, a natural, though unprovable at this point, increase in the size of the shrine's police forces would have been necessary. And the stock-breeding nomads who used the pastures of Balkh, especially the Qipchaq and Qalmaq groups, could have been a logical source of recruits. Zayn al-Din Shirwani, a Sufi intellectual and visitor to the region in 1800, observed that the nomadic population living around Balkh City numbered some 30,000 households.[42] We have at this point no evidence that the shrine recruited from the tribal groups, but, in light of the forces ultimately assembled by the mutawalli, it seems highly likely that it did.

It is clear that the mutawalli and his staff were unwilling to surrender their administrative prerogatives despite having no political authority to whom they could turn to back those rights. Probably in a gradual and circumstantial way, in response to events, the mutawalli began to equip the shrine with the means to guarantee its own security. Only the results of decisions made in the late eighteenth century are at all apparent to us today, and these come only in the impressionistic and impressionable accounts that foreign visitors to Balkh have left. Their reliability would be open to question were it not for the fact that they themselves had no idea of the significance of what they were seeing and reporting and thus could have had little motive for trying to embellish it.

Mountstuart Elphinstone, writing in the first decade of the century, is the first to record the shrine's emergence as a "petty state." According to his informants, "Mozaur" was one of the independent political units that Qilij 'Ali had incorporated under his jurisdiction at the beginning of the century.[43] When Qilij 'Ali died in 1817, the shrine reverted to the independent status it had enjoyed, or endured, before his consolidation of Balkh. The era of Mir Murad Beg, the Qataghan amir from Qunduz and the next prominent amirid figure, thrust the shrine back into the political limelight, and it is from this period that our information on its military resources comes. By 1824 at the latest, the shrine, under its mutawalli and backed by the economic resources of its waqf properties, had assembled an armed force of sufficient size to attract the notice of visitors to the region.

In the 1820s, two plucky but ill-fated entrepreneurs, William Moorcroft and George Trebeck, left India with grand schemes for getting rich in the Central Asian horse trade. En route to Bukhara, they were held

[42] Shirwani 1960, 156.
[43] Elphinstone 1815, 474.

up at Qunduz by a war that had erupted between Mir Murad Beg and an alliance of the amirid rulers of the petty town-states of the Balkh region. "While we were thus detained," they wrote in their journals, "a confederacy was formed against Murad Beg amongst whom were the Wali of Aibek; Zulfakar Sher of Siripol; Ishan Khan of Balkh; the chief of Mazar and others; who had raised a force of eight thousand men, better equipped and mounted than those of Murad Beg."[44]

The wali of Aibek (Aybak, Ay Bik, Ay Beg, Haibek, a begate south of Khulm/Tashqurghan commanding one of the main routes between Kabul and Balkh) at this time was Mir Baba, the son of Qilij 'Ali. Ishan Khan may be identified with Ishan Naqib and the "chief of Mazar" was probably none other than the mutawalli of the shrine. In the 1820s it may well have been a man named Shuja' al-Din. The coalition of Aybak, Sar-i Pul, Mazar, and Balkh forces did not actually engage Mir Murad's forces, and Moorcroft and Trebeck were able to proceed on.

In the early 1830s, another British visitor, Alexander Burnes, estimated that the military resources of the shrine included some 1,000 cavalrymen,[45] and in 1839 an American visitor placed the figure at 900 horsemen.[46] In 1845, another foreign observer asserted that the shrine's armed force was made up of a regular contingent of 250 cavalrymen with another 1,000 reserves that could be mobilized in a crisis.[47]

What the foreign visitors recorded in the first half of the nineteenth century was an unusual but certainly not unique phenomenon in the history of shrines, waqfs, and the people associated with them.

Certainly a parallel instance (but one with an ideological element not so apparent in the 'Alid shrine case) is found in the history of the Ardabil shrine of Shaykh Safi al-Din in the fifteenth century.[48] Another is the history of the Ridawi shrine at Mashhad in the middle of the eighteenth century.[49] Although one should not make too much of the similarities, it is interesting to note at least one of them, the change in titles that accompanied the change in function.

At Ardabil, the title "shaykh" was replaced by "sultan," signifying the different expectations and responsibilities associated with the head of the shrine and administrator of its properties.[50] At Mashhad, the mutawalli, Mir Sayyid Muhammad, adopted the throne name "Sulayman Shah" or "Shah Sulayman." At the 'Alid shrine at Balkh, the titulature also

[44] Moorcroft and Trebeck 1841, 2:444.
[45] Burnes 1834, 1:232.
[46] Harlan 1939, 33.
[47] Ferrier 1857, 209.
[48] Mazzaoui 1972, 71–77.
[49] Gulistanah 1965, 37–58.
[50] Mazzaoui 1972, 20.

changed. During the second half of the eighteenth century, the title "khan" was added to the name of the mutawalli. In the annexes up until the Nadirid occupation, the title "khan" never appears with the names of the mutawallis. This is hardly surprising. Not only did it have a political connotation, it was an exclusive prerogative of the Chingizid family and, before 1750, was not used even by Uzbek amirs. The mutawalli of the shrine during the Nadirid occupation is referred to as Khwajah Ni'mat by the one contemporary source in which his name appears.[51] But in a late-nineteenth-century document he is called Mirza Ni'mat Khan,[52] and by the end of the first quarter of the nineteenth century, his successors were already known by that title. As part of the general process of the extinction of the Chingizid mandate in Central Asia, the formerly exclusive titulature passed into more common usage. This transition was at first perhaps a sign that the bearer saw himself heir to the Chingizid tradition; then, as the Chingizid legacy lost all political meaning, use of the term "khan" was further generalized into a common honorific. In Afghanistan, the term was used both in local onomastica as a suffix equivalent to its contemporary "esquire" and in political terminology to describe a local leader. It was in this way that Moorcroft refers to the "chief of Mazar" when he calls him "the Khan."[53]

There are marked differences of course among the situations at Ardabil, Mashhad, and Balkh. Ideology played a more obvious role at Ardabil than at either of the other two shrine centers. More significantly, the transformation at Ardabil occurred under the aegis of two relatively powerful states, the Aq Qoyunlu and the Shirwanshahs.[54] At Balkh, there was no strong political force with which to contend, and had there been, there would have been no call for the militarization of the shrine. Far more analogous to the changing role of the mutawalli at Balkh was the situation in Mashhad.[55]

There, by the middle of the eighteenth century, the relations between the state and the Ridawi shrine had long been close. The political authorities were accustomed to appointing the mutawalli, and the position was at times little more than an office, although an important one, within the state bureaucracy. When Nadir Shah was assassinated in 1747, the various political factions sought out candidates with enough of the aura of legitimacy (still at this time rooted in the Safawid family) to enjoy some credibility as claimants of the shah's throne.

One who emerged in this turbulent period was Mir Sayyid Muham-

[51] Astarabadi 1848, 380.
[52] TMS, 74 (text), 81 (transcription).
[53] Moorcroft and Trebeck 1841, 2:489.
[54] Mazzaoui 1972, 76.
[55] Gulistanah 1965, 37–58.

mad, a man who had been mutawalli of the Ridawi shrine during Nadir Shah's regime. As far as family connections went, his credentials were impressive. His father's line was Ridawi and his mother's Safawid. (His mother was a daughter of the late Safawid shah, Sulayman [r. 1666–1694].) For a time after Nadir Shah's murder, the mutawalli had traveled in the entourages of various pretenders. At Qum, sometime before 1750, a number of political leaders encouraged him to seek the throne. His response was noncommittal but made another pretender, Shah Rukh, who was then in Mashhad, sufficiently apprehensive to lure the former mutawalli to Mashhad and there try to assassinate him.

But the ostensible backers of Shah Rukh now decided that Mir Sayyid Muhammad would make a better candidate and transferred their loyalties to him. Gulistanah has Mir Sayyid Muhammad only very reluctantly agreeing to their overtures. But whatever the interest or lack thereof in having the title of "shah," on 10 January A.D. 1749 or 30 December 1749 (either 20 Muharram A.H. 1162 or 1163)[56] he and his haram were placed under the protection of his new "Bayat, Khuzaymah, Kurd, Tatar, Mish Mast, Afshar, and Turk" supporters.[57]

On Nawruz, 20 March 1749 or 1750, following his astrologers' recommendation, he was enthroned and assumed the title "Shah Sulayman," no doubt in honor of his grandfather, and had coins minted under that name. His reign was of no great duration or political consequence but is noteworthy as a historical curiosity.

As far as I know, Shah Sulayman (the Second) is the first and last mutawalli to have taken the title and assumed the position of shah in Iran. There are numerous earlier and later examples of shahs who assume honorary and nominal mutawalli-ships,[58] but Mir Sayyid Muhammad/Shah Sulayman stands as a unique example of the reverse.

The transformations of the mutawalli at Mashhad and the mutawalli at Balkh into political leaders have more superficial than substantive similarities. Mir Muhammad Sayyid had "shah's blood" and thus an innate standing in the political sphere that no mutawalli at the 'Alid shrine had ever enjoyed. Nonetheless, the realization of the potential implicit in that inherited capacity could only have occurred in the political upheaval occasioned by Nadir Shah's assassination, just as the assumption and development of a political role by the Ansari mutawalli came about because of political conditions. Similar in both cases is the question of who legitimately can claim nominal authority. In Iran, the Safawid mandate was dying but not dead. Authentic Safawid blood carried political weight well

---

[56] Ibid., 46.

[57] Ibid., 45.

[58] For example, Shah 'Abbas for his 1602–03 waqf at Mashhad (McChesney 1981, 169).

into the second half of the eighteenth century. In Balkh, the Chingizid khanate was a not much dimmer memory. What distinguished the two cases was the apparent crowd of genuine Safawids in eighteenth-century Iran and the apparent absence of Tuqay-Timurid Chingizids in Balkh after the Nadirid invasion ended. Scattered to India, Iran, or the Hijaz, no Chingizid seems to have looked to Balkh after 1747 as a land of opportunity.

The position of the mutawalli in both Mashhad and Balkh was thus a product of, or part of the response to, the political conditions at work in both places. In neither case, in contrast to what happened at Ardabil in the fifteenth century, did the religious/ideological factor of being the head of a major shrine play a distinctive role. The similarity of administrative function and the concomitant loyalties, dependencies, and powers that it conferred seems to have been the predominant factor. There is little evidence to suggest that either the Ridawi shrine at Mashhad or the 'Alid shrine at what was increasingly by then being called Mazar or Mazar-i Sharif was a center for the kind of display of spiritual fervor that marked Ardabil.[59]

At Mazar no evidence of the mutawalli's spiritual role, if he had one, has survived to show that his followers and subjects considered him imbued with any of the divine grace that Shaykh Junayd's followers at Ardabil saw in him. The shrine itself, however, continued to exert a strong spiritual attraction. Since at least the early sixteenth century, when the Shibanid sultan at Balkh, Kistan Qara, had chosen to be buried within its sacred precincts, it had been a favorite place of interment. In addition, its fame as a place of divine intercession, especially in cases of physical problems, continued. There is a record of a visit paid by one former Durrani shah, Shah Zaman (r. 1793–1801). In 1814, the ex-shah, who had been blinded by his successor, Shah Mahmud, traveled by elephant from Kabul, where he was then living a relatively comfortable retirement. He was welcomed at the shrine by the chief political figure of Balkh, Qilij 'Ali. After a twenty-day stay at the shrine, the ex-shah went on to Bukhara.[60]

According to Bukhari, during this time pilgrims came from all over the region—"from Hindustan, Khurasan, and Turan"—to visit the shrine and "when 1,000 travelers have come, the mutawalli gives them food [ash wa nan] and pocket money."[61]

The influence that the shrine came to have in the political arena

[59] There was, for example, no raiding of non-Muslim districts organized by the shrines, even though, as at Ardabil, unbelievers lived within striking distance (in the case of the 'Alid shrine, in eastern Badakhshan and the region known today as Nuristan).

[60] Bukhari 1976, 73–74.

[61] Ibid.

stemmed in large part from the esteem in which the public held it. But no attempt ever seems to have been made by the administrators to transform that popular reverence for the shrine and its tradition into reverence for them as guardians of the tradition. The militarization of the shrine appears to have arisen not in response to a missionary call, as at Ardabil, but in answer to the more prosaic need to maintain regional security and to protect shrine properties in the absence of another source of authority to which they should appeal.

The buildup of armed forces to the 900–1250 cavalrymen that the shrine was said to command in the 1830s and 1840s was probably a gradual response to a growing need for security rather than a calculated effort to raise the shrine town and its region to a position of political prominence. That it eventually had the effect of politicizing the shrine and forcing it to play a larger regional role seems to have been an unintended consequence.

The headquarters of the shrine administration and the home of the mutawalli was a fort, the type of fortified structure called a qal‘ah—neither as complex nor as large as the citadel or arg common to large cities but an adequate symbol of political power. The would-be entrepreneur William Moorcroft was welcomed to the shrine in February 1825 and has left the following description:

> Mazar is enclosed by a mud wall and seems to be larger than Tash Kurghan. The houses are of clay, of one story, with either domed or flat roofs, surrounded by a court, but less separated by orchards than at Tash Kurghan. It takes its name from a tomb (Mazar) supposed to contain some of the bones of Ali. There is another mausoleum[62] which has been of some importance, but is now in a state of dilapidation. . . . On the following morning we waited on the Khan and were introduced to him in the fort in a long, low, and narrow apartment which seemed to have been intended for a stable: he was seated with many of his people on felts ranged along the wall, and rose, and embraced me; he welcomed me to Mazar and assured me of his friendship.[63]

By the time of Moorcroft's visit, the mutawalli/khan, Shuja‘ al-Din, was a person of substantial influence in the region. He was related by marriage to Ishan Naqib (also known as Ishan Khwajah), the governor of Balkh, and he maintained diplomatic relations with the Mangghit rulers of Bukhara. Somewhat later, about 1840 or so, after the Bukharan amir, Nasr Allah b. Amir Haydar, deposed Ishan Naqib, the latter's son, Ishan

---

[62] Probably the tomb of Kistan Qara Sultan, built by ‘Abd al-Mu’min b. ‘Abd Allah Khan, and called the Gunbad-i Kabud (Azure Dome) (TMS, 37, 94).

[63] Moorcroft and Trebeck 1841, 2:489–90.

Uraq, reportedly solicited and received Shuja' al-Din Khan's military help in recapturing the city.[64]

Shuja' al-Din Khan was seen by at least one contemporary as a shrewd politician and, by virtue of his association with the 'Alid tradition, able to play the role of mediator in regional disputes. Josiah Harlan, a soldier of fortune and native of Chester County, Pennsylvania, was obviously impressed by the mutawalli, whom he met on his travels through Balkh in 1839:

> He is a man of grave address and dignified deportment but his character is full of duplicity and political tergiversation. He is addicted to literary pursuits and said to be a good poet. He covets the reputation of a mediator and is frequently referred to for the settlement of feuds, in which occupation much of his time is spent. He is suspected of being in secret correspondence with the Bocharrah prince, and no doubt justly suspected. His policy would be to temporize with any power superior to and likely to conflict with his interest, but no political attachments are sufficiently strong to bias his judgement in the crafty pursuit of individual advantage.[65]

Judging by the rest of Harlan's memoirs, Shuja' al-Din was a man after his own heart.

Self-interest, entailing the security of the waqf and the shrine it supported, no doubt determined the overall policies of the mutawalli. His ability to adapt to rapidly changing political conditions appears to have spared the shrine catastrophic economic problems. Shuja' al-Din's ability to tack in shifting political winds is evident in the reports of his relations with the major regional power after Qilij 'Ali, Mir Murad Beg of Qataghan. Earlier there was mention of the mutawalli's involvement with a coalition that hoped to overthrow Murad Beg in the fall of 1824. But shortly thereafter, according to Harlan, Shuja' al-Din cooperated in (or in Harlan's inimitable phrasing "connived in") negotiations to settle the claims of Qilij 'Ali's heirs, Mir Baba and Mir Wali, to the benefit of Mir Murad.[66]

Shuja' al-Din not only managed to steer a course through the treacherous political waters of the first half of the nineteenth century, he also succeeded in keeping the main waqf properties, the Shahi Canal district, in apparently excellent condition. The more peripheral properties (those amirid donations, of the seventeenth century in particular, that were in the Aybak, Hadrat-i Sultan, or Samangan River valley) seem to have fared less well. By the early nineteenth century, it is fairly evident that

[64] *Gaz.* 4:109.
[65] Harlan 1939, 32–33.
[66] Ibid., 34–35.

at least some, if not all, of these parcels had passed from shrine control, although whether by sale or otherwise is unknown.

One example was in the Qush Ribat region near the old city of Khulm. In the seventeenth century, the shrine administered half of the irrigation system there as waqf; in the eighteenth century these water rights were reconfirmed. But when Harlan visited Qush Ribat in 1839, he saw only ruins:

> It was formerly a rich and fertile appurtenance of Khoolum but has become involved in the fatality that follows the track of Moorad [Murad Beg] and presents only the outlines of a ruined village. It was formerly watered by the Heibuck River, which now runs to waste and is absorbed from the desert sands.[67]

But the core of the waqf, the original grant made by Sultan Husayn Bayqara in 1480 of the Nahr-i Shahi and its appurtenances, was flourishing in the early nineteenth century. In the late 1790s, when Mughul Beg visited the area, the irrigation system made a strong impression on him.[68] In 1825, Moorcroft remarked on the irrigation system and the richness of the soil between the Abdu Pass (Kutal-i Abdu) and the shrine, a distance of some fifteen miles.[69] (Subhan Quli had defined the eastern border of the waqf land as the Kutal-i Abdu in 1668.) Moorcroft also visited Dih Dadi, which formed the western boundary of the waqf lands as defined by Subhan Quli's manshur. It was, he observed,

> a walled town about six miles west from Mazar; a very large body of water, the great canal of Mazar, flowed by it and was seen to come from a gorge in the hills at some distance. The orchards of Deh Dadeh are famous for pomegranates and plums. . . . Deh Dadeh is also celebrated for its breed of greyhounds, and for brown or Nankin cotton, called there the Mullah's cotton; vestments made of it unbleached being worn almost exclusively by that class of persons, many of whom reside at Mazar.[70]

To Moorcroft, the economy of the shrine stood in striking contrast to that of Balkh City. Many of the irrigation channels to and through Balkh were blocked up and the city itself was seriously dilapidated.[71]

Alexander Burnes, following Moorcroft's route seven years later, was somewhat less impressed with the conditions of the waqf lands.[72]

---

[67] Ibid., 34.
[68] Mirza Mughul Beg, fols. 21b–22a.
[69] Moorcroft and Trebeck 1841, 2:488.
[70] Ibid., 2:490–41.
[71] Ibid., 2:492–43.
[72] Burnes 1834, 1:232–33. It should be added, though, that Mohan Lal, a secretary or munshi employed by Burnes to write his Persian letters, left a description of Mazar and the region east of Balkh that suggests that the shrine and its waqf economy were thriving: "June

Burnes's outlook was that of an archaeologist and historian, concerned about the state of the monuments rather than the business prospects Moorcroft's entrepreneurial eye sought out. Seven years after Burnes, Josiah Harlan described the economy of both the shrine and Balkh City as quite prosperous: "The necessaries of life are more abundant and cheaper in the vicinity of Balkh and Mozar than in any other part of the province. This district is more fertile and has the advantage of a profuse supply of water for irrigation."[73] Corroborating the impression of a prospering shrine is his observation that, second to Murad Beg, the wealthiest man in the entire region was the mutawalli, Shuja' al-Din Khan.[74]

From these sources, scant and impressionistic though they may be, we may tentatively conclude that, at least in comparison with other parts of the region, the shrine enjoyed a high level of material prosperity during the first half of the nineteenth century. Moorcroft's passing mention of the ruined state of Kistan Qara's tomb introduces the only dissonant note to such a finding.[75] But it may be that the apparent failure of 'Abd al-Mu'min, the builder of the tomb, to provide a waqf endowment for it was the cause of its deterioration, not general economic conditions.[76]

The position that the shrine administration had come to occupy in the century after 1747 was largely determined by its response to the political circumstances in which it had to operate. The political situation created by the Nadirid occupation was perhaps the single most influential factor in the evolution of the shrine's political role. During the Nadirid occupation, the Chingizid mandate in the region was effectively eradicated. And the withdrawal of the Iranian forces after a decade left the area with no acknowledged legitimate political entity.

In the process of adapting to the new conditions, the shrine was militarized and politicized, and its mutawalli was forced to play an active political role, sometimes as mediator, sometimes as ally, and sometimes as opponent. Had a single political authority, legitimized by popular recognition, been able to establish itself in the former Chingizid appanage of Balkh after the Nadirid withdrawal, it is highly unlikely that the shrine would have developed in the way that it did. The structure of amirid or begid petty states that emerged after 1747 was an indispensable ingredient in the rise of the shrine as a political power.

---

11 [1831]—A march of fifteen miles brought us to the ancient place called Balk [sic], or Bactria. Our course was almost entirely through plains, bordered on both sides with beautiful gardens" (Mohan Lal 1846, 65).

[73] Harlan 1939, 31.

[74] Ibid.

[75] Moorcroft and Trebeck 1841, 2:489.

[76] TMS, which is generally careful to note the waqf endowments of the shrine buildings, makes no reference to any waqfs established to maintain Kistan Qara's tomb.

Similarly, when the conglomeration of minor states that had contested the region for a century began to feel pressure from the vigorous and expansionist Afghan state at Kabul, the shrine, too, was inevitably affected. In the intervening time, however, certain internal changes and developments took place that would have long-range consequences for the shrine and its waqf.

WAQF REVENUES AND ANSARI RIGHTS

One of these developments directly affected the income of the shrine and how it was disbursed. By the terms of the 1668–1669 manshur issued by Subhan Quli, the Ansari mutawalli was entitled to 20 percent of the gross revenues of the waqf as his salary. The document leaves somewhat ambiguous the question of whether or not all administrative salaries were to be paid out of this portion. The use of the phrase "for his own expenses"[77] strongly suggests that the sum was the mutawalli's own salary and that additional administrative costs were to be covered by the remaining waqf or other non-waqf income, such as the votive offerings brought by pilgrims. Until the late nineteenth century, we have no information on how the cash and valuables offered by worshippers were disbursed. In the early days of the shrine, these votive offerings appear to have been quite substantial. Khwandamir, describing the situation at the end of the fifteenth century and the beginning of the sixteenth century, reckoned the annual income from votive offerings alone at "one hundred kapaki tuman" worth of cash and goods.[78] He gives no information, though, on how this enormous sum was handled. The seventeenth-century documentation makes no separate provision for this type of income, a fact that suggests either that votive offerings were too trivial to mention or, as seems far more likely, that from an administrative standpoint all income was subsumed under the rubric "waqf."

The mutawalli's interest in the shrine's income was established by a document, Subhan Quli's manshur, and the legal instruments underlying it. The fact that the annexes offer no specific modification of the terms is presumptive evidence for their being in effect down to 1737, the date of the last annex.

But sometime during the last half of the eighteenth century, the disbursement of income changed from what the earlier documentation outlined. In the 1790s, Mirza Mughul Beg b. Muhammad (d. 1806), who collected topographical data for Lieutenant Colonel Francis Wilford, a member of the Asiatic Society of Bengal,[79] observed that the agricultural

[77] TMS, 59 (text), 67 (transcription).
[78] Khwandamir n.d., 4:173.
[79] For a bibliographic note on his work, see Storey 1927–84, 2:(1):148.

income from the shrine at Balkh was distributed among those employed at the shrine.[80] In and of itself this observation is only suggestive and not very enlightening. It takes on added significance, however, in light of a remark made by Alexander Burnes on the occasion of his visit to the shrine in 1832. He writes, "the priests sat at the door of the shrine and divided the proceeds of the day, copper by copper, among certain families who are entitled to it by hereditary right."[81] Although one might reasonably view such a remark, made by a stranger with no real understanding of the workings of the shrine, in a skeptical light, we know for certain that some process was underway by which the Ansari family would gain exclusive rights to the shrine's income. By 1889, even the Afghan state had recognized this right, and it is safe to assume that it was not a claim only recently advanced. By then the jurisdiction of the Ansari family was accepted as hereditary and extending to the entire income of the waqf income and to all the income from votive offerings, after the operating expenses of the shrine had been deducted.[82]

It is reasonable to assume that Ansari interest in the waqf income began with the first Ansari to take up residence at the shrine. Certainly by the end of the seventeenth century—by which time Ansari succession to the tawliyat was taken for granted—shrine and Ansari interests were inseparable. When the shrine was forced to assume increased administrative responsibilities in the first half of the eighteenth century, it is reasonable to infer that the Ansaris benefited. Taking the late-nineteenth-century situation as suggestive of Ansari prominence in the administration in earlier times as well, we find that all of the major officials at the shrine then—the mutawalli, the treasurer (*sanduqdar*), the auditor (*nazir*), the grounds and buildings supervisor (*farrash-bashi*), and the keeper of the keys (*kilidar*)—as well as most of their assistants were Ansaris.[83]

The exclusion of all but Ansaris from a share of waqf income would appear to be in violation of at least some of the earlier waqf conditions. In 1668–1669, the manshur of Subhan Quli had affirmed that what remained of waqf income after the mutawalli deducted his 20 percent was to be used for necessary building maintenance; for the hospice or residential quarters (khanaqah); and for the salaries of the imam, the muezzin, the preachers, the scholar-residents (*mujawiran*), and other employees (*khuddam*).[84]

[80] Mirza Mughul Beg, fols. 21b–22a.
[81] Burnes 1834, 1:233.
[82] *TMS*, 73 (text), 77 (transcription).
[83] See the list of shrine officials (*TMS*, 82–83) and the list of Ansari family members (Ibid., 78–81).
[84] *TMS*, 59 (text), 67 (transcription).

In 1889, on the other hand, the Afghan imam and muezzin were entitled only to a state salary and were not entitled to a share in either the votive income or the waqf income. In 1889, moreover, no mention is made of the khanaqah or of the mujawiran, who lived at the shrine but had no official duties. Obviously changes had occurred in the intervening two centuries, and what little evidence we have suggests that it was during the latter half of the eighteenth century that the Ansaris were establishing what would become an inalienable right to the revenues generated by the shrine's properties.

THE ISSUE OF SUCCESSION

A second development linked to the effect of political and economic circumstances on the internal order of the shrine administration is what might be characterized in a different context as a succession crisis, a struggle for control of the shrine and its waqf economy during the late eighteenth century. The evidence is mostly circumstantial but nonetheless persuasive that sometime during the post-Nadirid period the office of chief administrator, the tawliyat, was assumed, perhaps seized, by one Ansari line, which kept control of it to at least as late as 1889. The struggle appears to have been for a preeminent but not necessarily an exclusive role in administration of the shrine and its waqf properties.

Before delving into the shadowy evidence that suggests such an episode, it is first worth digressing a bit on the line of Ansari mutawallis and discussing the sources of this information and the problems in its interpretation.

The only source to enumerate the mutawallis at the 'Alid shrine begins its list with the founding of the shrine in 1480 and, although the work itself was compiled in the middle of the twentieth century, carries the list of mutawallis only down to the middle of the nineteenth:[85]

1. Shaykh Shams al-Din Miskin Ansari
2. Mirza Abu'l-Hasan Ansari
3. Mirza Abu Talib Ansari
4. Mirza Sanjar Ansari
5. Mirza Najm al-Din Ansari
6. Mirza Akhdar Ansari
7. Qadi Mir Muhammad Ya'qub Ansari
8. Mirza 'Aziz Khan
9. Mirza Shuja' al-Din Khan

Hafiz Nur Muhammad, the author of *TMS*, has taken most, if not all, of this list verbatim from another work. As the source(s) he used provides

[85] Ibid., 100 (note).

the line down to the penultimate mutawalli, Mirza 'Aziz Khan (Hafiz Nur Muhammad giving the name of Shuja' al-Din Khan, who flourished 1824–1845), it is possible to eliminate all of the works cited by the author except the *Tarikh-i Akabir al-Din*.[86] Nur Muhammad describes this work as a manuscript defective at both ends and he dates it circa 1240/1824–1825 on the basis of the information it gives about the amirs of Bukhara.[87] This dating corresponds with the fact that Mirza 'Aziz Khan is the last mutawalli mentioned in Hafiz Nur Muhammad's list. Furthermore, according to the author, the *Akabir al-Din* contains biographical material on fifty-nine "nobles and deceased [*buzurgan wa asudagan*] of Balkh" and the genealogies of fifty-one "people of God," including the mutawallis of the "mazar-i sharif."[88] There can be little doubt that this was the source of Hafiz Nur Muhammad's list.

It is by no means a complete or accurate list, however. Even the most cursory examination of it uncovers problems. Missing from the list is the name of Qadi Mir Muhammad Amin, the son and successor of Mir Muhammad Ya'qub Ansari. Muhammad Amin's name appears in the annexes to the 1668–1669 manshur dated 1720–1721, October–November 1721, April 1729, and September–October 1730.[89] His relationship to Mir Muhammad Ya'qub is explicitly stated in the second and fourth annexes. The name of Khwajah Ni'mat is likewise conspicuously absent from the list. Like Mir Muhammad Amin, Khwajah Ni'mat is twice mentioned elsewhere by Hafiz Nur Muhammad.[90] Further, Hafiz Nur Muhammad earlier (*TMS*, 36) says that Taj al-Din Andkhudi was the first mutawalli at the shrine (based on Khwandamir's account) but does not include his name in the list of mutawallis.

The inexplicably long periods between mutawallis whose dates are known or can be approximated are another problem that the author of TMS might have been expected to notice. For instance, we know that Mir Muhammad Ya'qub was deceased or out of office by 1721[91] and that Mirza Shuja' al-Din was the mutawalli between 1824[92] and 1845,[93] and yet in the intervening century only one mutawalli, Mirza 'Aziz Khan, is listed.[94] If, as Hafiz Nur Muhammad asserts, the latter was Shuja' al-

[86] The *Tarikh-i Akabir al-Din* is found neither in Storey nor Storey and Bregel'.

[87] *TMS*, 14.

[88] Ibid.

[89] Ibid., 52–55 (text), 69–70 (transcription).

[90] Ibid., 74, 81.

[91] According to the dates on the annexes issued in his son's name (*TMS*, 52 [text], 69 [transcription]).

[92] Moorcroft and Trebeck 1841, 2:488.

[93] Ferrier 1857, 209.

[94] Fufalza'i 1967, 1:302, citing the *Husayn Shahi* of Imam al-Din Husayn Chishti (see Storey and Bregel' 1972, 1223), says that Mirza 'Aziz was mutawalli in 1204/21 September

Din's father, then we are confronted with a period of some fifty or sixty years at least (between Mir Muhammad Ya'qub and Mirza 'Aziz) for which no mutawalli is named. A similar case occurs for the sixteenth century. The author of TMS claims to have had the "fourth volume" of BA "at hand"[95] and from it he should have known that the fourth mutawalli on his list, Mirza Sanjar, was appointed to the post by Nadhr Muhammad in 1624–1625.[96] If we then follow the information in the 1668–1669 manshur that Mirza Abu'l-Hasan Ansari was the first mutawalli,[97] we are faced with a 145-year period in which only Mirza Abu'l-Hasan and Mirza Abu Talib held the tawliyat. Even if we accept TMS's assertion that Shams al-Din was the first mutawalli, the period between 1480 and 1624 still seems rather long for only three mutawallis to have held office.

This list raises other more complex questions of verification for which no satisfactory answers are possible at this time. Of the eleven mutawallis mentioned, including the two not on the list (Mir Muhammad Amin and Khwajah Ni'mat), seven are attested historical figures, that is to say there is independent corroboration of their lives. These seven are Shaykh Shams al-Din, Mirza Sanjar, Mir Muhammad Ya'qub, Mir Muhammad Amin, Khwajah Ni'mat, Mirza 'Aziz Khan, and Mirza Shuja' al-Din Khan. Of the other four, Mirza Abu'l-Hasan is a marginal case. Although he is mentioned in a source other than Akabir al-Din (the 1668–1669 manshur), that document was drafted some two centuries after Abu'l-Hasan was alleged to have lived.

What follows is a revised list in which I have tried to take into account the obvious problems of the Akabir al-Din list. The names in square brackets are individuals for whom no independent evidence has yet been found. Names of individuals for whom some tenuous verification exists have been enclosed in parentheses. Where a father-son relationship is known to have existed, the names are linked thus: + . Where such a relationship is known *not* to have existed, the notation is: × . Dates where known are also given.

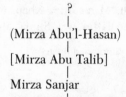

Mirza Sanjar   1034/1624–1625 to post-1045/1636

1789–9 September 1790. He also gives the name of another individual associated with the shrine, who is called "khadim" (servant) in an inscription in the shrine building. The name given is Bargaday Sultan, with dates of 1211–1213/7 July 1796–4 June 1799.

[95] TMS, 13.

[96] BA 4: fol. 304b.

[97] TMS, 56–57 (text), 65 (transcription).

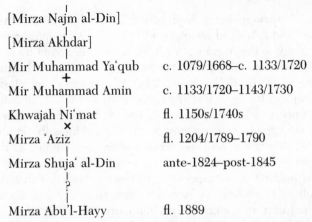

[Mirza Najm al-Din]	
[Mirza Akhdar]	
Mir Muhammad Ya'qub	c. 1079/1668–c. 1133/1720
Mir Muhammad Amin	c. 1133/1720–1143/1730
Khwajah Ni'mat	fl. 1150s/1740s
Mirza 'Aziz	fl. 1204/1789–1790
Mirza Shuja' al-Din	ante-1824–post-1845
Mirza Abu'l-Hayy	fl. 1889

There are other difficulties involved in attempting to identify the first mutawalli of the waqf. In the first place, the organization of the shrine's administration under the Timurids differed from what it became under the Shibanids and Tuqay-Timurids in the sixteenth and seventeenth centuries. In the second place, the retrospective view of documents and other historical materials tends toward the point of view that the contemporary circumstances were unchanged from the past. In the case of the tawliyat, while Subhan Quli's manshur of 1668–1669 posits the office of the mutawalli from the very founding of the shrine, authors contemporary with the founding—Khwandamir, Isfizari, and Lari—do not use the term. Instead the titles "shaykh" and "naqib" are used.

If we take conditions at Mashhad as somewhat analogous for the same period, we might conclude that the responsibilities associated with a mutawalli would have fallen on the naqib.[98] That being the case, the first person charged with administration of the waqf would have been Sayyid Taj al-Din, who came from Andkhud,[99] not Herat, as the Ansaris are supposed to have done. If we follow the *Akabir al-Din* list, the first mutawalli would have been the man whom Khwandamir styles "shaykh," Shams al-Din Muhammad. Furthermore, if we accept Shams al-Din Muhammad as the first mutawalli, we have the difficult problem of establishing Ansari connections for him.

Perhaps the simplest and most reasonable way out is to evade the complexities and assume that the Ansari line began with Abu'l-Hasan, as the 1668–1669 manshur asserts, but that his position in the early shrine administration was far less prominent than what his successors would enjoy in later centuries. Such a hypothesis seems to be supported by the information that in 1537–1538 a man named Mir 'Abd Allah Tirmidhi, "a Khu-

[98] Mu'tamin 1969, 225.

[99] Khwandamir n.d., 4:172.

dawand khwajah," was appointed naqib of the "Astanah-i 'Aliyah-i 'Ali" in Balkh.[100] Mir 'Abd Allah had no apparent links by geographical provenance or genealogy to the Ansaris. Nor is his name mentioned by later sources as an Ansari mutawalli, and it is reasonable to infer from this that he was not an Ansari. In 1573, during 'Abd Allah Khan's era, Hasan Khwajah, the naqib of Bukhara, was appointed shaykh of the 'Alid shrine for a period of uncertain length (he died in Jumada al-Awwal 991/May–June 1583).[101] Both appointments suggest that the "shaykh-naqib" administration was still in effect during the century after the founding of the shrine. The silence of the sixteenth-century sources on any appointments of mutawallis is indirect if not especially convincing evidence that the post of mutawalli, if there was one, was not yet particularly prominent. In Iran, it was not until the reign of Shah Tahmasp (1524–1576) that the office of mutawalli superseded the naqib as administrator of the Ridawi shrine at Mashhad.[102]

If nothing else, it should be clear that the seventeenth-century and later claims that Ansari origins and their administrative prerogatives go back to the foundation of the shrine are at best problematic. It is not until the third decade of the seventeenth century that we have substantial evidence of the existence of an office called the tawliyat at the 'Alid shrine. Mirza Sanjar, appointed in 1624–1625, is the first mutawalli of record.[103] His origins are rather interesting and suggest some of the complications of seventeenth-century religious affiliations that later writers had to explain away or gloss over. The nineteenth-century *Akabir al-Din* claims him as an Ansari and calls him the son of Mirza Abu Talib Ansari. But Mahmud b. Amir Wali, a contemporary of Mirza Sanjar, portrays him in quite a different light. In the first place, Mirza Sanjar was born in India. If his father had been mutawalli, why was Mirza Sanjar born in India? Further research may provide a perfectly plausible explanation. For now it seems somewhat incongruous. Moreover, Mahmud b. Amir Wali's silence regarding Sanjar's succession to his father's place seems even more incongruous, especially since one recurrent theme in the biographical sketches in his work is the importance of lineage in occupation succession. Had the oft-repeated aphorism "wealth and status are both inheritable" been applicable in the case of Mirza Sanjar, one would have expected the author to note it.

Mahmud b. Amir Wali's report, which Hafiz Nur Muhammad says he used, poses other questions about the Ansari origins of Mirza Sanjar. First he is characterized as "sayyid," that is, a descendant of the Prophet

[100] *TR*, fol. 126b.
[101] Tanish n.d. I: fol. 198b.
[102] Mu'tamin 1969, 226.
[103] *BA* 4: fol. 304b.

Muhammad. We have no record of any other mutawalli before or after Mirza Sanjar using that title. He also is described as a member of "a sublime house," which gave him "superiority over his peers." There is some evidence that the "sublime house" was that of the Ridawi sayyids of Mashhad, for further along in the account Mirza Sanjar is described as a relation (*az qarabatiyan*) of Nadhr Muhammad's mother, Shahr Banu Begum. She was the daughter (or half-sister) of a Ridawi shaykh at Mashhad and married Nadhr Muhammad's father there during the Shibanid/ Uzbek occupation in the 1590s.[104] It is a curious coincidence that Mirza Sanjar's predecessor (and father?) is named Mirza Abu Talib in the *Tarikh-i Akabir al-Din* list of mutawallis; that Shahr Banu's father (or brother), who was "mutawalli of the Imam 'Ali Musawi shrine" at Mashhad, was also named Mirza Abu Talib;[105] and that the mutawalli of the Ridawi shrine during the period 1031–1035/1621–1626 was also a Mirza Abu Talib.[106]

All of this may be nothing more than coincidence, but it does little to strengthen the assertion that the Ansaris had held the tawliyat of the 'Alid shrine in unbroken fashion, "generation after generation," from the year of the shrine's founding.

About the two mutawallis who followed Mirza Sanjar, Mirza Najm al-Din and Mirza Akhdar, I have no information whatsoever.

It is only with Mirza Muhammad Ya'qub that an Ansari connection is firmly established. In Subhan Quli's 1668–1669 decree, the lore of the Ansari tawliyat is first recorded. Explicitly, the document declares that the first mutawalli was Abu'l-Hasan Ansari. Implicitly, the document recognizes a past in which the tawliyat had passed down through the Ansari family to Mir Muhammad Ya'qub, the living representative of the tradition. The prerogatives of the Ansari family are likewise implied. The decree does not accord the family outright a legal or canonic right to the tawliyat; for example, no reference is made to a founder's stipulation that the tawliyat should be exercised only by the Ansari family. Yet by including the otherwise meaningless information that Abu'l-Hasan, the first mutawalli, had been a descendant of the legendary Hanbalite mystic, Khwajah 'Abd Allah Ansari, and that successors to Muhammad Ya'qub (by implication, likewise a descendant) would be of his line ("generation

---

[104] On the circumstances of the marriage of Nadhr Muhammad's mother, Shahr Banu Begum, to his father, Din Muhammad, see *BA* 4: fols. 161a–b, and Salim, fols. 137a–b. The latter calls her the half-sister (*hamshirah*) of Mirza Abu Talib. Munshi n.d., 1:572 (1978, 2:758) mentions Abu Talib's continuing association with Din Muhammad after the marriage of his daughter.

[105] Salim, fol. 137a.

[106] Mu'tamin 1969, 228.

after generation"),[107] Subhan Quli leaves little doubt that a sanction of the Ansari tradition was intended.

The mid-seventeenth-century documentary evidence is only the visible evidence of a process that had certainly been maturing and gathering authority for some time. Subhan Quli was not, as far as we can tell, attempting to impose a new tradition; he was simply putting down in writing what everyone knew to be the case, that through long tenure the Ansaris had forged their own tradition.

How does one reconcile the existence of such a tradition with the problematic Ansari origins of Mirza Sanjar, who after all preceded Mir Muhammad Ya'qub by no more than thirty-five years? In a time when genealogy was one of several important credentials for a position like that of mutawalli, would Subhan Quli have been unaware of Mirza Sanjar's apparent Ridawi genealogy, or was there no discrepancy between his lineage and that advanced by *Akabir al-Din* for the entire Ansari line back to the fifteenth century? It is not impossible that the silence of later sources regarding Imami-Shi'ite connections for the seventeenth-century mutawallis is simply the discretion required by a rise in anti-Shi'i public sentiment. As of now, however, the inconsistencies in the *Akabir al-Din* list make somewhat problematic its acceptance as an authoritative source on the Ansari lineage of the mutawallis before Mir Muhammad Ya'qub's line. From his time onward, however, the exclusively Ansari character of the tawliyat is well established despite the apparent gaps in the late eighteenth and mid-nineteenth centuries.

What is of immediate concern to us now is the effect the Ansari claim had on the evolution of the tawliyat in the late eighteenth century. Once such a genealogical claim is accepted as valid, competition for succession is not eliminated but refocused. In a bureaucracy in which selection is at least partly governed by kinship, and tenure and promotion by experience and competence, the ability of the head of the bureaucracy to influence succession is substantial. By selecting and training a son and then, once he had proven his competence, moving him into an administrative role, a mutawalli could insure that he received the experience that would make his succession virtually inevitable. Accidents and other unforeseen occurrences could at least partially be offset by training more than one successor. But the risk in that case was that the designated successor would be faced by a challenge from an experienced, competent rival whose claim only lacked the imprimatur of heir-apparency. In the case of two brothers, for example, a rival claim of right to succeed might not arise during the sibling's tenure but be advanced when the incumbent's son, for instance, attempted to succeed. At such a moment, the advan-

[107] *TMS*, 60 (text), 67 (transcription).

tages to the uncle might be considerable—experience and the bureaucratic loyalties formed over the years.

At the 'Alid shrine, control of succession to the tawliyat was not exclusively within the power of the mutawalli. The qadi's court could always intervene in the event of malfeasance and appoint its own administrator. The fact that the two mutawallis of the late seventeenth and early eighteenth centuries were both qadis might have forestalled any such intervention. The support of the political authorities, who had a final right to consent in the succession of the mutawalli, was also necessary. But given all that, the mutawalli still exercised for all practical purposes the right to choose his successor. It is probably safe to say that when the process unfolded as expected, when the designated son assumed the duties held by his father at an appropriate moment, no note of the fact would be taken. It was only when the process was disrupted, when things did not go as planned and conflict arose, that the events were likely to be recorded and a new resolution revealed.

In the case of the 'Alid shrine, there is evidence, postdating by perhaps a century or more the actual events, that points to a conflict over succession to the tawliyat sometime in the second half of the eighteenth century.

At about the midpoint of the eighteenth century, Khwajah Ni'mat (or Ni'mat Mirza Khan) was mutawalli at the shrine. Sometime in the last half of the century he was succeeded by Mirza 'Aziz Khan, a shadowy figure in history whom *Akabir al-Din* lists as predecessor, and probably father, of Shuja' al-Din, a fully attested historical personage.

In a farman-decree dated 25 Dhu'l-Qa'dah 1306/24 July 1889, the Afghan ruler, Amir 'Abd al-Rahman Khan, listed all those eligible for a share in the waqf income.[108] The list is divided into two parts, each of which is further subdivided into two. The first main division contains the names of 214 male descendants of Mirza 'Aziz Khan. Those names are subdivided into those descended through the male offspring (*awlad-i pasari*) of Mirza 'Aziz Khan, of whom there are 158, and those descended through the female offspring (*awlad-i dukhtari*), of whom there are 56. The second main division includes the names of the 43 male descendants of Khwajah Ni'mat entitled to a share of the waqf income in 1889. Those 43 further divide into 19 descended through male offspring and 24 through female.

In effect, this farman records the division of the Ansari house into two branches, the 'Azizi and the Ni'mati, a division that is prima facie evidence for a succession crisis at the end of Khwajah Ni'mat's tawliyat. The history of tawliyat succession down to Khwajah Ni'mat's time suggests

[108] *TMS*, 72–76 (text), 77–84 (transcription).

that father-to-son succession was, if not the norm, at least the ideal. From the 1889 farman we know that Khwajah Niʿmat had male offspring and that Mirza ʿAziz was not one of them. Both were Ansaris and perhaps shared a common father or grandfather.

It is worth noting again here that the nineteenth-century list of muta-wallis used by Hafiz Nur Muhammad does not mention Khwajah Niʿmat, although history books of his era refer to him, as does the 1889 farman. This is further circumstantial evidence pointing to the ousting of his line.

As yet there is no evidence of the nature, duration, or intensity of the succession conflict. That there was a succession conflict may be deduced from three facts. The first is that Khwajah Niʿmat was mutawalli in the middle of the eighteenth century. The second is that the mutawalli of the shrine in 1889 was Abuʾl-Hayy, an ʿAzizi Ansari and not a descendant of Khwajah Niʿmat. The third is that by the end of the nineteenth century the ʿAzizis far outweighed the Niʿmatis at the shrine, both in absolute numbers of people entitled to waqf income and more importantly in the number of official positions held at the shrine. When the shrine admin-istration in the 1880s is discussed, in chapter 13, I will expand on this point.

Here I would propose that either at or shortly before the death of Khwajah Niʿmat, a contest took place over his successor. The winner was Mirza ʿAziz Khan, perhaps a brother or perhaps a nephew, uncle, or cousin. The loser's name has vanished from history. By the time the struggle occurred, it would appear that already the Ansaris had fixed a claim to the shrine's revenues, waqf and nonwaqf alike. Though the Niʿmatis surrendered control of the tawliyat, they retained their rights as Ansaris to part of the income, a right that remained inviolate down to 1889 and beyond. The exercise of this right is what Burnes noted in 1832 in his description of the daily division of the shrine's proceeds "copper by copper."

To conclude, the period after the Nadirid withdrawal had a fundamen-tal and profound effect on the organization of the shrine and its economy. The political environment of the time led to the militarization and polit-icization of the shrine, which then evolved into a petty state like the states surrounding it. The period also witnessed the transformation of the Ansari family, by this period the historically legitimized administrators of the shrine, from mere officials to primary beneficiaries of the trust that supported the shrine. The shrine had become a state, its administrators had been transformed from "mirzas" into "khans," its waqf properties and revenue from votives had become the tax base of the shrine-state, and within this organism factionalism and political conflict had emerged, as if to give the final stamp of authenticity to the transformation.

CHAPTER ELEVEN

Shrine-State to Provincial Capital: The Muhammadza'i Mandate in Balkh, 1849–1889

FROM THE late 1840s to the late 1880s, the 'Alid shrine was caught up in the political upheaval occasioned by the Afghan state's aggressive claim of sovereignty over the former Chingizid appanage of Balkh. At the opening of the period, the region comprised the several, generally separate and autonomous, Uzbek amirates discussed earlier (Maymanah, Shibarghan, Andkhud, Ghuri, Aqchah, Balkh, Mazar, Sar-i Pul, Tashqurghan/Khulm, Aybak, and Qunduz). The policies of these entities were by and large defensive and nonexpansionist, less by choice than by force of circumstances. Occasional alliances, succession crises, or outside intervention encouraged sporadic military action against neighboring amirates, but for the most part the rulers of these principalities were limited, by virtue of their narrow political appeal, to enacting or reacting to the policies of outsiders.

This system of petty states survived the Afghan conquests and the imposition of the "sardar state" more or less intact. The Afghans engaged in no general purge of amirs nor did they attempt to transplant an Afghan-manned political apparatus into the towns. But Afghan military success in the region meant, at least in the long run, the demise of the amirid states. Initially, the Afghans were content to have the Uzbek amirs act as their surrogates. This was no doubt due to the general lack of popular backing for the Afghans, who as Pushtu speakers represented a new linguistic and ethnic intrusion into the region. Persian (Dari, Tajiki) was the language of cross-cultural communication, but bilingualism was not intended to bridge ethnic divisions. In the eastern part of the old appanage (Qataghan and western Badakhshan), the Turkophone Uzbeks, while politically dominant, were a minority in a sea of Tajiks. Farther west, the new Afghan permanent residents were in the same position vis-à-vis the Uzbek majority. There the Uzbek political leadership played a useful role in shaping and directing public opinion. In the east, the Afghans were able, to some extent, to manipulate the Uzbek overlords, whose popular support was always fragile. By and large, the Afghan sardars were content to accept tokens of submission and promises of tribute in exchange for permitting the amirs to remain in power.

But the Afghans had a history of imperial expansion and a predilection for a centrally organized state. They were thus constitutionally unable, nor did they ever show much desire, to accommodate for long the independent status of the amirates. By 1876 and the death of Na'ib Muhammad 'Alam Khan, a staunch supporter of the Kabul regime and a man whose career has particular importance for the 'Alid shrine, the handwriting must surely have been visible on the wall. The amirid states of Qunduz (Qataghan) and Maymanah were still recognizably intact, but, like the independent princes of India under British rule, their policies and politics were wholly subject to Afghan review. Some latitude was allowed them, but the Afghan internecine struggles that accompanied succession to the throne did not present these amirs with opportunities to assert their independence. Rather these moments placed them in the potentially fatal position of choosing the wrong side. The amirs were allowed to coexist with the Afghan state as long as their presence was of some use and as long as the Afghans were unwilling to pay the military price to put an end to them.

The earliest amirid states to pass into Afghan administrative control were the ones closest to Balkh City—Balkh, Mazar, and Aqchah. Those that survived the longest as independent entities and then as protectorates were those farthest from Balkh—Maymanah, Shibarghan, and Andkhud in the west, all three of which had ties to Herat, and Qunduz and Faydabad in the east. Maymanah and Qunduz were the first independent amirid offshoots of the Chingizid appanage system in the second half of the seventeenth century, Maymanah becoming the permanent iqta' of the Ming tribe and Qunduz the territory of the Qataghan. Between the political sentiment behind these principalities, with their roots in the Chingizid era, and the sentiments underpinning the Afghan state lay a wide, unbridgeable gulf. The Afghans, despite the importance of tribal identification and the kinds of factional alignments this produced, had adopted, without much modification, the monarchical system of Iran and Moghul India. The state was hierarchically and centrally organized with one head (shah or padshah), not a first among equals as the Chingizid system favored but a man whose writ theoretically prevailed throughout his dominions.

Under the Saduza'i Afghans, the titulature had reflected the Iranian model (Ahmad Shah, Zaman Shah, Timur Shah, Shah Mahmud, Shah Shuja'). Dust Muhammad, whose regime commenced the Muhammadza'i era, preferred the more evocatively Islamic "amir" (in the sense "amir al-mu'minin," the caliphal soubriquet), perhaps to distinguish the Muhammadza'i from the Saduza'i, but the regnal expectations were not similarly changed.

The Afghan tribal system did, to some extent, modify the monarchy, primarily by expanding the concept of royal family and thus increasing the controversy and conflict surrounding the fundamental issue of succession. The ideas engendered by belief in the tribe as a proper means of organizing society influenced the way in which the state was structured. Although the division of the mamlakah was not organized, strictly speaking, on the basis of appanages, as the Chingizid state had been, members of the royal tribe did still expect and receive appointments to govern regions within the state. The appointments of these sardars, a term prefixed to the names of Muhammadza'i males from Dust Muhammad onward, were theoretically revocable and were not inheritable, as were Chingizid appanages in sixteenth- and seventeenth-century Mawarannahr and Balkh. Such appointments did, however, provide ambitious sardars with the means to position themselves as future claimants of the monarchy. Thus the Afghan state was characterized by a fundamental tension, for it was a monarchy overlain with an almost religious adherence to tribal values, including genealogical fastidiousness, consultation and consensus, and mediation and corporate responsibility.

The rights of the monarch were effected through a centrally directed bureaucracy. At the pinnacle of the bureaucratic pyramid was the diwan-i a'la (central administration), headed by the chief wazir (called *sadr-i a'zam*, later *wazir-i a'la* and *wazir-i a'zam*).[1] The diwan-i a'la reported to and processed orders from the padshah. At the provincial level, the Afghan governing apparatus was headed by a governor (variously called *hakim*, *hukmran*, and *wali*), answerable directly to the padshah. Until the time of Amir 'Abd al-Rahman Khan (r. 1880–1901), the governorships were dominated by the Muhammadza'i sardars. The head of the provincial fiscal bureau was the *sar daftar*, answerable to the chief wazir in the capital. The third major provincial figure and one characteristic of an absolute monarchy was the *mushrif* or *nazir*, the "overseer" whose responsibility was to monitor the operations of both the governor's office and the *sar daftar*'s. No comparable figure is to be found in the regional fiscal apparatuses of the Chingizid appanages—nor would such a post have been conceivable within a system that recognized local prerogatives.

It was within the framework of Chingizid political values that the petty amirs of the former appanage of Balkh were accustomed to judge what was politically acceptable and what was not. The Afghans must have been initially seen as worthy heirs to the Chingizid mandate. The amirs probably expected that they would recognize Afghan sovereignty, present the usual tokens of fealty, and in turn be confirmed in their local prerogatives. Certainly the initial contact with the Afghans would have done nothing to contradict such a view. For almost three-quarters of a century,

---

[1] Fufalza'i 1955 is a study of the development of the *diwan-i a'la* in Afghanistan.

the Afghans were either invisible or only a distant force that needed occasional placating by a nominal gesture of obeisance.

From 1850 on, however, the Afghan state made it clearer and clearer that it was in Balkh not simply to reign but to govern. Sardar Muhammad Akram Khan, a son of Amir Dust Muhammad and the victor in the decisive battle for Balkh in 1849, undertook as one of his first administrative acts to assess the *maliyat* (taxes on land and livestock) and to give a portion of it as a service grant (*jaygir*) to the recently defeated amirs.[2] Whether the historical assertion is founded in fact or is merely rhetorical, it can be taken as symbolic of the kind of presence the Muhammadza'i Afghans intended. More customary in the Balkh context and perhaps more anticipated would have been for Muhammad Akram to have accepted gifts, tribute, and expressions of fealty from the amirs but not to have assumed so directly administrative a role.

The Afghans at first needed the cooperation of the Uzbek amirs. But given Afghan perceptions of how a state should be run, the amirs were ultimately redundant. They could not accept the impositions of a monarchic, bureaucratically centralized state and still maintain their traditional positions. Within a year of their submission to Afghan authority, the amirs refused, in the words of Fayd Muhammad, "to remit the diwan revenues and the royal taxes," an act signifying rebellion.[3] The amirs, however, again almost as a necessary product of the appanage system, lacked the unifying grounds that might have helped them successfully resist Afghan control. The years of inter-amirid conflict and the autonomy inherent in and necessary to the system of which the petty amirates were the products rendered them ineffective rivals to Afghan power.

The Afghans who were sent to Turkistan to rule used the amirs to further two specific ends: first, they made use of the amirs' armed forces to maintain Afghan control of Turkistan, and second, they recruited the amirs and their followers as allies in their own factional struggles for control of the Afghan state. But once the usefulness of the amirs ceased to compensate for the obstacles that they threw in the way of efficient provincial administration, they were eliminated as a political force.

The details of the complex and long process by which the Afghans established their power and erased that of the amirid remnants of the Chingizid system are given by Nur Muhammad Nuri, writing about 1870, and in the "Memorandum on Afghan Turkestan" drafted in 1869 by Tallboys Wheeler and updated by other writers to 1907. The sources for the latter were the journals of British agents in Kabul and Peshawar.[4] Fayd Mu-

[2] Fayd Muhammad Katib 1913–15, 2:206.
[3] Ibid., 209.
[4] Nuri 1956, 73ff.; *Gaz.* 4:18–36 (the Wheeler memorandum).

hammad Katib offers a broader, retrospective, more interpretive, and less detailed picture of the period from the late 1840s to the late 1880s.

Based on the material in these three works, it is possible to divide the period into four parts. In the first (c. 1845–1863), the Muhammadza'i state under the charismatic Dust Muhammad laid claim to cis-Oxine Turkistan and, after a full-scale military expedition that crushed the Uzbek-led opposition, made Balkh the seat of an Afghan governor. The ensuing conflict between the regional amirs and the bearers of the new political mandate was punctuated by internecine Muhammadza'i struggles for control of Turkistan.

The second part of the period covers the years between 1863 and 1869. It began with the death of Amir Dust Muhammad and the intense strife that followed, which engulfed all the major urban areas—Kabul, Herat, Qandahar, and Balkh—and ended with the victory of Shir 'Ali Khan and his appointment of Na'ib Muhammad 'Alam Khan as governor of Turkistan.

During these six years, Turkistan was the main base for Muhammadza'i forces opposed to Shir 'Ali. They were led by Muhammad Afdal, another son of Dust Muhammad, and his son, 'Abd al-Rahman.

The governorship of Na'ib Muhammad 'Alam Khan makes up most of the third segment (1869–1879) of the postconquest period. Muhammad 'Alam's tenure (1869–1876) was relatively long in comparison with those of other Afghan governors, and, although the Wheeler memorandum refers to violent reactions against his regime and its alleged repressiveness, the mere length of time he spent in charge of Turkistan is indicative of his effectiveness. His poor relations with the Uzbek amirs, especially the still powerful though much reduced amirs of Qataghan and Maymanah, are symptomatic of the friction existing between the Afghans and the guardians of the old autonomous principalities. In 1875, Na'ib Muhammad 'Alam was forced to besiege the Mir of Maymanah, who had tried to renounce his allegiance to Kabul. In the course of the campaign, in which the mirs of Qunduz, Andkhud, and Sar-i Pul assisted him, Na'ib Muhammad 'Alam is reported to have uncovered proof of their treachery to him and so managed to have all of them transported to Kabul and placed under house arrest.

In the fourth and final part of the postconquest period (1879–1889), Afghan Turkistan briefly revived its past autonomy. In 1879, after Shir 'Ali Khan's death, the people of Turkistan, that is, its surviving amirid elements and some of the newly settled Afghans, welcomed 'Abd al-Rahman Khan, the leader of the Muhammadza'i faction opposed to Shir 'Ali, from exile. The pledges of support that he received in 1879 convinced the powers in Kabul (a British occupying force) to hand over the capital to him and recognize his sovereignty.

'Abd al-Rahman appointed his cousin, Sardar Muhammad Ishaq Khan, governor of Turkistan. In August of 1888, after a peaceful and relatively unsupervised tenure as governor (the Wheeler memorandum asserts that Muhammad Ishaq alone of all of 'Abd al-Rahman's governors "enjoyed the whole revenue and had power of life and death"),[5] Muhammad Ishaq either actively led a secessionist movement or allowed himself to be maneuvered into appearing to lead such a movement. The motives behind it are not at all clear. In his autobiography, the *Pand-namah*, 'Abd al-Rahman laid the blame on the heads of the Naqshbandi order in Afghan Turkistan, who he said had instilled delusions of grandeur in Muhammad Ishaq's head.[6] Although this less than disinterested opinion is not corroborated elsewhere, it does have a certain historical resonance. In the history of mid-nineteenth-century Balkh, three leading actors on the political stage were Ishan Khwajah (also known as Ishan Naqib), his son Ishan Uraq, and Ishan Sudur. They had been more or less independent rulers of Balkh and Aqchah and had figured in Bukharan and Kabuli policies in the region. Ishan Khwajah had been transported into exile in Bukhara in the 1820s; Ishan Uraq and Ishan Sudur had been taken to Kabul in the 1860s. Their titles suggest affiliation with one or another of the Naqshbandi suborders operating in Balkh (the Parsa'i, Dahpidi, or Salihi). There is ample reason to think that Naqshbandism was a vital force in the social and religious life of the region and that it influenced politics. In 1864, Amir Shir 'Ali Khan attempted to use Naqshbandi influence to undercut support for his challenger, Muhammad Afdal.[7] And in 1865, the Amir of Bukhara, Muzaffar al-Din, in whose city Naqshbandism had been born and where it still retained a powerful grip, interceded with Shir 'Ali on behalf of the interned families of Ishan Sudur and Ishan Uraq.[8] These were regionally influential men who, we presume, could become the standard-bearers of local movements opposed to either Kabul or Bukhara. [9]

However, against the likelihood that Naqshbandi forces were a major factor in the secessionist movement should be weighed 'Abd al-Rahman's paranoia when it came to his opponents. In his autobiography and elsewhere, he shows a penchant for ascribing any opposition to his policies to the machinations of those whom he considers sectarian subversives—Naqshbandis, Shi'is, Wahhabis, and fanatical mullahs.[10]

---

[5] *Gaz.* 4:34.

[6] Mir Mohammed Monshi 1901, 1:264–65.

[7] *Gaz.* 4:27–28.

[8] Ibid. 4:27–28.

[9] An important source on the Naqshbandis of Turkistan is the work of Riyadi 1906 (Diya).

[10] See Mir Mohammed Monshi 1901, 1:264–65 on the Naqshbandis. In a private collection of farmans sent by 'Abd al-Rahman to Shirindil Khan, his governor at Khust (seen by this author in Qandahar in 1968 and partly photographed), one finds numerous references

The source closest to the Turkistan rebellion, Mirza Ya'qub 'Ali Khafi, blamed the secession on poor communications with Kabul, which caused rumors to circulate in Mazar-i Sharif of the dire fate awaiting anyone summoned to the capital.[11] Muhammad Ishaq, apparently affected by such rumors, refused to present himself in Kabul when ordered to do so. He had been recalled because of a dispute over revenues and how they had been accounted for.[12] Although the Wheeler memorandum portrays Muhammad Ishaq as exempt from any revenue obligations, Fayd Muhammad suggests either that a misunderstanding had arisen over this exemption or that none had ever in fact been granted.

The outbreak of fighting in early fall 1888 was the occasion for a final resurgence of amirid elements in the politics of Afghan Turkistan. Formerly harassed by both 'Abd al-Rahman and Muhammad Ishaq, the amirs of Qataghan and Badakhshan now returned to center stage in support of the rebellion. Sultan Murad, one of Muhammad Ishaq's most active supporters, was a direct descendant of Mahmud Bi Ataliq, the Qataghan amir who had made his tribe, settled in the territory around Qunduz, one of the most influential forces in the Balkh appanage at the end of the seventeenth century. Sultan Murad had succeeded his father in the 1860s and, by walking a political tightrope in the 1860s and 1870s, had managed to remain in power. But his backing for Muhammad Ishaq's unsuccessful rebellion cost him his position and removed Qunduz from the control of the Qataghan family. The mirs of Badakhshan suffered the same fate.[13]

The Afghan amir, 'Abd al-Rahman, spent nearly two years (from September 1888 until July 1890) in Turkistan overseeing the reorganization of provincial government. The period was decisive for eradicating the last traces of amirid political influence. 'Abd al-Rahman was an absolutist in the mainstream of the Irano-Islamic padshah tradition. He continued the Muhammadza'i practice of using the title "amir." But in his domestic policies, especially his unrelenting efforts to assert Kabul's fiscal and political control over the entire country, he modeled himself on the great Iranian and Indo-Iranian monarchs like Shah 'Abbas I and Akbar.

In order to restructure patterns of service loyalty and to break the harmful (from a centralizer's point of view) effects of tribal loyalties, he instituted what must have seemed to outsiders a rather anachronistic institution, the *ghulam bachchah* system. Apparently using the Ottoman *devshirme* and the Safawid *ghulam* institutions as models, 'Abd al-Rah-

---

to the "abominable Shi'ah" (*shi'ah shani'ah*), the Hazarahs of Central Afghanistan. Also see Fayd Muhammad Katib 1913–15, vol. 3.

[11] Khafi 1956, 2:173ff.

[12] Fayd Muhammad Katib 1913–15, 3:593–95.

[13] Mir Mohammed Monshi 1901, vol. 1.

man recruited young boys for the court, trained them as administrators and army officers, and assumed that they would have loyalties only to the court. Some of these boys were prisoners of war taken during the internal campaigns against the Hazarahs and the people of "Kafiristan." Others were hostage sons of tribal leaders who had been sent or brought to Kabul as bonds for their sires' good behavior.[14]

'Abd al-Rahman freely used other instruments of coercion to impose his policies. These included forced exile, public torture and execution, a well-developed network of informers, and his own reputation for arbitrariness and cruelty.

For the shrine, its waqf, and its administration as well as for Turkistan in particular, 'Abd al-Rahman's policies were the culmination of a process set in motion by the conquest and occupation of Turkistan in 1849 and the intentional incorporation of it within the country coming to be known as Afghanistan. During the forty years from 1849 to 1889, the authority of the local amirs was broken by the superior power and resources of the Muhammadza'i Afghans. Civil strife among the Muhammadza'i had periodically permitted a resurgence of the amirs, and for decades the Afghan state had been content to allow the rulers of Badakhshan, Qataghan, and Maymanah and their colleagues in Aqchah, Sar-i Pul, Balkh, Mazar, Aybak, Tashqurghan, Andkhud, and Shibarghan to remain in their positions as long as they were obedient. But 'Abd al-Rahman Khan used the secessionist movement of Muhammad Ishaq as an excuse for eliminating the last vestiges of the Chingizid amirid legacy.

The transformation of the old Balkh appanage into the Afghan province of Turkistan was of particular importance to the shrine, for it thrust it into a political prominence that it had not previously known. The Afghans found the 'Alid tradition of the shrine entirely in keeping with their own religiosity and showed the same kind of reverence for the shrine that their predecessors in Balkh had displayed. But partly as a result of the economic and political decline of the city of Balkh and the simultaneous emergence of the shrine city as an economic center, the "mazar-i sharif" had political and economic significance for the Afghans that it had not held for earlier politicians.

CO-OPTING A TRADITION

In 1869, the shrine city, by then known as Mazar-i Sharif ("Noble Shrine"), became the capital of Afghan Turkistan. There were many reasons for the transfer of the administrative center from Balkh City, the political and economic center of the region for more than two millenia, to Mazar-i Sharif. The relative prosperity of Mazar-i Sharif, its enduring

[14] For a description of the ghulam bachchah system, see Kakar 1979, 19–20.

allure as a pilgrimage spot, the Afghans' need for some local identity, and perhaps the pool of managerial expertise found at the shrine all may have contributed to its adoption as the political center. The relative importance of each of these factors will be sketched as we consider how the shrine became the capital of Afghan Turkistan.

The Afghan occupation of Turkistan after 1849 and the slow but steady transformation of the region, for a century dominated by petty amirates, into a more or less unified province subject to Kabul affected the shrine-state of Mazar as dramatically as it did any of the other amirates. For contemporary observers, especially for those Europeans who surveyed the region and scrutinized it in detail for military purposes, Mazar was no different from any of the other amirates or begates. Unaware of its history and therefore unable to distinguish between the Uzbek amirs who governed Qunduz or Aybak, for instance, and the Ansari mutawallis who governed the shrine-state, the authors of the journals and memoranda that provide much of our detailed information for the postconquest period have nothing to say about policies peculiar to the shrine-state and only slightly more to say about events connected with it during the period from 1849 to 1869, when it became the capital of Afghan Turkistan. We thus have to apply a little creative interpretation to what scanty information they do give.

When the Afghans completed the military phase of the occupation of Turkistan, they made their capital at Balkh, which was still viewed as the economic and political center of the region. We have no information about the steps taken by the Ansari mutawalli (apparently still Shuja' al-Din) to obtain Afghan recognition of his position as head of the shrine administration, but we must assume he did what he thought appropriate to obtain Afghan backing.

In 1852, the conqueror of Turkistan, Muhammad Akram Khan, died. The Afghan amir, Dust Muhammad, named another son, Muhammad Afdal, to succeed him. Tallboys Wheeler tells us, without giving any specifics or motives, that "The people of the holy shrine of Mazar-i Sharif . . . were especially refractory; and they gave Muhammad Afzal so much trouble, that at length he resolved on taking possession of the place. The Afghan occupation of the holy shrine appears, however, to have excited great hostility among the Uzbaks."[15] According to Wheeler, Muhammad Afdal was faced with a rebellion by the governor of Aqchah as well. Eventually, however, the Afghan sardar prevailed: "Muhammad Afdal succeeded in capturing both the governor of Mazar-i Sharif and the governor of Akcha, and put them to death, together with their sons."[16]

The execution of the "governor of Mazar-i Sharif" (by whom is proba-

[15] *Gaz.* 4:21.
[16] Ibid.

bly meant the mutawalli of the shrine, perhaps Shuja'al-Din Ansari) caused "great excitement" and led to a religiously inspired uprising, at least according to Wheeler. There was a holy man at the shrine styled "Khalifah" ("Caliph"). His followers rose against the Afghan occupiers but, for reasons that remain obscure (Wheeler's explanation is rather disjointed and unconvincing) the followers of "Khalifah," in Wheeler's words, "dispersed . . . and returned to their homes."[17]

This is an extremely curious piece of information. There is no independent corroboration of it, as far as I have been able to discover, in any other source. The depiction of Muhammad Afdal as occupier of the shrine is particularly anomalous in light of the way in which his feelings about the shrine are depicted in the semiofficial Afghan sources. It is quite possible, though improbable, that his son, 'Abd al-Rahman Khan, made an effort to rewrite the history of Afghan relations with the shrine in order to cover up his father's role.

The name or title of the holy man who led the uprising, the "Caliph," is intriguing, if accurate. It immediately recalls that earlier holy man, the "Hadrat-i Ishan," whose popular movement during the Nadirid occupation of the eighteenth century briefly threatened the Ansari administration of the shrine. The "Hadrat-i Ishan" was first known to the chroniclers of his movement as "Rasul" ("Messenger"), the title of the Prophet Muhammad, whose role as leader of the Muslim community, in the Sunni Muslim view, was taken on after his death by his caliphs.

The next piece of information concerning the shrine comes from 1853, the year after this uprising, and strikes a somewhat discordant note with the whole tenor of the alleged anti-Afghan uprising of the followers of the "Caliph." It recalls to the stage a familiar figure, Ishan Uraq, the former, apparently Naqshbandi, ruler of Aqchah. He had been released from Afghan custody in Qandahar and had gone to Maymanah in 1853, reportedly to rally the Uzbek population behind Amir Shir 'Ali and against the Muhammadza'i governor in Balkh, Muhammad Afdal. The Wheeler memorandum, again our lone source, asserts that Muhammad Afdal had very great difficulty suppressing the rebellion and managed it only with the assistance of "the son of the priest of Mazar-i Sharif."[18] No reason is given why "the son of the priest" would be collaborating with the man who had attacked the shrine the year before and killed its "governor" and his son.

Both stories are at odds with the way in which Fayd Muhammad Katib portrays Muhammad Afdal's relations with the shrine. It is important to note again that the *Siraj al-Tawarikh* was commissioned by Muhammad

---

[17] *Gaz.* 4:25.
[18] Ibid.

Afdal's grandson, Habib Allah Khan, the son of 'Abd al-Rahman Khan, and this might have played a part in Fayd Muhammad's omission of the material cited by Wheeler, assuming he knew of it. Moreover, it is obvious that Fayd Muhammad used 'Abd al-Rahman's autobiography as his source, perhaps his only source, for this passage.[19] 'Abd al-Rahman had even stronger motives for downplaying any conflict between his father and the shrine administrators.

Fayd Muhammad presents his material in the context of Muhammad Afdal's building a new administrative center at Takhtah Pul east of Balkh and his move there in 1852–1853, just about the time, as sketched by Wheeler, that he was having to confront the uprising of the "Caliph's" followers. The passage is brief and worth citing in full:

> Since with the passage of time the city of Balkh had fallen into ruins, since its climate was unhealthy and unwholesome, because Sardar Muhammad Afdal Khan considered Friday pilgrimage visits to the shrine of the Amir al-Mu'minin 'Ali, where he would prostrate and humble himself, as an obligatory duty, and because of the distance between Balkh and the mazar, therefore he decided to construct a city near the mazar-i sharif. In 1269 [1852–1853] he created the town of Takhtah Pul and oversaw its construction over a period of three years. . . .[20]

This hardly squares with the impression given in the Wheeler memorandum, and perhaps it was intended not to. Fayd Muhammad suggests that, whatever Muhammad Afdal's feelings toward the people associated with the shrine, for a mix of spiritual and political reasons he wanted to be seen as a full devotee of the shrine and its tradition.

There is at this point a gap of about a decade in the story of the shrine. In the meantime, Muhammad Afdal had, as governor of Turkistan, suppressed most local opposition and begun to create a political constituency. When his father, Dust Muhammad, died in 1863, he initially supported his brother Shir 'Ali as successor, but in 1864, from his base in Turkistan, he declared his own amirate by the usual symbols, striking coins and having his name inserted into the khutbah-sermon at Friday mosque services. In June of 1864, Shir 'Ali Khan led an expeditionary force to Turkistan and forced his brother to renounce his claims. In return, he was reconfirmed for a time as regent over a now-truncated Turkistan (Maymanah and the eastern regions, Qunduz and Badakhshan, being removed from his jurisdiction) before being arrested and taken to Kabul.

---

[19] Fayd Muhammad Katib 1913–15, 2:214; Mir Mohammed Monshi 1901, 1:2.
[20] Fayd Muhammad Katib 1913–15, 2:214.

In August 1864, the victorious Amir Shir 'Ali went to the 'Alid shrine, performed the ritual visitation ceremony (ziyarat), and then returned to Kabul.[21] Such symbolism was not lost on the populace there. True sovereignty was demonstrated by the ability to protect the religion and its sacred sites, and in Turkistan there was no site more important than the 'Alid shrine. To be in Turkistan meant an obligatory visit to the shrine to pay respects. Such visits gave substance to the ruler's claim of being the guardian of Islam. Furthermore, to conduct court at the shrine, to summon and dismiss other wielders of political power there, was to weave together the warp and weft of political life—the specific political legitimacy of the Muhammadza'i line on the one hand and the universal responsibilities of a Sunni Muslim monarch on the other. In addition, in this particular case, publicizing the visit was probably meant to leave no doubt in people's minds that Shir 'Ali Khan was devoted to the shrine as much as Muhammad Afdal was. This display of reverence became an unvarying theme in the public actions of Afghan political figures when in Turkistan. The wedding of political and spiritual motives had the consequence of further raising the significance of the mazar and, simultaneously, of suppressing the importance of Balkh's political heritage. This shift of attention and physical presence from Balkh was also a shifting away from the earlier political tradition, from appanage politics and Chingizid legitimacy.

Some foreign observers at this time did not hesitate to label the shrine "Shi'ite."[22] For them it seemed a straightforward designation in view of the fact that it was the shrine of 'Ali, the first imam in the Shi'i scheme. None of them, however, considered the implication of such a label in light of the warmth, even fervor, with which the devotedly Hanafi Afghans had embraced the shrine from Ahmad Shah's time onward. The tendency to focus on the Sunni-Shi'i polarity obscures a far more interesting manifestation of religious sentiment, that which we have called "ahl-al baytism," a popular ecumenical phenomenon that focused spiritual feeling on the significant five members of the Prophet Muhammad's family—the "People of the House" (ahl-al bayt): the Prophet himself, his daughter Fatimah, his son-in-law 'Ali, and his grandsons Hasan and Husayn. The phenomenon of ahl-al baytism in Balkh and Mawarannahr arose from both the universal phenomenon of saint worship and the often concomitant syncretism particular to specific regions. In Afghan Turkistan, the proximity of Hanafi Sunni Muslims and Ja'fari Imami Shi'ites (as well as some Isma'ili Shi'ites) encouraged the evolution of cult forms and cult sites appealing to both groups. The 'Alid shrine was, and still is, a

---

[21] Ibid., 267.
[22] Hamilton 1906, 257; Ferrier 1857, 209.

major realization of the phenomenon. It has proved as attractive to Sunni Afghans and Uzbeks as it has to Shi'i Hazarahs. In some ways, the parallels with the Ridawi shrine at Mashhad in the seventeenth and eighteenth centuries are striking.

The next appearance of the shrine in the literature, after Shir 'Ali Khan's use of it to assert his political preeminence, is the signing of a pact at the shrine in August 1867 between Shir 'Ali and an Afghan governor whose loyalty had been transferred from Shir 'Ali to his rivals and then back again in the space of two years.[23] In this case, too, the shrine serves a symbolic role, emphasizing the solemn nature of the covenant and again publicly displaying the reverence of the amir for the shrine's authority. More indicative of the political role of the shrine and how it may have changed is the list of gubernatorial appointments made by Shir 'Ali during this visit. One particular appointment stands out, that of a certain "Rustam Khan Mazari" to be governor of Balkh and Mazar-i Sharif.[24]

The appointment is odd for a number of reasons. The Wheeler memorandum gives two lists of gubernatorial appointments, one for 1864, when Muhammad Afdal Khan was preparing to press his claim for the Kabul throne and was handing out governorships in Afghan Turkistan to his supporters, and one for 1867, when Shir 'Ali Khan, after defeating Muhammad Afdal and his backers, named his own governors. In the 1864 list and elsewhere in the discussion of the history of Turkistan, there is no mention of a governorship at Mazar-i Sharif. After the Afghan conquest of 1849, the government of Balkh appears to have absorbed the previously independent mutawalliate of Mazar. The 1867 reference to "Balkh and Mazar-i Sharif" perhaps indicates the rising political importance (relative to Balkh) of the shrine.

Rustam Khan Mazari makes only this one appearance in the record. The designation "Mazari" suggests affiliation not with the town but with the shrine, for no other governor is given such a soubriquet as a consequence of service there. Whether Rustam Khan was mutawalli of the shrine and its waqf at this time or even an Ansari is simply a matter of conjecture. The record of his appointment is tantalizing but not very helpful in further clarifying the shrine's role in the politics of the period.

That the shrine was exerting a major political pull is clear, however. In the first place, we have the motives, perhaps apocryphal, ascribed to Muhammad Afdal Khan's building Takhtah Pul halfway between Balkh and the mazar and moving his headquarters out of Balkh sometime in the mid-1850s. The lists of governors of 1864 and 1867 suggest that as late as 1867 Mazar-i Sharif was not yet the political center of Afghan Turkistan.

[23] *Gaz.* 4:30.
[24] Ibid., 4:31.

But in A.H. 1285/A.D. 1868–1869, there is some evidence that Mazar-i Sharif had become an independent governorate when 'Abd al-Rahman, momentarily regaining control of Afghan Turkistan, appointed a man called Nazir Jahandar as governor.[25]

Although there is at least one reference to Mazar-i Sharif's becoming capital of Afghan Turkistan in 1866,[26] the actual date seems to be later. When Shir 'Ali Khan sent Muhammad 'Alam Khan from Herat to take over the government of Turkistan, Nur Muhammad Nuri reports that the sardar was sent "to Balkh and Takhtah Pul."[27] In recounting the flight of 'Abd al-Rahman's chargé d'affaires in Turkistan at that same time, Nuri says that he fled Takhtah Pul and that Muhammad 'Alam Khan took over "that governorship," by which is clearly meant Takhtah Pul.[28] The actual transition from Takhtah Pul to Mazar-i Sharif, which was probably gradual, occurred sometime between July 1869[29] and 1873–1874.[30]

The man responsible for making Mazar-i Sharif the capital of Afghan Turkistan would therefore appear to be Na'ib Muhammad 'Alam Khan. From at least 1873 onwards, Mazar-i Sharif was the administrative center of Afghan Turkistan. Balkh receded in both political and economic importance until it remained a great city only in memory—completely eclipsed by the shrine, its economy, and the force of its attractiveness as an urban center.

SHRINE EXPANSION AND RENOVATION

Muhammadza'i interest in the shrine produced major changes in its physical state. Muhammad 'Alam Khan, in particular, took an intense and life-long interest in the shrine after his appointment there as governor. When he moved into the city, the buildings at the shrine had a whitewashed brick exterior, a facade that Hafiz Nur Muhammad attributes to Sultan Husayn Mirza Bayqara.[31] Muhammad 'Alam set up a tile factory at the shrine under the supervision of Ustad Sami' Khan Samarqandi, whom he recruited from Balkh, where tile-making still flourished (perhaps to maintain the exterior of the Parsa'i mosque).[32] After training apprentices, Ustad Sami' began a four-year project to revet the shrine buildings with blue tile, a process called "Kashan work" (kashi-kari).[33] Besides the Ka-

25 Fayd Muhammad Katib 1913–15, 2:303.
26 N. Dupree 1977, 391.
27 Nuri 1956, 165.
28 Ibid., 170.
29 Ibid., 173.
30 Fayd Muhammad Katib 1913–15, 2:335.
31 TMS, 38.
32 Ibid.
33 Ibid.

shan work, Ustad Sami' supervised construction of outer domes over each of the two main domes of the shrine. These outer domes appear to have been erected to weatherproof the shrine roof. When completed these were also revetted.[34] Muhammad 'Alam Khan memorialized his own patronage in two inscriptions dated 1287/1870–1871 and 1288/1871–1872. (The earlier inscription was destroyed when another Afghan governor renovated the portico where it was engraved.)[35]

To the existing shrine complex, which had not undergone much building since the early seventeenth century, the Afghan governor added a thirty-three-room madrasah, which he endowed with waqf. Part of the waqf grant included building a commercial building, a saray, the income of which was to help pay the stipends of the students, a professor's salary, and part of the maintenance expenses. The saray had fifty-six rooms for commercial travelers.[36] (The waqf will be discussed in chapter 12.)

Na'ib Muhammad 'Alam Khan died in 1874–1875[37] (or 1876),[38] but his successors continued to spend money on the shrine. In 1877, the governor Shirin Dil Khan renovated the shrine's north gate, the Chaharbagh Gate, with a tile revetment. The tiling of the shrine was carried on through the rest of the nineteenth century and into the twentieth by 'Abd al-Rahman Khan.[39] During the reign of his son and successor, Habib Allah Khan (r. 1901–1919), the governor of Mazar-i Sharif, 'Abd Allah Tukhi, renovated the Nazargah Arcade (riwaq), the western entry to the shrine building.[40] When 'Abd al-Rahman succeeded in quelling Muhammad Ishaq Khan's secessionist movement in 1888, he marked the victory with a salam-namah for 'Ali b. Abi Talib: a series of salaams following the pattern "al-salam 'alayka ya————" or "al-salam 'alayka ayyuha————" ("peace be upon you, oh————," the "oh" being followed by appropriate epithets). The salam-namah was inscribed on two stone tablets mounted on either side of the entrance to the tomb building.[41]

The site remained a popular burial place throughout the Muhammad-za'i era. Three of Dust Muhammad's twenty-seven sons were buried there, including Muhammad Akram Khan, the conqueror of Turkistan, and Amir Shir 'Ali Khan, who died in Mazar-i Sharif while en route to exile in Bukhara.[42] His tomb is a small domed annex attached to the west-

[34] Ibid.

[35] Ibid., 39.

[36] Ibid., 40, 42.

[37] Fayd Muhammad Katib 1913–15, 2:335.

[38] Gaz. 4:34.

[39] TMS, 102.

[40] Ibid., 100; N. Dupree 1977, 393 mentions an Aslan Khan Kabuli and Ahmad Khan Ghaznawi, who did work on the interior decoration during Shir 'Ali Khan's time.

[41] TMS, 42, 47–49.

[42] Fayd Muhammad Katib 1913–15, 2:251; N. Dupree 1977, 393.

ern wall of the main shrine building; it stands just a few yards north of a similar annex, the tomb of Wazir Muhammad Akbar Khan, the third of Dust Muhammad's sons buried there and the man credited with the defeat of the British army at Kabul in 1841–1842.[43] Numerous other lesser Afghan luminaries of the nineteenth century are also buried at the shrine.

By 1886, the town of Mazar was estimated to contain three thousand households. If one adds the suburbs, the population was about six thousand households or some twenty-five thousand people.[44] The shrine and the town around it were still dependent on the Shahi Canal, the core of the original endowment, for agricultural production. The Hazhdah Nahr region, in which the Shahi Canal now ranked as the most important water source, was a grain-producing and -exporting area. When British intelligence surveyed the area in the mid-1880s, it noted that virtually all the grain of Afghan Turkistan was grown in the Hazhdah Nahr district and that, if troops were ever to occupy northern Afghanistan, that would be their source of food.[45]

At a point some five miles west of the shrine, the Shahi Canal was about twenty feet wide. At Dih Dadi, the village marking the western limits of Mazar-i Sharif, the canal was crossed by brick bridges, and, at several points where it was necessary to allow cattle to cross, the depth of the water in the canal was limited to about three feet. Captain R. E. Peacocke of the Afghan Boundary Commission (1884–1886) received information that led him to believe that the Shahi Canal was not providing a water supply adequate to cope with the growth of Mazar-i Sharif. There was talk at the time of cutting another canal from Imam Bakri, the site of the barrage on the Balkh River for the Shahi Canal.[46]

The emergence of the shrine, the mazar-i sharif, as the political capital of Afghan Turkistan, Mazar-i Sharif, was gradual. The ingredients for an urban center had long been there—a functioning economy, a major cultural attraction, and a managerial elite. Balkh in the meantime had lost its political and economic luster. The ancient city was encumbered with a history linked to the fortunes of Bukhara, now Kabul's regional rival. The years of the amirates had cost it its economic leadership as well. Mazar-i Sharif offered itself to the Afghans—who took nearly a generation to accept the offer wholeheartedly—as a means for developing a local constituency. Patronage of the shrine and political consolidation of Afghan Turkistan proceeded simultaneously. For the shrine itself the consequences were dramatic.

---

[43] For a photograph of both, see *TMS*, 101.

[44] *Gaz.* 4:413.

[45] Ibid., 4:251, 263.

[46] Ibid., 4:413.

CHAPTER TWELVE

Waqf under the Afghans

WAQF AS an institution tends to be of greater or lesser administrative concern to Muslim governments and accordingly incorporated into their domestic policies in direct proportion to the governments' bureaucratic and centralizing tendencies. The legal consensus on waqf has placed ultimate responsibility for insuring the integrity of the institution on the shoulders of the secular authorities, whose instrument for resolving litigation or other conflict was the qadi court. Governments have varied in their willingness to create and maintain supervisory agencies whose functions ranged from registering waqfs and routinely confirming personnel changes to annual budget and administrative review.

As far as we can tell from the surviving evidence, the Chingizid successor states, from the end of the fifteenth to the middle of the eighteenth centuries, saw waqf foundations as semiautonomous institutions subject to qadi-court jurisdiction in litigation (or through appeal to the political authorities) and not requiring the supervision of a state directorate of waqfs, a *diwan*, or any other bureaucratic office.

The Saduza'i Afghans beginning with Ahmad Shah were heirs to Irano-Indian policies of administration. Generally speaking, the Afghan rulers maintained large bureaucratic establishments, including fiscal and military (diwan-i a'la), judicial (dar al-qudat), and police (darughah, dabit, kutwal) components. Initially, the office of sadr or *khan-i 'ulum* was responsible for the efficient and honest operation of waqfs under Saduza'i jurisdiction.[1] The official worked in close conjunction with the qadi and had overall responsibility for the cult and matters pertaining to it.

Although evidence about the extent of waqf in the Saduza'i period is scattered, it was clearly a common form of property tenure. A sale document of 9 Safar A.H. 1168/25 November A.D. 1754, in listing the boundaries of twenty-five parcels of land for sale in Diyudi Baghbanan and Dih-i Mubarak, mentions two adjoining parcels of land as the waqf of two different foundations, for example.[2]

The first half of the nineteenth century, for now at least, is something of a clean slate when it comes to information about waqf and its administration. But the evidence from the latter half of the century indicates

---

[1] Elphinstone 1815, 539; Kakar 1979, 35–36; Gregorian 1969, 70.
[2] Fufalza'i 1958, 282.

considerable administrative continuity from the late eighteenth century. The state offices in charge of waqf were still sought after, and therefore there must have been waqf to supervise. Sometime in 1865–1866, for example, while Muhammad Afdal Khan and his brother, Muhammad Aʿzam Khan, were struggling to wrest control of Kabul and the Muhammadzaʾi throne from Amir Shir ʿAli Khan, Muhammad Aʿzam was approached by two prominent citizens of the capital, Mulla ʿUzayr of the Dih-i Afghanan quarter and Mulla Mir Aftab. In return for their help in delivering up the city, they asked that he appoint them chief qadi (*qadi al-qudat*) and mutawalli of waqfs, respectively. He agreed and gave them a written undertaking to that effect.[3] In May-June 1866, soon after the two sardars had taken Kabul and Muhammad Afdal had assumed the amirate, the mullas presented him with the signed document promising them the posts of "khan-i ʿulum and tawliyat of the waqfs." Muhammad Afdal is said to have told them, "I will never dismiss my kinsmen from a judicial position and appoint someone else to it. You can take this document to whoever gave it to you and make your demands to him."[4] The apparent identification of the office of qadi al-qudat with that of khan-i ʿulum and the apparent close link between that office and supervision of waqfs emerges from these passages. The actual appointee to the tawliyat of waqfs is never named, but the office of khan-i ʿulum was given to Saʿd al-Din Khan, son of the qadi al-qudat ʿAbd al-Rahman.[5]

Under the amir ʿAbd al-Rahman Khan, whose reign was long (twenty-one years) and who was obsessed with the formation of a strong central monarchy and bureaucracy, much more data on waqf emerge. Recent scholarship has concluded that ʿAbd al-Rahman was the architect of major waqf reforms in Afghanistan. One scholar has asserted that the Afghan amir confiscated all waqfs and stripped the religious figures of Afghanistan of their incomes.[6] Other more moderate assessments suggest only that he took administrative control of waqfs and in so doing destroyed the economic independence of the religious classes.[7] Both views are in need of revision based on the available evidence. Administrative control of waqfs by the Afghan state had a long and respectable history, beginning with the Saduzaʾi shahs and, although the evidence is circumstantial, continuing right through the Barakzaʾi and Muhammadzaʾi amirates. ʿAbd al-

---

[3] Fayd Muhammad Katib 1913–15, 2:283.

[4] Ibid., 2:289.

[5] Ibid.; Fufalzaʾi 1967, 2:326, where other titles associated with the supervision of waqfs are also given. These include *mulla-bashi, aʿlam al-ʿulama, sadr al-ʿulama,* and *mudarris-bashi.*

[6] Busson de Janssens 1951, 13–14.

[7] Gregorian 1969, 135; Wilber 1952, 44.

Rahman's initiatives on waqf are by no means a departure from the policies of his predecessors.

In 1884–1885, he issued a farman-decree extending his administrative control over all waqf properties. In the farman, he proclaimed that henceforth the income from all waqfs supporting mosques would be used only for the salaries of mosque officials, the imams and muezzins, and for mosque maintenance.[8] No mention is made of waqfs whose purpose was other than the support of a mosque, although the text of the farman itself is not available and therefore it is not certain how completely Fayd Muhammad quoted its contents.

Three years later, in 1887–1888, the Afghan amir formally established a new administrative office for waqfs called *diwan-i awqaf*,[9] perhaps, in part, to implement the earlier farman. The stated responsibilities of the office were to keep records of all waqfs and make sure that all waqf income was spent according to the conditions set by the donor.[10]

In neither case is there anything to warrant the suggestion that the amir was confiscating waqfs or attempting to curb the means of the religious figures who received waqf income. Quite the contrary in fact. Both decrees fall well within what was expected of a good Muslim sovereign and, if we were to speculate on his motives for issuing them based on the evidence, it would be far more reasonable to conclude that 'Abd al-Rahman, pursuing tried and true policies of waqf supervision, was only interested in making sure that the waqfs operated as they were intended to and that the recipients of waqf income were not deprived of their entitlements by corrupt waqf administrators.

The Mazar-i Sharif Waqf under the Afghans, 1869–1889

More specific information on Muhammadza'i waqf policies is to be found in two documents pertaining to the 'Alid shrine itself and to the city of Mazar-i Sharif. The first of these is the 1873 waqfnamah of Na'ib Muhammad 'Alam Khan. The second is 'Abd al-Rahman Khan's 1889 farman pertaining to the organization of the shrine and its waqf.[11] Taken together, the documents offer direct evidence of the state of the shrine waqf properties in the latter part of the nineteenth century and provide a comparative basis for assessing the evolution of the 'Alid waqfs in both the short run (between 1873 and 1889) and the long run (between 1668–1669 and 1889). They also highlight the issue of relations between the political administration and the waqf administration and offer some basis for conclu-

---

[8] Fayd Muhammad Katib 1913–15, 3:475.
[9] Ibid., 3:586.
[10] Ibid.
[11] *TMS*, 72–76 (text), 77–84 (transcription).

sions about Muhammadza'i Afghan administrative policies on waqf. In turn the documents shed a certain amount of light on the economic conditions of the region around Mazar-i Sharif, especially agricultural conditions and the relative importance of the commercial and service sectors in the regional economy.

The two documents allow us to identify four trends in the waqf holdings of the 'Alid shrine. First, there had been, over the long term, a significant decrease in the amount of land held as waqf. We know nothing, however, about relative income, that is, whether or not the lesser amount of land actually produced substantially more yield because of the urbanization of the region and the transformation of land use from agricultural to commercial. Second, we note an administrative distinction drawn by the Afghan administration in 1889 between commercial properties and property rights and agricultural properties held as waqf. The 1889 document appears to restrict use of the word *waqf* to the latter, although the former made up perhaps the greatest part of the shrine's wealth. Third, the documents show a much more complex pattern of land tenure than do any of the earlier materials. This complexity arises not so much from any increasing sophistication in land use law but rather from the intricacies engendered by urbanization and the pressure toward "highest and best" use of the existing land stock. Finally, the two documents provide indirect evidence, if any were needed in light of the unambiguous jurisdictional policies of the Muhammadza'i Afghans, that the shrine had surrendered all its nonproperty prerogatives. No more references to tax rights nor to the rights to collect police fees appear in the surviving archival record.

LAND USE AND THE 'ALID WAQF

We will begin with a consideration of the apparent evolution of the use of waqf land at Mazar-i Sharif. Over the centuries, the shrine and waqf administrators had been comparatively successful in maintaining the economic prosperity of the Shahi Canal and the land watered by it. That single branch of the Hazhdah Nahr (Eighteen-Canal) irrigation system had had, as far as we can tell, an unbroken four-hundred-year history of channeling water from the Balkh River to the region around the shrine and beyond. Year in and year out, since the founding of the waqf in 1480, the canal had been the heart of the waqf endowment, pumping the region's lifeblood along its twenty-mile length.

All of the Balkh region depended on the efficient canalization of snowmelt from deep in the Hindu Kush. The elaborate Hazhdah Nahr system had developed over time to serve the region's water needs. Yet during the century after the Nadirid occupation, the system as a whole deteriorated enormously. Any irrigation system, of course, is in a state of constant deterioration owing to erosion and silting. The banks of the Hazhdah Nahr canals had to be constantly shored up against erosion and the canal beds, from the eighteen trunk canals to the myriad aqueducts and feeders that branched off, had to be repeatedly dredged because of silting. Controlling the diversion of waters from the Balkh River into the trunk canals, from the trunks into the feeders, and from the feeders into the fields placed cyclical and unremitting demands on the administrative authorities. When recognized authority vanished or was crippled by internal struggles, the most vulnerable regions lost control of their water. A regional authority was needed to levy the manpower required to maintain the canals; to arbitrate conflicting claims; and to prevent the powerful (those upstream) from depriving the vulnerable (those downstream) of their rights.

If we take the fairly striking prosperity of the shrine as evidence, then we can assume that the administrators of the shrine had been able to provide or to obtain the necessary authority to safeguard shrine water rights. An inventory of the Hazhdah Nahr system compiled in the middle of the seventeenth century listing the canals with the names of the villages they watered places the Shahi Canal far down the list in terms of numbers of villages. In the seventeenth century, Balkh (both the region and the city) enjoyed a substantial degree of political calm and economic vitality. The Hazhdah Nahr canal with the largest number of villages was the 'Abd Allah Canal, with twenty-six villages, while the Shahi Canal supported only ten.[12] But when members of the British delegation to the Afghan Boundary Commission surveyed the area two hundred years later, in 1884–1886, they could find only seven villages on the 'Abd Allah Canal, while there were now eighteen on the Shahi. Moreover, it was estimated then that the Shahi Canal supported about 18 percent of the entire population of the Hazhdah Nahr system (2,745 of 14,925 households).[13] This rise in relative importance, which was one of the reasons the city became the commercial and political center of Afghan Turkistan, must have been due to the administrative skills of the mutawallis and to the continuity of the shrine's appeal as a center of pilgrimage. The pilgrims brought a steady flow of wealth, which, along with the waqf income, sustained the shrine administration in fat times and lean.

The waqf administrators undoubtedly benefited from the fact that the head of the Shahi Canal was the farthest upstream of the main trunk canals into which the Balkh River divided. It received first flood and, to

[12] Mukhtarov 1980, 102–3.
[13] *Gaz.* 4:260.

some extent, control of the barrage where its water was diverted affected downstream water rights.

The relationship between political authority and an economy based on irrigation is a complex one, and establishing cause-effect links is extremely difficult. There were several related factors in the peculiar circumstances of the Balkh basin, however, that deserve to be mentioned again. Each undoubtedly played some part in the relative rise of the shrine's economy, which in turn must be linked to its irrigation resources. These include a vigorous pastoralism, which placed fewer demands on a system of artificial irrigation; the concomitant trade-off in agricultural productivity; the disappearance of a single Hazhdah Nahr–wide political authority in the century after 1747; and the shrine's development of military capabilities.

With a weak or nonexistent political authority to mediate disputes over water distribution, it is reasonable to think that the mutawallis and their officials were able to assert increased power over the distribution of water. The link between political assertiveness and the protection of vital water supplies is exemplified by the case of the amir Qilij 'Ali Khan of Khulm/Tashqurghan. History connects his rise and the validation of his political coming of age to victory in a struggle with the amir of Aybak over the water supply of Khulm.[14] The rise of petty amirates in Aqchah and Sar-i Pul, as well as Mazar, is another probable case of a local response to the need to protect water supplies. In the Hazhdah Nahr basin, besides Mazar, the two main political entities during the century before Afghan dominion were at Aqchah and Balkh. Among them the Hazhdah Nahr system was more or less neatly divided into the western trunks (Aqchah), the central trunks (Balkh), and the eastern trunks (Mazar).

By creating a state apparatus with a military wing, the shrine administration secured the water supplies of the Shahi Canal, the core of the shrine's waqf and the resource on which much of its economic prosperity depended.

We have three reference points for assessing changes in the extent of the agricultural economy of the 'Alid waqf, and the development of land use on the waqf properties within the water district of the Nahr-i Shahi. One is the 1668–1669 manshur of Subhan Quli, the second is Muhammad 'Alam Khan's 1873 waqfnamah, and the last is 'Abd al-Rahman's 1889 farman. The latter two, because of their extreme remove from the seventeenth-century material and near contemporaneity, are probably best viewed in tandem.

The extent of the waqf agricultural lands included in the 1668–1669 manshur, despite a certain vagueness in the description, is enormous.

[14] *Gaz.* 4:572.

The boundaries of the waqf lands of the shrine, treated for all intents and purposes as a contiguous whole, are listed as Kutal-i Abdu in the east; Dih Dadi, Karamlik, and Takhtah Pul on the Quddar Canal in the west; Ranjaktu and Fuladi, also on the Quddar Canal, to the north; and the Shadyan Plain (Dasht-i Shadyan) to the south. The east-west axis (the line between Kutal-i Abdu and Dih Dadi) is about twenty-one or twenty-two miles long. The length of the north-south axis is more difficult to fix and probably varied enormously as one moved from east to west. There is some indication that, in the nineteenth century at least, the land immediately south of the Shahi Canal was wasteland. If one imagines the face of a clock (twelve o'clock being north) with the shrine at the point of rotation of the hands, then the area radiating out from the center and covering the distance between eight and eleven o'clock and between two and three o'clock represents the irrigated agricultural lands, the Nahr-i Shahi following a line roughly connecting eight o'clock with half past two. The land south of the Shahi Canal, as well as the lands between eleven and two o'clock, were mixed pasture and salt wasteland in the nineteenth and twentieth centuries. The salt lands were probably once irrigated and consequently salinized.

In Muhammad 'Alam Khan's waqfnamah of 1873, one of the endowed properties is a grist mill [asyab] bounded "on the west by appurtenances of [tawabi'] the mazar-i sharif; on the south by unowned 'dead' land; on the east by a public road, and on the north by land belonging to the wards [saghirha] of Mirza Badal."[15] Grist mills had to be located on waterways with sufficient rates of flow to turn millstones. If we assume that the mill was located on the Shahi Canal, then the canal itself and perhaps land on its left bank were what was meant by the "appurtenances of the mazar-i sharif." The name of the place where the mill stood, Harim Bagh,[16] also suggests proximity to the shrine. Such being the case, the fact that the southern edge of the parcel on which the mill stood abutted unowned wasteland leads to the conclusion that the southern edge of the waqf territory as described by Subhan Quli Khan in 1668–1669 was the right bank of the Shahi Canal itself.

In his manshur, the northern limits were Ranjaktu and Fuladi on the Quddar Canal, the next trunk canal in the Hazhdah Nahr system as one moves west from the Shahi Canal. Ranjaktu, or Janjaktu as the mid-seventeenth-century description of the system spells it, was the eleventh village along the Quddar Canal and Fuladi was eighteenth and last.[17] By

---

[15] *TMS*, 90.

[16] Ibid. According to Abu Yusuf 1969, the *harim* was a reserved area around a water source that extended from forty to sixty cubits (dhar') from the source, depending on whether it was for watering livestock or crops.

[17] Salakhetdinova 1970, 224; Mukhtarov 1980, 102.

1886 neither name appears on the list of the five villages then watered by the Quddar.[18] On the 1942 Survey of India Map GSGS, Sheet J-42T, a place called Chah-i Polati (the well of Polati/Fuladi) is situated seven miles north of the shrine, at approximately the same place at which Fuladi on the Quddar Canal would have been. By 1969, not only are the names no longer to be found but the canal itself had ceased functioning and vanished.[19]

The maximum extent of the waqf lands included within the limits set down in the 1668–1669 manshur was thus twenty-one or twenty-two miles from east to west and seven or eight miles from north to south. Seen as a rectangle, the area would have been approximately 154 square miles or nearly 100,000 acres. Certainly such a figure bears little resemblance to what must have been the reality. Waqf lands were directly dependent on the irrigation system, and if one could have viewed the Nahr-i Shahi waqf from the air in the seventeenth century, the parcels of cultivated lands would have probably appeared massed around the shrine itself and to the north and west of the shrine along the eight-to-eleven-o'clock arc described by the Quddar Canal (Dih Dadi at eight o'clock, Fuladi at eleven o'clock). East of the shrine, the waqf territories would have closely followed the course of the Shahi Canal to the Kutal-i 'Abdu.

What the manshur shows is an irregularly shaped, rather elongated but contiguous area. 'Abd al-Rahman Khan's 1889 farman, on the other hand, presents a dramatically different picture of the waqf lands under cultivation. The farman's main purpose was to settle the issue of eligibility for waqf income, and in doing so it discloses how drastically the corpus of income-producing properties classified as "waqf" had been reduced. According to the Afghan amir, the waqf properties of the shrine all came under the rubric of the "Eight-Paykal Waqf."[20] No other source of shrine income is referred to as "waqf." The Eight-Paykal Waqf was distributed over five regions: there was one paykal in Dih Dadi; one in Qal'ah-yi Qul Muhammad; and two each in Juy Siyah Gird, Shirabad, and Chughdak.

The term *paykal*, a unit of area, evolved over many centuries but appears to have always been associated with irrigated land. In the tenth-century encyclopedia *Mafatih al-'ulum*, the term *faykal* is used as a unit of water measurement.[21] Barthold believed there was a connection between the terms paykal/faykal and *finjan*, a device used to meter the flow of water from the trunk canal to the branch canals that carried water to

---

[18] *Gaz.* 4:251–52.

[19] Mukhtarov 1980, 106.

[20] *TMS*, 76 (text), 84 (transcription).

[21] Al-Khwarazmi 1895, 69 (Bosworth 1969, 152–53); Barthold 1963–77, 3:109. On the term *finjan* (glass or cup) and its use as a technical term in irrigation, see Lambton 1938, 672, and Qasim b. Yusuf Harawi 1968, 159.

the fields. In the sixteenth century, the term *faykal* as a unit of land appears in a sale deed from Bukhara: "I have sold . . . to Khwajah Muhammad Islam . . . the entirety of seventy mulberry trees belonging to me and located in the district of Qara Kul on the Arghunshah Canal, in the village of Suk Suk, on the faykal of Khwajah 'Ali. . . ."[22]

By the end of the sixteenth century, the term *paykal* at Balkh described a more or less standard area of irrigated land capable of producing enough grain to fill twelve (presumably standard) silos (*anbar*).[23] For nineteenth-century Bukhara, paykal was defined as an "irrigation grid," or series of irrigated fields all tied to a single network of irrigation ditches.[24] On at least one occasion, Amir Haydar (r. 1800–1826) made service grants to his soldiers of three or four paykals each.[25]

Within the Hazhdah Nahr system of Balkh, according to British intelligence reports, the paykal was equivalent to four "plows" ("kulba," i.e., qulbah or ghulbah). Each plow was about thirty acres.[26] The 1889 farman, however, clearly distinguishes two different paykals. The paykal of Dih Dadi was the largest of the eight paykals making up the waqf fund. It comprised eight "units" (*fard*), in contrast to the other seven paykals, which were only six units each. Again according to the 1889 farman, each unit equaled one "ox" (gaw). One of the standard units of measurement in nineteenth-century Afghanistan was the "team [juft or zawj] of oxen," that is, the average amount of land that a team of oxen could plow in a fixed period of time, usually a season. In nineteenth-century Bukhara, the team was about 50 tanabs,[27] but in the Hazhdah Nahr system, where it is equated with the plow, it was about 60.[28] The plow or team being two of 'Abd al-Rahman's units and the tanab being equal to about a half acre, we can calculate the paykal at Dih Dadi at 120 acres, but only 90 acres for each of the other seven paykals. Other calculations, using the Bukharan or Afghan equivalents for the tanab,[29] do not significantly change the overall amount of land included within the Eight-Paykal Waqf.

The total amount of land involved is probably no less than 750 acres and no more than 1,000 acres. The intelligence reports from the Afghan Boundary Commissioners estimate all the cultivated land in the Hazhdah Nahr system at approximately 2,030 paykals or nearly a quarter of a mil-

[22] Document number 320 in Bertel's 1938 and Ivanov 1954.
[23] Ivanov 1954, 61–62.
[24] Abduraimov 1970, 176.
[25] Ibid., 138, note.
[26] *Gaz.* 4:263.
[27] Abduraimov 1970, 43, note.
[28] *Gaz.* 4:263.
[29] Gregorian 1969, Appendix B.

lion acres. The Shahi Canal, the heart of the waqf, at the same time supported about 18 percent of the total population of the Hazhdah Nahr system, while the waqf agricultural lands amounted to less than four-tenths of 1 percent of total cultivated lands.

The 1889 farman underscores the difference in the designated waqf properties between the middle of the seventeenth century and the end of the nineteenth. Subhan Quli's manshur describes a single contiguous area of land over which the shrine administrators exercised their waqf rights. 'Abd al-Rahman's farman just as clearly describes five noncontiguous parcels scattered around the shrine. The Dih Dadi, Shirabad, and Chughdak[30] parcels were five to seven miles west of the shrine, the Qal'ah-yi Qul Muhammad about six miles to the east, and the Juy Siyahgird (Siyahjird) some six miles north.

The question that naturally arises is: what happened? How did a large endowment of irrigated land, a unified area extending for miles in all directions, diminish to the point that only scattered parcels of one hundred to two hundred acres remained?

The answer cannot be given with any certainty, but a number of factors must be considered. The first has to do with the possible different interpretations placed on the word *waqf* by the seventeenth-century authorities in Balkh and the nineteenth-century politicians in Kabul. Both states were Hanafi-Sunni and operated under the same legal precepts—those stemming from the eleventh- to twelfth-century Bukharan school (Marghinani, the Mahbubis, et al.), school as interpreted in the fatwa and shurut manuals found in the qadi courts of Mawarannahr and Afghanistan.[31] But from an administrative standpoint, the matter was more complicated. The shrine administrators managed the waqf. They also administered the votive offerings as well as the revenue privileges that friendly politicians gave them in the form of tax exemptions and miscellaneous revenues (sales of souvenirs, sales of licenses to peddle within the shrine precincts, revenue derived from the two- to three-month-long trade fair that followed the annual spring festival of Gul-i Surkh and income from the lands and properties they purchased with revenues from waqf and nonwaqf sources). From an administrative perspective, there was little to differentiate the various income sources, nor is there any evidence that the administrators tried to keep separate accounts or treasuries for waqf and nonwaqf income. Rather, all income was probably thought of as waqf at least by the politicians. The manshur of 1668–1669—in the phrasing "the entire Shahi canal lengthwise and breadthwise, including all villages

---

[30] Chughdak may be identical with the seventeenth-century Chughzak (Salakhetdinova 1970, 224), one of the few places under the control of the mutawalli when Subhan Quli issued the manshur in 1668–69.

[31] Ghani 1978.

and estates, dwellings and farms, boundaries and roads"—glosses over a congeries of administrative arrangements, some waqf, some nonwaqf, but all for ease of reference called "waqf." Such tendencies were naturally intensified in the absence of a strong central government for most of the eighteenth and early nineteenth centuries.

The farman of 'Abd al-Rahman, who was heir to a more rigorously bureaucratic state than was Subhan Quli, reflects a bureaucratic interest in separating the revenue stream both by source and by object. As a consequence, three categories are identified: (1) waqf income, or the income from the "Eight-Paykal Waqf;" (2) votive income, the money brought by pilgrims; and (3) rents and fees collected from urban properties, properties that were in all likelihood originally waqf but which, for reasons I will attempt to explain, may have effectively passed out of the category of waqf, at least as viewed by the Afghan administration of the late nineteenth century.

The latter circumstance, in particular the administrative decision to stop classifying certain revenue sources as waqf, may have had the effect of obscuring the actual yield to the shrine from its revenue sources, whatever administrative label happened to be hung on them.

Another reason for the apparent decline in the waqf endowment was the natural depreciation and deterioration that affected all real property. Irrigation increases the saline content of the soil. Without repeated flushing and drainage, the salinity of the soil rises to a point at which crops cannot be cultivated. A perusal of the maps of the Mazar-i Sharif region from 1942 and 1979 quickly reveals the ubiquitous word *salt* sprinkled liberally over the landscape to designate areas of high salinity. In addition, some place names appear that indicate salt lands, such as *shuristan*, *shurak*, and *namakzar*. One of the areas that was probably most seriously affected by salinization by the end of the nineteenth century was the eastern end of the Shahi Canal. Presumably, because of evaporation, the water that reached that end of the canal was more saturated with minerals than was the water anywhere else along it.

When Alexander Burnes traveled through the eastern part of the Shahi Canal district in the early part of the nineteenth century, he commented favorably on the vast extent of cultivation. Fifty years later, in 1888, Dr. John Gray, who had recently been hired by 'Abd al-Rahman as personal physician, traveled the same route taken by Burnes. This is how he describes the eastern end of the Shahi Canal: "In one place the road dipped down between some low clay hills, the defile of Abdu [Kutal-i Abdu]. . . . The plain became gradually flatter and more dusty, till, finally, it was little more than a desert with the scantiest vegetation."[32] Gray was traveling in late August or early September, certainly the least verdant

[32] Gray 1895, 149–50.

time of the year, a circumstance that no doubt had some effect on his impressions.

Other evidence, more indirect, also suggests a decline in waqf revenue from agricultural sources. In the 1889 farman, discussion of waqf revenue is relegated to the very end of the document, but, more significantly, the explanation in that section of the disbursement of the agricultural income, the only income now designated "waqf," shows what the shrine was able to dispense with. As of July 1889 (and probably long before, judging by the matter-of-fact presentation of the information), income from the Eight-Paykal waqf was distributed to members of the Ansari family who had no government salaries. The fact that the shrine officials were by now all on government salaries, and that the vast majority of those officials were from the Ansari family, tells us that, when given a choice between government salaries and a share in the waqf income, it was the former that was most attractive. Had it been otherwise, we assume that the positions at the shrine would have been filled by non-Ansaris.

The classification of only the Eight-Paykal agricultural land as waqf is misleading if we conclude from it that the old sources of income from which the shrine had long derived its prosperity had been seriously reduced. What seems to have happened instead is linked to the overall transformation of the shrine into the main urban center of the old Balkh appanage under Afghan hegemony. With the urbanization of Mazar-i Sharif, the need for a permanent bazaar, and the creation of all the ancillary institutions to which a bazaar gives rise, the commercial pressure on the agricultural waqf immediately adjacent to the shrine must have increased. The two- or three-month-long fair that followed the Gul-i Surkh festival at the shrine required space and probably certain structures of a more or less permanent nature providing stable, warehouse, and hotel space (the khans, sarays, or caravansaries). A growing permanent population required larger residential areas, and making Mazar-i Sharif the regional capital must have created new needs for government office space. (Takhtah Pul, at least through this period, seems to have been adequate to house the garrison.) In short, the usual pressures for a change in land use must have arisen as Mazar-i Sharif eclipsed Balkh as the principal urban center of Afghan Turkistan. And if the bulk of the land was held in waqf or controlled by the shrine, then it was the waqf land, we have every reason to believe, that was transformed by these pressures.

There has been very little work devoted to the evolution of waqf property.[33] A readiness to assume—because waqfs were perpetual in law and

[33] Some important exceptions are Baer 1979; Schoem 1985; and Deguilhem-Schoem 1988.

because the waqf deeds often contained legal language forbidding exchange, sale, or other divestment—that waqfs either did not change or were only transformed by illegal means has produced a gap in our knowledge about the legal devices by which trustees of waqfs were permitted to meet changing economic pressures.

The legal literature is quite rich. Some of the best information for the Hanafi school, the one whose manuals would have been referred to by qadi-judges in Mazar-i Sharif, comes from the Ottoman state and is more or less contemporary with the Afghan period in the history of the 'Alid shrine and its waqf. [34]

For now, it will have to suffice simply to identify some of the legitimate means by which divestment could occur. At this stage, we have no documentary evidence that the shrine administration had been divesting itself of its waqf lands, either exchanging valuable urban locations for more distant agricultural land of equivalent value, selling development rights, or exchanging development rights for a percentage of the income of the improvement.

One of the best-known of the transactions permitted on waqf property by the Hanafi school was the double rent (*ijaratayn*), [35] whereby a large advance payment was made in exchange for a long-term, below-market-rent lease. The large advance payment, like "key money" or "furnishings and fixtures money," was recoverable by the tenant by "sale" to a new tenant. The advantages to the parties to the transaction are straightforward. The lessor received a large payment for his property without actually alienating it while the tenant received long-term security and a favorable rent. Sometimes such arrangements called for periodic renegotiation of the rent, a condition that it would have been only prudent for the lessor to require in an inflationary environment . The disadvantage of the double rent was that in practice it removed control of the property from the lessor and furthermore established a kind of quasi-lien against the property in the form of the advance, which gave the lessee a claim.

The effective sale of development rights was another means by which the administrator of a waqf was allowed to improve the value of his land or other real estate without having to raise investment capital himself. Such a "sale" appears under different names (*sukna, hikr, gedik wa khulu*). [36] A tenant wishing to make improvements on a piece of waqf

[34] Two of the most accessible and useful works are Qadri Pasha 1902 and Hilmi Effendi 1922.

[35] Qadri Pasha 1902, article (*maddah*) 277 and Hilmi Effendi 1922, index. Qadri Pasha uses the term *extended* or *long* rent (*ijarah tawilah*). Gerber 1981, 4 discusses Ottoman attempts to reform the double rent and Baer 1979, 221–22 examines the consequences of the reform.

[36] Baer 1979; Deguilhem-Schoem 1988; Mukminova 1968.

property whose administrator may have lacked either the desire or the means to do so would, with the administrator's and sometimes the qadi's consent, perform agreed-upon improvements and negotiate a higher rent with the mutawalli. The improvement, for example a building built on a piece of waqf land, became the property of the tenant and could be rented, sold, given away (as waqf, for instance), or left as part of the owner's estate. The mutawalli may have retained certain preemptive rights (right of first refusal on a sale, for example), but if a new use was established with the improvement (for example, a caravansary where there had once been an orchard), the mutawalli's control of the waqf property for all intents and purposes disappeared. But with such an improvement, his gain from such a transaction presumably would have outweighed any passing worry about loss of control of the land.

A third important device, one often specifically prohibited by the language of the waqf deed, was outright exchange of waqf property (istibdal).[37] No doubt exchanges raised the possibility of corrupt dealings with the property, and an anxious donor might have tried, as founders of perpetual trusts are wont to do, to bind future administrators so tightly that they could not, deliberately or otherwise, squander the trust. In most actual cases, we must assume, the exchange of property for that of comparable or greater value, if not greater potential value, served the best interests of the waqf. Waqfs, by their more or less nonprofit nature, did not have large surpluses of capital. Indeed, where one can follow the cash flow of a waqf, it is usually deficits that characterize the budget, simply because depreciation reduces the yield of the endowment while raising the cost of maintaining the object of the waqf.

Raising investment capital to develop a piece of land was difficult enough when cash flow was a problem. But beyond that, the assets of the waqf could not be used as collateral to borrow money. Mortgage loans were impossible on waqf property because the ownership of the property could not be transferred in the event of a default.[38] On the question of legal ownership, there were at least two points of view: (1) that the land was given, and therefore belonged, to God and (2) that "ownership" belonged to the beneficiaries as the designated recipients of the usufruct.[39]

In any event, it was not the mutawalli who owned the waqf, and therefore he could not mortgage it. He was permitted to borrow money, but only against that part of the income assigned to maintaining the foundation. A poor cash flow made for a depressed credit line, hence the attrac-

[37] Qadri Pasha 1902, articles 129–43.

[38] FA (Baillie translation), 563–64.

[39] Heffening 1961, 625a–b.

tiveness of dealing with outside investors when the waqf was short of cash.

The right to sell or lease development rights and the right to exchange property both had the potential to weaken the administrative control of the mutawalli. Both created irrevocable rights of ownership either superimposed on waqf tenure (in the case of the former) or replacing waqf tenure (in the case of the latter). Another somewhat different instrument, the *mursad* or redeemable lien,[40] also over time and under the right circumstances led to a de facto divestment of waqf rights.

The redeemable lien was like the "repair and deduct" provision in modern tenancy laws. If a waqf house had a collapsing staircase, for example, and the mutawalli was unable or unwilling to fix it, the tenant, either with or without the mutawalli's consent (in the latter case with a qadi's decree), could make the necessary repairs and thereby establish a lien on the property in the amount of the repair or renegotiate a lower rent to amortize the repair. Unlike the sale of development rights, the mursad was redeemable at any time by the waqf administration. However, it is clear that, as time passed, property deteriorated, and repair costs mounted, the mursad liens could eventually exceed the value of the original waqf property, at which point there was de facto divestment.

We have no direct proof at this time that any of these legal forms either existed or were sanctioned in nineteenth-century Mazar-i Sharif. We do know that under Hanafi law, as codified by Ottoman lawyers of the time, these legal forms had a sound theoretical basis and that in contemporary Ottoman jurisdictions they were in fact functioning. Further research into Afghan court records may provide a definitive answer as to whether they were known to and practiced by the Hanafi courts of Afghanistan.

Our indirect evidence, on the other hand, suggests very strongly that some such legal devices were helping shape property tenure in nineteenth-century Mazar-i Sharif. The farman of 1889, by classifying income to the shrine from commercial property in the city as distinct from the waqf income, is almost prima facie evidence that a process of divestment had been going on for a long time.

The 1873 waqfnamah of Muhammad 'Alam Khan[41] provides more concrete evidence of an ongoing process in which agricultural uses of waqf land were superseded by commercial and residential uses. By virtue of this transformation, the waqf administrators had consciously, and perhaps beneficially both to the shrine and to themselves, divested the shrine of some of its waqf properties.

[40] Deguilhem-Schoem 1988.
[41] *TMS*, 89–92. According to the author, the waqfnamah is kept in the Mazar-i Sharif Museum.

According to what we know from material surviving from the seventeenth, eighteenth, and early nineteenth centuries, all the land dependent on the Shahi Canal was controlled as waqf land and had agricultural uses. The mid-seventeenth-century amirid additions to the waqf are the strongest evidence we have that the waqf was an agricultural one, every one of the seven endowments being of either water rights or pasturage. The only commercial waqf we know of is the bazaar with shops and a bath that Khwandamir included in Sultan Husayn Bayqara's original endowment of 1480.[42] The existence of the village of Khwajah Khayran, or al-Khayr, which stood on the site at the time of the 1480 rediscovery, means that some forms of property tenure there pre-dated the establishment of the waqf. Had the village been state land, or the private land of Sultan Husayn Bayqara, then it could have simply been conveyed to waqf at that point along with the canal. Even had there been surviving private property rights in the region watered by the canal, the long-term effect of waqf control of the Shahi Canal combined with the longevity of the shrine administration itself would have been to gradually diminish the relative importance of privately held agricultural land. The Qur'anically fixed shares of heirs would have tended toward the breakup of larger estates and the sale of smaller ones in order to meet the requirements of Muslim law governing the distribution of the estate. It is therefore reasonable to assume that the shrine's control of the agricultural economy in the surrounding area through its administration of the Shahi Canal would have meant that more and more agricultural land passed into its hands through either purchase, foreclosure, or waqf donations. If one accepts the assumption that, because the mutawalli was compensated on a percentage basis, he would have been encouraged to expand the waqf holdings, then it follows that the shrine would have generally tended to buy up private holdings and turn them into what was considered waqf, from an administrative standpoint at least. This is a practice that may be observed elsewhere.[43]

Subhan Quli's manshur appears to reflect a kind of culmination of this process, when all the territory and the improvements on it around the shrine were considered waqf.[44] Political conditions in the second half of the eighteenth and the first half of the nineteenth century cost the shrine control of its waqf rights in distant regions—Khulm, Sultan Bayazid, and Darrah-i Juz, for instance—while probably tightening its control (because of its own creation of a state apparatus) on the land adjacent to it. "Mazar"

[42] Khwandamir n.d., 4:172.

[43] See, for example, the purchase of land and the conveyance of it into waqf by the mutawalli at the shrine of Shaykh Safi al-Din at Ardabil (Papazian 1968, 473–75).

[44] TMS, 56 (text), 65 (transcription).

in the early nineteenth century was a state in which waqf lands were the state lands.

But by the time Muhammad 'Alam Khan issued his waqf deed on 14 December 1873, the waqf holdings of the shrine had undergone a long and profound process of change. Private property was widespread, including both land and improvements, as was waqf founded for objects other than the shrine. These phenomena are our clearest evidence that some means of divestiture of waqf rights had been in use, perhaps the instruments mentioned above, perhaps similar legal vehicles yet to be discovered in the legal literature.

Muhammad 'Alam's waqfnamah discloses a reality of property tenure in Mazar-i Sharif in 1873 quite distinct from that found in Subhan Quli's manshur. First there were sizeable amounts of private property. Within five years of his own arrival in the city, he had acquired or built as his own private property (*milk-i khalis*)

1. A water-driven grist mill (asyab) located in or on Harim Bagh.
2. Twenty-five shops in the city in the Royal Bazaar (Rastah-i Shahi). (This "Royal Bazaar" may have been the same, or on the same site, as the one attributed to Sultan Husayn Bayqara in the fifteenth century.)
3. A fifty-six-room saray apparently built just west of the shrine's precincts, for it was bordered on the north and east by cemeteries.
4. A bath comprising one hot room and one cold room located in the Mutton Bazaar (Bazar-i Gusfand), which was the property of the shrine.
5. Ten shops in the Mutton Bazaar.
6. Five shops in the Perfumers' Bazaar (Rastah-i 'Attari).
7. Eight shops (six in one group, two in another) at the entrance to the 'Ala al-Din Khan saray, known as the "Old Saray," of Mazar-i Sharif.
8. One-half of a shop owned jointly with a man named Husayn and located in the Public Bazaar (Rastah-i 'Amm).
9. Nine shops (groups of five and four) in the Greengrocers' Bazaar (Rastah-i Baqqaliha).

These properties did not represent the full extent of Muhammad 'Alam's private holdings in Mazar-i Sharif. The waqf deed was founded to endow a thirty-three-room madrasah, and he also owned the land on which it was built.

Private holdings were not limited to the Afghan politicians in Mazar-i Sharif. The description of each property in the waqf deed is accompanied by the requisite listing of abutting properties, and these offer more evidence of private property ownership near the shrine. One of the parcels of land abutting the grist mill belonged to the wards (saghirha)[45] of a cer-

---

[45] On the term *saghir* in a Central Asian context, see Troitskaia 1960.

tain Mirza Badal. A private water channel (*juy khass*) is listed as one of the properties abutting the group of shops in the Mutton Bazaar.

Shops were the most prevalent form of private property in the city. Muhammad 'Alam Khan owned the fifty-seven and one-half shops put into the madrasah endowment as well as at least one other shop conveyed earlier to waqf to endow a mosque. (This shop is mentioned because it abuts one of the madrasah shops.) Husayn, owner of the other half of one of Muhammad 'Alam's shops, also owned an adjacent shop. Other owners of single shops, mentioned because they stood on adjacent property, were an Arab named 'Ali; 'Abd al-Razzaq; Shaqil Chakman, a clothing dealer (*jallab*); 'Abbas; and 'Azim Allah. Two persons are described as owning more than one shop: Asad Khan, whose unspecified shops abutted the ten shops on the west in the Mutton Bazaar, and Usta(d) Latif, whose shops (number unspecified) abutted the Afghan governor's five shops in the Perfumers' Bazaar on the west.

From the waqf deed a picture is also provided of the extent of the shrine's waqf holdings in Mazar-i Sharif. The ten shops and the bath in the Mutton Bazaar with which Muhammad 'Alam Khan endowed his madrasah stood on the shrine's waqf land. Here we have an example of private development rights superimposed on waqf property. The mill in Harim Bagh abutted property belonging to the shrine. Although it was not specifically designated as waqf land, administratively there would have been little to distinguish it. The shrine also owned commercial property. The half-shop donated by Muhammad 'Alam Khan was abutted on the north by a shop that "was waqf of the rawdah."

The fact that the shrine is not mentioned in connection with other properties, the Perfumers' Bazaar, for instance, or the land near the entrance to the Old Saray, strongly suggests that that land was owned by others. Although it cannot be said with absolute certainty, it seems very likely that in those cases in which Muhammad 'Alam does not mention the shrine in conjunction with his description of abutting properties, then the land under his commercial properties was not under shrine control as waqf.

If we take the ratio of shrine-owned shops to privately owned shops in the waqf deed as typical of Mazar-i Sharif as a whole, then the shrine was a very small participant in commercial real estate. The shrine owned the land under the Mutton Bazaar, but is not referred to as the owner of a single shop in it.

We should not, however, conclude from this that the shrine's revenues from commercial or related properties were either unimportant or even less than they had been when the shrine administrators were the sole local authorities and the shrine controlled all the land in the area. In fact, there is fairly strong evidence that the shrine's commercial income was very significant and had far outstripped its agricultural income. 'Abd al-

Rahman's 1889 farman refers to two commercially derived income sources for the shrine, neither classified as waqf. These were the *tahja'i* and the *girayah*.[46]

According to a recent Tajik source, the *tahja'i* was "a fee for a spot to trade in the bazaar."[47] The term probably originally referred to the ground under shops built on waqf or other inalienable land and then was extended to the fees paid for the use of the land, i.e., the ground rents. It is possible too that the term applied to fees charged for doing business, whether in permanent quarters or not, on waqf land. In the nineteenth century, the city had, of course, a permanent bazaar area (in 1873 comprising at least the Perfumers' Bazaar, the Mutton Bazaar, and the Royal Bazaar) and other indications of commercial prominence (a government customs house—*chabutarah-i sarkari*). It also had an annual two- or three-month long fair following the Gul-i Surkh festival and weekly market days.[48] These might have been held partly in permanent structures and partly out of doors, and it is reasonable to think that the shrine collected the tahja'i for use of its land and facilities for such markets.

The term may have also been used for ground rents on residences. In the 1873 waqf deed, three references are made to residential compounds (*hawili*) as abutting properties. They are also all connected with private individuals (Hamid-i Sarhang, Nasr Allah, and "Hazarah Qadam," the latter probably the name of the building.) The likelihood that some of these residences were erected on shrine land seems large, and if so then it is also likely that tahja'i would have covered their ground rents, too.

The second income source referred to by 'Abd al-Rahman was the rental income from shops (*girayah-i dukkanha*). Use of the term tells us that the shrine still owned shops and probably other commercial premises (khans, sarays, and baths, for instance), which it leased. How significant this category of income was (it is not treated to the same detailed breakdown by appropriation as the votive offerings are) is difficult to say.

By the end of the nineteenth century, the evidence leads us to the conclusion that the shrine had a substantial but perhaps not predominant role in the commercial life of the city. Muhammad 'Alam Khan's waqf deed, in fact, indicates that the bulk of urban real estate, particularly commercial real estate, was in private hands by the 1870s.

The arrival of the Afghans in 1849, with their more inclusive sense of the role of government, and, probably more importantly, their transfer of urban functions from Balkh to Mazar-i Sharif in the 1860s and 1870s, had a profound effect on the administrative prerogatives of the shrine and therefore on what was considered waqf. Perhaps as much as anything,

---

[46] *TMS*, 73 (text), 77 (transcription).

[47] Rakhimi and Uspenskoi 1954, 375; Mukminova 1968, 127–34.

[48] On the Gul-i Surkh festival, see Muhammad Badi', fol. 182b; N. Dupree 1967, 54; *TMS*, 92–93.

the changed administrative role of the shrine under Afghan aegis shaped the evolution of the 'Alid waqf. Under the Tuqay-Timurids, fiscal prerogatives on the land under the shrine's jurisdiction were all or mostly ceded to it as "waqf." But the superseding of the shrine-state by the Afghan state removed those fiscal prerogatives from the mutawalli's account books. 'Abd al-Rahman's farman is unambiguous proof of the process, for nowhere in it do we find mention either of the right of the shrine to certain tax fees or of the exemption of shrine properties, whether classified as waqf or not, from taxation.

With the eventual surrender, probably gradual, of fiscal rights, the mutawalli and his administration and the Ansari family (which by the Afghan period had become the primary beneficiary, at least of the income of the shrine) refined their interest in the waqf. The administrators, who may have foreseen the diminished importance of waqf revenues as the Afghans reestablished fiscal controls and as urban development reduced the relative importance of the agricultural economy dependent on the Shahi Canal, shifted their attention to the other revenue sources, especially the votive offerings, which the 1889 farman treats as the most substantial source of income in 1889.

In taking over responsibility for political administration, part of the Afghan policy was to incorporate the shrine officials into the state apparatus by assigning them salaries. Whether this predates the 1889 farman, where it is first mentioned, or not, the change naturally reinforced the view that waqf income was less important under the Afghans than were other nonwaqf sources. In earlier times, the fortunes of the administration had been directly linked to the prosperity of the shrine economy. Now, with 'Abd al-Rahman assigning or reconfirming fixed annual salaries for the shrine officials to be paid from the state treasury, the importance of the condition of the waqf economy diminished.

THE ADMINISTRATION OF THE 'ALID SHRINE UNDER AFGHAN DOMINION

The battle that took place north of Bamyan in 1849 between the Afghans and a coalition of the amirs of the former Balkh appanage was the last military adventure for the 'Alid shrine administration. The establishment of a strong political authority at Balkh did away with the need for the shrine to maintain a coercive arm of its own. Despite the close ties between shrine administration and state officials that had characterized the period before 1747, the shrine had become accustomed to its autonomy and did not immediately acknowledge the political authority of the new standard-bearers. But after the Afghans crushed an uprising at the shrine in 1852 and dispersed the "Khalifah" disturbances of that same year, the shrine administrators seem to have accepted the inevitable and been prepared to make the best of it. Perhaps there was an expectation that, like earlier authorities operating from Balkh, the Afghans would allow the shrine administration to continue to function as a corporate entity while accepting the obligation to affirm and protect the shrine's interests. But earlier authorities had been the products of an entirely different system of state. The Chingizid legacy that shaped the governing attitudes of the Balkh authorities from the founding of the shrine until the middle of the eighteenth century, a period of 250 years, encouraged local autonomy and institutional development, whether private land ownership, service land tenure (iqta' and tiyul), or waqf.

The Afghans, however, brought with them a very different view of the role of the state. Despite the overtly tribal origins of the Afghan state, it was the imperial apparatus of Nadir Shah Afshar that had the most profound effect on the organization of the Afghan state. The first Afghan ruler, Ahmad Shah Durrani, inherited the administrative machinery of the Iranian "world-conqueror," and the governments of his successors also utilized sophisticated and extensive bureaucracies.[49]

When the Saduza'i, then Muhammadza'i, Afghans acquired new territories, they brought their bureaucratic policies to bear on the administration of the new lands. Land and revenue surveys would be carried out, financial officials sent to every town, and garrisons of troops under an Afghan governor assigned to enforce collections. The newly conquered region would soon be politically and fiscally linked to the provincial center.

For the shrine administration at Mazar-i Sharif, Afghan policies meant important changes from what it had been accustomed to. If the mutawalli of the 'Alid shrine—probably Shuja' al-Din Khan until the fateful rebellion of 1852[50]—expected to revive the kind of laissez-faire relationship his ancestors and predecessors had enjoyed with the Balkh authorities contemporary with them, he received a rude shock. The anti-Afghan disturbances of 1852 and their outcome removed any misconceptions the Ansaris may have harbored about the direction of future relations with the new political authorities. The gradual move of the political administration from Balkh to Mazar-i Sharif following the rise of the latter as the preeminent urban center made the possibility of a reprise of the seventeenth- and eighteenth-century relations between state and shrine even more remote.

[49] Fufalza'i 1967, 2:313–69 (for Timur Shah, r. 1773–93) and Fufalzai 1958, 221ff. (for Shah Zaman, r. 1793–1800).

[50] Ferrier 1857, 209, the last source prior to the final Afghan conquest, says that Shuja' al-Din Khan was still mutawalli in 1845.

CHAPTER THIRTEEN

Shrine-State to State Shrine

THE CENTRAL THEME of this chapter is the incorporation of the entire shrine apparatus into the Afghan state in the late nineteenth century and the consequences for the Ansari family. The takeover meant state salaries for officials at the shrine, the supervision and audit of its budget, and the publication of regulations governing its revenues and appropriations.

What we know of the shrine administration during this period comes from the 1889 farman-decree issued by 'Abd al-Rahman.[1] The farman has four distinct though related sections: the first is a five-paragraph discussion of shrine income from nonwaqf sources and the appropriation of that income; the second is a list of 257 Ansaris eligible for a share of the votive income as established in paragraph 5 of the appropriations schedule; the third lists all the salaried officials of the shrine; and the fourth gives a description of the waqf properties and the distribution of income from them.

In the preceding chapter, the fourth section (on shrine waqf) was discussed. Here the remaining three sections will be dealt with, but not in sequence. We will begin with the first section on nonwaqf revenues, proceed to the third section on the administrative structure of the shrine, and conclude with the second section on the Ansaris eligible for a share of the waqf income.

Before considering the contents of the farman, it is important to note that the way in which the farman is composed and its language both suggest that no radical departure from existing procedures is being offered. Rather, the amir appears to have been regularizing or reconfirming established procedures and structures. Certain specific items, such as the criteria of eligibility for those who deserved a share in the waqf, may in fact signify a new state of affairs and not merely be a recapitulation of the status quo ante.[2] Given the nature of the information, it is impossible to know when the shrine administration was first incorporated into the provincial government. A likely moment would have been in the aftermath of the failed 1852 uprising, but we have no evidence that this was the case. What is particularly interesting about the assumption by the state of administrative control of the shrine is how little apparent effect

---

[1] TMS, 72–76 (text) 77–84 (transcription).

[2] See especially ibid., 74 (text), 82 (transcription).

there was on the staffing of the administration or on the division of offices between the Ni'mati and 'Azizi branches of the Ansari family.

The occasion for the 1889 farman was, as mentioned earlier, the failed secessionist movement of Muhammad Ishaq Khan, 'Abd al-Rahman Khan's cousin, and the administrative reorganization that the Afghan amir undertook during his two-year stay in Afghan Turkistan following victory over the secessionists. The farman partly reflects as well 'Abd al-Rahman's own commitment to an integrated autocratic state in which the religious establishment and the institution of waqf were both deemed appropriate objects for state supervision and management.

By 1889, 'Abd al-Rahman had made substantial efforts to extend state supervision to waqfs and those who benefited from them.[3] His dedication to reorganizing a state-supervised religious hierarchy similar to that which had existed under earlier Afghan rulers[4] was decidedly single-minded and went hand in hand with the waqf reforms. It was natural, therefore, that when he arrived in Mazar-i Sharif toward the end of 1889, he would turn his attention to the shrine and its administration.

His own connection with the shrine went back to the early 1860s, when as a boy he lived with his father in Turkistan and attended Friday services at the shrine. There is no reason to doubt the authenticity of the speech attributed to him by Hafiz Nur Muhammad in which the amir asserts that he had used the shrine, as thousands before him had, as a place to seek divine assistance in gaining a desired goal and in exchange had made a solemn vow. The vow itself as recorded was somewhat un-usual:

> When I first set out to gain the throne, I made a pact with the Hadrat-i Shah [i.e., 'Ali b. Abi Talib] that if I were successful, I would make myself mutawalli of his threshold pro bono and would gain honor thereby. Today I am padshah and having once been a supplicant at the threshold I now come to fulfill my promise. Henceforth you will consider me chief mutawalli [mutawalli-bashi] of this pure sanctuary; you will refer to me all matters pertaining to the votive offerings, the alms, the waqfs, the buildings, devotees, and pilgrims; and you will obey me in this.[5]

Hafiz Nur Muhammad says that the Afghan amir's motive for naming himself mutawalli was to correct abuses that had crept into the manage-ment of the waqf property of the shrine[6] and because the only form of land tenure in and around Mazar-i Sharif in 1889 was tenure in waqf.[7]

---

[3] See Kakar 1979 for a wide-ranging study of 'Abd al-Rahman Khan's domestic policies.
[4] Fufalza'i 1967, 2:319–30; Fufalza'i 1958, 252–54.
[5] *TMS*, 71.
[6] Ibid., 71.
[7] Ibid., 49.

That this latter assertion has little basis in fact is immediately apparent from Muhammad 'Alam Khan's 1873 waqfnamah, in which numerous references to private property are made. There is no reason to believe that the highly complex picture of land tenure presented there had somehow been rendered completely uniform only sixteen years later. Nor do we find, either in the 1889 farman or in this statement attributed to him, any indication that the shrine administrators had been charged with or suspected of financial misconduct. In fact, the terms of the farman and the effective confirmation of the Ansari officials in their offices and the Ansaris who were not officeholders in their waqf rights at least imply the confidence of the amir in the Ansari family in general, and in its members who held administrative posts in particular.

When 'Abd al-Rahman made his speech, he already possessed, as head of state, all the powers he was now assigning himself. But there also seems to have been a message within the message. The assumption of the tawliyat was largely symbolic, and there is no evidence that he thereafter had any direct role in running the shrine. Instead, by issuing his proclamation, he was identifying himself, his personal honor, and the prestige of his throne with the well-being of the shrine and its waqf. In so doing, he was first asserting his sovereignty and second trying to mend political fences in the region that had only recently sought to throw off his authority. The routine administration of the shrine, however, remained lodged firmly in the hands of the Ansaris, but subject now to provincial government supervision.

THE INCOME AND APPROPRIATIONS OF THE SHRINE IN 1889

We begin our discussion of the administration of the shrine as it appears in the 1889 farman with the first section after the preamble, the five paragraphs devoted to the nonwaqf income and its disbursement:

> Para. 1. Votive offerings in the form of cash brought as gifts to the shrine should be added up and then divided into three parts. One part should be deposited in the treasury of the noble shrine [mazar-i sharif] for repairs and furnishings. The other two parts should be [combined and] divided by five. One of these parts should be deposited in the treasury of the mazar-i sharif for medicine for the hospital that is to be built and for shrouds for strangers [who die on ziyarat-pilgrimage to the shrine]. The four remaining parts should then be combined and divided by ten, one part of which should be spent on candles. The remaining nine should then be combined and divided by ten again. One of those shares belongs to the mutawalli of the shrine and the other nine are to be divided equally among the shaykhs of the shrine [see below, paragraph 5]
>
> [In percentages, the budget appropriations are:

Maintenance	33.33 percent
Medical and funeral	13.33 percent
Lighting	5.33 percent
Mutawalli	4.80 percent
"Shaykhs of the shrine"	43.20 percent

Para. 2. Noncash votive offerings like carpets, gilims [flat-woven rugs], and tapestries for the sepulcher, and gold and silver objects, etc. should be handed over to the treasurer of the shrine.

Para. 3. Revenue from ground rents (tahja'i) and leases (girayah) of shops that belong to the shrine should also be remitted to the treasurer of the shrine.

Para. 4. Regarding burial of the dead, whoever dies and wants to be buried near the Lion of God, by necessity no tomb should be created for them [surat-i qabr-ra daruran nasazand] [i.e., they should be interred without marker or tomb because of space limitations].

A full explanation of these four preceding paragraphs is recorded in the royal farman in the treasury of the mazar-i sharif. Anyone needing more details should refer to it. Here we only summarize it.

Para. 5. With respect to the division of the votive offerings brought to the shrine, since after some inquiries it has been ascertained by the Royal Justice-Dispensing Presence that from ancient times and from the days of previous sultans—May God cast light on their tombs—those refuges of nobility and perfection, Mirza 'Aziz Khan and Mirza Ni'mat Khan Ansari, were the mutawallis of the Blessed Shrine, and this is perfectly plain to the royal mind, therefore the distribution of the votives belongs especially to the descendants of those two deceased men. No one else has any right to it and we [here] write down the names of the descendants of those two men. Only [faqat]."

This section of the farman is a straightforward and clear statement of the way in which the annual budget of the shrine should be organized. Although the existence of a more complete farman on the subject has at this point not been established, the reference to it suggests two things: first that the formalizing of the principles of the shrine budget predates the issuance of this farman, and second that paragraph 5 is a new item and was needed to clarify the question of who was in the category "shaykhs of the shrine" and therefore entitled to a share in the votives.

THE STRUCTURE OF THE ADMINISTRATION

We turn now to the third section of the farman, which lists each of the offices at the shrine, the number of officeholders, and the salary of each officeholder. The reason for the inclusion of this list, besides simply confirming the designated officeholders was to make clear who, as recipient of a government salary, was ineligible for a share in the Eight-Paykal Waqf income (a discussion of which forms the last part of the farman).

The offices of the shrine, in the order they are given in the farman, are summarized in the table.

Shrine Offices According to the 1889 Farman

		Salary	
Office	Number of Officials	Tangahs (+ Grain [mann])	Percent Votive Offerings[a]
1. *Amin*	1	1,500	4.8
Staff	10	100 (ea.)	0.167 (ea.)
2. *Nazir*	1	1,000	0.167
Staff	10	100 (ea.)	0.167 (ea.)
3. Treasurer (*sanduqdar*)	1	500	0.167
Staff	5	200 (ea.)	0.167 (ea.)
4. Head Custodian (*farrash-bashi*)	1	800	0.167
Staff	50	100	0.167 (ea.)
5. Keeper of the keys (*kilidar*)	1	300	0.167
Staff	2	80 (ea.)	0.167 (ea.)
6. Imam (*Uzbaki*)	1	240 + 22	0.167
Na'ib	1	210 + 11	0.167
Muezzin	6	100 (ea.)	0.167
Imam (*Afghani*)	1	200	—
Na'ib	1	200	—
7. Gatekeepers (*darbanan*)	7		
Hukumat Khan		170 + 4	0.167
Ulugh Beg		60 + 2	0.167
Khwajah Jan		40 + 4	0.167
4 others		40 + 2 (ea.)	0.167 (ea.)
8. Head sweeper (*chandalbashi*)	1	200	0.167
Staff	8	60	0.167 (ea.)

[a] Only for those of Ansari lineage.

The shrine administration was divided into five main departments, the heads of which (amin, nazir, treasurer, head custodian, and keeper of the keys) made up a board of governors, and three lesser departments (imams and muezzins, gatekeepers, and sweepers), the senior members of which were not part of the governing board.

I infer the existence of such a board from the format of the 1889 document, although it does not explicitly identify one. Instead, the section it devotes to the administration begins with a list of seven officials, five of whom are the heads of what are clearly the main departments and the other two of whom (apparently staff of the board) are secretaries (*muharrir, nawisandah*). This group I believe constituted the governing board. The document then separately lists the employees attached to each of the five in order. Finally, it lists the three other departments, beneath the five main sections and in a smaller script, perhaps to indicate their lower status in the administration. The names of the employees of each of these three divisions are arranged in separate parallel columns on the farman directly below the names of their respective sections.[8]

The Amin

The working head of the administration in 1889 is given the title "amin" in the farman. Although it appears here for the first time as the title of the head of the shrine administration, it is probably derived from the standard legal formulation that a mutawalli must be "qadir wa amin" ("competent and trustworthy").[9] There is no difference in function between mutawalli and amin. But since 'Abd al-Rahman had named himself chief mutawalli, it perhaps was necessary for him to assign the former mutawalli another title. That the two were synonymous as far as the actual administration of the shrine is concerned may be seen by the fact that at one point in the farman the amin is referred to as the mutawalli.[10]

The decree states that the salary of the amin was fifteen hundred tangahs, which was paid not by the treasury of the shrine itself but by the state, specifically the Daftar Khanah-i Padshahi (State Accounting Office). The farman does not say whether the salaries listed are monthly or annual salaries; however, after comparing them with contemporary state salaries, I conclude with some uncertainty that the figures represent annual amounts. In comparison with other official salaries, fifteen hundred tangahs per year was fairly modest. In 1882–1883, top army officers received salaries in the range of five to ten thousand Kabuli rupees[11] (the Kabuli rupee was then equivalent to three tangahs)[12] or some ten to

---

[8] Ibid., 75. The document gives salaries, in both grain and money, in *siyaq* notation. I have relied on the reading made by the editor and transcriber of the document, Hafiz Nur Muhammad.

[9] Qadri Pasha 1902, article 144.

[10] *TMS*, 72 (text), 77 (transcription).

[11] Fayd Muhammad Katib 1913–15, 3:420.

[12] Gregorian 1969, Appendix B has compiled the available European and British Indian material on monetary values. On the relative value of the tangah, see also Mir Mohammed

twenty times the amin's salary. In 1883, the mirshabb (chief of the night-
watchmen) of Herat was paid a salary about triple the designated salary
of the mutawalli.[13] In 1889, governors of small provinces received approximately two thousand rupees (equivalent to six thousand tangahs).[14]
At first glance, the salary of the amin, the head of a bureaucracy with
more than one hundred employees, appears rather meager. But the state
salary was probably little more than a token of his subordination to the
Afghan administration. His real income came from his 4.8 percent of the
gross votive income (nudhurat).

The office of amin was held by Mirza Abu'l-Hayy Ansari, a descendant
through the male line of Mirza 'Aziz Khan. Mirza Abu'l-Hayy had a personal staff of ten, each of whom received a salary of one hundred tangahs
supplemented by a share in the votive income. Eight of the ten members
of Mirza Abu'l-Hayy's staff were also agnatic descendants of Mirza 'Aziz
Khan. A ninth, Mirza Nizam al-Din, may also have been an 'Azizi. In the
list of officials on or associated with the governing board, a Nizam al-Din
is named as the secretary (nawisandah), but no salary is given for him,
despite the inclusion of his name among those who received a salary
(tankhwah) from the state. This may have been because he was the same
Nizam al-Din listed farther along in the farman as being on the staff of
the amin, for which post he received a one-hundred-tangah salary. In the
second section of the farman, the lists of 'Azizi and Ni'mati Ansaris, a
Nizam al-Din "nawisandah" is listed among the agnatic descendants of
Mirza 'Aziz Khan.

The name of the tenth member of Mirza Abu'l-Hayy's staff, Muhammad Khan, does not appear, at least in that form, on the lists of Ansaris.
If he was not an Ansari, then he was the highest-ranking non-Ansari employed at the shrine.

The farman does not define the specific duties of the amin's staff. Nizam al-Din seems to have been clerk or secretary to the board. The rest
no doubt served the kinds of administrative functions one would expect
of the staff of the manager of a large institution.

The Nazir

The exact function of the nazir at the 'Alid shrine is uncertain at this
point. In the Muslim West, the title had long served to designate the
overall manager of a waqf. In Mamluk Egypt the jurisdiction of the nazir

---

Monshi 1901, 1:39, note. Fayd Muhammad Katib 1913–15, 3:916 mentions that in 1892–93
a single qarakul pelt cost nearly ten tangahs. The value of the tangah before the end of the
eighteenth century is discussed by Ivanov 1954, 49, note.

[13] Fayd Muhammad Katib 1913–15, 3:420.

[14] Ibid., 3:534.

included all aspects of the financial management of a waqf—its revenues, appropriations, and record-keeping.[15] At Mazar-i Sharif, the amin, not the nazir, appears to have had overall authority for the shrine and its waqf. There is no clear indication yet of how the nazir and amin cooperated and the duties of each. It is possible that the amin had more responsibility for the shrine itself and the nazir for the waqf, but there is no persuasive evidence yet that such was the case. Their respective salaries and their positions in the list of offices on the farman amply suggest the subordinate position of the nazir. The nazir's staff was at least as large in numbers and overall budget as the amin's[16] but the nazir received a state salary of only one thousand tangahs and a share, equivalent to those of other authentic Ansaris, in the votive offerings. Not only was the amin's state salary 50 percent higher, he was also the beneficiary of the lion's share of the votive offering income.

It is quite possible that the nazir's function was that of controller, his role being to check the fiscal power of the amin by auditing the shrine's accounts. A constant theme in the detailed administrative history of 'Abd al-Rahman Khan's regime written by Fayd Muhammad Katib is administrative mismanagement and allegations of embezzlement and fraud. It would not be surprising at all if the nazir's office performed some kind of oversight function, in line with the meaning of the title itself—supervisor, observer.

We have no evidence that the office predated the arrival of the Afghans in Turkistan or even that it predated Muhammad Ishaq Khan's failed secession attempt. In 1889, the nazir was Mirza Ghulam Haydar Khan, a descendant through the male line of Mirza Ni'mat Khan and the first recorded officeholder. The appointment of a Ni'mati as nazir is circumstantial evidence for the argument that the office audited the performance of other shrine departments on behalf of the state. As will be discussed more fully shortly, the dominant position of the 'Azizis, in shrine offices as well as in sheer numbers, would have made a Ni'mati a logical choice to serve as an auditor on behalf of the state.

We have no information as to the recipient of the nazir's reports, if any. The Daftar Khanah-i Padshahi is one possibility. But far more likely is 'Abd al-Rahman Khan himself, a man of paranoid tendencies with intelligence agents (*waqayi'-nigaran*) working throughout the country, whose appetite for information on the performance of his officials was nearly insatiable.

[15] Fernandes 1988, 60–63.

[16] The daftar list (intended for the records of the Daftar Khanah-i Padshahi) in the 1889 farman lists ten assistants to the nazir, the same number as on the amin's staff. The genealogical lists in the farman, however, identify twelve persons as "attached to the nazir."

The Sanduqdar

The third-ranking department (following the order given in the farman) was the treasury (sanduq). From the farman we know that the treasury was where all cash revenues, from votives, rents, and waqf, were deposited. Goods brought as offerings were also under the treasury's jurisdiction. The sanduq also contained the shrine archives, for the 1889 edict mentions a previous farman that was in the "sanduqkhanah," the treasury building. A photograph from the 1940s shows what appears to be a hexagonal one-story annex to the main shrine complex on its east side, called the "treasury" (khizanah), perhaps the same as the sanduqkhanah.[17]

In 1889, the treasurer was Mirza Muhammad Khan, an agnatic descendant of Mirza Ni'mat Khan. He received a government salary of five hundred tangahs. He had a staff of five whose combined salaries were budgeted at one thousand tangahs.[18]

The farman charges the treasurer with the collection and allocation of funds according to the prescribed formulas. It leaves open the question of whether the rental income should also be included with the votive offerings, a point that lends weight to the hypothesis that the rental income was not very significant. Noncash income in the form of carpets, gilims, tomb covers, and gold and silver objects was inventoried, stored, and presumably used where appropriate.

Although the farman does not specifically charge the treasurer with the Eight-Paykal Waqf accounts, someone had to collect, record, and distribute those revenues, and the sanduqdar seems an obvious choice. Perhaps the earlier, reportedly more detailed, farman contained those instructions.

The Farrashbashi

In 1889, the office of custodian (farrashbashi) was held by Ichildi Khan, an agnatic descendant of Mirza 'Aziz Khan. His department was the largest at the shrine. It had a staff of fifty employees, each of whom received a one-hundred-tangah salary. Ichildi Khan was paid eight hundred tangahs as well as his share in the votive offerings. The department he headed was, judging by his title, responsible for the physical plant, the grounds and buildings of the shrine, furnishings, maintenance, and renovation.

---

[17] TMS, 95.

[18] In the transcribed text (TMS, 82), the editor, Hafiz Nur Muhammad, has entered the figure 400 next to the name Ataliq, as if indicating that this individual received four hundred of the one thousand tangahs allocated to the entire staff. This number does not appear on the photographic reproduction of the text, although now-illegible smudges might indicate its presence. The term Ataliq does appear here to be a proper name and not a title.

The Kilidar

The smallest of the five departments whose heads formed the governing board was under the "keeper of the keys," the kilidar, Mulla Baba Khan. Its function is self-evident. The head keeper received three hundred tangahs in salary and his two assistants earned eighty tangahs each.

The Muharrir and the Nawisandah

The last two men associated with the governing board, the muharrir (recorder), Mulla Rahmat Allah, and the nawisandah (scribe or clerk), Mirza Nizam al-Din, had no staffs of their own.

The Imams and Muezzins

According to the order of listing in the farman, the first of the departments without representation on the governing board, and the only one with ceremonial duties, comprised two imams, two assistant imams, and six muezzins.[19] (The imams conducted the ritual prayers—the *salat*—and the muezzins called the believers to prayer at each of the five daily prayer periods.)

The first entry in this column under the heading "imam [*sic*] and muezzins" is the figure of 450 tangahs and 33 mann of grain. This represents the combined salaries of the next two offices listed, although why they should stand alone while the individual salaries are also listed is not clear. Next comes the heading "Uzbaki," beneath which are the names of one of the imams and one of the assistant imams with their salaries. Next, six names are listed without titles. These are the muezzins. Although they are not identified by title, three of the six appear in the list of Ansaris with the title "muezzin" next to their names. Below the six muezzins is the heading "Afghani" and beneath that two more names. Although no title is appended to either name, I have assumed that the first is an imam and the second an assistant imam, both on the evidence of their salaries (which are twice as high as those of the muezzins and comparable to those of the "Uzbaki" imam and assistant imam) and on the grounds that the heading "Afghani" is meant to be analogous to the heading "Uzbaki" and the names beneath the latter intended as the counterparts of those beneath the former.

By *Uzbaki* seems to have been meant only a long-standing resident of Mazar-i Sharif. There is no evidence that the term had anything to do with ethnicity. Both the Uzbaki imam and his assistant (*na'ib-i imam*)

---

[19] In transcribing the text, Hafiz Nur Muhammad moved the sweepers (chandalan) ahead of the imams and muezzins (*TMS*, 83), although the text clearly places the latter first.

were agnatic descendants of Mirza Ni'mat Khan though their lineage went back to Khwajah 'Abd Allah Ansari. There is no link with the concept of Uzbek as it is used for the Turkish-speaking peoples of northern Afghanistan and Central Asia.

Similarly, there is little to suggest that the term *Afghani* referred to anything more specific than more recent arrivals in Mazar-i Sharif, perhaps individuals associated with the settling of Pushtuns in northern Afghanistan. We do not know the lineages of the two men in this category (they do not appear in the lists of Ansaris), and their names, Mir 'Alam and Mir Kamal, provide no clues to their ethnic origin.

The Uzbaki imam, Mirza 'Aziz, was paid a salary made up of both a cash stipend of 240 tangahs and a 22-mann allocation of grain.[20] His assistant, Mulla Mir Kamal, earned 210 tangahs and 11 mann of grain. Their Afghani counterparts each received 200 tangahs with no grain allocation. In addition to their higher salaries, the Uzbaki imam and his na'ib also received a share in the votive offerings.

The six muezzins received state salaries of one hundred tangahs each. Three of them, 'Abd al-Sa'id, Ghiyath al-Din, and Mirza (or Mir) Muhammad, were Ansaris and thus also entitled to a share (0.167 percent) of the votive income each year.

The Darbanan

Another department without a board representative was that of the gatekeepers (darbanan). There were seven gatekeepers receiving salaries from the state. Although none is singled out as the head gatekeeper, there is a gradation in salaries. The highest paid was Hukumat Khan, who received 170 tangahs and 4 mann of grain, two and a half times more than the next highest paid, Ulugh Beg Khan, who received 60 tangahs and 2 mann. The other five—Khwajah Khurd Turk, Khwajah Jan, Mirza Sanjar, Sulayman Khan, and Amir Khan—each received 40 tangahs and 2 mann of grain, except for Khwajah Jan, whose grain allocation was 4 mann.

The Chandalan

The last of the smaller departments was composed of the sweepers (chandalan). The head sweeper, the *chandalbashi*, was Muhammad Akram, who received a salary from the state of two hundred tangahs. He super-

---

[20] According to Gregorian 1969, Appendix B, a Mazari mann was equivalent to some 427.5 pounds avoirdupois; 22 mann would thus have amounted to more than 4 tons. Even using Kabuli equivalents, the amount would have been nearly 1½ tons. *Gaz.* 4:11 and 262 says that the Mazari mann was equivalent to 4 maunds and 20 seer (British Indian weight), or about 368 pounds avoirdupois.

vised a group of eight sweepers who received salaries of sixty tangahs each.

. . .

This completes the picture of the shrine administration as set out in the 1889 farman. Except perhaps for the office of nazir, the offices and their functions were long-standing ones. The structure of the administration shows the extent now of the penetration of the state into the operations of the shrine. At the highest level, the state had given its jurisdictional claims institutional form in the office of the nazir. And at all levels, from amin down to sweeper and doorkeeper, the state's influence was assured through the salaries it paid.

The shrine administration had undergone a fundamental change from its days of effective independence in the seventeenth and eighteenth centuries and its real, if not necessarily desired, autonomy from the middle of the eighteenth to the middle of the nineteenth centuries. By 1889, there is little question about the right of the state, through its provincial government, to set policy for the shrine.

But as in any such institution in which a potential exists for forming new loyalties and coalitions, it was not enough to simply decree structure, salary, and policy. Behind what is set down on paper, one can make out other dynamics at work in the process of the incorporation of the shrine under state control.

There are at least three discernible phenomena in the farman that hint at the options available to the state, here personified by the amir, 'Abd al-Rahman, in its efforts to eliminate independent institutions. One of these is finding and exploiting internal divisions. In the case of the Ansari family, the farman recognizes and in a way formalizes the Ansari factions of the 'Azizis and Ni'matis. The second phenomenon is the official recognition of Ansari entitlements vis-à-vis the votive and waqf income. The third, somewhat more problematic, is the issue, only vaguely hinted at, of local tensions and divisions between the Afghan newcomers and the older Turkic-speaking Uzbek and Persian-speaking Tajik populations.

The first issue, formalizing and thereby officially exploiting the 'Azizi-Ni'mati divisions within the family, is revealed in the second section of the farman, where a list is given of 257 male Ansaris at the shrine on or about 22 July 1889. (The fact that one man named in the list is described as having died, probably after the list was drafted, and that three others are "Bukhara-gone"[21] is indirect evidence that the rest were alive and living at Mazar-i Sharif.) The purpose of the list was to establish eligibility

---

[21] *TMS*, 73 (text), 79 and 81 (transcription).

for a share in the cash votive income and in the Eight-Paykal Waqf revenues. People whose names were on the list were entitled to both kinds of income, except for those who received a state salary as officials at the shrine. They were not permitted to draw from the waqf revenues.

The list has four unequal sections. The first, and by far the longest (somewhat more than 60 percent of the whole) contains the names of 158 agnatic descendants (*awlad-i pasari*) of Mirza ʿAziz Khan, who flourished, as far as we can tell, during the second half of the eighteenth century. The second section has the names of 56 descendants of Mirza ʿAziz Khan through the female line. In the third section are listed the names of 19 agnatic descendants of Mirza (Khwajah) Niʿmat Khan, mutawalli of the shrine during the Nadirid occupation (1737–1747). The fourth and final section has the names of Mirza Niʿmat Khan's cognatic descendants, 24 in all.

Since the whole list includes the titles of those who were officials at the shrine, a comparison of it with the third section of the farman, the organizational chart of the shrine, is an obvious way of determining, first, how extensive, Ansari control of the shrine was, second, how much of a part the ʿAzizi-Niʿmati division played in the composition of the shrine administration, and third, the importance of non-Ansaris in the administration.

Before collating these lists, however, certain problems arising from discrepancies between them must be resolved. One of the more perplexing is that a name appearing with an official title on the first list, the list of male Ansaris, does not always appear on the organizational chart. For example, two agnatic descendants of Mirza ʿAziz Khan, Mirza Padshah and Mirza Khwajah, and Saʿd al-Din Khan, a cognatic descendant of Mirza ʿAziz Khan, are all characterized on the Ansari list as "attached to the nazir" (*taʿalluq-i nazir*). Their names do not appear, however, on the organizational chart among those "attached to the nazir." But it is among the custodial staff (farrashan) that the problem is most pronounced. There seven persons described as "farrash" in the Ansari list do not reappear in the organizational table. Five of them are of the male-descent line from Mirza ʿAziz Khan and two are through his female line.

A potential resolution of this problem is to ignore attributions of office given in the Ansari list unless the person is also included on the organizational chart. There is one compelling reason for arriving at this solution. The organizational chart lists state salaries along with the names. Although the Ansari list also had revenue implications (eligibility for votive and waqf income), the organizational chart would probably have been more carefully scrutinized and kept current by provincial officials because state monies were involved.

A related problem arises from the fact that titles are usually, but not always, included on the Ansari list, thereby raising the question of whether the same individual was actually meant when the title did not appear. For instance, there is a sweeper named Jalal on the organizational chart receiving sixty tangahs. Among the 'Azizis is a man named Mirza Jalal, sans title. Likewise, there is a certain 'Adalat listed among the farrashan. The same name is given among the 'Azizis but without the title.

Since the numbers involved here are small, and since the reliability of the title attribution in the first list is in some doubt, to remain consistent with the principle that the organizational chart is probably more reliable, I have assumed that identical names refer to the same individual when no title is given in the Ansari list.

The last problem in collating the two lists is orthographic, involving slight variations in the name from one list to the other. The most common variation is the omission of honorific, as opposed to job, titles, such as "mirza" or "khan," in either the organizational chart or the Ansari family list. There are also problems in the placement of diacritics, part of which may be the fault of the scribe and part due to faulty reading by the author of *Tarikh-i Mazar-i Sharif*, Hafiz Nur Muhammad. There are names for which the unpointed orthography is identical: Yar Khan, a farrash, appears as Nar Khan, farrash, on the Ansari list (neither pointing is clear from the document facsimile), and Ghulam Khan, farrash, on the organizational table appears as Ghulam Jan on the Ansari family list. Other names show greater discrepancies from one list to the other, for example Sharaf and Sharraf, Mirza Warith and Warith Shah.

In order to resolve this problem, I have had to rely to some extent on the title attribution on the Ansari family list. In all cases where a name appearing with a job title on the Ansari list can be reasonably identified with a similar name under the appropriate departmental heading on the organizational chart, I have accepted the two as identical. The line has been drawn, however, at identifying such names as Fayd al-Din with Fadl al-Din, Mirza Hamid with Mirza Ahmad, or 'Izzat Khan with 'Aziz Allah or A'izz al-Din. In these latter cases, the orthographic changes are so major as to rule out identification.

THE ANSARIS: 'AZIZI AND NI'MATI

The most striking finding from a collation of the Ansari family list and the organizational chart is the wholly dominant and nearly exclusive position of the Ansari family in the shrine administration. As organized in 1889, there were 109 official salaried positions at the shrine. Among these we can identify at least 83 Ansaris, following the above criteria.[22] Moreover, the Ansari hold was disproportionately tight on the upper echelons of the administration. Every department head from the amin down to the head sweeper was an Ansari. Only among the religious functionaries, the imams and muezzins, and the contingent of sweepers did the number of non-Ansaris equal (in the former case) or outnumber (in the latter) that of Ansaris.

In terms of their share in the salaries budgeted for the shrine, the Ansaris' position again was disproportionate to their overall numbers. Although they held 75 percent of the offices at the shrine, they received some 80 percent of the amount paid in cash by the state (11,750 out of 14,820 tangahs) and 100 percent of the grain allocations (51 mann). In addition, unlike their non-Ansari colleagues, they received shares in the votive offerings.

Those Ansaris without official title (168 if we include the 12 given a title in the Ansari list but not found on the organizational chart) received both a votive share and a share in the waqf revenues.

It should be remembered that the 1889 farman was prompted by the reorganization of the administration of Afghan Turkistan following Muhammad Ishaq's failed attempt at creating an independent region. From the decree, it would appear that neither the rebellion nor the reorganization that came in its wake noticeably affected the position of the Ansari family. The shrine's history shows that the mutawalli usually trimmed his sails to the prevailing political winds, was discreet in his political allegiances, and was usually predisposed to support whatever group seemed likely to be permanently in power in the region. We can assume, therefore, that the eight-year tenure of Muhammad Ishaq Khan at Mazar-i Sharif was supported by the shrine administration.

Yet we find that in the Ansari list only 3 of the 257 family members are described as "Bukhara-gone." (Muhammad Ishaq and his loyalists first took refuge in Bukhara after their defeat at the hands of 'Abd al-Rahman's forces.) Whether the "going to Bukhara" by Qari Nasir Khan, Muhyi al-Din Khan, and Mir Ayyub was associated with Muhammad Ishaq's defeat is not clear. In any event, by the time the farman of 22 July 1889 was drafted, the Ansaris as a whole had sufficiently ingratiated themselves with the Afghan amir to maintain their administrative hold. Obviously, the long administrative tradition, the expertise it had bred, and the local prominence and influence that must have accrued to it all weighed against any wholesale purge of the shrine administration.

[22] Another dozen or so might be added if we were less stringent about the identification of names—for instance, Ghulam Muhyi al-Din and Mirza Muhyi al-Din, Sayyid 'Ali and Shah 'Ali and similar cases.

But the Afghan amir had the means to shape the administration in such a way as to best insure its future malleability and allegiance. For this he had the instrument of the 'Azizi-Ni'mati factionalism to work with.

Earlier I suggested a cause for the split of the Ansari family into the 'Azizi and Ni'mati factions. To reiterate briefly, up until the tawliyat of Khwajah Ni'mat in the fourth and fifth decades of the eighteenth century, or at least from the late seventeenth century to that point, all indications are that the tawliyat, the office of the mutawalli, had passed from father to son. But either during or immediately after Khwajah Ni'mat's administration, during the turbulent post-Nadirid period, the tawliyat passed, perhaps as the result of a conflict, into the hands of Mirza 'Aziz Khan, not a descendant but a collateral of Khwajah Ni'mat. The evidence for this is circumstantial and based on the recognition of two eponymous Ansari groups in the 1889 farman and on the reduced numbers and status of the Ni'matis in comparison with the 'Azizis by the late nineteenth century. From the second half of the eighteenth century onward, the 'Azizis controlled the major offices of the shrine and thus its revenues, while the Ni'matis were apparently allowed to continue as beneficiaries of various kinds of income, probably what Burnes describes in the 1820s: the gate receipts from votive offerings and perhaps income from the waqf. This tradition was maintained throughout the nineteenth century in such a way as to impell the Afghan amir 'Abd al-Rahman Khan to refer to the Ansaris as the "rightful heirs in equal measure" (warathah 'ala al-sawiyah) to the waqf income and earlier, by inference, to the votives (nudhurat).

The preeminence of the 'Azizis over time is indicated by their overwhelming numerical superiority in 1889, by which time they outnumbered the Ni'matis by almost exactly five to one (214 male 'Azizis to 43 Ni'matis).

The political conditions during the period from the withdrawal of the Nadirid forces and their political claims until the final Afghan conquest and occupation undoubtedly gave impetus to the shift of authority from one line to the other. Besides control of the tawliyat, the 'Azizis, to meet the political exigencies of the time, had to create a full governing apparatus, including a military wing and a fiscal department—a step that in turn would have encouraged any dynastic pretensions. For some three generations, the 'Azizis would have been the sole voice of authority in the shrine region, and it would appear that the effect of this was to disenfranchise and drive away Ni'matis.

If 'Abd al-Rahman's response is indicative, the Afghans found the factionalism and imbalance between the branches of the family very useful. Looked at one way, 'Abd al-Rahman's farman might be seen as an attempt to redress the imbalance by guaranteeing the waqf and votive rights to which both Ni'matis and 'Azizis were entitled. But considered from the standpoint of 'Abd al-Rahman's *realpolitik*, the 1889 farman can be more convincingly viewed as an effort to exploit the division between the two lines in order to strengthen state authority over the shrine administration.

The shrine was dominated by the 'Azizis, of that there should be no question. Three of the five positions on the governing board were held by 'Azizis, including the position of amin, held by Abu'l-Hayy. His own staff of ten included nine 'Azizis and one non-Ansari; the staffs of the other board members showed a similar imbalance between 'Azizis and Ni'matis, one even greater than the 5:1 ratio among Ansaris as a whole. The 'Azizis held seventy-three official positions while the Ni'matis occupied only ten. In terms of salary budgeted, the Ni'matis took home 2,700 tangahs while the 'Azizis received 9,050 (a ratio slightly more favorable, proportionately, to the Ni'matis).

But numbers alone are deceptive and tend to give but one side of the picture. The dominance of the 'Azizis, all other things being equal, was natural considering their numerical superiority. What one should look for in assessing Afghan policies is the placement of Ni'matis in positions of strategic value to the Afghan administration.

The office of nazir draws immediate attention when we look for Ni'mati-held positions of strategic importance. As noted earlier, the title of "nazir" appears in other contexts as a synonym for mutawalli. But at Mazar-i Sharif, the function of mutawalli was now performed by the amin, the title "mutawalli" having evolved into a more ceremonial one when it was assumed by 'Abd al-Rahman Khan. I realize it is somewhat circular to argue that the nazir probably audited and monitored the amin and his administration because the office was held by a Ni'mati, while proposing at the same time that the Ni'matis were used to check the power of the 'Azizis as evidenced by the fact the office of nazir was conferred on them. Nevertheless, the administrative circumstances at Mazar-i Sharif seem to point toward those two conclusions.

Ghulam Haydar Khan, the nazir in 1889, was the lone Ni'mati on the governing board and, as mentioned earlier, was one of only ten Ni'matis in salaried positions, two of whom were on his staff.

Unfortunately, we have no information on how long a Ni'mati had held the position of nazir nor even of how long the office had functioned. The political conditions prior to the Afghan conquest tend to rule out the likelihood that the office or its functions predated 1849. Once the Afghans were ensconced at Mazar-i Sharif during the governorship of Muhammad 'Alam Khan, it is reasonable to assume that some kind of supervisory, or at least liaison, office was set up. The tone of the 1889 farman does not suggest that Ghulam Haydar was a recent appointment, but that may only be because the earlier farman to which it refers established the office.

If, as we have every reason to believe, the Ni'mati nazir, Ghulam Haydar Khan, served to check the abuse of power by the amin, Abu'l-Hayy 'Azizi, his power, too, was subject in turn to checks. His ten-man staff included nine Ansaris, of whom only two were Ni'matis.

The contention that a division between 'Azizi and Ni'mati existed and that it was used by the Afghan government to help assure state authority is supported by another circumstance. The third-ranking official on the shrine's governing board and the one who may have had the most extensive constant and routine contact with the provincial administration was the treasurer (sanduqdar), also a Ni'mati. While the nazir's relations with the state remain somewhat enigmatic, in line with the somewhat covert nature of the position, the treasurer's relations were quite straightforward and rooted in mutual accounting interests. Because the Daftar Khanah-i Padshahi paid the salaries of the shrine officials, there must have been a constant exchange of information between that office and the shrine treasurer. His records of those receiving payments from the Eight-Paykal Waqf had to be periodically correlated with the rolls of the state office to insure that individuals collecting state salaries were not receiving a share of the waqf proceeds. The treasury was the repository of the documentary record for its transactions, and that record had to be revised from time to time to reflect changed circumstances (appointments, dismissals, deaths) that affected state and shrine disbursements.

Further evidence that relations between the shrine treasurer and the Daftar Khanah-i Padshahi were close is the 1889 decree itself. 'Abd al-Rahman could not have put forth such a detailed and comprehensive statement about the shrine's finances had the state not had full access to the shrine's records. To make sure that this cooperation continued, it would have been sensible to have a treasurer whose position at the shrine was, at least in one respect, marginal. Given the minority status of the Ni'matis, it seems fitting that the treasurer is from that lineage. The Ni'matis had had long and close involvement with the shrine. They knew its affairs and its history probably as well as the 'Azizis and certainly better than any outsider could have. If they harbored resentment about their status and their exclusion from the tawliyat since the "succession crisis" of the mid-eighteenth century, so much the more useful for the Afghans.

Besides exploiting internal divisions in the administration, the Afghans encouraged the cooperation of the shrine administration in its absorption into the state bureaucracy by confirming and reasserting Ansari rights to certain entitlements.

The issue of Ansari claims on some of the shrine revenues is murky and raises several questions. In the first place, there is the legal issue of the charter of the charitable trust, the waqf. Were there waqf deeds that stipulated that the Ansari family as administrators of the shrine were also to be the beneficiaries of the waqf income? The only documentary references we find to Ansari rights stipulate the mutawalli's management fee (20 percent in the seventeenth century). Waqf income typically was dedicated to maintaining the object of a trust, paying for renovations, upkeep, and the salaries of ceremonial and custodial employees. It is not difficult to see how, by performing those functions, an individual or group could wind up as the eventual beneficiary of the trust without, in any way, violating legal norms.

But the case of the Ansaris goes beyond this, for we find the 1889 farman assigning waqf revenues "by right" to the Ansaris but limiting that assignment to those who were not employees of the shrine, i.e., those who performed no trust-sanctioned role. We perhaps should not draw the lines too narrowly around what the original deeds did or did not allow, particularly since we do not have them to examine.

What we seem to be seeing in the provisions of the 1889 farman are the consequences of a long tradition in which the Ansaris have become the de facto if not de jure beneficiaries of the waqf revenues, a tradition that the Afghan amir—who elsewhere is reported to have specifically condemned the diversion of waqf monies from the "imams and the mosques"—here is willing not only to tolerate but actually to give official approval to. Why he did so is difficult to say. In all probability, the need to build local loyalties in the wake of the secessionist movement played a major part.

Giving official recognition to Ansari entitlements in the votives presents less of a legal problem, for the kinds of legal stipulations that a waqf entails do not affect such gifts. Again, probably to encourage local support, the amir was willing to regularize an existing practice that rewarded a specific lineage. The fact that the Ansari officials at the shrine also received a share of the votives may have helped hold down the salaries paid by the state.

Another problem raised by the Ansari entitlements is the Ansari list itself. The waqf revenues, according to the farman, were to be divided equally among the heirs. The same is not said about the votives, which may be a clue as to why the list is divided between 'Azizi and Ni'mati and within each of those categories between descent through the son and descent through the daughter. None of those listed, as far as we can tell, are women. Those with "daughter" descent were the male lines succeeding the daughters of the two eponyms.

Succession is one of the most rational of all areas of Islamic law, and perhaps what the list represents is the gender-based inheritance principle of "to the male, the like of two females." That is, male heirs of the female heirs of the eponyms would have a share half as great as that of the male heirs of the male heirs of the eponyms. At this point there is no other more persuasive explanation for the division of the lists. It is possible here that the format of the Ansari list is an old one, merely being used here because it is familiar, with no legal implications attached. Because of the wording of the last section of the farman, in which the waqf shares are assigned on an equal basis, there is at least some indication that the votives are also to be distributed, after the amin's 4.8 percent, on an equal basis, i.e., 1/257th of the 43.2 percent of the gross votive income that was the Ansari share according to 'Abd al-Rahman.

Without being able at this point to discover all that lay behind the provisions of the decree, or to know how much represented new policy and how much a confirmation of an existing state of affairs, it is possible to conclude that the provisions were generous toward the Ansari family as a whole and particularly so toward those employed at the shrine.

The farman shows no evidence of 'Abd al-Rahman's purported policy of "confiscating" waqfs. To the contrary, it reaffirms old waqf rights and acknowledges the Ansari position at the shrine while at the same time establishing the state's claim to jurisdictional precedence in matters pertaining to the shrine.

LOCAL ETHNICITY

How much the farman may be taken as an indicator of ethnic tensions in Afghan Turkistan is a very problematic question. The designation of "Uzbaki" and "Afghani" imams and muezzins is certainly suggestive. But without additional information on Afghan settlement prior to 1889 and the local conflicts it may have created, it is impossible to say anything substantive about the meaning of a double imamate and muezzinate at the shrine.

The *Historical and Political Gazetteer of Afghanistan* shows a heterogeneous population in the Shahi Canal district in the late nineteenth century. Of the 2,745 families said to reside in its villages, 1,385 are called "Uzbak" and 270 "Pathans" or Afghans. Even though the Afghan numbers may not have necessitated an "Afghan" imam, perhaps the fact that they were the politically dominant element in the 1880s did. A recent study of 'Abd al-Rahman's resettlement of Afghan farmers and nomads, especially in the northwestern regions—(Badghis, Bala Murghab, and the Maymanah area) underscores the conflicts that arose between the new settlers and people already on the land.[23] But such documentation still needs to be compiled for the area around Mazar-i Sharif.[24]

MISCELLANEOUS OBSERVATIONS

The farman of 1889 offers a few additional pieces of information that do not fit neatly into any of the above issues but help flesh out the picture of life at the shrine in the 1880s from both a social and an administrative standpoint.

1. Given the long involvement of the Ansari family with the shrine, we would expect that sons would tend to follow fathers in a career at the shrine. The farman contains three instances in which father and son held positions simultaneously. In two cases, both were employed in the same department. Mirza Ahmad and his father, Mirza Muhammad, who were both 'Azizis, served as farrashan. Yar (Nar?) Khan and his father Najm al-Din are also listed as farrashan. Luqman, the son of Munawwar, on the other hand, was a farrash while his father is listed as "attached to the nazir."

2. The Ansari family list has information on men who served in the Afghan military. No other careers are mentioned in the list, and perhaps the reason for inclusion of the names of the army men has to do with their being recipients of a state salary and hence barred from a share in the waqf income. Only 4 of the 257 Ansaris are described as military men. Nasr al-Din Khan, an 'Azizi, was a soldier (nawkar) in a "regular battalion" (paltan-i nizam). Another 'Azizi, Muhammad Khan b. Baba Khan (a farrash?) is characterized as attached to "a battalion" (ta'alluq-i paltan).[25] Mirza Yunus and Qamar Khan b. Amir Khan were both cavalrymen, Qamar Khan in the "Qandahar Troop" (risalah-i Qandahar)[26] and Mirza Yunus in an unspecified troop.

3. One of the Ansaris, an 'Azizi named Turah, the son of 'Ala al-Din, is described in the farman as "majdhub," literally "drawn" or "attracted" (to

---

[23] Tapper 1983.

[24] Mukhtarov 1980, 6–7 has information on the involuntary migrations into and out of Balkh in the latter part of the nineteenth and early twentieth centuries.

[25] According to the *Military Report of Afghanistan* (India Office Library 1/MIL/17), a battalion comprised six companies of one hundred men each. For the most recent studies of nineteenth-century Afghan military affairs, see Babakhodzhaev 1970 and Kakar 1979, 93–114.

[26] There was a regular Qandahari infantry regiment (fawj-i piyadah-yi nizam-i Qandahari) in Mazar-i Sharif at this time (Fayd Muhammad Katib 1913–15, 3:657, 772), but I have no information about a cavalry unit.

God). Here it means an ascetic, probably an extreme anchorite. Of all the Ansaris on the list as well as the non-Ansaris employed at the shrine, only he and the religious functionaries at the shrine (the imams and muezzins and their assistants) are accorded spiritual attributes or titles. Perhaps the drafter of the farman added the word "majdhub" as a memo to government or shrine officials so that they would not be surprised if he failed to collect his waqf and votive shares. The adjective may also have been added because Turah represented such a contrast to the other members of his family and to his ancestors.

CHAPTER FOURTEEN

Conclusions

THE FARMAN of 1889 marked the end of one phase and the beginning of another in the evolution of the shrine and its waqf. The history of the shrine in the century since 'Abd al-Rahman issued his decree awaits study and analysis. It is probably safe, if not very imaginative, to assume that the shrine, which remains a preeminent regional institution, and its economy have continued to evolve and adapt to changing economic, social, and political conditions. Change and adaptation are the constant themes of the shrine's long history. From the rediscovery of the gravesite of 'Ali b. Abi Talib in 1480 and its endowment until the attempt by the Afghan amir to bring it under state regulation four hundred years later, the shrine and its economic underpinnings, the corpus of waqf endowments, underwent a process of often gradual but sometimes rapid and unexpected transformation.

From the end of the fifteenth to the end of the nineteenth century, the region of Balkh, later Afghan Turkistan, witnessed numerous and occasionally dramatic political changes. The legacy of the Mongol world-conqueror, Chingiz Khan, in the form of political structures—the system of appanages, the khanate with its succession by seniority, and the amirid class—left the most influential imprint on popular political thought. The realm of the possible and the limits of the permissible in politics were shaped by the ideas and the ideals introduced by the Chingizids. Not until the very end of the period, that is, toward the middle of the nineteenth century, were those vestiges of the Chingizid mandate that were still operative supplanted by a new political reality, the Muhammadza'i Afghan mandate.

The shrine administration was, of course, affected, and its operating procedures in large measure determined, by the political conditions under which it lived. The mutawallis routinely sought confirmation of their prerogatives from the authorities at Balkh, both at moments of political succession there and when a new mutawalli succeeded to leadership of the shrine. The administrators relied on the shrine's aura to elicit financial and political support from the wealthy and powerful. As the shrine's wealth increased, its own political influence was enhanced. Signs of the shrine's importance to the political authorities and its mutual reliance on their backing may be seen at least as early as the middle of the seventeenth century in the now somewhat obscured but obviously important part played by the shrine in the Moghul occupation of Balkh. Far clearer are the actions of the shrine administration a century later when an Iranian army conquered and then occupied Balkh for a decade. The shrine administrators openly supported the Iranian efforts to keep order during this period, but were equally ready to withdraw that support when indications appeared that Iranian control over the region was becoming untenable.

The foundation of the shrine's wealth and thus the ultimate material basis of its influence were its waqf properties, the main form in which the shrine received and managed its wealth. Waqf proved remarkably durable as a way in which to maintain capital. An inherent contradiction in the institution, the irreconcilability of the legal notion of waqf as permanent and immutable with the impermanent nature of all material things, always had to be overcome. When any individual waqf survived for long periods, there was a presumption of periodic capital reinvestment, new capital infusion, or some transformation of the original use of the waqf to a more efficient form. For an endowed institution, longevity and permanence meant continually finding new income, new endowments, or new ways to increase the income of existing endowments. In the case of the 'Alid shrine at Balkh, new sources of income came from the votive offerings brought by pilgrims, fees collected from shrine users, and occasional tax remissions or exemptions (in Subhan Quli's manshur, tax exemptions appear at the forefront, while they play no role in the farman issued by 'Abd al-Rahman Khan). The conversion of waqf property to more lucrative uses provided additional new capital: the development of Mazar-i Sharif as the main commercial center of Afghan Turkistan in the nineteenth century undoubtedly increased the shrine's share of commercial income from rents and fees.

It was not enough just to protect waqf property from the ravages of time and nature. Unremitting efforts had to be made to be protect the properties from human encroachments as well. This seems to have been particularly true when the rubric "waqf" encompassed revenue rights to which government officials also laid claim. The reconfirmations sought for the rights of the shrine vis-à-vis this part of its waqf during the early part of the eighteenth century depict the presence of, or the potential for, this kind of conflict between waqf administrators and tax collectors.

Success in the incessant jockeying for rights and prerogatives and then, once they were gained, in maintaining them required skillful management. As a group, the mutawallis of the 'Alid shrine displayed the requisite administrative ability. As managers of a large economic entity, they also needed some political aptitude. They had to be able to summon support when needed and to cultivate those same forces during the times when direct assistance or intervention was not needed.

This combination of political savvy and administrative know-how created the philosophical and institutional prerequisites of a quasi-state apparatus, at least of a fully fledged bureaucracy. Its constitutional base was devotion to and protection of the 'Alid legacy. Its executive arm was the mutawalli and his staff. Its constituents were those who acknowledged the aura and spiritual legacy of the shrine. And its policies evolved to insure the longevity of the first two through the support of the third.

One of these policies addressed the question of succession, the most basic issue for institutional longevity. The origins of the Ansari tawliyat-administration are now obscure. But by 1668 at the latest, the family's right to succeed to leadership of the shrine administration was acknowledged and received official sanction. The Ansari family remained in control of the administration at least to the end of the nineteenth century. The documentary evidence shows a policy of lineal succession. To the extent that we know the course of succession over the two centuries from 1668 until 1885, the rule was for the tawliyat to pass from father to son.

But any institution in which the system of succession determines not only institutional leadership but also decisive control of the institution's wealth will experience some degree of dissension from those constitutionally excluded as well as some pressure to revise the policy of succession in favor of those excluded. When such attempts have sufficient backing, a crisis occurs, and in the ensuing competition, a new policy may indeed be forged. It is clear that in the period after the end of the Iranian occupation just such a succession crisis was played out. Although the evidence as to exactly what happened remains tantalizingly vague, it appears that one line of the Ansaris, the Ni'mati mutawallis, who had held the position for the preceding seventy years at least, were displaced by the 'Azizi line, which maintained its dominance at least until the end of the nineteenth century. We have no evidence that similar crises occurred at other times, but given the less than wholly satisfactory nature of the evidence to begin with, its absence should not be taken as proof that no other crises did occur. In view of what was at stake, it might be safer to assume that the potential if not the reality of a succession crisis and ensuing struggle was always present.

Waqf, its administration, and the institution it is designed to support form, as I have tried to show, an integral whole. It is difficult to speak of one without reference to the circumstances of the other two. To paraphrase Köprülü, it is impossible to understand waqf completely without accounting for its history, administration, and economic, social, and political environment.

Waqf is an Islamic institution made accessible to the historian by its documentary record. But to appreciate fully the way it is woven into the fabric of human society and to assess its place in the achievements of Muslim communities, the documentary record is only a beginning. The temporal and spatial dimensions of waqf, the geographical and historical realities, must also be examined. Waqf deeds form both a legal contract and a statement of hope of the way the founder would like things to be. It is only through other records that touch in one way or another on the waqf in question—narrative histories, biographies, and royal court and Shar'i court decisions—that the degree to which the intent was fulfilled may be seen.

Glossary

ahl al-bayt — The "People of the House," the holy family—the Prophet Muḥam-mad, his daughter Fāṭimah, her husband ʿAlī b. Abī Ṭālib, and their sons, Ḥasan and Ḥusayn.

amīr — Commander; a common title for male members of the Mongol-Turkic groups (the Uzbeks) of the sixteenth through eighteenth centuries. In the nine-teenth century, the official title of the Afghan head of state. See also *mir*.

āsyāb — A water-driven mill.

atālīq — A high amirid official.

aywān, ayvān — See *īwān*.

dārūghah — A police officer or garrison commander.

dharʿ — A cubit; a unit of linear measurement approximately equivalent to the *gaz*. See chapter 2, note 15.

dih — A village.

dīnār — (1) A monetary unit of account. (2) A copper coin.

dīwān — (1) A government office or bureau. (2) The title of a government official.

farmān — A royal decree.

farrāsh — A janitor or custodian.

farsakh (also *farsang*) — A unit of distance approximately equal to six kilometers.

fatwa — A formal legal opinion, issued by a *muftī*.

fiqh — Muslim jurisprudence.

fuqahā (sing. *faqīh*) — Specialists in jurisprudence or *fiqh*.

gaz — A variable unit of linear measurement approximately equivalent to the *dharʿ*. See chapter 2, note 15.

ghāzī — A generic term for a religious warrior.

ghulbah, kulbah, qulbah — The "plow," a unit of surface measurement suppos-edly equivalent to the area that could be plowed by one team of oxen in a given period, such as a season, and approximately equal to twenty-five to thirty acres.

ḥadīth — A saying or action ascribed to the Prophet Muḥammad.

ḥajj — The pilgrimage to Mecca obligatory on all Muslims.

ḥikr — A type of lien on waqf property.

imām — (1) The prayer leader at a mosque. (2) A term of respect for individuals especially accomplished in religious studies. (3) The title of the Shīʿī successors to the Prophet Muḥammad as head of the Islamic community.

ʿināyatnāmah — A decree of confirmation or attestation.

iqrār — A court affidavit or registration of a transaction.

iqṭāʿ — A fief, or region granted with its revenues as a subinfeudation, usually to an *amīr*.

īwān (also *aywan*) — A section of a building opening into the building's courtyard and distinguished by an arched entry (*ṭāq*).

jarīb — A unit of surface measurement approximately equal to one-half acre and equivalent to the *ṭanāb*.

khān — (1) In the sixteenth through eighteenth centuries, the sovereign in a Mongol-Turkic context, a person of Chingīzid descent. (2) In the nineteenth century, a common honorific appended to personal names. (3) In architecture, a commercial building, warehouse, or caravansary.

khānaqāh — A hostel usually associated with a Ṣūfī order.

kharwār — Literally, a donkey load. A unit of weight, usually two-thirds of an *ushturwār*.

khaṭīb — The mosque official who delivers the *khuṭbah*.

khums — Literally, "one-fifth," a tax associated with land and with spoils of war.

khuṭbah — The homily delivered at the Friday congregational service, in the course of which the current head of state was traditionally recognized by name.

khwājah — A common title for members of Central Asian religious orders.

madrasah — A college or seminary.

maḥfal, majlis — An assembly or gathering.

mālah — A harrow.

mamlakah — A country, state, or kingdom. A favorite term in pre-modern Central Asia for the realm.

mann — A unit of weight. See chapter 13, note 20.

manshūr — A royal decree.

masjid — A parish or quarter mosque.

masjid-i jāmiʻ — A congregational mosque or Friday mosque.

maṣlaḥah — The legal concept of a "general good" or "common weal."

mazār — A shrine; the place where one performs *ziyārat*.

miḥrāb — The niche in the mosque that indicates the direction of the Kaʻbah in Mecca, hence the direction to face when praying.

mīr — The short form of *amīr* and *mīrzā*.

mīrzā (contraction of *amīrzādah* = "born of an amir") — (1) In the fifteenth century, the title of a Tīmūrid prince. (2) In the sixteenth through nineteenth centuries, a title in more generalized use among scholars and bureaucrats.

muezzin (muʾadhdhin) — The mosque official who gives the call to prayer.

muftī — A person learned in the law (*Sharīʻah*) who issues legal opinions (*fatwas*).

muḥtasib — A market inspector.

mullā, mullāh (variant of *mawlā*) — In the nineteenth century, a common title for local religious leaders.

mutawallī — The chief trustee or administrator of a waqf foundation.

nadhr (pl. *nudhūr, nudhūrāt*) — Votive offerings of cash or gifts brought to a shrine.

nahr — A large canal.

naqīb — A high office associated with the royal court, usually held by an individual with credentials in law and religious learning.

parwānajī — The court official (generally an *amīr*) responsible for delivering *parwānahs* (royal investitutres, grant deeds).

paykāl — A unit of irrigated land. See chapter 12.

pīshṭāq — An arched entryway.

qaʻalkhān, qaʻlkhān — The heir-apparent to the khanate.

qāḍī — A Muslim judge.

qāḍī al-quḍāt, aqḍā al-quḍāt — A Muslim chief judge.

qariyah — A village or hamlet.

qaṣīdah — A type of poem.

quriltāy (also *kangāsh, kūrunush*) — An assembly or convention of Chingizids.

riwāq — An arcade or cloister.

ṣadaqah — A voluntary gift for a charitable purpose.

ṣandūq — A treasury.

ṣandūqdār — A treasurer.

sardār — A male member of one of the ruling Afghan clans in the eighteenth and nineteenth centuries.

shāh, pādshāh — The king or sovereign in an Irano-Islamic context.

sharʿī — Pertaining to the *Sharīʿah*.

Sharīʿah — Literally, "The Way:" Islamic law.

shaykh — (1) A leader of a Ṣūfi order. (2) A well-regarded religious personage in general. (3) One of the high officers at the ʿAlid shrine in the fifteenth and sixteenth centuries.

shaykh al-islām — In the sixteenth and seventeenth centuries, a high appointive office for the learned.

shurūṭ (sing. *sharṭ*) — Conditions, stipulations. In law, forms and formularies.

siyāq — A system of bureaucratic notation for rendering numbers in letter form.

suknā — Development rights on waqf or other property not controlled by the developer.

sūl — See *ūng and sūl*

sulṭān — Specifically in the sixteenth through eighteenth centuries in Central Asia, a male of Chingīzid lineage.

suyūrghāl — A tax revenue grant usually for services rendered or anticipated.

ṭanāb — A unit of surface measurement approximately equal to one-half acre and equivalent to the *jarīb*.

tangah — (1) A monetary unit of account. (2) A silver coin.

ṭāq — An arch.

tawliyat — The trusteeship or administration of a waqf (held by the *mutawallī*).

tiyūl — A tax revenue grant usually for services rendered or anticipated.

tūmān — (1) A quantity of 10,000, used to denote military and monetary units. (2) In Central Asian administration, a district or subdivision of a province.

tūrah — (1) Mongol customary law. (2) A Chingīzid prince.

ʿulamā — (sing. *ʿālim*) — Muslim scholars, the learned class.

ūlūs, ulūs — In the Mongol context, a people given to a Chingīzid prince. Generally, a distinct group of people or a tribal organization.

ūng and sūl — The right and left wings of the army.

ʿushr — A tithe; a tax associated with land.

ushturwār (*shuturwār*) — Literally, a camel load. A unit of weight equal to ten *mann*.

uymāq (*aymāq*) — A tribal organization.

waqfnāmah (*waqfiyah*) — A waqf document, usually a charter or foundation deed.

yarlīgh — A royal decree.

yāsā, yāsāq, yāsā and yūsūn — The formal and customary political and penal law attributed to Chingiz Khan.

yūrt, yūrtgāh — The territory of an *amīr* or Chingīzid *sulṭān*.

zakāt — The Muslim obligatory alms tax.

ziyārat — A pilgrimage to a shrine (*mazār*) and the rituals associated with it.

Bibliography

'Abd Allāh b. Muḥammad 'Ali Naṣr Allāh. 1904. *Zubdat al-athar*. Excerpted and translated by V. V. Barthold in "Otchet o komandirovke v Turkestan." *Zapiski Vostochnogo otdeleniia Russkogo Arkheologicheskogo Obshchestva*, 15 (2–3). Reprinted in his *Sochineniia*, vol. 8, 119–210 (130–45 for the selections from *Zubdat al-athar*). Moscow, 1973.

'Abd al-Razzāq b. Isḥāq al-Samarqandī. 1941–44. *Maṭla' al-sa'dayn wa majma'-i baḥrayn*. Lahore.

Abdur Rahim. 1937. "Mughal Relations with Central Asia." *Islamic Culture* (Hyderabad) 9:81–94, 188–99.

Abduraimov, M. A. 1970. *Ocherki agrarnykh otnoshenii v Bukharskom khanstve*, vol. 2, Tashkent.

Abū Yūsuf [Abū Yūsuf Ya'qūb b. Ibrāhīm al-Anṣārī]. 1969. *Kitab al-kharaj*. Translated by A. Ben Shemesh as *Taxation in Islam*, vol. 3. Leiden.

Abū'l-Fidā. 1970. *Taqwīm al-buldān*. Translated into Persian by 'Abd al-Muḥammad Ayātī. Tehran, A.H. 1349 (A.D. 1970).

Abū'l-Faḍl al-'Allāmī. 1897–1939. *The Akbar Nama of Abu'l-Fazl*. 3 vols. Translated from Persian by H. Beveridge. Fourth Indian reprint. New Delhi 1987.

Abū'l-Ghāzī. 1871–74. *Shajarah-yi Turk (Histoire des Mongols et des Tartares par Aboul-Ghazi Behadour Khan)*. 2 vols. in 1. Edited and translated by Baron P. I. Desmaisons. St. Petersburg. (Vol. 1 is the Chaghatay text; vol. 2, the translation.)

Adamec, Ludwig W., ed. 1972–79. *Historical and Political Gazetteer of Afghanistan*. 6 vols. Graz. Vol. 1 (1972), *Badakhshan Province and Northeastern Afghanistan*. Vol. 4 (1979), *Mazar-i Sharif and Northern Afghanistan*.

Adamec, Ludwig W. 1975. *Who's Who of Afghanistan*. Graz.

Afghānī Nawīs, 'Abd Allāh. 1961. *Lughāt-i 'Amyānah-i Fārsī Afghānistān*. Kabul, A.H. 1340 (A.D. 1961).

Akhmedov, B. A. 1965. *Gosudarstvo Kochevykh Uzbekov*. Moscow.

Akhmedov, B. A. 1982. *Istoriia Balkha (XVI–pervaia polovina XVII v.)*. Tashkent.

Akhmedov, B. A. 1985. *Istoriko-geograficheskaia literatura Srednei Azii XVI–XVII vv. (Pis'mennye pamiatniki)*. Tashkent.

Akimushkin, O. A. 1970. "K voprosu o vneshnepoliticheskikh sviazakh Mogol'skogo gosudarstua s Uzbekami i Kazakhami v 30-kh godakh XVI v.–60-kh godakh XVII v." *Palestinskii sbornik*, 21:233–48.

Allan, J. 1978. "Khatam." *EI(2)*, vol. 4. Leiden.

Allen, Terry. 1981. *A Catalogue of Toponyms and Monuments of Timurid Herat*. Cambridge, Mass.

Aminova, R. Kh., M. A. Akhunova, Ia. G. Guliamov, K. E. Zhitov, Kh. Z. Ziiaev, Kh. Sh. Inoiatov, T. N. Kary-Niiazov, I. M. Muminov, V. Ia. Nepomnin, M. K. Nurmukhamedov, S. P. Tolstov, Sh. Z. Urazaev, and B. A. Shishkin. 1967. *Istoriia Uzbekskoi SSR*. 4 vols. Tashkent.

Arendarenko, G. A. 1974. *Bukhara i Afganistan v nachale 80-kh godov XIX veka* (Zhurnaly komandirovok G. A. Arendarenko). Edited by N. A. Khalfin. Moscow.

Arunova, M. R. and K. A. Ashrafi. 1958. *Gosudarstvo Nadir Shakha Afshara.* Moscow.

Al-Aṣīl, Aḥmad b. Shams al-Dīn. *Miftāḥ al-qulūb,* vol. 3. Cambridge University Library. (See E. G. Browne, *A supplementary hand-list of the Muhammadan manuscripts . . . in the Library of the University of Cambridge,* Cambridge 1896, No. 1227.)

Aṣīl al-Dīn, 'Abd Allāh b. 'Abd al-Raḥmān al-Ḥusaynī. 1931. *Risālah-i mazārāt-i Harāt.* Edited by Muhammad 'Aẓīm Khān. A.H. 1310 (A.D. 1931). Herat.

Astarābādī, Muḥammad Mahdī Khān. 1848. *Tārīkh-i jahāngushā-yi Nādirī.* Bombay, A.H. 1265 (A.D. 1848).

―――. 1876. *Durrah-i Nādirah.* Bombay, A.H. 1293 (A.D.1876).

Aubin, Jean. 1956. "Notes sur quelques documents Aq Qoyunlu." In *Mélanges Louis Massignon,* vol. 1, 123–47. Damascus.

Babakhodzhaev, M. A. 1963. "Russko-Afganskie torgovye otnosheniia v 80–90ykh godakh XIX v." *Kratkie Soobshcheniia Instituta Vostokovedeniia* (Moscow) 73:11–18.

―――. 1970. "Afghanistan's Armed Forces and Amir Abdur Rahman's Military Reform." *Afghanistan* (Kabul) 23(2):8–20; (3):9–23.

―――. 1975. *Ocherki sotsial'no-ekonomicheskoi i politicheskoi istorii Afganistana (konets XIX v.).* Tashkent.

Bābur, Ẓahīr al-Dīn. 1922. *Babur-Nama (Memoirs of Babur).* 2 vols. in 1. Translated from the original Turki Text of Zahiru'd-din Muhammad Babur Padshah Ghazi by Annette Susannah Beveridge. Reprint. New Delhi 1979.

Bacqué-Grammont, Jean-Louis. 1970. "Une liste Ottomane de princes et d'apanages Abu'l-Khayrides." *Cahiers du monde russe et sovietique* (Paris) 11:423–53.

―――. 1971. "Les événements d'Asie Centrale en 1510 d'après un document Ottoman." *Cahiers du monde russe et sovietique* (Paris) 12:189–207.

Badakhshī, Sang Muhammad. 1959. *Tārīkh-i Badakhshān (Istoriia Badakhshana.* Edited and translated by A. N. Boldyrev (with *Tatimmah* by Fāḍil Beg). Leningrad.

Al-Badā'ūnī, 'Abd al-Qādir b. Mulūk Shāh. 1884–1925. *Muntakhabu-t-tawārīkh.* 3 vols. Vol. 1 translated by C. Ranking; vol. 2 by W. M. Lowe; vol. 3 by Wolseley Haig. Calcutta.

Baer, G. 1979. "The Dismemberment of Awqāf in Early 19th Century Jerusalem," *Asian and African Studies* (Haifa) 13:220–41.

―――. 1982. "Ḥikr," *EI*(2), supplement. Leiden.

―――. 1983. "Women and Waqf: An Analysis of the Istanbul *Taḥrīr* of 1546." *Asian and African Studies* (Haifa) 17:9–27.

Bāfiqī, Muḥammad Mufid Mustawfi. 1967. *Jāmi'-i Mufīdī* vol. 3. Edited by Īraj Afshār. Tehran.

Barnes, John Robert. 1987. *An Introduction to Religious Foundations in the Ottoman Empire.* Leiden.

Barthold, V. V. 1904. "Otchet o komandirovke v Turkestan" in *Sochineniia*, vol. 8, 119–210. Reprint. Moscow, 1973.

———. 1914. "K Istorii orosheniia Turkestana" in *Sochineniia*, vol. 3:97–233. Reprint. Moscow, 1965.

———. 1962. *Four Studies on the History of Central Asia*. Vol. 3, *Mir 'Ali-Shir* [and] *A History of the Turkman People*. Translated from the Russian by V. Minorsky and T. Minorsky. Leiden.

———. 1963. *Four Studies on the History of Central Asia*. Vol. 2, *Ulugh-Beg*. Translated from the Russian by V. Minorsky and T. Minorsky. Leiden.

———. [V. V. Bartol'd]. 1963–77. *Sochineniia*, 9 vols. in 10. Moscow.

———. 1968. *Turkestan Down to the Mongol Invasion*. 3rd ed. Edited by C. E. Bosworth. E.J.W. Gibb Memorial Series, n.s., vol. 5. London.

———. [Barthold, V. V. W.]. 1981. "Kuramah." *EI(2)*, vol. 5. Leiden.

———. [W. Barthold]. 1984. *An Historical Geography of Iran*. Translated by Svat Soucek and edited by C. E. Bosworth. Princeton.

Barthold, V. V., A. Bennigsen, and H. Carrère d'Encausse. 1960. "Badakhshān." *EI(2)* vol. 1. Leiden.

Al-Baṣrī, Hilāl b. Yaḥyā. 1936–37. *Kitāb aḥkām al-waqf*. Hyderabad, A.H. 1355 (A.D. 1936–37).

Beisembiev, T. K. 1987. *"Ta'rikh-i Shakhrukhi" kak istoricheskii istochnik*. Alma-Ata.

Berki, Ali Himmet. 1946. *Vakıflar*. Istanbul.

Bertel's, E. E. 1938. *Iz Arkhivov Sheikhov Dzhuibari*. Moscow-Leningrad.

Bilgrami, Rafat M. 1984. *Religious and Quasi-Religious Departments of the Mughal Period 1556–1707* A.D. Aligarh.

Blair, Sheila. 1984. "Ilkhanid Architecture and Society: An Analysis of the Endowment Deed of the Rab'i Rashīdī." *Iran: Journal of the British Society of Persian Studies* (London) 22:67–90.

Bonine, Michael. 1979. "Vaqf and Commercial Land Use. The Bazaar of Yazd, Iran." Paper presented at the International Conference on Waqf, The Hebrew University of Jerusalem, June 1979.

Bosworth, C. E. 1969. "Abū 'Abdallāh al-Khwārazmī on the Technical Terms of the Secretary's Art." *Journal of the Economic and Social History of the Orient* (Leiden) 20:113–64.

———. 1980. "Kotwal." *EI(2)*, vol 5. Leiden.

Braudel, Fernand. 1981. *The Structure of Everyday Life*. Civilization and Capitalism 15th–18th Century, vol. 1. New York.

Bregel, Yuri, 1980. "Kosh-Begī," *EI(2)*, vol. 5.

———. 1982. "Tribal Traditions and Dynastic History." *Asian and African Studies* (Haifa) 16:357–98.

———. 1983. "Abu'l-Kayr Khan." *EIr.*, vol. 1. London.

Bretschneider, Emilii V. 1876. *Medieval Researches from Eastern Asiatic Sources*. 2 vols. Leiden.

Brockelmann, Carl. 1937–42. *Geschichte der Arabischen Literatur*, supplement vols. I–III. Leiden.

Brockelmann, Carl. 1943–49. *Geschichte der Arabischen Literatur*, vols. 1 and 2. Leiden.

Browne, E. G. 1902–24. *A Literary History of Persia*. 4 vols. Reprint 1964. Cambridge.

Bukhārī, Mīr ʿAbd al-Karīm. 1876. *Histoire de l'Asie Centrale*. Edited and translated by C. Schefer. Paris.

Burnes, Alexander. 1834. *Travels into Bokhara*. 3 vols. London.

Burton, J. Audrey. 1988a. "The Fall of Herat to the Uzbegs in 1588." *Iran: Journal of the British Society of Persian Studies* (London) 26:119–23.

———. 1988b. "Who Were the First Ashtarkhānid Rulers of Bukhara?" *Bulletin of the School of Oriental and African Studies* (London) 51:482–88.

Busse, Heribert. 1959. *Untersuchungen zum Islamischen Kanzleiwesen*. Cairo.

Busson de Janssens, G. 1951–53. "Les Wakfs dans l'Islam Contemporain." *Revue des Etudes Islamiques* (Paris) 1951:1–71; 1953:43–76.

Cahen, Claude. 1965. *Jean Sauvaget's Introduction to the History of the Muslim East*. Berkeley and Los Angeles.

Chekhovich, O. D. 1947. "Sobraniia vostochnykh aktov v Uzbekistane." *Biulleten' Akademii Nauk Uzbekskoi SSR* (Tashkent) 4:26–28.

———. 1948. "Sobranie vostochnykh aktov Akademii Nauk Uzbekistana." *Istoricheskie zapiski* (Moscow) 26:306–11.

———. 1951. "Novaia kollektsiia dokumentov po istorii Uzbekistana." *Istoricheskie zapiski* (Moscow) 36:263–68.

———. 1954. *Dokumenty k istorii agrarnykh otnoshenii v Bukharskoi khanstve XVII–XIX vv.* vol. 1, *Akty feodal'noi sobstvennosti na zemliu XVII–XIX vv.* Tashkent.

———. 1955. "Bukharskie pozemel'nye akty XVI–XX vv." *Problemy istochnikovedeniia* (Moscow) 4:223–240.

———. 1964. "Materialy po terminologii istoricheskikh istochnikov." *Narody Azii i Afriki* (Moscow) 6:69–74.

———. 1965. *Bukharskie Dokumenty XIV v.* Tashkent.

———. 1969. "Zadachi Sredneaziatskoi diplomatiki." *Narody Azii i Afriki* (Moscow) 6:75–82.

———. 1972. "Novye nakhodki dokumentov Khodzha Akhrara XV–XVI vv." *Philologia Orientalis* (Tbilisi) 2:135–46.

———. 1974. *Samarkandskie Dokumenty XV–XVI vv.* Moscow.

———. 1976. "K probleme zemel'noi sobstvennosti v feodal'noi Srednei Azii." *Obshchestvennye Nauki v Uzbekistane* (Tashkent) 11:36–44.

———. 1979. *Bukharskii Vakf XIII v.* Moscow.

———. 1980a. "Cherty ekonomicheskoi zhizny Maverrannakhra v sochineniiakh po 'fikkhu' i 'shurutu'." In *Blizhnyi i srednyi vostok: Tovarno-denezhnye otnosheniia pri feodalizme*, edited by G. F. Girs and E. A. Davidovich. Bartol'dskie chteniia 1978. Moscow.

———. 1980b. "Obzor arkheografii Srednei Azii." In *Srednevekovyi Vostok: Istoriia, Kul'tura, Istochnikovedenie*, edited by G. F. Girs, E. A. Davidovich, S. B. Pevsner, and I. V. Stebleva, 267–280. Moscow.

———. 1984. "O diplomatike i periodizatsii sredneaziatskikh aktov." In *Istochnikovedenie i tekstologiia srednevekovogo Blizhnego i Srednego Vostoka*, edited by G. F. Girs and E. A. Davidovich. Bartol'dskie chteniia 1981. Moscow.

Chekhovich, O.D., and A. B. Vil'danova. 1979. "Vakf Subkhan-kulikhana Bukharskogo 1693 g." *Pis'mennye Pamiatniki Vostoka* (Moscow) 1973:213–25.

Chingi, Muḥammad Yaʿqub. 1982. *Kelur-Name (Starouzbeksko-tadzhiksko-persidskii slovar' XVII v.)*. Introduction, transcription, translation of the text, glossaries, lexical and grammatical notes, and grammatical index by A. Ibragimova. Tashkent.

Cohen, Amnon. 1984. "Sixteenth Century Egypt and Palestine: The Jewish Connection as Reflected in the *Sijill* of Jerusalem." In *Egypt and Palestine*, edited by Amnon Cohen and Gabriel Baer. Jerusalem and New York.

Coulson, N. J. 1964. *A History of Islamic Law*. Islamic Surveys, 2. Edinburgh.

Dānish, Ākhūnd Makhdūm. 1960. *Risālah yā mukhtaṣarī az tā'rīkh-i salṭanat-i khāndān-i Manghītīyah*. Stalinabad.

Dārāshukūh, Muḥammad. 1965. *Safīnat al-awliyā*. Edited by Dr. Tara Chand and Sayyid Muḥammad Riḍā Jalīlī Nā'īnī. Tehran.

Davidovich, E. A. 1953. "Nadpisi na sredneaziatskikh serebrianykh monetakh XVI v." *Epigrafika Vostoka* (Dushanbe) 7:30–40.

———. 1960. "O merakh vesa pozdnesrednevekovoi Bukhary." *Izvestie Otdeleniia obshchestvennykh nauk* (Dushanbe) 22:99–114.

———. 1964a. *Istoriia monetnogo dela Srednei Azii XVII–XVIII vv.* Dushanbe.

———. 1964b. "Some Social and Economic Aspects of 16th Century Central Asia." *Central Asian Review* (London) 12:265–70.

———. 1968. "Klad serebrianykh monet XVI v. iz Bukhary." In *Material'naia Kul'tura Tadzhikistana*, edited by B. A. Litvinskii, 209–29. Dushanbe.

———. 1970. *Materialy po metrologii srednevekovoi Srednei Azii*. (Published with Hinz 1970.) Moscow.

———. 1975. "Feodal'nyi zemel'nyi milk v Srednei Azii XVI–XIX vv." In *Formy feodal'noi zemel'noi sobstvennosti i vladeniia na Blizhnem i Srednem Vostoke*, edited by B. G. Gafurov, G. F. Girs, and E. A. Davidovich. Bartol'dskie chteniia 1975. Moscow.

———. 1979. "Serebrianye monety udel'nykh vladetelei kak istochnik po istorii Srednei Azii XVI vv." *Pis'mennye Pamiatniki Vostoka* (Moscow) 1973:55–100.

———. 1983. *Istoriia denezhnogo obrashcheniia srednevekovoi Srednei Azii*. Moscow.

Davidovich, E. A., A. A. Egani, and O. D. Chekhovich. 1976. "Novye materialy po metrologii Srednei Azii." In *Istoriia i kul'tura narodov Srednei Azii*, edited by B. A. Litvinski, 161–67. Moscow.

Davydov, A. D. 1960. "Imeniia medrese Subkhankuli-khana v Balkhe (po vakfnoi gramote XVII v.)." *Kratkie Soobshcheniia Instituta Vostokovedeniia* (Moscow) 37:82–128.

———. 1967. *Agrarnyi stroi Afganistana*. Moscow.

———. 1969. *Afganskaia derevnia*. Moscow.

———. 1976. *Sotsial'no-ekonomicheskaia struktura derevni Afganistana (Osobennosti evoliutsii)*. Moscow.

de Beaurecueil, S. 1960. "Al-Anṣārī al-Harawī." *EI*(2), vol. 1. Leiden.

Deguilhem-Schoem, Randi. 1988. "The Loan of *Murṣad* on Waqf Properties." In *A Way Prepared: Essays on Islamic Culture in Honor of Richard Bayly Winder*, edited by Farhad Kazemi and R. D. McChesney. New York.

Deny, J. 1913–36. "Muhr." *EI*(1), vol. 6. Reprint. Leiden, 1987.

Dhikr-i taʿdād-i padshāhān-i Uzbek. Ms. N. T4468, fols. 136b–176a. IVAN Uzbekshoi SSR, Tashkent.

Dickson, Martin B. 1958. "Shāh Tahmāsb and the Uzbeks." Ph.D. diss., Princeton University.

————. 1960. "Uzbek Dynastic Theory in the Sixteenth Century." *Trudy XXV-ogo Mezhdunarodnogo Kongressa Vostokovedov* (Moscow) 3:208–216.

Dihkhudā, ʿAlī Akbar. 1946– . *Lughatnamah*. Tehran.

Doerfer, Gerhard 1963–76. *Turkische und Mongolische Element im Neuper-sichen*. 4 vols. Wiesbaden.

Dughlat, Muhammad Haydar. 1895. *A History of the Moghuls of Central Asia, Being The Tarikh-i-Rashidi of Mirza Muhammad Haidar, Dughlát*. Edited with commentary, notes, and map by N. Elias. Translated by E. Denison Ross. Reprint. London., 1972.

Dupree, Louis. 1976. *Saint Cults in Afghanistan*. American Universities Field Staff Reports, vol. 20, no. 1. Hanover, N.H.

Dupree, Nancy Hatch. 1967. *The Road to Balkh*. Kabul.

————. 1977. *An Historical Guide to Afghanistan*. Kabul.

Dzhalilov, A. 1989. "Dokumenty ob obrashchenii deneg v vakf v Khivinskom khanstve (XIX–nachalo XX veka)." *Obshchestvennye Nauki v Uzbekistane* 1:45–49.

Elphinstone, Mountstuart. 1815. *An Account of the Kingdom of Caubul*. Reprint. Graz, 1969.

Encyclopaedia of Islam. 1st ed. 1913–36. Reprint. Leiden, 1987.

Encyclopaedia of Islam. New ed. 1960– . Leiden.

Erskine, William. 1854. *A History of India Under the First Two Sovereigns of the House of Taimur, Baber and Humayun*. 2 vols. London.

Faroqhi, Suraiya. 1974. "Vakif Administration in Sixteenth Century Konya." *Journal of the Economic and Social History of the Orient* (Leiden) 17:145–72.

————. 1981. "Sayyid Gazi Revisited." *Turcica: Revue des Etudes Turques* (Leiden) 13:90–122.

————. 1984. *Towns and Townsmen in Ottoman Anatolia*. Cambridge.

Fasīḥī-i Khwāfī, Faṣīḥ al-Dīn Aḥmad b. Muḥammad. 1960–61. *Mujmal-i Faṣīḥī*. 3 vols. Edited by Maḥmūd Farrukh. Mashhad.

Al-Fatāwā al-ʿĀlamgīrīyah (alternately *al-Fatāwā al-Hindīyah*). 1892. 6 vols. Compiled by Shaykh Niẓām Burhānpūrī. Reprint of 1892 Būlāq edition. (Published with *Fatāwā Qāḍī Khān* and *al-Fatāwā al-Bazzāzīyah*.) Cairo, 1973. Partly translated into English by N. Baillie as *A Digest of Moohummudan Law*, Third Impression, 1957. Lahore.

Fayḍ Muḥammad Kātib. 1913–15. *Sirāj al-tawārīkh*. 3 vols. in 2. Kabul, A.H. 1331–1333 (A.D. 1913–1915).

Fernandes, Leonor, 1980. "The Evolution of the Khanqah Institution in Egypt." Ph.D. diss., Princeton University.

————. 1981. "Three Ṣūfī Foundations in a 15th Century Waqfiyya." *Annales Islamologiques* (Cairo) 17:141–56.

————. 1985. "Notes on a New Source for the Study of Religious Architecture During the Mamlūk Period: The Waqfiya." *Al-Abhath* (Beirut) 33:3–12.

————. 1988. *The Evolution of a Sufi Institution in Mamluk Egypt: The Khanqah.* Berlin.

————. 1987. "Mamluk Politics and Education: The Evidence from Two Fourteenth Century Waqfiyya." *Annales Islamologiques* (Cairo) 23:87–98.

Ferrier, J. P. 1857. *Caravan Journeys and Wanderings in Persia, Afghanistan, Turkistan, and Beloochistan.* London.

Fletcher, Joseph. 1978. "Ch'ing Inner Asia." Chap. 2 in *The Cambridge History of China*, vol. 10, part 1, edited by John K. Fairbank and Denis Twitchett. Cambridge.

————. 1986. "The Mongols: Ecological and Social Perspectives." *Harvard Journal of Asiatic Studies* (Cambridge, Mass.) 46:11–50.

Frye, Richard. 1960a. "Balkh." *EI*(2), vol. 1. Leiden.

————. 1960b. "Bisṭām." *EI*(2), vol. 1. Leiden.

Fūfalzā'ī, ʿAzīz al-Dīn Wakīlī. 1955. *Tidhkār-i dīwān-i humāyūn-i aʿlā yā wizārat-i māliyah.* Kabul, A.H. 1334 (A.D. 1955).

————. 1958. *Durrat al-zamān.* Kabul, A.H. 1337 (A.D. 1958).

————. 1967. *Tīmūr Shāh Durrānī.* 2 vols. Kabul, A.H. 1346 (A.D. 1967).

Geertz, Clifford, Hildred Geertz, and Lawrence Rosen. 1979. *Meaning and Order in Moroccan Society.* Cambridge.

Gerber, Haim. 1981. "Late 19th Century Wakf Reform in the Ottoman Empire." Paper presented at the Workshop on Waqf, Harry S. Truman Institute of Advanced Studies, The Hebrew University of Jerusalem, February 1981.

————. 1983. "The Waqf Institution in Early Ottoman Edirne." *Asian and African Studies* (Haifa) 17:29–45.

Ghani, Ashraf. 1978. "Islam and State Building in a Tribal Society. Afghanistan 1880–1901." *Modern Asian Studies* (London) 12:269–284. London.

Al-Gharnaṭī, Abū Ḥāmid. 1925. *Tuhfat al-albāb wa nukhbat al-aʿjāb.* Edited by G. Ferrand. *Journal Asiatique* (Paris) 1925: 1–148, 195–303.

Al-Ghazzāli. 1966. *The Mysteries of Almsgiving.* Translated by Nabih Amin Faris. Beirut.

Gibb, H.A.R., and Harold Bowen. 1957. *Islamic Society and the West.* 1 vol. in 2. Oxford.

Goldziher, Ignace. 1971. "The Veneration of Saints in Islam." In *Muslim Studies (Muhammedanische Studien)*, vol. 2, edited by S. M. Stern, 255–341. London.

Golombek, Lisa. 1969. "Abbasid Mosque at Balkh." *Oriental Art*, n.s. 15 (3)179–89. London.

————. c. 1969. *The Timurid Shrine at Gazur Gah.* Toronto.

————. 1977. "Mazar-i Sharif: A Case of Mistaken Identity?" In *Studies in Memory of Gaston Wiet*, edited by Miriam Rosen-Ayalon, 335–43. Jerusalem.

Golombek, Lisa, and Donald Wilber. 1988. *The Timurid Architecture of Iran and Turan.* 2 vols. Princeton.

Gray, John Alfred. 1895. *My Residence at the Court of the Amir.* London.

Gregorian, Vartan. 1969. *The Emergence of Modern Afghanistan.* Stanford.

Gross, JoAnn. 1982. "Khoja Ahrar: A Study of the Perceptions of Religious Power and Prestige in the Late Timurid Period." Ph.D. diss., New York University.

Gulbadan Begam. 1902. *The History of Humāyūn (Humāyūn Nāma).* Translated with introduction and notes by Annette S. Beveridge. Reprint of the 1902 London edition. New Delhi, 1983.

Gulchīn-i Ma'ānī, Ahmad. 1969. *Tārīkh-i tadhkirah-hā-yi Fārsī.* 2 vols. Tehran, A.H. 1348 (A.D. 1969).

Gulistānah, Abū'l-Hasan b. Muhammad. 1965. *Mujmal al-tawārīkh.* Edited by Mudarris-i Ridawī. Tehran, A.H. 1334 (A.D. 1965).

Habib, Irfan. 1982. *An Atlas of the Mughal Empire.* Delhi.

Hāfiz-i Ābrū. 1970. *Jughrāfiyā. Qismat-i rub'-i Khurāsān-i Harāt.* Edited by Māyil Harawī. Tehran, A.H. 1349 (A.D. 1970).

Haider, Mansura. 1975. "Agrarian System in the Uzbek Khanates." *Turcica: Revue des Etudes Turques* (Leiden) 5–7:157–78.

Hambly, Gavin, ed. 1969. *Central Asia.* New York.

Hamidi, Hakim. 1967. *A Catalog of Modern Coins of Afghanistan.* Kabul.

Hamilton, Angus. 1906. *Afghanistan.* London.

Harawī, 'Alī b. Abī Bakr. 1953–57. *Kitāb al-ishārāt ilā ma'rifat al-ziyārāt (Guide des lieux pèlerinages).* 2 vols. Edited and translated by J. Sourdel-Thomine. Damascus.

Harawī, Fādil. 1965. "Irshād al-zirā'ah." Edited by Iraj Afshar. *Farhang-i Īrān Zamīn* (Tehran) 13:7–67.

Harlan, Josiah. 1939. *Central Asia: A Personal Narrative of General Josiah Harlan 1824–1841.* Edited by Frank E. Ross. London.

Hasan-i Rūmlū. 1931–34. *Ahsan al-tawārīkh.* 2 vols. Edited and translated by C. N. Seddon as *A Chronicle of the Early Safawis being the Ahsanu't-tawarikh of Hasan-i Rumlu.* The Gaekwad Series, vols. 57 and 69. Baroda (vol. 57 is the Persian text; vol. 69, the English translation.)

Heffening, W. 1961. "Wakf." *EI*(S). Leiden.

Hilmi Effendi, Omar. 1922. *A Gift to Posterity or the Laws of Evkaf.* Translated by C. R. Tyser. Nicosia.

Hinz, W. 1970. *Musul'manskie mery i vesa s perevodom v metricheskuiu sistemu.* Translated from the German (*Islamische Masse und Gewichte*) by E. A. Davidovich. (Published with Davidovich 1970.) Moscow.

Hoexter, Miriam. 1979. "Wakf al-Haramayn and the Turkish Government in Algiers." Paper presented at the International Conference on Waqf, The Hebrew University of Jerusalem, June 1979.

Hofman H. F. 1969. *Turkish Literature: A Bio-Bibliographical Survey,* sect. 3, pt. 1. 6 vols. Utrecht.

Howorth, Sir Henry 1876–88. *History of the Mongols.* Pt. 2, Div. 2, *The Mongols of Russia and Central Asia.* London.

Hudūd al-'Ālam. *The Regions of the World: A Persian Geography.* 1937. Translated and explained by V. M. Minorsky. E.J.W. Gibb Memorial Series, n.s., vol. 9. London.

Ḥusayn b. 'Alī. 1961. "Zib-i tarikhha: Maloizvestnyi istochnik po istorii Afganistana i Severo-Zapadnoi Indii." Edited and translated by G. A. Voloshina. *Kratkie Soobshcheniia Instituta Vostokovedeniia* (Moscow) 42:3–18.

Hutteroth, Wolf-Dieter. 1977. *Historical Geography of Palestine, Trans-Jordan, and Southern Syria in the Late 16th Century.* Erlangen.

Ibn al-Athīr, 'Izz al-Dīn. 1867–77. *al-Kāmil fī'l-ta'rīkh.* 12 vols. and 1-vol. index. Edited by C. Tornberg. Reprint of 1867–77 Leiden edition. Beirut, 1965–67.

Ibn Bābūyah. 1956–57. *Kitāb man lā yaḥḍuruhu'l-faqīh.* 4 vols. Edited by Sayyid Ḥasan al-Murawī al-Khurasan. Najaf, A.H. 1376 (A.D. 1956–1957).

Ibn Baṭṭūṭah. 1853–58. *Voyages d'Ibn Batoutah.* 4 vols. Edited and translated by C. Defremery and B. R. Sanguinetti. Paris.

Ibn Ḥasan. 1933. *The Central Structure of the Mughal Empire.* Reprint. Delhi, 1967.

Ibragimov, S. K., N. N. Mingulov, K. A. Pishchulina, and V. P. Iudin. 1969. *Materialy po istorii Kazakhskikh Khanstv XV–XVII vekov.* Alma-Ata.

Isfizārī, Mu'īn al-Dīn Muḥammad Zamchī. 1959–60. *Rawḍat al-jannāt fī awṣāf madīnat-i Harāt.* 2 vols. Edited by Sayyid Muḥammad Kāẓim-i Imām. Tehran.

Iskandarov, B. I. 1958. *Istoriia Bukharskogo Emirata.* Moscow.

Ivanov, P. P. 1940. *Arkhiv Khivinskikh Khanov XIX v.* Leningrad.

———. 1954. *Khoziaistvo Dzhuibarskikh Sheikhov.* Moscow-Leningrad.

———. 1958. *Ocherki po istorii Srednei Azii (XVI–seredina XIX v.).* Moscow.

Jalāl-i Munajjim Yazdī. *Tārīkh-i 'Abbāsī.* British Library Ms. No. Or. Add. 27,241.

Jāmī, 'Abd al-Raḥmān. 1957. *Nafaḥāt al-uns.* Edited by Mahdī Tawḥīdī-pur. Tehran, A.H. 1336 (A.D. 1957).

———. 1982. *Pis'ma-avtografy Abdarrakhmana Dzhami iz "Al'boma Navoi."* Edited by A. U. Urunbaev. Tashkent.

Jones, William R. 1980. "Pious Endowments in Medieval Christianity and Islam." *Diogenes* (Montreal) 109:23–36.

Junābādī, Mīrzā Beg. *Rawḍat al-Ṣafawīyah.* British Museum Ms. No. Or. No. 3338.

"K.D." *Inventarnaia kniga rukopisnykh dokumentov feodal'nogo-kolonial'nogo perioda Uzbekskogo Gosudarstvennogo Istoricheskogo Muzeiia goroda Samarkanda.* State Historical Museum, Samarkand.

Kakar, Hasan. 1979. *Government and Society in Afghanistan: The Reign of Amir 'Abd al-Rahman Khan.* Austin.

Kanbūh, Muḥammad Ṣāliḥ. 1923–29. *'Amal-i ṣāliḥ.* 3 vols. Calcutta.

Kashmīrī, Badr al-Dīn. *Rawḍat al-riḍwān fī ḥadīqat al-ghilmān.* Ms. no. 2094. IVAN Uzbekskoi SSR, Tashkent.

Kāẓim-i Imām, Sayyid Muḥammad. 1970. *Mashhad-i Ṭūs.* Tehran.

Khadduri, Madjid. "Maṣlaḥa." *EI*(2), vol. 6. Leiden.

Khāfī, Mīrzā Ya'qūb 'Alī. 1956. *Padshāhān-i muta'akhkhirīn-i Afghānistān.* 2 vols. Kabul, A.H. 1334 (A.D. 1956).

Khāfī Khān, Muḥammad Hāshim. 1860–74. *Muntakhab al-lubāb*, vol. 2, pts. 1 and 2. Calcutta.

Khamraev, A. Kh. 1976. "Nekotorye cherty feodal'nogo sposoba proizvodstva v Bukhare XIX veka." In *Iz Istorii Uzbekistana XIX–XX vv.* (*Sbornik nauchnykh trudov*), 3–36. Tashkent.

Al-Khaṣṣāf. *Kitāb aḥkām al-awqāf*. Ms. No. 987. The Yahuda Collection, Princeton University Library.

Al-Khaṭīb, Aḥmad 'Alī. 1968. *al-Waqf wa'l-waṣāyā*. Baghdad.

Khunjī, Faḍl Allāh b. Rūzbihān. 1962. *Mihmān-nāmah-yi Bukhārā*. Edited by M. Sutūdah. Tehran.

———. 1976. *Mihmān-nāmah-yi Bukhārā*. Edited and translated by A. K. Arends. Moscow.

Khwāndamīr, Ghiyāth al-Dīn b. Humām al-Dīn al-Husaynī. n.d. *Ḥabib al-siyar fī akhbār afrād al-bashar*. 7 vols. in 4. Tehran.

———. 1883. *Rawḍat al-ṣafā*, pt. 7. Lucknow. (His continuation of his grandfather, Mīr Khwānd's, work.)

———. 1945. *Rijāl-i kitāb-i Ḥabib al-siyar*. Edited by 'Abd al-Ḥusayn Nawā'ī. Tehran, A.H. 1324 (A.D. 1945).

Al-Khwārazmī, Abū 'Abd Allāh Muḥammad b. Aḥmad b. Yūsuf. 1895. *Kitāb Mafātīh al-'Ulūm*. Edited by F. van Vloten. Leiden.

Al-Khwārazmī, 'Alī b. Muḥammad 'Alī. *al-Fatāwā al-Shībānīyah* (*Fatāwā Shībani Khān*). IVAN, Uzbek SSR. MS. no. 11282.

Köprülü, Fuad. 1938. "L'Institution de Vakf et l'importance historique des documents de Vakf." *Vakıflar Dergisi* (Ankara) 1:3–9 (Partie Francaise).

———. 1942. "L'Institution du Vakouf, sa nature juridique et son évolution historique." *Vakıflar Dergisi* (Ankara) 2:3–44 (Partie Francaise).

Kozlowski, Gregory. 1985. *Muslim Endowments in British India*. Cambridge.

Kunt, Metin. 1979. "The Vakıf as Instrument of Public Policy: Notes on the Köprülü Family Vakıfs." Paper presented at the International Conference on Waqf, The Hebrew University of Jerusalem, June 1979.

Kushkakī, Burhān al-Dīn. 1924. *Rāhnamā-yi Qaṭaghān wa Badakhshān*. Kabul, A.H. 1302 (A.D. 1924).

Lāhūrī, 'Abd al-Ḥamīd. 1867–72. *Bādshāhnāmah*. 2 vols. Calcutta.

Lambton, A.K.S. 1938. "The Regulation of the Waters of the Zāyande Rūd." *Bulletin of the School of Oriental and African Studies* (London) 9:663–73.

———. 1957. "The Administration of Sanjar's Empire as illustrated in the '*Atabat al-katabah.*" *Bulletin of the School of Oriental and African Studies* (London) 20:367–88.

———. 1969. *Landlord and Peasant in Persia*. Oxford.

Lane-Poole, Stanley. 1882. *The Catalogue of Oriental Coins*. Vol. 7, *The Coinage of Bukhara (Transoxiana) in the British Museum from the Time of Timur to the Present Day*, classes XXII, XXIII. Edited by Reginald Stuart Poole. London.

Lārī, 'Abd al-Ghafūr. 1971. *Tārīkhchah-i Mazār-i Sharīf mansūb bih Mawlānā 'Abd al-Ghafūr Lārī Shāgird-i Ḥaḍrat-i Jāmī*. Edited by Māyil Harawī. Kabul.

Lee, Jonathan. 1987. "The History of Maimana in Northern Afghanistan 1731–1893." *Iran: Journal of the British Society of Persian Studies* (London) 25:107–24.

LeStrange, Guy. 1905. *The Lands of the Eastern Caliphate*, Cambridge.

Levi-Provencal, E. 1960. "Abū Ḥāmid al-Gharnaṭī." *EI*(2), vol. 1. Leiden.

Lockhart, Laurence. 1938. *Nadir Shah*. London.

Lowick, N. M. 1966. "Shaybanid Silver Coins." *Numismatic Chronicle* (New York) 6(ser. 7):251–330.

McChesney, R. D. 1980a. "The 'Reforms' of Bāqī Muḥammad Khān." *Central Asiatic Journal* (Vienna) 24:69–84.

———. 1980b. "A Note on Iskandar Beg's Chronology." *Journal of Near Eastern Studies* (Chicago) 39(1):53–63.

———. 1981. "Waqf and Public Policy: The Waqfs of Shāh 'Abbās: 1011–1023/ 1602–1614." *Asian and African Studies* (Haifa) 15:165–90.

———. 1982. " 'Abd al-mo'men b. 'Abdallah." *EIr* vol 1. London.

———. 1983. "The Amirs of Seventeenth Century Muslim Central Asia." *Journal of the Economic and Social History of the Orient* (Leiden) 26:33–70.

———. 1987. "Economic and Social Aspects of the Public Architecture of Bukhara in the 1560's and 1570's." *Islamic Art* (New York and Genoa) 2:217–42.

———. 1988. "Ilyas Qudsi on the Craft Organizations of Damascus." In *A Way Prepared: Essays on Islamic Culture in Honor of Richard Bayly Winder*, edited by Farhad Kazemi and R. D. McChesney. New York.

Al-Maḥbūbī, 'Ubayd Allāh b. Mas'ūd, al-Ṣadr al-Sharī'ah. n.d. *Sharḥ al-Wiqāyah*. 2 vols. in 1. Lucknow.

———. 1879. *Mukhtaṣar al-Wiqāyah fī masā'il al-Hidāyah*. Qazan, A.H. 1296 (A.D. 1879).

Maḥmūd al-Ḥusaynī. 1974. *Tārīkh-i Aḥmad Shāhī*. 2 vols. Edited by Dūst Muḥammad Sayyid Muradov. Moscow.

Maḥmūd b. Amīr Walī. 1977. *More Tain Otnositel'no Doblestei Blagorodnykh (Geografiia)*. Introduction, translation, notes, and indices by B. A. Akhmedov. Tashkent.

Maḥmūd b. Amīr Walī. 1980. *The Bahr ul-Asrar. Travelogue of South Asia*. Introduced, edited, and annotated by Riazul Islam. Karachi.

Maḥmud b. Amīr Walī. *Baḥr al-asrār fī manāqib al-akhyār*. Second part (*rukn*) of vol. 6: Ms. No. 1375. IVAN Uzbekskoi SSR, Tashkent. Third part of vol. 6: Ms. No. 1375. IVAN Uzbekskoi SSR, Tashkent. Fourth part of vol. 6. Ms. No. 575. India Office Library, London.

Mandaville, Jon E. 1979. "Usurious Piety: The Cash Waqf Controversy in the Ottoman Empire." *International Journal of Middle East Studies* (Cambridge) 10:289–308.

Al-Marghinānī, Burhan al-Din 'Ali. 1908. "Kitāb al-waqf." In *Kitāb al-Hidāyah fī sharh Bidāyat al-mubtadi'*, vol. 3, 10–17. Cairo, A.H. 1326 (A.D. 1908).

———. 1957. "Kitāb al-waqf." In *Hedaya or Guide: A Commentary on the Mussulman Laws*. Translated by Charles Hamilton. Reprint of 1870 edition. Lahore.

Martin, Frank A. 1907. *Under the Absolute Amir*. London and New York.

Masefield, G. R. 1967. "Crops and livestock." In *The Cambridge Economic History of Europe*, vol. 4, edited by E. E. Rich and C. H. Wilson. 276–301. Cambridge.

Masson, V. M., and V. A. Romodin. 1964–65. *Istoriia Afganistana*. 2 vols. Moscow.

Mazzaoui, Michel. 1972. *The Origins of the Safavids*. Wiesbaden.

Miklukho-Maklai, N. D. 1975. *Opisanie persidskikh i tadzhikskikh rukopisei Instituta Vostokovedeniia*, vol. 3. Moscow.

Minorsky, V. M. 1943. *Tadhkirat al-Muluk: A Manual of Safavid Administration*. Translated and explained by V. Minorsky. E.J.W. Gibb Memorial Series, n.s., vol. 16. London.

Mir Mohammed Monshi. 1901. *The Life of Abdur Rahman Khan*. 2 vols. London.

Mīrzā Badīʿ Dīwān. 1981. *Majmaʾ al-arqām (Madzhmaʾ al-arkam)*. Edited and translated by A. B. Vilʾdanova. Moscow.

Mīrzā Mughūl Beg b. Muhammad Beg. *Kitāb dar ahwāl-i manzilhā*. London. (Storey 1927–84 2(1)148 calls it *Risālah-i Mister Wilford*.) (See *Catalogue of the Arabic, Persian, Hindustani, and Turkish MSS. in the Library of the Royal Asiatic Society*, p. 176.)

Mirzoev, A. M. 1976. *Kamal al-Din Binai*. Moscow.

Mohan Lal. 1846. *Travel in the Punjab, Afghanistan and Turkistan to Balk, Bokhara, and Herat and a Visit to Great Britain and Germany*. With an introduction by Dr. S. Hasan Ahmad. Revised edition of 1846 London publication. Calcutta, 1977.

Moorcroft, W., and G. Trebeck. 1841. *Travels in the Himalayan Provinces of Hindustan and the Punjab; in Ladakh and Kashmir; in Peshawar, Kabul, Kunduz, and Bokhara*. 2 vols. London.

Morgan, David 1986a. "The 'Great Yāsā of Chingiz Khān' and Mongol Law in the Īlkhānate." *Bulletin of the School of Oriental and African Studies* (London) 49:163–76.

————. 1986b. *The Mongols*. London.

Morley, W. H. 1854. *A Descriptive Catalogue of the Historical Manuscripts in the Arabic and Persian Languages Preserved in the Library of the Royal Asiatic Society of Great Britain and Ireland*. London.

Moynihan, Elizabeth. 1979. *Paradise as a Garden in Persia and Mughal India*. New York.

Muhammad Amīn b. Mīrzā Zamān Bukhārī, Mīr. 1957. *Ubaidulla-Name*. Translated by A. A. Semenov. Tashkent.

Muhammad Amīn b. Muhammad Zamān Bukhārī Sūfiyānī Kīrāk-yarāqchī. *Muhīt al-tawārīkh* Ms. No. 472. Bibliotheque Nationale. Ms. No. 835. IVAN Uzbekskoi SSR, Tashkent. (*Tārīkh-i Subhān Qulī Khān* according to Storey 1927–84, 1:379.)

Muhammad Badīʿ Samarqandī "Malīhā." *Mudhakkir al-ashāb*. Ms. Nos. 4270, 58. IVAN Uzbekskoi SSR, Tashkent. Ms. No. 610. IVAN Tadzhikskoi SSR, Dushanbe.

Muhammad Kāzim 1962–66. *Nāmah-i ʿĀlam-ārā-yi Nādirī*. 3 vols. Facsimile edition by N. D. Miklukho-Maklai. Indices and annotated chapter headings by G. V. Shitov (vol. 1) and O. P. Shcheglova (vols. 2 and 3). Moscow.

Muhammad Kāzim b. Muhammad Amīn. 1968. *ʿĀlamgir-nāmah*. Calcutta.

Muhammad Murīd Muhyi al-Dīn al-Hanafi al-Qādirī. A.H. 1319 A.D. 1901–2. *Hujjat al-Baydā*. Bombay.

Muḥammad Ṭāhir b. Abī'l-Qāsim Balkhī, Mawlānā Ākhūnd Khwājah. 'Ajā'ib al-ṭabaqāt fī bayān 'ajā'ib al-'ālam. Ms. No. 179. Royal Asiatic Society. Ms. Catalog No. 686. IVAN, Uzbekskoi SSR, Tashkent. (Vol. 1 of A. A. Semenov 1952–75.)

Muḥammad Tālib b. Khwājah Tāj al-Dīn Jūybārī. Maṭlab al-ṭālibīn. Ms. Nos. 3757, 10809. IVAN Uzbekskoi SSR, Tashkent.

Muḥammad Ya'qūb b. Dānyāl Beg. Gulshan al-mulūk. Ms. No. 1507/II. IVAN Uzbekskoi SSR, Tashkent.

Muḥammad Yūsuf Munshī b. Khwājah Baqā. Tārīkh-i Muqīm Khānī (or Tadhkirah-i Muqīm Khānī). Ms. No. 160. Royal Asiatic Society.

Muḥammad Yūsuf Munshī. 1956. Mukimkhanskaia Istoriia. Translated by A. A. Semenov. Tashkent.

Muḥammadzādah, Qurbān and Maḥabbat Shāhzādah. 1973. Tārīkh-i Badakhshān (Istoriia Badakhshana). Edited, with notes and indices by A. A. Egani. Moscow.

Mukhtarov, A. 1963. Materialy po istorii Ura-Tiube: Sbornik Aktov XVII–XIX vv. Moscow.

———. 1980. Pozdne-srednevekovyi Balkh. Dushanbe.

———. 1982. Po sledam proshlogo. Dushanbe.

Mukminova, R. G. 1960. "Iz istorii vakfnogo zemlevladeniia v Srednei Azii v XVI v." In Issledovaniia po istorii kul'tury narodov Vostoka (Sbornik v chest' semidesiatiletiia Ak. I. A. Orbeli), edited by V. V. Struve et al., 215–18. Moscow-Leningrad.

———. 1966. K Istorii agrarnykh otnoshenii v Uzbekistane XVI v. Po Materialam "Vakf-name." Tashkent.

———. 1968. "K Izuchenii sredneaziatskikh terminov tagdzha, sukniiat, ichki." Pis'mennye Pamiatniki Vostoka 1968:127–134. Moscow, 1970.

———. 1976. Ocherki po istorii remesla v Samarkande i Bukhare v XVI veke. Tashkent.

———. 1985. "Dukhovenstvo i vakfy v Srednei Azii XVI veka." In Dukhovenstvo i politicheskaia zhizn' na Blizhnem i Srednem Vostoke v period feodalizma, edited by G. F. Girs and E. A. Davidovich, 141–46. Bartol'dskie chteniia 1982. Moscow.

Muminov, I. M., ed., with V. A. Abdullaev, M. U. Aminov, M. A. Akhunova, K. A. Akilov, Ia. G. Guliamov, Kh. Z. Ziiaev, Kh. Sh. Inoiatov, T. N. Kary-Niiazov, B. V. Lunin, M. K. Nurmukhamedov, G. R. Rashidov, I. I. Umniakov, and A. F. Iatsyshina.

———. 1969–70. Istoriia Samarkanda. 2 vols. Tashkent.

Munshī, Iskandar Beg. n.d. Tārīkh-i 'Ālam-ārā-yi 'Abbāsī. 2 vols. Edited by Īraj Afshār. Isfahan.

———. 1978. Eskandar Monshi. History of Shah 'Abbas the Great. 2 vols. Translated by Roger M. Savory. Boulder, Colo.

Musta'idd Khān, Muḥammad Sāqī. 1871. Ma'āthir-i 'Alamgīrī. Calcutta.

Mu'tamin, 'Ali. 1969. Rāhnamā yā tārīkh wa ṭawāf-i darbār-i wilāyat madār-i Riḍawī. Mashhad, A.H. 1348 (A.D. 1969).

Naficy, Said. 1960. "Bannā'ī." EI(2), vol. 1. Leiden.

Nāhid, Muḥammad Ḥakīm. 1951–60. *Qāmūs-i jughrāfiyā-yi Afghānistān*. 4 vols. Kabul.

Nazarov, Khaknazar. 1963. *Ravabiti Bukhoro va Afganiston az barpo shudani davlati to ghaltidani amorati Bukhoro*. Dushanbe.

Nūr Muḥammad, Ḥāfiẓ. 1946. *Tārīkh-i Mazār-i Sharif*. Kabul, A.H. 1325 (A.D. 1946).

Nūrī, Nūr Muḥammad. 1956. *Gulshan al-imārah*. Kabul, A.H. 1335 (A.D. 1956).

O'Kane, Bernard. 1987. *Timurid Architecture in Khurasan*. Costa Mesa, Calif.

Papazian, A. D. 1968. *Persidskie dokumenty Matenadarana*, vol. 2 ("Kupchie"). Erevan.

Peri, Oded. 1983. "The Waqf as an Instrument to Increase and Consolidate Political Power: The Case of Khāṣṣekī Sulṭān Waqf in Late Eighteenth-Century Ottoman Jerusalem." *Asian and African Studies* (Haifa) 17:47–62.

Petrushevskii, I. P. 1949. *Ocherki po istorii feodal'nykh otnoshenii v Azerbaidzhane i Armenii v XVI-nachale XIX vv*. Leningrad.

———. 1960. *Zemledelie i agrarnye otnosheniia v Irane XIII–XIV vekov*. Moscow.

———[I. P. Petrushevsky]. 1970. "Rashid al-Din's Conception of State." *Central Asiatic Journal* (Vienna) 14:148–62.

Pishchulina, K. A. 1977. *Iugo-vostochny Kazakhstan v seredine XIV–nachale XVI vekov*. Alma-Ata.

Pugachenkova, G. A. 1951. "Sadovo-parkovoe iskusstvo Srednei Azii v epokhe Timura i Timuridov." *Trudy Sredneaziatskogo Gosudarstvennogo Universiteta* (Tashkent) 23:143–62.

———. 1968. "Les Monuments peu inconnus de l'architecture médiévale de l'Afghanistan." *Afghanistan* (Kabul) 21:18–27.

———. 1970. "Nu-Gumbad v Balkhe (Afganistan)." *Sovetskaia Arkheologiia* (Moscow) 3:241–50.

Pugachenkova, G. A., and E. V. Rtveladze. 1986. "Archaeology. Central Asia." *EIr*, vol 1. London.

Qadrī Pāshā, Muḥammad. 1902. *Qānūn al-'adl wa'l-inṣāf lil-qaḍā 'ala mushkilat al-awqāf*. Būlāq, A.H. 1320 (A.D. 1902).

Qāsim b. Yūsuf Harawī 1968. *Ṭarīq-i qismat-i āb-i qulb*. Edited by Māyil Harawī. Tehran.

Qāṭi'ī Harawī, Mullā, 1979. *Tadhkirah-i majma' al-shu'arā-yi Jahāngīr Shāhī*. Edited, introduced, and annotated by Dr. Muḥammad Saleem Akhtar. Karachi.

Qudāmah b. Ja'far. 1965. *Kitāb al-kharāj*. Translated by A. Ben Shemesh as *Taxation in Islam*, vol. 2. Leiden.

Qūzānlū, Jamīl. 1892. *Qushūn kashī bih mamālik-i Tūrān*. Tehran, A.H. 1310 (A.D. 1892).

Rabino di Borgomale, H. L. 1945. *Coins, Medals and Seals of the Shahs of Iran, 1500–1941*. Hertford.

Raffi'ā, Mīrzā. n.d. *Dastūr al-mulūk*. Edited by Muḥammad Taqī Dānishpazhuh. [n.p.]

Rakhimi, M. V. and L. V. Uspenskoi. 1954. *Tadzhikso-Russki slovar'*. Moscow.

Rashīd al-Dīn. 1971. *The Successors of Genghis Khan.* Edited and translated by J. A. Boyle. New York.

Rashidov, R. T. 1977. *Aimaki.* Tashkent.

Riḍā Qulī Khān Hidāyat. 1960. *Mulḥaqāt-i Rawḍat al-safā-yi Nāṣirī,* vols. 8–10. Tehran, A.H. 1339 (A.D. 1960).

Risālah dar bayān-i binā'i Balkh. Ms. no. 3638. IVAN Uzbekskoi SSR, Tashkent.

Ritter, H. 1960. "Abū Yazīd Bisṭāmī." *EI*(2), vol. 1. Leiden.

Riyāḍī, Muḥammad Yūsuf. 1906. *Baḥr al-fawā'id* (also known as *Kulliyat-i Riyāḍī*). Mashhad, A.H. 1324 (A.D. 1906). (A compendium comprising eleven separately titled works, a conclusion [*khatimah*], and appendixes [*mulḥaqāt*]: *Bayān al-wāqi'ah, Ḍiyā al-ma'rifah, 'Ayn al-waqā'i', Daftar dānish, Pursish wa pāsikh, Fayḍ-i rūḥānī, Manba' al-bukā', Takhmīsāt, Barayāt-i Riyāḍī, Parī-shān-i Riyāḍī,* and *Awḍā' al-bilād.*)

Rustam al-Ḥukamā, Muḥammad Hāshim. 1969. *Rustam al-tawārīkh.* Edited by Muḥammad Mushīrī. Tehran, A.H. 1348 (A.D. 1969).

Salakhetdinova, M. A. 1968. "Pokhody Anusha-khana na zemli Bukharskogo khanstva." In *Blizhnyi i Srednii Vostok (Sbornik statei v chest' . . . I. P. Petrushevskogo),* edited by Iu. A. Petrosian and V. A. Romodin, 123–33. Moscow.

————. 1970. "K istoricheskoi toponomike Balkhskoi Oblasti." *Palestinskii Sbornik* (Moscow) 21:222–28.

Salīm, Ḥājī Mīr. Muḥammad. *Silsilat al-salaṭīn.* Ms. No. 169. Bodleian Library.

Saljūqī, Fikrī. 1976. *Gāzar Gāh.* Kabul, A.H. 1355 (A.D. 1976).

Samandar Tirmidhī, Khwājah. 1977. *Dastūr al-mulūk.* Edited and translated by M. A. Salakhetdinova. Moscow.

Ṣamṣām al-Dawlah, Shāh Nawāz Khān. 1888–91. *Ma'āthir al-umarā'.* 3 vols. Calcutta.

Sāmī, Mīrzā 'Abd al-Laṭīf. 1962. *Tārīkh-i salāṭīn-i Manghītīyah.* Edited and translated by L. M. Epifanova. Moscow.

Schimkoreit, Renate. 1982. *Regesten publizierter safawidischer Herrscherurkunden.* Berlin.

Schmitz, M. 1978. "Ka'b al-Aḥbār." *EI*(2), vol. 4. Leiden.

Schoem, Randi. 1985. "Waqf in 19th and 20th Century Syria." Ph.D. diss., New York University.

Semenov, A. A. 1948. "Bukharskii traktat o chinakh i zvaniiakh i ob obiazannostiakh nositelei ikh v srednevekovoi Bukhare." *Sovetskoe Vostokovedenie* (Moscow-Leningrad) 5:137–53.

Semenov, A. A., A. Urunbaev, L. M. Epifanova, and D. G. Voronovskii. 1952–75. *Sobranie vostochnykh rukopisei Akademii Nauk Uzbekskoi SSR.* 10 vols. Tashkent.

Al-Shahrastānī. 1948–49. *Kitāb al-milal wa'l-niḥal.* Edited by Aḥmad Fahmī Muḥammad. Cairo.

Sharaf al-Dīn b. Nūr al-Dīn Andijānī, Ākhūnd Mullā. *Tārīkh-i Mīr Sayyid Sharīf Rāqim* (or *Tārīkh-i Rāqimī*). Ms. No. 163. Royal Asiatic Society. (This work is continued by Muḥammad Badī' Samarqandī, *Mudhakkir al-aṣḥāb.* Ms. No. 4270, fols. 129a–135b. IVAN Uzbekskoi SSR, Tashkent.)

Shinar, P. 1982. "Inzāl." *EI*(2), supplement. Leiden.

Shirwānī, Ḥājī Zayn al-Dīn. 1960. *Riyāḍ al-siyāḥah*. Tehran, A.H. 1339 (A.D. 1960).

Shorter Encyclopaedia of Islam. 1961. Leiden.

Shokhumorov, S. 1980. "*Akhkam huzur*" *kak istochnik po istorii Afganistana na-chala XX v*. Moscow.

Shushtarī, Nūr Allāh. n.d. *Majālis al-mu'minīn*. Tabriz.

Singh, Ganda. 1959. *Aḥmad Shāh Durrānī*. Bombay.

Sipintā, 'Abd al-Ḥusayn. 1969. *Tārīkhchah-yi awqāf-i Iṣfahān*. Iṣfahān.

Sīstānī, Malik Shāh Ḥusayn. 1965. *Iḥyā al-mulūk*. Edited by M. Sutūdah. Tehran, A.H. 1344 (A.D. 1965).

Skrine, F. H., and E. D. Ross. 1899. *The Heart of Asia. A History of Russian Turkestan and the Central Asian Khanates from the Earliest Times*. London.

Sourdel-Thomine, J. 1971. "al-Harawi al-Mawṣilī." *EI*(2) vol. 3. Leiden.

Spuler, B. 1965. "Djanids." *EI*(2), vol. 2. Leiden.

―――. 1969. "Central Asia: The Last Centuries of Independence." In *The Muslim World*, pt. 3, edited by F.R.C. Bagley, 219–59. Leiden.

Storey, C. A. 1927–84. *Persian Literature: A Bio-Bibliographical Survey*, vol. 1, pt. 1–vol. 3, pt. 1. London.

Storey, C. A. and Iu. E. Bregel'. 1972. *Persidskaia Literatura: Bio-Bibliografi-cheskii Obzor*. 3 vols. Moscow.

Subḥān Qulī Khān. *Iḥyā al-ṭibb-i Subḥānī*. Ms. No. 9750. IVAN Uzbekskoi SSR, Tashkent.

Subtelny, Maria Eva. 1983. "Art and Politics in Early 16th Century Central Asia." *Central Asiatic Journal* (Vienna) 27:121–48.

―――. 1984. "Scenes from the Literary Life of Timurid Herat." In *Logos Islamikos: Studia Islamica in honorem Georgii Michaelis Wickens*, edited by Roger M. Savory and Dionisius A. Agius, pp. 137–55. Papers in Medieval Studies, vol. 6. Toronto.

―――. 1988a. "Centralizing Reform and Its Opponents in the Late Timurid Period." *Iranian Studies* (New York) 21:123–51.

―――. 1988b. "Socioeconomic Bases of Cultural Patronage under the Later Timurids." *International Journal of Middle East Studies* (Cambridge) 20:479–505.

―――. 1990. "A Timurid Educational and Charitable Foundation: The Ikhlā-ṣiyya Complex of 'Alī Shīr Navā'ī in 15th Century Herat and its Endowment." *Journal of the American Oriental Society* (in press).

Suhaylā. *Imam Quli Namah*. Ms. No. 89. IVAN Uzbekskoi SSR, Tashkent.

Sukhareva, O. A. 1976. *Kvartal'naia obshchina pozdne-feodal'nogo goroda Bukhary*. Moscow.

Sulṭān Maḥmūd Khan b. Mūsā Khān Durrānī. 1881. *Tārīkh-i Sulṭānī*. Bombay, A.H. 1298 (A.D. 1881).

Sultanov, T. I. 1977. "Opyt analiza traditsionnykh spiskov 92 plemeni ilatiia." In *Sredniaia Aziia v drevnosti i srednevekov'e*, edited by B. A. Litvinskii and B. G. Gafurov. Moscow.

Al-Suwaydī, 'Abd Allāh. 1905–06. *Kitāb al-ḥujaj al-qaṭ'īyah lil-ittifāq al-firaq al-Islāmīyah*. Cairo, A.H. 1323 (A.D. 1905–1906).

Ṭāhir Muḥammad b. 'Imād al-Dīn Ḥasan b. Sulṭān 'Alī b. Ḥājī Muḥammad Ḥasan Sabzawārī. *Rawḍat al-ṭāhirīn*, vol. 2. Ms. No. HIST. 291. Salar Jung Library. Hyderabad.

Ṭāli', 'Abd al-Raḥmān. *Tārīkh-i Abū'l-Fayḍ Khān*. Ms. No. 194. IVAN Uzbekskoi SSR, Tashkent.

Tanīsh, Ḥāfiẓ. *Sharaf-nāmah-i shāhī* (also known as '*Abd Allāh Nāmah*). Ms. No. 574. India Office Library, London. Ms. No. 778/II. IVAN Tadzhikskoi SSR, Dushanbe.

———. 1983– . *Sharaf-nama-yi shakhi*, vols. 1– . Edited and translated by M. A. Salakhetdinova. Moscow.

Tapper, Nancy. 1983. " 'Abd al-Rahman's North-West Frontier: The Pashtun Colonisation of Afghan Turkistan." In *The Conflict of Tribe and State in Iran and Afghanistan*, edited by Richard Tapper, 233–61. London.

Al-Ṭarābulusī, Burhān al-Dīn. 1952. *Kitāb al-is'āf fī aḥkām al-awqāf*. Cairo.

Tārīkh-i Shībanī Khān wa mu'āmalāt bā awlād-i Amīr Tīmūr. n.d. Ms. No. 4468/II. IVAN Uzbekskoi SSR, Tashkent.

Tauer, F. 1971. "Ḥāfiẓ-i Abrū." *EI(2)*, vol. 3. Leiden.

Teufel, F. 1884. "Quellenstudien zur neuren Geschichte der Chanate." *Zeitschrift der Deutschen Morgenlandischen Gesellschaft* Leipzig. 38:235–81.

Togan, A. Zeki Velidi. 1942–47. *Bugünkü Türkili (Türkistan) ve Yakïn Tarihi*. Istanbul.

———. 1946. *Umumi Türk Tarihine Giriş*, vol. 1. Istanbul.

———. 1950. "Herat." *İslâm Ansiklopedisi*, vol. 5. Istanbul.

———. 1970a. *Tarihde sul*. Istanbul.

———. 1970b. "The Topography of Balkh down to the Middle of the Seventeenth Century." *Central Asiatic Journal* (Vienna) 14:277–88.

Tolstov, S. P., R. N. Nabiev, Ia. G. Guliamov, and V. A. Shishkin. 1955–56. *Istoriia Uzbekskoi SSR*, vol. 1. In 2 parts. Tashkent.

Tolybekov, S. E. 1959. *Obshchestvenno-ekonomicheskii stroi Kazakhov v XVII–XIX vekakh*. Alma-Ata.

———. 1971. *Kochevoe obshchestvo Kazakhov v XVII–nachale XX veka*. Alma-Ata.

Troitskaia, A. L. 1960. "Sagira v Kokandskom Khanstve (XIX v.)." In *Issledovaniia po istorii kul'tury narodov Vostoka (Sbornik v chest' semidesiatiletiia Ak. I. A. Orbeli)*, edited by V. V. Struve et al., 271–82. Moscow-Leningrad.

Turan, Osman. 1941. *Oniki hayvanli Türk takvimi*. Istanbul.

Turkestanskie Vedomosti. A newspaper published in Tashkent in the Tsarist period.

Vambery, Arminius. 1868. *Sketches of Central Asia*. Philadelphia.

———. 1873. *History of Bokhara*, 2d ed.

Vaysi. 1977. *Khwāb-nāmah: Kniga snovideniia*. Edited and translated by F. A. Salimzhianova. Moscow.

Veccia-Vaglieri, L. 1960. " 'Alī b. Abī Ṭālib." *EI(2)*, vol. 1. Leiden.

Viatkin, V. L. 1899. "Samariia'. Opisanie drevnostei i musul'manskikh sviatyn'

Samarkanda Abu Takhir Khodzhei." *Spravochnaia Knizhka Samarkandskoi Oblasti*, (Samarkand) 6:153–259.

Viatkin, V. L. 1958. "Vakufny dokument Ishrat Khany." *Samarkandskii Mavzolei izvestny pod nazvaniem Ishrat khana*, edited by M. E. Masson, 109–36. Tashkent.

Vil'danova, A. B. 1968. "Podlinnik Bukharskogo Traktata o chinakh i zvaniiakh." *Pis'mennye Pamiatniki Vostoka* 1968:40–67. Moscow, 1970.

Vorotin, L. N. 1950. "Ustroistvo v pamiatnikakh arkhitektury Srednei Azii." *Materialy po istorii i teorii arkhitektury Uzbekistana* (Tashkent) 1:14–24.

Wā'iẓ-i Kāshifī, ʿAlī b. Ḥusayn. 1912. *Rashaḥāt ʿayn al-ḥayāt*. Cawnpore.

Wakin, Jeanette. 1972. *The Function of Documents in Islamic Law: The Chapter on Sales from al-Tahawi's Kitab al-shurut al-kabir*. Albany.

Wāṣifī, Zayn al-Din. 1961. *Badāʾiʿ al-waqāʾiʿ*. 2 vols. Edited by A. N. Boldyrev. Moscow.

Wilber, Donald. 1952. "The Structure and Position of Islam in Afghanistan." *Middle East Journal* (Washington, D.C.) Winter:41–48.

Winter, Michael. 1984. "Military Connections between Egypt and Syria (Including Palestine) in the Early Ottoman Period."

In *Egypt and Palestine*, edited by Amnon Cohen and Gabriel Baer, 139–49. Jerusalem and New York.

Wood, John. 1841. *A Personal Narrative of a Journey to the Source of the River Oxus*. London.

Yaḥyā b. Ādam. 1967. *Kitāb al-kharaj*. Translated by A. Ben Shemesh as *Taxation in Islam*, vol. 1. Leiden.

Yāqūt al-Ḥamawī. 1886. *Kitāb Muʿjam al-Buldān*. 6 vols. Edited by F. Wüstenfeld. Leipzig.

Yarshater, E., ed. 1982– . *Encyclopaedia Iranica*. London.

Yegar, Moshe 1972. "Islam and Islamic Institutions in British Malaya 1874–1941: Policies and Implementation." Ph.D. diss., The Hebrew University of Jerusalem.

Index

2